MW00963521

The Erosion of Democracy in Education

Critique to Possibilities

*John P. Portelli and
R. Patrick Solomon (Editors)*

With a foreword by Roger Simon

Detselig Enterprises Ltd.

Calgary, Alberta, Canada

The Erosion of Democracy in Education

© 2001 Detselig Enterprises Ltd.

National Library of Canada Cataloguing in Publication Data

Main entry under title:

The erosion of democracy in education

Includes bibliographical references.

ISBN 1-55059-214-9

1. Education--Social aspects--Canada. 2. Education--Aims and objectives. 3. Educational sociology--Canada. 4. Education and state--Canada. I. Portelli, John P. (John Peter) II. Solomon, Rovell Patrick.

LC191.8.C2E76 2001   306.43'0971   C2001-910149-X

Detselig Enterprises Ltd.

210, 1220 Kensington Rd. N.W., Calgary, Alberta, T2N 3P5

Phone: (403) 283-0900/Fax: (403) 283-6947

e-mail: temeron@telusplanet.net

www.temerondetselig.com

We acknowledge the financial support of the Government of Canada through the Book Publishing Industry Development Program (BPIDP) for our publishing activities.

ISBN 1-55059-214-9

SAN 115-0324

Printed in Canada

Table of Contents

Dedication

"To my parents, Paul and Lily Portelli, whose humility and compassion taught me a lot about democracy."

"To my parents, Egbert and Eunice, and the rest of the Solomon clan for whom democracy was an unattainable ideal."

Acknowledgements

We are grateful to the contributors who made their material available for this collection. Their co-operation and encouragement made the task of editing this collection an enjoyable one.

We are also grateful to Roger Simon, who generously accepted to write the foreword notwithstanding time limitations.

We are indebted to our institutions: The University of Toronto for a Connaught Grant, York University for personnel assistance, and the Canadian Race Relations Foundation for its research grant. Our thanks to Nola James, Kristen Ligers, Archana Sharma, Jordan Singer, and Debbie Simms for secretarial and editorial assistance – their kind assistance helped make it possible for this project to be completed on time. We also benefited from comments and suggestions from our colleagues Amanda Datnow and Sharon Murphy. In every respect, this project has been a collaborative effort of both editors.

We are also grateful to the following journals for permission to reprint in this collection those essays which have been previously published: *The Canadian Journal of Education* ("Limited vision: The Ontario curriculum and outcome-based learning," by Wein and Dudley-Marling), and *The Alberta Journal of Educational Research* ("School reform in Ontario: The marketization of education and the resulting silence on equity," by Dei and Karumanchery).

Our heartfelt thanks to Ted Giles of Detselig Enterprises Ltd., whose unswerving support made this project possible.

Finally, our sincere thanks to our families for their understanding and support for their dads/spouses who became preoccupied with this book project and retreated from holiday festivities to contemplate, write about, and put the final touches to a collection of essays on the nature of democracy and schooling in Canada.

John P. Portelli

R. Patrick Solomon

Toronto, January 2001.

Contributors

Andrew Allen teaches in the Faculty of Education at York University. He is completing his doctorate at the Ontario Institute for Studies in Education of the University of Toronto. His research interests include anti-racist education and educational equity; multicultural children's literature; and critical teacher education. He is the author of "Creating Space for Discussions about Social Justice and Equity Issues in an Elementary Classroom," *Language Arts* (1997), and "'I don't want to read this': Students Respond to Illustrations of Black Characters," in K. S. Brathwaite and C. E. James (Eds.), *Educating African Canadians* (1996).

Nina Bascia is an Associate Professor and Associate Chair in the Department of Theory and Policy Studies at the Ontario Institute for Studies in Education of the University of Toronto, where her teaching and program development efforts focus on issues of social diversity and the impact of educational policy on teachers' work. She is the author of *Unions in Teachers' Professional Lives* (1994) and co-editor of *The Contexts of Teaching in Secondary Schools* (1990), *Making a Difference About Difference: The Lives and Careers of Racial Minority Immigrant Teachers* (1996), and *The Sharp Edge of Educational Change: Teaching, Leading and the Realities of Reform* (2000).

George J. Sefa Dei is a Professor and Associate Chair in the Department of Sociology and Equity Studies in Education at the Ontario Institute for Studies in Education of the University of Toronto. His teaching interests are in the areas of antiracism studies, indigenous knowledge and anti-colonial thought, and development education. His most recent co-authored publications include: *Removing the Margins: The Challenges and Possibilities of Inclusive Schooling* (with I. James, S. James-Wilson, L. Karumanchery, and J. Zine) (2000). His co-edited books in the year 2000 include: *Power, Knowledge and Anti-racism Education: A Critical Reader* (with A. Calliste); and *Anti-racism Feminism: Critical Race and Gender Studies* (with A. Calliste).

Curt Dudley-Marling is Professor of Education at Boston College in Chestnut Hill, Massachusetts. Dudley-Marling has published numerous articles and books focusing on teaching and teacher education, the politics of literacy, and students for whom school is a struggle. His most recent book is *A Family Affair: When School Troubles Come Home*, published by Heinemann.

Alison I. Griffith is the Associate Dean for Field Development in the Faculty of Education at York University. She has published extensively in journals such as *Human Studies, Educational Policy, Educational Policy Archives* (online). Her published books include *Families in Schools: A Chorus of Voices* (1997) (with E. St. John and L. Allen-Haynes). She researches and writes in the areas of textual analysis, educational leadership, feminist methodology, and the family-school relation.

Dick Henley is an Associate Professor at the University of Brandon teaching in the Brandon University Northern Teacher Education Program (BUNTEP). His research interests are in the history of education in Canada and in cross-cultural and antiracist education. Recent publications include: "Public Schooling in English Canada: Addressing Difference in the Context of Globalization" (with R. Bruno-Jofré), *Canadian Ethnic Studies*: 2001.

Leeno Luke Karumanchery is a Ph.D. candidate at the Ontario Institute for Studies in Education of the University of Toronto. He has been published in academic journals, is co-author of *Removing the Margins: The Challenges and Possibilities of Inclusive Schooling* (2000) and he is engaged in community work around issues of antiracism and social justice. Leeno is currently working on a co-authored text titled *See No Evil, Hear No Evil: Speaking Out About Racism.*

Bill Maynes is a Professor in the Department of Educational Policy Studies at the University of Alberta. His current interest in examining Canadian educational poverty programming connects with a more general policy-oriented program of research. The broader program of research is aimed at exploring factors that influence educational policy-makers as they consider poverty-related issues.

Sharon Murphy is an Associate Professor in the Faculty of Education and Associate Dean of the Faculty of Graduate Studies at York University. Her research interests include educational assessment, classroom discourse, and the relationship between art and print as semiotic systems. Her most recent books, *Fragile Evidence: A Critique of Reading Assessment* and *Telling Pieces: Art as Literacy in Middle School Classes,* are published by Lawrence Erlbaum.

Ken Osborne is Professor Emeritus of Education at the University of Manitoba. His main professional interest throughout his career lay in the role and status of history in the schools and he remains actively involved in the debates on the teaching of history in Canadian schools. His publications include: *Education: A Guide to* *the Canadian School Debate – or, Who Wants What and Why?* (1999) and *Teaching for Democratic Citizenship* (1991).

John P. Portelli is a Professor in the Department of Theory and Policy Studies at the Ontario Institute for Studies in Education of the University of Toronto. His research interests include: democratic values and critical leadership; student engagement and critical pedagogy; philosophical issues in educational administration and policy studies; developing critical/philosophical discussions in schools. He has co-authored *What to Do? Case Studies for Teachers* (1998), and co-edited *Reason and Values* (1993), *Children, Philosophy, and Democracy* (1995), and *Philosophy of Education: Introductory Readings* (1996).

R. Patrick Solomon is an Associate Professor in the Faculty of Education, York University, where his teaching focuses on social and cultural foundations of education; race, culture, and schooling; and teacher preparation for urban diversity. He is the author of *Black Resistance in High School: Forging a Separatist Culture* (1992), and is a regular contributor to teacher education journals. His current research interests include racialized minorities and access to teacher education and teaching.

Alison Taylor is an Assistant Professor in the Department of Educational Policy Studies at the University of Alberta. Her current research examines high school work education programs. She has published a number of articles relating to school-business partnerships and recently authored a book titled *The Politics of Educational Reform in Alberta*.

Ann B. Vibert is an Associate Professor and Associate Chair of Graduate Studies in the Department of Education, Mount St. Vincent University. She researches and teaches in the areas of literacy education, critical literacy and social justice, and educational and professional change. She has been involved in a number of school-based research projects in the provincial and national context. Her publications in the area of literacy education and educational change include analysis of curriculum and policy effects across categories of social difference.

Carol Anne Wien is an Associate Professor in the Faculty of Education at York University. Most of her work is in Early Childhood Education and includes her book *Developmentally Appropriate Practice in 'Real Life': Stories of Teacher Practical Knowledge* (1995), and various articles on emergent curriculum and the inspiration of Reggio Emilia. She is also interested in integrating the arts at all levels of education and is a published writer of short fiction.

Jon Young is a Professor and Head of the Department of Educational Administration, Foundations, and Psychology at the University of Manitoba. His research interests are in the areas of antiracist teacher education, school reform, and school improvement. His recent publications include the text *Understanding Canadian Schools: An Introduction to Educational Administration* (with B. Levin), and "Education in Transition: Canada" (with B. Levin) in *Education in Times of Transition*, World Yearbook of Education 2000.

Now's the Time

*The always irrecusable inadequation between the 'idea of democracy'
and that which presents itself in its name remains forever ambiguous.
...It commands the most concrete urgency, here and now. If I keep its
old name of 'democracy' nevertheless, and often speak of a 'democracy to come', it is because that is the only name for a political regime
which declares its historicity and its perfectibility, in that it carries in
its concept the dimension of inadequation and of that which is to come.
Democracy allows us in all liberty to invoke these two openings publicly in order to criticize the current state of all so-called democracy.
(Jacques Derrida, 2000)*

There couldn't be a book more timely. As I opened my *Globe and
Mail* this morning I read of a new study providing evidence that the
sweeping changes to Ontario's high schools appear destined to fail,
that in fact, school improvement was being undermined by legislated reform (*Globe and Mail*, March 17, 2001). The legislated reforms
referred to here have become increasingly familiar to Canadians:
streamlining of school services through budget cuts, adoption of
province-wide standardized testing, re-written mandatory curricula
with a focus on a profusion of fragmented learning outcomes, the
cutback of teacher development support and preparation time, and
the vast reduction in structures that enable local participation in
school governance. These have become the conditions under which
education is taking place in most schools in the country. As a result,
teachers are massively demoralized, forced into compromising
forms of pedagogy which negate what they understand is required
for excellence in education. This has led to vast numbers of teachers
leaving the profession, emptying many schools of experienced leadership. Increasingly pressured by the quick march through often
confusing curriculum, students are becoming disinterested as learning is reduced to one's ability to display narrowly defined, dis-
aggregated behaviors. Inevitably, parents' anxiety is increasing not
only in regard to the economic future of their children but, as well,
to the social and environmental viability of the society these children
shall inherit.

What brought us to this state of affairs is no secret. Across Canada, government reforms have been put in place with the justification of re-organizing education to enable our citizens to compete in what is assumed to be an increasingly competitive global economy. This justification seemed to be common sense. The inevitable logic of the necessity of global competition appeared to bring to a close the century and half debate on the purpose of public education. Yet no one is celebrating. The corporate agenda for school reform has gone awry. We are all worried that the future is slipping from our hands and the hands of our children, and it is not just a management problem. It is far more fundamental than that. If we can agree that the core of public education is to enable a society's future citizens, then we had better come back to a reconsideration of what this must mean. No serious educator would advocate a school system that would reduce the citizen to a passive subject; to a person subject to requirements that one must simply master, a pre-determined set of facts and skills that others have presumed necessary (despite the well-embraced notion that the necessities of the future remain uncertain). Yet educational planning based on the logic of the marketplace seems to be leading us to just this impoverished view of education. What is at issue are the very terms on which we think the institution of schooling should address its students. Education is very much the strategic and positional mechanism through which such students are addressed; positioned within social spaces, located within particular histories and experiences; leaving the least privileged displaced and decentered as part of a pedagogical process.

To be a citizen is not just to hold a legal status in relation to a particular nation state; rather it is to possess the capacities, and have access to the opportunities, to participate with others in the determination of life in one's society. This means being able to take into account the inter-related character of culture, politics, and economics. If we want people to be citizens, not subjects (i.e., those to whom economics, politics, and schooling simply happen), we will need to have young people think critically and be able to participate in society so as to transform inequities that impede full participation in democratic life. This is a tradition that signals the importance of investing in education as part of a broader effort to revitalize notions of democratic citizenship, social justice, and the public good. Linking such a broad-based definition of education to issues of power and agency raises fundamental questions that go to the heart of any substantive notion of democracy: how do issues of history, language, culture, and identity work to articulate and legitimate particular exclusions? Education, in the broadest sense, is a principal feature of politics because it provides the capacities, knowledge, skills, and social relations through which individuals recognize themselves as social and political agents capable of struggling for a just society. It means developing the capacities for self development, political agency, and moral leadership, without sacrificing the necessary competencies to determine the frames of the future economic viability of our communities (Giroux, 2000).

Surely it is time to re-open public discussion about the aims of education and ensure that our current policies and practices are consistent with the core qualities of democracy; democracy not narrowly defined as a form of government, but as Dewey characterized it – as a way of life, as an ethical conception, and hence always about the democracy still to come. If this sounds utopian, so be it. As Norman Geras (1999, p. 42) writes:

We should be, without hesitation or embarrassment, utopians. At the end of the twentieth century it is the only acceptable political option. ...The realities of our time are morally intolerable....The facts of widespread human privation and those of political oppression and atrocity are available to all who want them. They are unavoidable unless you wilfully shut them out. To those who would suggest that things might be yet worse, one answer is that of course they might be. But another answer is that for too many people they are already quite bad enough; and the sponsors of this type of suggestion are for their part almost always pretty comfortable.

There is a time in the incessant endeavor to change the world, when alternative visions provide the grist for shaping powerful political forces for change. We are precisely at such a moment. The times require more than the language of critique. Combining the discourse of critique and possibility is crucial to the affirmation of that critical activity which offers the prospect for change. This is precisely what the essays collected in this book set out to do. Thanks to Portelli, Solomon, and all their contributors for re-animating what we must maintain as a lively public debate.

Roger I. Simon

Professor

**Ontario Institute for Studies in Education
of the University of Toronto**

References

Derrida, J. (2000). Intellectual courage: An interview (Trans. Peter Krapp). *Culture Machine, 2,* http://culturemachine.tees.ac.uk/articles/art_derr.htm.

Geras, N. (1999). Minimum utopia: Ten theses. In L. Panitch and S. Gindin (Eds.), *Necessary and unnecessary utopias.* New York: Monthly Review Press.

Giroux, H. (2000). 'Something's missing': From utopianism to a politics of educated hope. In *Public space, private lives: Beyond the culture of cynicism.* Lanham, MD: Rowman and Littlefield.

Introduction

The topic of democracy and education has again become a promi-nent one in educational literature and discourse. Educators, academ-ics, policy analysts, and critics from different ideological stances are debating this topic. While none has argued against the importance of the relationship between democracy and education, different and conflicting views and recommendations have emerged. Given the nature of the concepts in question, this should not be surprising. However, from the perspectives presented in this collection, recent educational reforms in several regions of Canada are troubling because, in our view, they have undermined some basic democratic principles, beliefs, and practices. These reforms in Canada (Davis, 2000; Dehli, 1996; Harrison & Kachur, 1999; Robertson, 1995) are an echo of similar or identical reforms promoted in other parts of the world, particularly in English-speaking countries like Australia, the United Kingdom, and the United States (Gerwitz, Ball & Bowe, 1995; Hatcher, 1998; Kenway, 1995; McNeil, 2000). While such countries continue to present themselves as bastions of democracy, some recent educational reforms have been questioned because they contradict some basic democratic qualities.

This collection focuses on the Canadian context. By highlighting different regions of Canada and their reform movements, the essays in this book present an extended argument that the democratic tra-dition in education is being eroded. At face value this may sound like a doubtful claim, given the popular image of Canada as a liber-al democracy. It is less in doubt when one analyzes several of the recent conservative educational reforms that have been proposed in Canada. The essays in this collection consider emerging themes of reform: the plea for common curriculum standards; the design and implementation of standardized testing; the urge for outcomes-based education; the increased involvement or intervention of busi-ness in determining educational purposes; and the lack of support for programs or initiatives in schools that focus on issues of equity and diversity, and curriculum of life. These essays are written from a critical perspective that interrogates the capacity of reform initia-tives to provide democratic schooling. More importantly, the essays move beyond critique to offer alternative possibilities for schooling. Such possibilities embrace a democratic stance that seriously and honestly acknowledges the importance of equity, diversity, and social justice. Since there are different conceptions of democracy, it is crucial that we clarify our democratic stance. We believe that democracy is an ideal, which, by definition, is not fully attainable or at least very difficult to attain completely. Following Dewey (1951) and Greene (1985), we believe in the ongoing reconstructive nature of democracy. Living the democratic spirit is not easy or straightforward; we need to continue the struggle of reconstructing democracy. The fact that it is difficult to achieve and that there are different conceptions of democracy does not imply that anything can count as being democratic. Despite disagreement over the concept of democracy, we believe that there are some core qualities and values associated with democracy – otherwise democracy becomes an empty concept. What are these core qualities and how are they achieved? In response to this question we offer the thinking of leading 20th century and contemporary scholars who have written widely on this topic.

> *One of the most important functions of a vibrant democratic culture is to provide the institutional and symbolic resources necessary for young people and adults to develop their capacity to think critically, to participate in power relations and policy decisions that affect their lives, and to transform those racial, social, and economic inequities that impede democratic social relations. (Giroux, 2000, pp. 37-38)*

> *[D]emocratic dispositions [include] the disposition to listen to others,…a disposition toward tolerance,…the disposition to question, criticize, and debate; the disposition to respect the public matter that among us comes to be treated as a private matter but that as a private matter is not valued. (Freire, 1998a, p. 66)*

> *The democratic ideal is that of an open and dynamic society…antithetical to the notion of a fixed class of rulers, with privileges resting upon social myths which it is forbidden to question. It envisions rather a society that sustains itself not by the indoctrination of myth, but by reasoned choices of its citizens, who continue to favour it in the light of a critical scrutiny both of it and its alternatives. (Scheffler, 1973, p. 137)*

> *To develop democratically means to move ourselves and our students from our original position of seeing ourselves as **objects**, who believe that economics, politics, and schooling happen to us, to a new position of seeing ourselves as **subjects**, who have the right, ability, and responsibility to participate in the decision making that affects our lives. (Shannon, 1993, p. 91)*

> *The reconciliation of education and democracy rests…on a vision of society in which reflection, dialogue, critical thinking, and mutual care are central. (Levin, 1998, p. 73)*

We naturally associate democracy, to be sure, with freedom of action, but freedom of action without freed capacity of thought behind it is only chaos. (Dewey, 1903/1997, p. 229)

Emerging from these visions of democracy are common elements such as critical thinking, dialogue and discussion, tolerance, free and reasoned choices, and public participation. The arguments developed in this book rest on a conception of democracy which is associated with equity, community, creativity, and taking difference seriously. This conception is contrasted with a notion of democracy that is minimalist, protectionist, and marginalist (Parker, 1996) and hence promotes a narrow notion of individualism (Goodman, 1992) and spectator citizenship (Martin, 1992).

How does education through the schooling process go about preparing citizens for notions of democracy that value self-determination and equity? Contemporary scholars have offered their views on education for democracy, while at the same time warning against forms of education that are counter-productive to democratic values. Darling-Hammond (1998), for instance, argues that "democratic life requires access to empowering forms of knowledge that enable creative life and thought, and access to a social dialogue that enables democratic communication and participation" (p. 85). According to her, from this perspective, it follows that schools develop "humanity and decency,…cultivate appreciation,…create social community, …and support deep learning about things that matter to the people in them" (p. 86). Kohli (2000) focuses on an education that "teaches about democracy in a more truthful, more complete way" (p. 33), while Carr and Hartlett (1996) call for an education that "seeks to empower its future members to participate collectively in the process through which their society is being shaped and reproduced" (p. 43).

All these scholars denounce bureaucratic and factory-model schooling, characterized by the assumed neutrality, fragmentation, segregation of groups, and differential education that are the requirements of a market economy. Carr and Hartlett argue that this marketization of schooling often materializes into a two-tier system of education:

…one offering a minority an education appropriate to future political leaders; the other preparing the mass of ordinary individuals for their primary social roles as producers, workers and consumers in a modern market economy. For the same reason, it is always likely that mass education will have a strong emphasis on preparation for the world of work and that curriculum content will be regarded as a body of knowledge and skills which have some market value. (p. 44)

Two different conceptions of democracy lie at the heart of much of the debate in education. One is referred to as classical, participatory, public, and critical democracy; the other as contemporary, representative, privatized, and managed democracy. This collection is based on the former conception, which builds on Dewey's characterization of democracy as a way of life rather than as a form of government. These different notions of democracy result in different understandings of the purposes of education.

Purposes of Education

Recent theorization in education distinguishes several purposes of education that are central to the arguments developed in this book: education as cultural capital, education for individual growth, and education for democratic transformation (Smith et al., 1998). The notion of education as cultural capital originated from cultural reproduction theorists such as Basil Bernstein (1977) and Pierre Bourdieu (1977). They argue that schools tend to value, reward, reproduce, and transmit certain knowledge forms, skills, aptitudes, and experiences that are required to function in predetermined social and economic structures. Students' social class backgrounds and home environments are key factors in the acquisition and nurturing of these requirements; middle class students come to school with these valued commodities already in place. Working class students, on the other hand, are placed at a disadvantage because their "cultural capital" is perceived to be less valuable in formal schooling. Education through formal schooling then becomes the vehicle for providing the technical base for productive participation in a market economy, and the cultural competence to attain social status in society. Such cultural and academic capital is later translated into economic power and privileged positions in the labor market.

Education for the purpose of acquiring cultural capital has a series of problems associated with it. First, schools reproduce the inequities of a class-stratified society by privileging and rewarding what some students bring to school while marginalizing what others have. Schools, perceived as great equalizers, fail to work for equity, social justice, and democracy. Second, if education is viewed as cultural capital, then school knowledge must be considered to be static; that is, the work of schools is to prepare future citizens to fit into the world *as it is,* not for the world as it might become (Smith et al., 1998). If official school knowledge is constructed as relatively stable and people's statuses are determined by the acquisition and mastery of such knowledge, it is problematic because it serves the interests of those who create and credentialize such knowledge. In addition, if democratic life is always in a state of renewal, static knowledge does not foster democracy. Third, if cultural capital is defined narrowly, the purpose of education appears to reflect the ideology of the technical functionalism that Burton Clark described about 40 years ago in his book *Educating the Expert Society*. Here he comments, "our age demands army upon army of skilled technicians and professional experts, and to the task of preparing these men the educational system is increasingly dedicated" (1962, p. 3). The functionalist vision of schooling that Clark critiqued four decades ago has come full circle and has continued to operate in ways that erode aspects of democratic education.

Education for the purpose of individual growth is embraced by many students, educators, and their institutions as their operating philosophy (Smith et al., 1998). This vision of education has as its core a child-centred kind of pedagogy where the classroom curriculum and pedagogy cater to students' particular learning needs and experiences. Students engage actively in the exploration of ideas and knowledge that are relevant to them. But when Smith et al. (1998) considered the breadth of students' curricular choices and areas of knowledge exploration, they found this approach to education to be potentially limiting. For example, often unexplored in homogeneous student populations are Canadian societal issues of diversity and social difference. Excessive preoccupation with individual autonomy, as seems to be the case when the purpose of education is individual growth, is problematic in a society that claims to be democratic.

The third purpose of education reported in Smith et al. (1998) is that of "preparing students not to fit into a given world so much as to understand and transform the world as given" (p. 71). The conception of education as democratic transformation was found to be more prevalent in socio-economically marginalized and culturally diverse communities. Forms of emancipatory education, such as inclusive education, feminist pedagogy, and antiracism, are designed and implemented to achieve equity, social justice, and social transformation. Here, democratic schooling is exemplified in student voice rather than student choice; communal and social concerns take precedence over individual interests and experiences. Education as democratic transformation does not deny the importance of knowledge and a required curriculum or individual growth. Instead, these are not seen as fixed and static but as socially constructed and organic; individual growth is not seen from an individualistic perspective but from its relation to communal growth.

The prevalent forms of schooling that support the first two aims of education discussed above, education as cultural capital and education for individual growth, emerge from the conception of democracy that Carr and Hartnett (1996) label "contemporary democracy" which, according to several of the authors already referred to, is associated with the modern market economy, competition, a narrow notion of usefulness, a technicist approach to teaching, functionalism, assumed neutrality, and excessive individualism. Paulo Freire (1998b) associated these qualities with "neoliberal pragmatism." He warned of the dangers of this stance: cynical fatalism, a discouragement of utopia and dreams, and a feeling that we have to accept the status quo and hence students have to be given simply technical training to fit in what is deemed, according to neoliberal pragmatism, to be "inevitable [and] cannot be changed" (p. 27). According to Freire, this fatalistic and anti-utopian ideology

> *proposes a purely technical kind of education in which the teacher distinguishes himself or herself not by a desire to change the world but to accept it as it is. Such a teacher possesses very little capacity for critical education but quite a lot for 'training' for transferring contents. An expert in 'know-how'. (p. 126)*

Given the conceptions of democracy and education we adhere to and the nature and implications of contemporary conservative educational reform, we believe it is imperative and timely to critically assess aspects of these reforms as they are manifested in policies and practices in particular educational jurisdictions in Canada. It is indeed crucial that we re-open public discussions about aims of education and ensure that the aims that guide our current policies and practices are consistent with the core qualities of democracy.

From the stance that we ascribe to, it follows that:

(a) there is a necessary, intrinsic connection between democracy and education (Carr and Hartnett, 1996; Levin, 2000);

(b) the relationship between democracy and education is not a linear causal one but a reciprocal one (Dewey, 1958; Greene, 1995; Gutman, 1990; Portelli, 1996);

(c) the relationship between education and the future is not envisaged in a narrow, utilitarian manner (Dewey, 1938);

(d) policy-making would not be located centrally (Darling-Hammond, 1996);

(e) open, informed, and public discourses about equity, diversity, and social justice would be encouraged (Giroux, 2000; Kohli, 2000); and,

(f) policies and practices that support full and equitable access to education, an education that acknowledges and realistically supports different constructions of knowledge, different forms of learning, and different values, would be established and supported (Darling-Hammond, 1996).

These arguments are further explored in the chapters presented in this collection.

Overview of chapters

The first two chapters provide theoretical and conceptual frameworks that situate the issue of democracy and schooling in particular historical and political contexts. The first essay by Osborne traces the connections between democracy and democratic citizenship, on the one hand, and schooling, on the other. It examines the contested meanings of democracy and citizenship in the Canadian context, both past and present, and what they have meant for the organization, content, and delivery of public education. In doing so, the essay also explores the ways in which schools can contribute to the enhancement of democracy in Canada.

The next chapter by Portelli and Vibert clarifies issues involved in popular discourse that calls for common standards in education by examining the concept of standards and its ethical and political implications. The essay offers a critical examination of the assumptions underlying popular arguments for common standards in education. This critique is offered from a critical pedagogy perspective that values equity and social justice. Further, the chapter offers alternative perspectives on educational standards and justification for these perspectives. These alternative perspectives rest on the conception of the "curriculum of life," a curriculum that is grounded in the immediate daily world of students as well as in the larger and social political contexts of their lives. Portelli and Vibert conclude that it would be more worthwhile to direct the efforts spent on establishing and monitoring common standards on support needed to enact a curriculum of life. Such a re-direction would provide better opportunities for creating equity in schools.

The essays by Griffith, Wein and Dudley-Marling, and Mackinnon critically interrogate the philosophy, policies, and texts of outcomes-based learning in Ontario and the Atlantic Provinces of

Canada, while the essay by Murphy focuses on the nation's preoccupation with measuring schooling outcomes. Griffith's chapter analyses the texts of restructuring education in the province of Ontario, and more specifically, the textually co-ordinated activities through which restructuring, marketization, and globalization become the everyday task of parents, teachers, and particularly local school administrators. The author contends that these reform texts are a marked shift away from education for democracy and citizenship. Ontario's major text for restructuring, *Bill 160: The Education Improvement Act* (1997) signals, in rather contradictory ways, a retreat from the possibilities of emancipatory or critical leadership to the tyranny of bureaucratic managerial leadership. Griffith advocates a style of leadership that links textually-mediated administration to the teaching and learning of democratic education.

In their chapter, Wien and Dudley-Marling critique Ontario's outcomes-based learning and its narrow, controlling vision of teachers and learners, and of diversity and ecology. The authors' analysis of the province's policy documents found them superficial in their treatment of cultural diversity and broader ecological communities, and their failure to acknowledge the experiences of either learners and teachers. In more pedagogically-specific ways, Wien and Dudley-Marling critique the imposed curriculum as a rigid, lock-step system with lists of "expectations" that students are required to obtain. They suggest that educating the young is more complex than outcomes-based curriculum dictates and offer alternative approaches to pedagogy based on the principles of Italian educators in Reggio Emilia.

Mackinnon's chapter provides both an overview and critique of the Atlantic Provinces Education Foundation program, an outcomes-based educational initiative that is meant to transform curriculum and teaching practice in Nova Scotia. The outgrowth of the initiative is the creation of a common core curriculum for New Brunswick, Prince Edward Island, Nova Scotia, Newfoundland, and Labrador, currently in place for selected subject areas. Integral to the core curriculum is the specification of "essential graduation learnings" and a series of general and key-stage curriculum outcomes, all stated in terms of student performance, and an increasing visibility of standardized exams. Mackinnon points out that while having the positive effect of focusing educational evaluation on student accomplishment, the initiative suffers from a variety of serious problems such as the contestable assumptions of an outcomes-based program, the contradictory messages established by juxtaposing constructivist language and behaviorist measures, and the ubiquitous issue of establishing standards.

Murphy's chapter interrogates the nation's preoccupation with student testing and evaluation. She argues that over the past several years, the use of standardized tests has risen dramatically in Canada. Using primarily Canadian newspaper sources as evidence, she considers what lessons Canadians might learn from the use of standardized tests over the past few years. Specifically considered are whether the inferences taken from tests exceed the boundaries of good educational measurement practice, whether the media's desire for catchy news inflates the importance of tests, whether business ways of thinking have contributed to a numerically-driven balance-sheet approach to assessing the effectiveness of education, and whether standardized tests inherently include biases against certain groups. She further examines whether politicians use tests results to bolster solutions that serve immediate political ends without consideration as to how such use may contribute to the eventual dismantling of a democratic public education system. The chapter concludes with a discussion of the burgeoning anti-testing movement that has begun both in Canada and the United States.

The essays by Taylor, and Dei and Karumanchery explore the potential impact of corporate sponsorship and the marketization of education on democractic schooling in the provinces of Alberta and Ontario. Taylor's chapter documents the increased interest in formal education shown by national and provincial level corporate-sponsored groups in the 1980s and 1990s. It demonstrates the apparent convergence between government and business visions for education around the role of schools in producing a labor force that can ensure economic competitiveness in the 21st century. Given this situation, two questions are considered: why has there been so little resistance from education groups, and what are the implications of increased business involvement for democratic processes? Three reasons for the lack of apparent resistance are: the futurist tone of knowledge economy discourse, the appeal of progressive vocational discourse, and the pragmatic realities of under-funding facing teachers and schools. Taylor argues that increased private sector involvement in education through partnerships and multi-stakeholder collaboration poses a threat to democratic participation and concludes with recommendations for educators and others to strengthen the democratic and egalitarian side of education in the current climate.

The chapter by Dei and Karumanchery recounts ways in which market dynamics have begun to entrench themselves in educational systems around the world, and the encroachment of market forms, relations, and concepts on educational sites. Using an integrative antiracist perspective, this chapter critically examines these ongoing reforms in the Canadian context, specifically in relation to the recent reforms in Ontario's educational system. They draw on knowledge about race and difference to argue for serious questioning of these reforms and their impact on socially disadvantaged groups. They assert that this movement toward the "marketization of education" will be felt most severely in the areas of equity and access to education. Through the rhetoric of cost-effectiveness and bureaucratic efficiency, the "official" agenda for educational change shifts focus away from equity considerations in schooling to those of capital, market forces, and big business. The authors interrogate the rhetoric of reform and call for equity to be placed at the centre of educational change. In conclusion, they suggest new ways of examining and addressing genuine educational options in Canadian contexts.

The next three essays by Solomon and Allen, Bascia, and Maynes are presented as case studies on the impact of school reform and standardized curricula on three marginalized groups in the Ontario school system. The chapter by Solomon and Allen provides insights into the lived experiences of teacher candidates in practicum schools that are implementing a state-imposed standardized curriculum, and highlights three interrelated issues: the discontinuity of educational theory from teacher education curriculum to classroom practice; the culture of power within schools and the resulting "silences" it creates among equity-conscious candidates; and the unique strategies candidates employ to create spaces for a pedagogy of equity, diversity, and social justice. The authors raise important questions about the ecology of teacher education and the volatile mix of political, pedagogical, and institutional factors that conspire against learning to teach for democracy and social justice. They recommend particular forms of professional development schools as alternatives to the current learning environment.

Bascia's chapter is a close-up examination of the conditions of English as a Second Language (ESL) teaching and learning. It provides a conceptual framework to describe how educational policy affects practice, then describes the major policies that have shaped and reshaped ESL programs over the past decade, through what some see as two distinct and diametrically opposed policy "waves" or "swings." A description of ESL programs in four typical public schools in Ontario reveals the impact of various layers of policy history on ESL delivery.

Maynes' chapter explores possibilities for educating children who live in poverty, and the challenges associated with efforts to realize those possibilities. Beginning with a review of established program- and district-level perspectives on these matters, he constructs a complementary school-level perspective utilizing case studies of two Toronto inner-city schools. The "lessons" he extracts from these case studies relate to the sense of "wholeness" in these schools, democratic leadership, collaborative cultures, resources, orientations to curriculum, and orientations toward student achievement. These lessons, Maynes contends, provide insight into conditions which serve to enable schools in their efforts to provide more equitable programming for children living in poverty.

In the closing chapter, Henley and Young look critically at school reform initiatives in the province of Manitoba, as they were proposed and implemented during the 1990s. This is done against a backdrop of competing versions of democracy and public schooling, and the historical development of liberalism in Canada. The analysis that develops is that the reform initiatives of the 1990s were intended to provide the foundation upon which a neo-liberal market democracy would eventually be constructed. Here, primacy would be afforded to the largely unfettered rights of the individual, superseding earlier efforts in the 1960s and 1970s to forge a pluralist moral democracy where primacy was given to issues of equity over those of individual liberty. They argue that despite claims that the educational reforms introduced in Manitoba in the 1990s were "commonsense," or "a necessary response to the irresistible pressures of globalization," they were, in fact, far from inevitable. Nor were they a desirable direction for public education in a compassionate liberal democracy. They contend that "progressive possibilities" are to be found in (a) the egalitarian reforms of the 1970s and 1980s, (b) the more moderate approaches to reform taken by the province during the 1990s by the ruling Progressive Conservative Party, and (c) some early initiatives taken by the newly elected New Democratic Party.

Emerging from these essays are insights into ideologically driven policies and practices and the re-entrenchment of economic functionalism that are eroding the democratic tradition in education. To reverse these trends, writing from their various theoretical locations – philosophy and history, curriculum studies, language and literacy, sociology and equity studies, and policy studies and leadership – the authors have posited alternative visions and progressive possibilities. We hope that these essays will prove to be stimulating and informative to educators, policy-makers, and citizens at various levels in the schooling enterprise, and inspire democratic action.

References

Bernstein, B. (1977). Social class, language and socialization. In J. Karabel & A. H. Halsey (Eds.), *Power and ideology in education* (pp. 473-486). New York: Oxford Press.

Bourdieu, P. (1977). Cultural reproduction and social reproduction. In J. Karabel & A. H. Halsey (Eds.), *Power and ideology in education* (pp. 487-510). New York: Oxford Press.

Carr, W. & Hartnett, A. (1996). *Education and the struggle for democracy: The politics of educational ideas.* Buckingham: Open University Press.

Clark, B. K. (1962). *Educating the expert society.* San Francisco: Chandler.

Darling-Hammond, L. (1997). Reframing the school reform agenda: Developing capacity for school transformation. In E. Clinchy (Ed.), *Transforming public education: A new course for America's future* (pp. 38-55). New York: Teachers College Press.

Darling-Hammond, L. (1998). Education for democracy. In W. C. Ayers & J. L. Miller (Eds.), *A light in dark times: Maxine Greene and the unfinished conversation* (pp. 78-91). New York: Teachers College Press.

Davis, B. (2000). *Skills mania: Snake oil in our schools?* Toronto: Between the Lines.

Dewey, J. (1903/1977). Democracy in education. In J. A. Boydston (Ed.), *John Dewey: The middle works.* Vol. 3, 1903-1906 (pp. 229-239). Carbondale, IL: Southern Illinois University Press.

Dewey, J. (1938). *Experience and education.* New York: Macmillan.

Dewey, J. (1951). Creative democracy: The task before us. In M. H. Fisch (Ed.), *Classic American philosophers* (pp. 389-394). New York: Prentice Hall.

Dewey, J. (1958). Democracy and educational administration. In *Philosophy of education: Problems of men* (pp. 57-69). Totawa, NJ: Littlefield Adams & Co.

Dehli, K. (1996). Between "market" and "state"? Engendering education change in the 1990s. *Discourse: Studies in the cultural politics of education, 17*(3), 363-376.

Freire, P. (1998a). *Teachers as cultural workers: Letters to those who dare teach.* Boulder, CO: Westview Press.

Freire, P. (1998b). *Pedagogy of freedom: Ethics, democracy, and courage.* Lanham: Rowman & Littlefield Publishers, Inc.

Gerwitz, S., Ball, S. J. & Bowe, R. (1995). *Markets, choice and equity in education.* Milton Keynes, UK: Open University Press.

Giroux, H. (2000), *Impure acts: The practical politics of cultural studies.* New York: Routledge.

Goodman, J. (1992). *Elementary schooling for critical democracy*. Albany, NY: State University Press of New York.

Greene, M. (1985). The role of education in democracy. *Educational Horizons, 63,* 3-9.

Gutman, A. (1990). Democratic education in difficult times. *Teachers College Record, 92*(1), 7-20.

Harrison, T. W. & Kachur, J. L. (Eds.) (1999). *Contested classrooms: Education, globalization, and democracy in Alberta*. Edmonton: University of Alberta Press.

Hatcher, R. (1998). Social justice and the politics of school effectiveness and improvement. *British Race, Ethnicity and Education, 1*(2), 267-289.

Kenway, J. (1995). The marketization of education: Mapping the contours of a feminist perspective. Paper presented to the British Educational Research Association, Bath.

Kohli, W. (2000). Teaching in the danger zone: Democracy and difference. In D. W. Hursch & E. W. Ross (Eds.), *Democratic social education: Social studies for social change* (pp. 23-42). New York: Falmer Press.

Levin, B. (1998). The educational requirement for democracy. *Curriculum Inquiry, 28*(1), 57-79.

Levin, B. (2000). Democracy and schools: For citizenship. *Education Canada, 40*(3), 4-7.

Martin, J. (1992). Critical thinking for a humane world. In S. P. Norris (Ed.), *The generalizability of critical thinking: Multiple perspectives on an educational ideal* (pp. 163-180). New York: Teachers College Press.

McNeil, L. M. (2000). *Contradictions of school reform: Educational costs of standardized testing*. New York : Routledge.

Parker, W. C. (1996). Curriculum for democracy. In R. Soder (Ed.), *Democracy, education, and the schools* (pp. 182-210). San Francisco, CA: Jossey-Bass Publishers.

Portelli, J. P. (1996). Democracy in education: Beyond the conservative or progressive stances. *Inquiry: Critical Thinking Across the Disciplines, 16* (1), 9-21.

Robertson, H. J. (1995). Hyenas at the oasis: Corporate marketing to captive students. *Our Schools/Our Selves, 7*(2), 16-39.

Scheffler, I. (1973). Moral education and the democratic ideal. In *Reason and teaching* (pp. 136-145). London: Routledge & Kegan.

Shannon, P. (1993). Developing democratic voices. *The Reading Teacher, 47*(2), 86-94.

Smith, W. J., Butler-Kisber, L., LaRocque, L. J., Portelli, J. P., Shields, C. M., Sturge Sparks, C. & Vibert, A. B. (1998). *Student engagement in learning and school life: National project report*. Montreal, QC: Office of Research on Educational Policy, McGill University.

Chapter 1
Democracy, Democratic Citizenship, and Education

Ken Osborne

Introduction

In recent years schools have come under increasing public scrutiny. Much of this criticism has come from the political right, though some of it is echoed by at least some voices on the left, and forms part of a wider political, economic, and social agenda. As is well known, the neo-liberal and neo-conservative right distrusts government and public institutions, including public schools, believing that greater efficiency and effectiveness are delivered by private enterprise operating according to the procedures of competitive market economics. This turning away from government is accompanied by a belief that individual and national success is best secured by greater competitiveness in all aspects of life. Thus education must be geared to making students more competitive and entrepreneurial and to teaching them the skills and dispositions required by an increasingly competitive global economic order.

This view of education has proved attractive to the corporate world and to governments. It has also drawn support from students and parents who understandably see education as the key to a good job in a world where good jobs are increasingly hard to find. The result has been, however, to impoverish our view of education. Not least, it has ignored, sometimes unknowingly but often deliberately, the contribution that education can make to the strengthening and perhaps even the transformation of democracy.

Thus, this chapter is written in the conviction that there is a tension between the demands of democracy and the imperatives of capitalism, that the present and future of democracy are at risk, and that education has some part to play in ensuring its survival and good health. In what follows, I have tried to survey the questions, arguments, and considerations that have to be taken into account by anyone who sees an important link between education and democracy.

Education, Politics, and the State

The idea that a political system, whatever its ideological complexion, should have an education system appropriate to its values and beliefs has a long history, stretching back to Plato and Aristotle, but only in the 19th century was the state able to take control of education. It did so in response to three forces that it sought to harness to its own use: nationalism, liberalism, and industrialism.

In the 19th century, nationalism became a major force in European politics. Increasingly Europeans accepted the idea that people could more or less naturally be divided into nations, defined in terms of language and culture, and that every nation was entitled to its own territory, government, and sovereignty. Hence, of course, the now-familiar concept of the nation-state. Usually, however, nationalists found that nations were not so much discovered as invented. In Benedict Anderson's formulation, they are "imagined communities" (Anderson, 1991) and nationalists saw the creation and maintenance of nationhood as depending crucially on education. It was in school that citizens would learn of the past glories of their nation, to speak and write its language, to love its customs and traditions, to identify with its people, and to gain that sense of shared national identity upon which a nation depends for its existence.

Though nationalism often came to be associated with the right rather than the left in politics, it initially appeared as a liberal and liberating force. For liberal nationalists, the people were supreme. People were no longer to be subjects of king or emperor; they were to be self-governing citizens. Moreover, as the American and French revolutionaries proclaimed, citizens were entitled to rights, both to inalienable rights as human beings and to specific rights as national citizens.

Not the least of these rights was the right to vote, and, as an understandable corollary, the idea grew that voters had to be educated so that they would vote intelligently. Thus, nationalism, in its liberal form, strengthened the state's determination to control education, for the education of citizen voters could not be left to chance. It also made education something of a popular cause as citizens came to understand the connection between education and material success and political influence. Ruling elites usually tried to ensure that citizens got only the barest minimum of elementary education, but citizens learned to push for more. The resulting struggle to extend and direct the provision of education, and to widen citizenship rights generally, served to increase the state's interest in education, both positively, to control and shape it, and negatively, to keep its direction out of the hands of those it did not trust.

The third force that directed the state's attention to education was the Industrial Revolution which, as the process of industrialism became more complex and scientifically-based, called for at least a minimum of literacy and skill from its work-force, and for the training of the innovators, researchers, and others upon whom competitive industrial and commercial success was thought to depend. More fundamentally, industrial capitalism demanded a new labor discipline, new values, and new habits of mind from its citizens. Clock time replaced traditional rhythms of months and seasons. The factory called for a more regimented and disciplined pace of work than the farm. The city demanded new ways of living. The logic of the market-place challenged more traditional loyalties. Capitalist values invaded almost every corner of personal life.

The combination of nationalism, liberalism, and industrialism ensured that education became a matter, not only of public concern, but of public policy. By the end of the century there was general agreement that some degree of elementary education should be provided for all boys and girls, though there was much disagreement as to how much and what kind and who should actually provide it. Equally important, the growing capacity of the national state, based on the bureaucratization of administration, the ability to raise taxes efficiently, and on technological developments in transportation and communications, made it possible for the state to take charge of education, thus turning it also into a subject for political debate. In short, education entered the arena of democratic politics.

By the end of the 19th century, a broad, though contested, consensus existed that schools existed primarily to train citizens and to produce workers. Of these two goals, citizenship was generally seen as the more important, though it was often honored more in theory than in practice. There was also widespread agreement that education was as much a moral as an intellectual exercise. Schools existed to shape character, to teach morality, to instil values, though this sometimes provoked considerable disagreement between secularists and those who saw morality as inseparable from religion. This said, however, all sides agreed that schools existed in large part to prepare the young for life in contemporary society. As the Winnipeg School Board noted in 1913:

> *Until a comparatively recent period the schools were organized on purely academic lines and the avowed aim of education was culture and discipline. This aim has, however, been greatly enlarged within the past few years, by including within its scope the development of a sense of social and civic duty, the stimulation of national and patriot-*

ic spirit, the promotion of public health, and direct preparation for the occupations of life. (Manitoba Dept. of Education, 1913, 23).

Democrats, Democracy, and Education

These developments in education were of particular interest to democrats. Once the idea that government should be of, for, and particularly by the people became part of political debate, it became possible to argue about just who constituted the people in a political or citizenship sense, until bit by bit, and with considerable struggle, the idea was established that the people included all adult men and women, regardless of wealth, race, religion, or property, so that citizenship became a matter not of status, but of birth, or naturalization in the case of those immigrants who were judged suitable for inclusion in the community of citizens. At the same time, most democrats accepted the argument that if the people were to rule, they had to be qualified to do so.

This is why many, though not all, democrats believed – and believe today – that schooling should not be left to private initiative, whether to churches, to parents, to fee-for-service entrepreneurs, or to any other private group. As they see it, education is a social more than an individual matter and thus has to be brought under public control (Gutmann & Thompson, 1996, pp. 63-69; but see also Galston, 1999).

Historically, democrats have sought to make politics more democratic by encouraging more direct popular participation in the political process; by seeking to make politicians more responsive to citizens; by devolving government down to the level of the people most directly affected by its decisions. At the same time they have moved beyond such measures in at least two ways, both of which have important consequences for education. One, they have widened the scope and operation of politics; and, two, they have seen democracy as embracing more than politics as usually understood.

The widening of the scope of politics has meant that the political agenda is no longer confined, as it once was, to matters of high policy, notably war and peace, international relations more generally, law and order, and the like. It now includes, indeed is dominated by, far more immediate and personal concerns: sewage and sanitation, clean water, public health, pensions, housing, child-rearing, roads, land use, and the thousand and one other aspects of people's daily lives. This development has resulted in large part from democrats' insistence that the state is the most appropriate institution to deal with such subjects in ways that are comprehensive, effective, and socially just, though in recent years neo-conservatives, libertarians, and even left-inclined proponents of the "third way" between social-ism and capitalism have been suggesting that perhaps government is part of the problem as much as it is any solution. It is also the result of the democratization of politics, whereby so-called ordinary people, once they had the right to vote, pressed for action to deal with their needs and priorities.

This widening of the scope of politics went hand in hand with a second development: a widening of the concept of democracy. Traditionally, democracy was seen as a set of political arrangements, comprising whatever institutions were thought necessary to turn the idea of self-rule into reality. As the 19th century proceeded, however, the concept of liberty was enlarged to include equity, so that democracy was seen, at least on the left, as including a concern for social justice – hence, of course, the term "social democracy," which a hundred years ago enjoyed a far more radical connotation than it has today. In 1888 John Dewey spoke for many on the liberal-left when he rejected any purely political conception of democracy:

> To say that democracy is **only** a form of government is like saying that home is a more or less geometrical arrangement of bricks and mortar; that the church is a building with pews, pulpit, and spire. It is true; they are certainly so much. But it is false; they are so infinitely more. Democracy, like any other polity, has been finely termed the memory of an historic past, the consciousness of a living present, the ideal of the coming future. Democracy, in a word, is a social, that is to say, an ethical conception, and upon its ethical significance is based its significance as governmental. (Dewey, 1888, p. 240; see also Dewey, 1916; Westbrook, 1991; Caspary, 2000)

It is in this spirit that today democratic theorists speak of democratic values or virtues. The political philosopher, Carol Gould, for example, writes of "the democratic character," which she sees as consisting of reliance on reason, reciprocity, and mutuality in dealing with other people, openness to diverse viewpoints, respect for human rights, flexibility, open-mindedness, responsibility, co-operativeness, and a concern for community (Gould. 1988, pp. 283-9; see also Dagger, 1997; Galston, 1991, pp. 220-7). In a similar vein, Eamonn Callan sees "justice as reasonableness" as the "cardinal personal virtue of liberal democratic politics" and describes it as including imaginative sympathy with others, respect for reasonable difference, a spirit of moderation and compromise, imaginativeness and empathy, reciprocity and an awareness of the limits of reason (Callan, 1997, pp. 8, 26, 42).

Both of these developments – the widening of the scope of politics and the broadening of the understanding of democracy – heightened democrats' interest in and commitment to education in at least two ways. One, both developments created disagreement and controversy over specific issues and led to citizens mobilizing for or against some preferred option or policy, so that politics became less the concern of elites and more the concern of citizens in general. Two, these controversies over specific issues stimulated debate over the scope and meaning of democracy and citizenship. In both cases the result was that education was increasingly seen as necessary for the preparation of democratic citizens.

Democratic Citizenship

Throughout the 20th century schools have been seen as shapers of citizenship (Heater, 1990). Indeed, in the early decades of the century, citizenship was seen as the primary goal of the public schools. As a British Columbia Royal Commission put it in 1925: "The development of a united and intelligent citizenship should be accepted without question as the fundamental aim of our schools" (Putman & Weir, 1925, pp. 38).

The conception of citizenship that lay behind this and similar formulations was often prophylactic, designed to prevent what was seen as an undesirable state of affairs from coming to pass as much as to promote something more positive. In the words of the Royal Commission of 1925: "From the viewpoint of self-preservation alone, society recognizes that the best form of state insurance against anarchy and bolshevism is an efficient system of public education" (Putman & Weir, 1925, pp. 57).

Official-style citizenship was also usually narrow and coercive. It was in the name of citizenship that Aboriginal children were forced into residential schools where they could be duly Canadianized, and minorities were coerced into an assimilative Canadianism, sometimes described by historians as "Anglo-conformity." Citizenship was also seen in gendered terms, with girls being trained for a maternal, domestic, and inward-looking social role different from that intended for boys. As organized labor, farmer radicals, and assorted socialists recognized, citizenship was also a code-word for hiding the realities of social class behind a smokescreen of national consensus.

Nonetheless, the critics of official citizenship education did not turn their backs on it. Rather, they took its rhetoric at face value and sought to use it for their own advantage, with the result that bit by bit the definition of citizenship broadened beyond the imposition of ideological orthodoxy and calls for "service" to the community, to include the possibility of a critical analysis of social realities. At the very least, it became an arena where competing definitions and conceptions of society could struggle for acceptance.

By the 1920s there was general agreement that education for citizenship in the context of Canada's parliamentary democracy consisted of some seven elements (Osborne, 1996; see also Sears, 1994). The first was a sense of Canadian identity and non-chauvinist patriotism, combined with a sense of internationalism. The second was an awareness of one's rights and respect for the rights of others, initially defined within the context of British legal and historical traditions and since 1982, the Canadian Charter of Rights and Freedoms. The third was a commitment to carry out the obligations of citizenship, not simply in the minimal sense of paying taxes, obeying the law, and the rest, but more positively in the sense of service to the community at large, ranging from military service in time of war to volunteer work in the local community. The fourth was an internalization of dominant social values, for example honesty, non-violence, respect for property, a willingness to work, a sense of fair play, and the like, but also including some more critical consideration of what those values represented, of their strengths and their limitations. The fifth was what the British political theorist Bernard Crick (1978) has called in another context "political literacy," an awareness of political issues, an understanding of the political process, a sense of political efficacy, and a willingness to become politically involved. The sixth was a broad general knowledge and command of basic skills so that one could in fact play an active part in society. The seventh was a capacity to reflect on the implications of the previous six components of citizenship, to think for oneself, to follow one's conscience, and to act appropriately.

These seven elements of citizenship and citizenship education were and are obviously highly contestable and have often been the subject of considerable debate. They have been variously interpreted and assigned different degrees of importance in different regions at different times. For example, Quebec has always been highly sceptical of any attempt to define citizenship in pan-Canadian terms, seeing it as an attempt to submerge Quebec's distinctiveness in a wider Canadian identity. Citizenship is also a word that arouses ambivalent feelings in many Aboriginal people, who increasingly prefer to identify themselves as members of their own indigenous nations rather than as members of the Canadian polity. It was in this spirit, for example, that the Royal Commission on Aboriginal Peoples argued in 1996 that Aboriginal people should be connected with Canada not so much through a common citizenship as through a nation to nation relationship (Royal Commission, 1996).

In very general terms, until sometime in the 1920s the primary thrust of citizenship was Canadianization, as represented by the use of the schools to promote a British-oriented definition of pan-Canadian unity. In the 1930s this was to some extent replaced, or at least overlaid, by an emphasis on service to the community, usually seen in non-political terms as characterized by volunteer work, being a good neighbor, and so on. In the 1940s a win-the-war mood prevailed but, in the context of the fight against Fascism and Nazism, this also produced an emphasis on Anglo-American style liberal democracy, an emphasis that was given further impetus by the post-1945 Cold War with the Soviet Union. In the 1970s came a renewed emphasis on Canadianism, or "pan-Canadian understanding" as it was called, this time with a pronounced multicultural flavor, sparked by fears that the future of the country was in doubt and by surveys that revealed that students knew very little about Canada compared to what they knew about the United States. The 1970s also saw a move in some classrooms to get students involved in explicitly political activities, whether in elections, environmental campaigns, global development programs, antiracist and antisexist projects, or some other form of action program. In the 1980s and continuing today, these emphases were supplanted by an economic agenda in which the claims of citizenship largely disappeared, as political and economic elites pushed for education to prepare students for the new global economy (Osborne, 1996; Robertson, 1998).

It should perhaps be added that all this describes the official world of schooling, as embodied in curricula, programs of study, ministerial statements, and the like. The real world of the classroom was not necessarily affected by them all that much. Most teachers saw themselves, not as promoters of citizenship, but as trying to do whatever they could to meet the needs of their students. Even when teachers were inclined to define their work in terms of preparation for citizenship, as some did, their working conditions and lack of training and resources often worked against them, especially in smaller, financially-strapped, resource-poor rural school districts, which were the Canadian norm until the 1960s. One of the many paradoxes of citizenship education in Canada is that although for much of the last hundred years policy makers have spoken eloquently of the need to prepare students for citizenship in a democracy, they have at the same time starved schools of the resources and denied teachers the working conditions that would turn the rhetoric into reality.

The Democratic Deficit and the Decline of Social Capital

That there is a worrying gap between the rhetoric of education for democratic citizenship and the reality of the classroom is suggested by the existence of what has come to be called the "democratic deficit." This consists of a widespread and apparently increasing disillusionment with and cynicism about politics and the political process that surveys indicate exists in all the liberal democracies, including Canada. It has long been recognized that, despite its egalitarian ideals, democracy has been unable to redress the inequities of social class. Indeed, the orthodox Marxist criticism of liberal democracy for many years was that it was not democratic at all, but merely a legitimizing facade for the inequities of capitalism (Femia, 1993). Certainly, the evidence shows that political participation, trust, and sense of efficacy increase with wealth, in large part because the political system is more responsive to those with power and influence than it is to those without them. In years past, however, this systemic weakness of democracy was seen as a reason for seeking to improve its working. The discourse of democratic citizenship was one way by which men and women excluded or marginalized from the political process sought to find a place within it. Today, by contrast, increasing numbers of citizens appear to have given up.

Some observers link the democratic deficit with a decline in what they describe as "social capital." Social capital consists of people's willingness to work together, to join clubs and associations, to get involved in community affairs, and generally to form a dense network of associational life which, while often not ostensibly political, nonetheless contributes to a spirit of social solidarity and shared citizenship which spills over into higher rates of political participation and a greater interest in politics generally. As Benjamin Barber puts it, social capital is produced in "the free space in which democratic attitudes are cultivated and democratic behaviour is conditioned" (Barber, 1998, p. 6). According to some researchers, social capital has markedly declined in the last 30 or so years, with unwelcome consequences for the health of democracy (Putnam, 2000).

If citizens are disillusioned with the political process, it is because they have reason to be. If they do not vote in the numbers that they should, it is not because they are selfish or lazy, but because they see that voting often does not change very much. The democratic deficit is the symptom of a structural problem that cannot be fixed through better citizenship education, but only through changes in the political system, and, more fundamentally, in the socio-economic order we call capitalism. Nonetheless, there is a role for education in alerting students to the problems that exist, and leading them to reflect on alternative ways of conceptualizing and organizing democracy to make it more socially just and inclusively participatory; and in providing them with the kinds of participatory experiences that will lead them to become democratically active citizens in adult life.

Concern over the erosion of public life has a particular edge in Canada, arising from a widespread anxiety about the very future of Canada itself. Quebec sovereignty, Aboriginal nationalism, provincial assertiveness, multiculturalism, neo-liberal opposition to big government, the pressures of globalization, and North American economic integration have combined to cast into doubt the continued existence of Canada. As the political theorist, Alan Cairns, puts it, Canadian citizenship has become "fragmented" (Cairns, 1995, pp. 157-185). This is not necessarily an unwelcome development and "fragmented" is obviously a loaded word. The traditional idea of a standardized Canadian citizenship was often used to ride roughshod over the cultural distinctiveness of Aboriginal Canadians, francophones, and other minorities, and it might well be that a new conception of citizenship, based on diversity and differential rights, will be integral to a new and more diverse Canada (Ignatieff, 2000; Kymlicka, 1998).

Even so, Canada's uncertain present, while offering us a different future, carries with it considerable risks, and thereby puts enormous responsibilities on its citizens. To quote Alan Cairns: "If we survive as one country, we must accommodate diversity without so destroying inter-connectedness that we shall be incapable of undertaking future civic tasks together. Since the latter will be more demanding than yesterday's challenges, we must hope that a citizen body lacking the bond of a standardized citizenship but nevertheless participating in common civic endeavours is not an oxymoron" (Cairns, 1995, p. 185). In the circumstances that face us we must do more than hope. As Lazar and McIntosh (1999, pp. 7-8) recently

observed: "Canadian notions of citizenship are undergoing important changes that, while they may have positive effects, require
Canadians to confront traditional understandings of what it means
to be a Canadian." Without expecting more from education than it
can ever deliver, it seems obvious that it has a role to play in creating the kind of citizens that Canada now needs.

Democracy, Hegemony, and Schooling

Democrats often view education with a certain ambivalence.
Full of hope for its democratic potential, they know full well that it
has often been used as an instrument of ideological indoctrination
and cultural imposition. Historians have repeatedly shown that
public schooling was designed to serve the needs of the state more
than it was the needs of children or their parents. Citizenship similarly was defined in terms of the state's priorities, which, in operational terms, meant in terms of those who controlled the state, namely its dominant elites. A generation ago historians and social scientists described this use of schooling as a form of social control. The
underlying ideas were, one, that any society depends for its cohesion
upon its members internalizing a set of shared values and dispositions; two, that these values are neither neutral nor self-evident; and,
three, that they reflect the priorities of those in positions of power
and influence. There was always something paradoxical about seeing schooling in these terms, when Marx and Engels had made compulsory schooling one of their revolutionary demands in the
Communist Manifesto, and empirical research into the history of
education revealed that the concept of social control did not correspond to reality.

As a result, the concept of social control was abandoned for that
of hegemony, a term taken from Antonio Gramsci to describe the
processes by which people come to see a given state of affairs as natural or irresistible, even when it works to their disadvantage
(Adamson 1980; Femia, 1993). It describes a much more nuanced
state of affairs than did the older concept of social control.
Hegemony is not simply imposed in some top-down fashion; it has
to be negotiated, attended to, and shaped. Those at the receiving end
of the hegemonic process often resist it, manipulate it, appropriate it
to their own purposes, and in a thousand different ways contest it.
In short, hegemony is a process, not an end-state. As the British his-
torian and educationist Brian Simon has observed, "Education is an
area of struggle, an arena where opposing (or at least differing)

objectives meet – objectives reflecting the interests of different social classes and groups" (Simon, 1978, p. 29).

The concept of hegemony helps us to understand the present state of affairs in education, where in recent years talk of democracy and citizenship has largely disappeared. Instead, schools these days are expected to prepare students to be flexible and adaptable workers in the emerging global economy. In the words of the 1987 Radwanski report on Ontario drop-outs, education is now seen, not as a training ground for democratic citizenship, but as "the paramount ingredient for success in the competitive world economy" and thus essential to "our very survival as an economically competitive society" (Radwanski, 1987, p. 11). Policy-makers in education now think in terms of producing workers, not citizens, of retooling Canadian schools so as to produce the kind of work-force that will guarantee success in the new global economy.

The implications of this argument for education are clear (Robertson, 1998; Davis, 2000). They include closer links between schools and business; an emphasis on skills over knowledge (literacy but not literature, for example); a concentration on economically oriented subjects such as mathematics, science, and computer science, at the expense of history, literature, and the arts; a general vocationalization of the curriculum; and a tightening up of accountability measures to ensure that teachers and students are doing what is expected of them. In the process, democratic citizenship comes a poor second. Education for democracy is counter-productive in the era of the global marketplace. Democratic citizenship creates imperatives of heritage and tradition, of rights and obligations, of community and responsibility, of equality and justice, of popular sovereignty, that obstruct market efficiency and global competitiveness.

All of which is another way of saying that we are in the midst of a struggle to determine the shape of education and its contribution to the health of democracy. Those of us who see in education a means of maintaining and, better yet, extending and redefining democracy, must therefore become involved in the day-to-day politics of education. We must revive the discourse of citizenship, not the exclusionary, assimilative and often coercive citizenship of the past, but a citizenship that is built on diversity, equity, social justice, inclusiveness, and participation. The advocates of the new vocationalism, with their insistence of reshaping schools to serve the global economy, have largely captured the vocabulary of education: effectiveness, excellence, accountability, standards, quality – these and other words have come to represent a particular view of education. Those of us who value democratic citizenship need to recapture and redefine them.

It remains to consider what taking democracy seriously means for education. Against the view of education offered by the proponents of the new global economy, what have democrats to offer?

A Democratic Program for Education

There is no space here to present a detailed answer to this question, and, in any event, it has been thoroughly discussed over the years (for some recent examples, see Apple & Beane, 1995; Arnstine, 1995; Butts, 1989; Callan, 1997; Carlson & Apple, 1998; Goodman, 1992; Gutmann, 1987; McDonnell, Timpane & Benjamin, 2000; Parker, 1996; Sehr, 1997; Steiner, 1994). Suffice it to say that if education is to contribute to the flourishing of democracy, there are six aspects of it that are of interest to democrats: (1) the determination and control of education policy; (2) the choice of educational goals; (3) the content of the curriculum; (4) teaching and learning; (5) the organization of schooling; and (6) access to and provision of education.

So far as the first is concerned, the conventional wisdom is that, in a parliamentary system such as Canada's, democratic control of education is ensured through the office of a minister of education responsible to an elected legislature. In practice, however, things are not so clear cut. Typically, elected governments represent not an absolute majority of voters, but a plurality only. More fundamentally, the theory and practice of majority government say nothing about the interests of the minority who did not vote for the majority party and it can easily happen that a government sees itself as responsible, not to society as a whole, but to those groups to whom it feels politically obligated or ideologically committed. Moreover, once appointed, ministers of education can easily find themselves hamstrung by party discipline or at the mercy of officials who know more about their portfolio than they do themselves.

Historically, a partial solution to such difficulties has been found in school boards which, at least in theory, are supposed to represent local interests. In reality, however, school boards attract little attention from voters and have not provided much of a forum for democratic discussion of education, and governments in recent years have moved to reduce or eliminate them, as in New Brunswick, Ontario, Alberta, and, potentially, Manitoba. These provinces claim to have delegated power to individual schools and to school councils, arguing that this makes the school system more economical (by eliminating unnecessary school boards) and more democratic (by giving control to parents). There are three problems with this argument. One is that local school councils are unlikely to be able to resist the mandates of a provincial ministry of education, whereas school boards potentially could and sometimes did. Two, school councils represent the interests of parents, but parents are not the only stakeholders in education, which in a democracy must be the responsibility of all citizens. Three, those provinces that have eliminated or reduced school boards have at the same time moved to concentrate more power in their ministries of education, for example through examinations and assessment, tighter curriculum controls, teacher testing, and other such accountability measures. As things stand, there is no obvious mechanism to secure the democratic control of education, but it is a problem with which democrats must wrestle. If nothing else, democrats must use all available forums to give the problem the public visibility it requires so as to ensure that education policy is subject to truly democratic deliberation.

The second element of education for democracy addresses the choice of educational goals. For democrats the priority is obvious: while not neglecting the role of education in helping the young make the most of their lives and in finding good jobs, the primary task of schooling in a democracy is to produce democratic citizens. The equally obvious question is how this is best done. I have suggested elsewhere (Osborne, 1999) that education for democratic citizenship should meet the following criteria, which for purely mnemonic purposes I describe as the "twelve C's." The first C is *Canadian* and it proposes that schools should teach students enough about Canada, its history and geography, its institutional structures, its artistic and cultural achievements, its current problems, and so on, to enable them to understand and participate in the continuing debate about what kind of society Canada is and should become. The second C is *cosmopolitan*, in the strict sense of the word, and proposes that students also learn enough about the world as a whole, past and present, to see themselves as not only Canadian, but global citizens. The third C is *communication* and proposes that students should learn how to communicate effectively, through speech, writing, graphics, and all the other media. The fourth C is *content* and proposes that all students must gain a thorough all-round grounding of general knowledge. The fifth C is *curiosity* and proposes that schools must teach students to be intellectually curious, to want to keep on learning. The sixth C is *critical*, and proposes that students must learn to think critically, to question the status quo, and to see learning as continual inquiry. The seventh C is *creativity* and proposes that schooling develops the creative spirit which is present, but too often stifled, in all human beings. The eighth C is *civilizations* (in the plural) and proposes that schooling must give students an adequate knowledge and appreciation of human civilizations (again in the plural) of which we are all both the heirs and the trustees for the future. The ninth C is *community* and proposes that students must learn to see themselves as informed and involved members of their communities, locally, nationally, and globally. The tenth C is *concern* or *caring* and proposes that education teach students to care for other people and for the environment that makes life possible in the first place. The eleventh C stands for *character*, the development of which years ago was seen as one of the key purposes of education, standing for the willingness to shoulder responsibilities, to follow one's conscience, and to act morally. Finally, the twelfth C stands for *competence*, meaning that education must equip students to play their part as competent and effective citizens in the world in which they live.

In recent years, neo-liberals have rejected the need for any such formulations, arguing that there need be no overarching goals in education, that goals should be left to the choice of parents and students, and that schools should offer whatever the marketplace will support, for example through vouchers, through charter schools, or through the privatization of schooling (Chubb & Moe, 1990; Murphy, 1996; Nathan, 1996). In one sense, such suggestions seem to offer the ultimate in democratic freedom by giving parents total control of how their education dollars should be spent. Such an argument, however, equates democracy with individual choice while ignoring the claims of community. It also totally ignores the reality that we are not disembodied beings, that our individual desires and our ability to satisfy them derive from and depend on the community that nourishes us, so that education for democracy concerns not just children and their parents, but society as a whole.

The third element of education for democracy involves the content of the curriculum that is to be taught in schools. The twelve C's, as described above, provide a general philosophy of education; they do not answer the question of how best to deliver it in the classroom. For much of the 20th century, especially in North America, democratic educationists equated education for democracy with so-called progressive education, defined in terms of adjusting the curriculum to the needs of students, of defining education as promoting students' growth and development, often leading to a rejection of conventional academic curricula as intellectually elitist and culturally hegemonic.

Critics of the conventional academic curriculum are correct to attack its rigidities, but they ignore its many strengths. George Orwell's *Nineteen Eighty-Four* vividly illustrates what can happen in a society where people lack knowledge and so have no basis from which to challenge what they are told. This is why a liberal education is still the most valuable form of education for democratic citizenship. To quote the political philosopher, Alan Ryan:

> At its best, liberal education opens a conversation between ourselves and the immortal dead, gives us voices at our shoulders, asking us to think again and try harder...Liberal education in the conventional sense also rests on the thought that an acquaintance with intellectual, literary and artistic excellence is in some (debatable and hotly debated) fashion good for us, and that one of the ways it is so is in teaching us to measure ourselves against touchstones of cultural and intellectual excellence. (Ryan, 1997, p. 47)

A democratic liberal education consists not of stockpiling the knowledge of the past, an approach that Paolo Freire condemned as a "banking" concept of education in which students amass knowledge/capital for later use, but of using knowledge to evaluate and participate in the life of the present with the aim of shaping the future. There is no contradiction between liberal education as understood in this sense, and critical pedagogy as defined by such writers as Freire, Giroux, McLaren, Simon, and others, with their insistence that schooling must be used to interrogate the world as it exists in order to pursue greater social justice (Freire, 1970; Giroux, 1988; Giroux & McLaren, 1989; McLaren, 1994; Simon, 1985). Nor is there necessarily a contradiction between liberal education and Freire's concept of problem-posing education. As Freire himself noted: "I am not against a curriculum or a program, but only against the authoritarian and elitist ways of organizing the studies. I am defending the critical participation of the students in their education" (Schor & Freire, 1987, p. 21). As I have argued elsewhere, a liberal education, when appropriately taught, raises the problems that lie at the heart of democratic living (Osborne, 1988, 1991). Moreover, liberal education can be organized and taught in many different ways. Martha Nussbaum and others have shown how liberal education today can be organized into multiform curricula that address the concerns of contemporary society (Nussbaum, 1997; Orrill, 1997; Proctor, 1999).

Liberal education draws on the global heritage of human achievement. Properly understood and taught, it contains the seeds of its own deconstruction. As Gerald Graff (1992) has suggested with regard to debates over the literary canon, insofar as a curriculum is the subject of conflict, that very conflict can form a valuable part of its study. It is not a case of drilling into students the belief that some forms of cultural expression are inherently superior to others, but of showing them the variety of forms that exist so that they come to appreciate the diversity of the human heritage, to apply what they learn to the present, and to begin to make informed choices for themselves. We sometimes forget that the great theorists of democracy did not have what is commonly thought of these days as a democratic education. What they did have was a solid liberal education that gave them a rich fund of knowledge and the ability to reflect on what they knew. In the same way, all citizens deserve to have a broad and comprehensive knowledge of how human beings, past and present, have sought to understand and change their world. Only in this way can they avoid the presentism and parochialism that too often strips democratic deliberation of its true potential (Jacoby, 1999).

Knowledge also has to be organized and taught in ways that incorporate both skills and values. It is obvious that democratic deliberation, like democratic life generally, requires the exercise of skills, ranging from the three Rs to critical thinking, problem solving, decision making, and working with other people. Such skills have been staples of educational discussion for decades and need no elaboration here. What democrats must resist is the current tendency to define skills in "generic" terms, divorced from worthwhile subject matter. With skills people will know how to do what they are told, but without knowledge they will have no basis for questioning anything, no sense of alternatives, and no field of choice (Davis, 2000).

Besides knowledge and skills, schools obviously teach values. Equally obvious, values are central to the practice of democracy. Few people object to the schools teaching honesty, respect for others, mutuality, co-operation, and the like, all of which are at the basis of democratic life. Controversy begins where more substantive value conflicts arise: evolution versus creationism in science; the treatment of race and gender in literature; controversial issues in social studies; the presence of certain books in school libraries – these are only the best known examples of value issues that can create problems for schools. Problems or not, however, schools in a democracy have an obligation to teach students to explore issues and to consider viewpoints that they otherwise might not encounter. To quote the philosopher, Eamonn Callan: "The essential demand is that schooling properly involves at some stage sympathetic and critical engagement with beliefs and ways of life at odds with the culture of the family or religious or ethnic group into which the child is born" (Callan, 1997, p. 133). Democracy requires schools to observe such procedural values as tolerance, fairness, and respect for evidence and rules of argument, and it is difficult to do this in the absence of genuine controversy and challenges to cherished beliefs.

Schools also have to take a stand on more substantive values. In 1994, for example, Ontario's Royal Commission on Learning held schools responsible for teaching "some sense of honesty, truth, civility, social justice and co-operation, and a determination to combat violence, racism, gender inequity, and environmental degradation" (Royal Commission on Learning, 1994, pp. 1, 61). Like everyone else, democrats want schools to teach children to behave properly, though we do not always agree on just what that entails. We want them to teach the value of work, responsibility, respect for human rights. But we also want them to explore controversial and sensitive value questions. Democracy requires no less.

The fourth component of education for democracy deals with teaching and learning: what teaching strategies should democrats favor and how do they connect with what we know about how students learn? It has long been a commonplace of democratic education that if students are to learn the principles and practices of democracy, they will do so most successfully in the "democratic classroom" through the experience of "democratic pedagogy." Everything depends, however, on how these concepts are understood.

The democratic classroom is too easily equated with any teaching strategy that can be said to be activity-based and student-centred. If students have some sort of say in what they are learning, and if they are involved in something more active than listening to their teacher or filling out worksheets, then they are considered to be learning democratically. For example, in a recent study of democratic teacher education, the researchers looked for classrooms that exemplified the democratic principles they espoused, "defined by us as practising such strategies as Whole Language learning, co-operative learning, authentic assessment, and other techniques that ensure equitable learning opportunities in classrooms" (McEwan, 1994, p. 105).

This one-to-one equation of democratic education with student-centred pedagogy is far too simple, however. Mere activity, no matter how student-centred and participative, can be profoundly undemocratic. Group work, co-operative learning, inquiry learning, and activity methods are techniques only. They can be used to foster democracy or to cripple it. In and of themselves they are democratically neutral.

What matters is the spirit in which teachers use their various teaching techniques and the purpose for which they employ them. A generation ago Massialas and Cox made a distinction between "method" and "technique" which deserves a wider hearing than it has received. "Method" they defined as "the overarching attitude the teacher takes towards knowledge, the materials at hand, the learning situation, and the roles that students are to perform," while "technique" describes the specific teaching methods used at any given moment, such as lecturing, note-taking, discussion, and the rest (Massialas & Cox, 1966, p. 62). What matters is not so much whether teachers use this or that technique, but whether they deliberately espouse democratic citizenship, with all its implications and possibilities, as a fundamental goal and organize their subject-matter, their pedagogy, and their classrooms to attain it.

This distinction between method and technique is also consistent with what we know about how students learn about, for example, the nature of multiple intelligences, of constructivist learning, of Vygotsky's concept of the zone of proximal development, and all the other psychological discoveries which reveal what good teachers have always known: that students are meaning-makers, that in their own way they are inquirers and theory builders. If the schools are to contribute to democracy, teachers must see their students as participants in the process of learning, as people who have a contribution to make to the inquiry being pursued in the classroom, which is, of course, one of the central tenets of critical and feminist pedagogy.

The fifth component of education for democracy addresses, not so much the curriculum and the way it is taught and learned, but the general organization of schooling. It is generally agreed that some of what we learn from our schooling derives from the general everyday routines of school life. It is partly through their schooling, for example, that children learn to co-operate or to compete, to settle disputes amicably or violently, to accept or to question discipline and authority, to respect or ignore the rights of others, and to internalize (or not) the thousand other dispositions and values that make democratic life possible.

Researchers usually describe this process as comprising the "hidden curriculum" and, broadly speaking, it comes in two forms. The first consists of the rules of conduct that schools knowingly enforce on students, rules about attendance, punctuality, dress, hallway behavior, smoking, and the rest. The second lies more below the surface and can be much less obvious to students and even to teachers. It consists of the social interactions among students, the interchanges between teachers and students, the implicit and often unspoken signals through which teachers reveal their expectations, and the many occurrences that impinge on a student's day without anyone necessarily doing anything from deliberate intent, but which combine to shape the character traits and behavior patterns that have an impact on the kind of adult citizen a student might become.

Too often the hidden curriculum serves to promote qualities that are the antithesis of democratic citizenship. Whatever schools might say about the importance of critical thinking, social participation, personal autonomy, social responsibility, and the like, the message of the hidden curriculum can often be one of conformity, obedience, hierarchy, and order. Indeed, an international survey of civic education some years ago came close to concluding that the organizational imperatives of schools are almost by definition antidemocratic, suggesting that "perhaps a hierarchical organization such as the school is not the best setting for inculcating democratic values" (Oppenheim & Torney, 1975, p. 21).

Equally troubling, the evidence shows that the democratic and citizenship values that students learn in school often vary according to their social background. Thus, girls are often treated differently from boys and traditional gender-roles are reinforced by teachers, with the result that boys can think of citizenship differently from girls, as in Carol Gilligan's well-known, though contested, argument that men think primarily in terms of an ethic of rights and duties, while women think more in terms of caring and responsibility (Gilligan, 1982; Hekman, 1995). Social class is also an important factor in determining the kind of schooling offered to students and how they respond to it. To date, schools have not proved able to compensate for the inequities of class with the result that academic and educational success, with all that it means for adult life, still strongly correlates with students' class background. Students are tracked into different programs, allegedly for reasons of aptitude and ability, but in fact in terms of social class and race, and researchers have shown that middle class students receive an education that emphasizes participation and efficacy, while working class students are fed a message of compliance and deference, thus establishing a type of anticipatory political socialization that is all too clearly reflected in the over-representation of the middle class in the political system. As with class, so with race, as students from racial minorities similarly too often find themselves receiving not only an inferior education, but one that fails to acknowledge their particular cultural identity (Anyon, 1980; Curtis, Livingstone & Smaller, 1992; Oakes, 1985; Willis, 1976).

In short, if schools are to serve as training grounds for democracy, they cannot ignore the so-called hidden curriculum. Democracy depends in large part on students feeling sufficiently capable and competent to involve themselves in the affairs of their society, to work for their preferred cause without trampling on the rights of others – and these and many other such traits are learned, or not learned, as much through the everyday experience of schooling as through any particular lessons.

Finally, the sixth component of education for democracy concerns the provision of and access to education. No society can properly be called democratic if it denies its citizens, whether deliberately or otherwise, equal access to the highest possible quality of education. The concept of equality of opportunity is central to even the narrowest conception of democracy and lies behind the many attempts undertaken over the years to ensure that all children enjoy the same start in life. It is no secret that Canada has a long way to go in this regard, as shown, for example, by the failure to eliminate unacceptably high levels of child poverty and to provide adequately funded day-care, but, this said, at least the concept of equality of opportunity is inscribed on the mainstream political agenda.

Whether it is adequate is another question. As critics on the left have long pointed out, equality of opportunity, even if it could be perfectly realized, does not solve the problem of democratic equality, since it usually results in people becoming progressively unequal. At best, it allows for the circulation of inequality by creating a talent-based meritocracy whose membership changes with each new generation. But, as Michael Young (1958) pointed out over a generation ago, meritocracies have their problems too, not least in their leaving those who do not "make it" with no-one to blame for their lack of success but themselves. For such critics, the goal to strive for is not equality of opportunity but equality of result. To this end, they advocate the reallocation of resources such that those most in need are seen as the highest priority (which is rarely the case in education today). In the context of schooling, this means rethinking the organization and delivery (and some would say the content also) of education so that students who for whatever reason do not feel comfortable in conventional school settings can nonetheless receive a worthwhile education. It also means redefining the notion and criteria of educational achievement so that a variety of outcomes can reasonably be regarded as equal in quality and value.

There is also a considerable history behind attempts to compensate for inequities that arise from difference in parental income and social class, though enormous problems still remain. The most obvious and earliest remedy was to make education free up to the end of high school, so that no-one would be disadvantaged by an inability to pay school fees. Outside the realm of schooling, redistributive tax policies and family allowances were intended to put more money into the pockets of lower-income families. All such policies, however, failed to address the substantial differences that existed between schools for the children of the well-to-do and those for the children of the poor. This was and is much more than a problem of private, elite schools. Within the public school system the institution of the local, neighborhood school, combined with a de facto segregation of neighborhoods by income and social class, means that some school boards, or schools within the same school district, are more advantaged than others. The proposals to deal with this kind of inequality have included differential allocation of resources; head start and other assisted learning programs; open school boundaries; family support; community schools; educational priority areas; and many other such policies, but to date the problems have proved largely intractable and the inequalities largely remain in place. This is one reason why in today's market-driven political climate, we see suggestions that the very concept of public schooling is at fault, with market-oriented critics urging its replacement by charter schools, vouchers and an overall privatization of education.

In recent years less obvious issues of educational equality have arisen. Though it was always obvious that class and income often intersected with race and ethnicity, it is now widely recognized that there is a cultural dimension to race and ethnicity that operates independently of class. Some Aboriginal and Black Canadians argue that the mainstream school curriculum reflects white European values and assumptions that deny the validity of their own cultural traditions, while also imposing an alien barrier to their children's willingness to learn. Though to a lesser extent than in the United States, Canadian schools have responded by instituting curricula based on Black and Native Studies and Aboriginal Canadians increasingly control their own schools and determine their own curricula. In one sense, this represents a democratic extension of multiculturalism, but it raises some problems for those who believe that democracy depends, at least in part, on citizens sharing some elements of a common culture (Entwistle, 1978; Lawton, 1975; Whitty, 1985). The answer, presumably, lies in designing curricula that reflect both the cultures to which students belong and the culture of the broader national society.

Another dimension of educational equality that has become increasingly obvious in recent years and that must be of concern to democrats revolves around gender. Historically, citizenship, democratic or otherwise, excluded women and feminists today view the concept with some suspicion (Okin, 1992; Phillips, 1989 & 1993). As a concept based on activity in the public sphere, it inevitably privileged men and excluded women, who were confined to the private sphere of home and family, which were kept distinct from the public, political realm. This public-private distinction had educational consequences. Girls were denied educational opportunities open to boys. They were shunted into programs designed to prepare them for gender-based roles. Textbooks and curricula displayed a gender-biased view of the world. Teachers often interacted more positively with boys than with girls. None of these inequities has been completely eliminated, but most schools now seek to ensure that girls are treated equally with boys.

Some researchers argue that the problem goes much deeper than equality of access and provision. They suggest that girls have a different learning style from boys and that schools privilege masculine learning styles over feminine ones, thereby denying girls, especially in early adolescence, the chance to develop their full potential as adults, and therefore as citizens, while also denying to boys a different way of learning, based more on caring and co-operation, that would be of benefit to them (Belenky, Clinchy, Goldberger & Rule, 1986; Gilligan, Lyons & Hammer, 1990). In practical terms, this has meant a growing popularity for single-sex, girls-only classes and has led to some rethinking of curriculum content and pedagogy. Feminist researchers, for example, have developed a feminist pedagogy, aimed primarily at girls but intended also to be of benefit to boys, and centred on such attributes as "care, concern and connection" (Martin, 1987, pp. 406-9), of "community, communication, equality and mutual nurturance" (Schniedewind, 1983, p. 262; see also Briskin, 1994).

In other words, the provision of equal access to education involves more than ensuring equal access to all. It raises questions of curriculum content, pedagogy, and school organization which do not permit easy answers in a democratic society, especially when democracy is coupled with cultural diversity and respect for difference. Perhaps the most obvious example is that of the "mainstreaming" of students with special needs. In recent years, schools have largely abandoned the belief that such students are best taught in segregated schools or classes, believing instead that they are entitled, as citizens in the making, to be integrated with students at large. Experience suggests, however, that simply putting special needs students into existing classrooms, even with teacher aides, individual learning plans and other supports in place, is not enough. To be successful, it involves redesigning teacher training, rethinking class sizes, re-organizing teachers' working conditions, and a host of other considerations.

The solution to educational inequity lies not in some universally applicable policy formulation or some foundationalist claim, for the problem manifests itself in some concrete, context-specific arena and must be dealt with in the light of local circumstances. It embodies the very essence of democracy: difficult problems of public policy that divide people and which revolve around conflicting value priorities while admitting of no simple solutions. As Amy Gutmann (1987) and others have argued, dealing with such questions is itself a form of education for democracy.

Conclusion

In describing John Dewey's philosophy of education, Alan Ryan said that Dewey's aim was "always to socialize children into an American society that could be created by radical political and economic change" (Ryan, 1998, p. 131). This idea of socializing children into a society that has yet to be created, and by so doing making its creation possible, applies with particular force to education for democracy. A problem with many discussions of democratic reform is that though they present attractive visions of what democracy could be – more participatory, more deliberative, more critical, more inclusive, and so on – they rarely offer any suggestions for how to turn their visions into reality (Barber, 1984 & 1998; Budge, 1996; Dryzek, 1990; Elster, 1994; Fishkin, 1991; Held, 1993; Hirst, 1994; Mouffe, 1993). Nonetheless, visions of what might be are important for helping us reflect on what actually is. Robert Dahl is obviously correct when he observes that even the most developed "actual democracy" falls considerably short of the top of the scale of "ideal democracy," but he is equally correct to note that this does not mean that "actual democracy" is not worth preserving and extending (Dahl, 1999: 21). Democracy is, in part, a process of and a commitment to continual debate and deliberation in which the ultimate goal is more debate and deliberation. As John Dewey once noted:

> *The very idea of democracy, the meaning of democracy, must be continually explored afresh; it has to be constantly rediscovered, remade and re-organized; while the political and economic and social institutions in which it is embodied have to be remade and re-organized to meet the changes that are going on in the development of new needs on the part of human beings and new resources for satisfying those needs. (Dewey, 1937, p. 182)*

It is obvious, for example, that Canadian democracy is capable of substantial improvement. Canadian society remains highly inequitable in terms of the distribution of wealth and power. Political participation continues to be largely a function of gender, race, and social class. Many Canadians take a very passive view of citizenship and have little engagement with the political process. Moreover, Canada faces a number of pressing problems that will demand the utmost from citizens if they are to be manageable: the place of Quebec in Confederation; the place of the First Nations in the Canadian polity; the challenge of globalization; the protection of the environment; the abolition of poverty; the role and nature of government – these are only some of the most obvious. As John Ralston Saul (1998) has observed, Canada is not a conventional nation-state on the American or European model and, as such, it demands special qualities from its citizens.

This has long been true, but it is especially the case in the circumstances in which we find ourselves today. As Reg Whitaker has observed, older political narratives of Canada, through which citizens deciphered their society and defined their hopes for its future, were largely associated with political ideologies (conservative, liberal, and socialist primarily) which, despite their differences, all assumed "a consensual notion of community that transcended politics." These older narratives, however, are today being replaced by what Whitaker calls a "neo-populism," an amalgam of faith in the market, neo-liberal economics, and social conservatism, interacting with pressures for the strengthening of cultural identity and heritage, which, in combination, tend to "weaken consensual identification with the community, as it is the very boundaries of the community itself, the terms of citizenship, that are part of the problematic of political controversy" (Whitaker, 1999, p. 47; but see also Graves, Dugas & Beauchamp, 1999).

Perhaps the most fundamental fact about Canada is that it is a country that is continually debating the terms of its own existence. It has been doing so ever since 1763. To participate in this debate, to avoid false solutions, to accept that there might in fact not be any once-for-all solutions at all, and above all not to turn one's back on its frustration, is perhaps the ultimate exercise in democracy. As the political scientist John Dryzek (1996) puts it:

> *If there is no debate about what its future direction should be and about how further democratization might be possible, then democracy itself will be impoverished. There is an important sense in which one of the goals of democracy always has to be more democracy....[T]he democratic life consists in large part of searching for democracy. (p. 4)*

This searching for democracy is more than ever necessary today, when the health of democracy is threatened by the very success of the capitalism that provides its economic foundation. Culturally, capitalism holds little sacred. It thrives on innovation and subjects everything to the logic of the marketplace.

As Marx and Engels put it in 1848:

> *Constant revolutionizing of production, uninterrupted disturbance of all social conditions, everlasting uncertainty and agitation distinguish the bourgeois epoch from all earlier ones. All fixed, fast-frozen relations, with their train of venerable prejudices and opinions are swept away, all new-formed ones become antiquated before they can ossify. All that is solid melts in air, all that is holy is profaned, and man is at last compelled to face with sober sense, his real conditions of life, and his relations with his kind. (p. 83)*

The phenomenal success of capitalism has largely depended on the existence of pre-capitalist values such as trust, frugality, loyalty, and obligation, which the very logic of capitalism serves to erode. Capitalism calls almost everything into question, and creates and depends on a self-interested, profit-driven, let's-make-a-deal personality type that thinks in terms of material acquisition and personal well-being without regard to the social consequences of its activities, and that explains in considerable part the democratic deficit and the decline of social capital described earlier in this chapter.

By contrast, democracy requires its citizens to possess a sense of community, to be public spirited, devoted to the common good, and able to balance personal interest against the welfare and needs of their fellow citizens, both present and future. To quote Dryzek (1996) once more: "...the more that capitalism and its associated discourses, political ideologies, and public policies produce rational egoists, the more instability, arbitrariness, authoritarian drift, and loss of legitimacy that liberal democratic political institutions are likely to experience" (p. 145).

There is a contradiction in capitalism between the imperatives of capital accumulation and of legitimation. The first includes all the policies necessary for the economic well-being of the capitalist order; the second consists of the measures through which capitalism meets the needs of people; and they periodically come into conflict, as when the drive to control inflation or maintain credit ratings creates unemployment and insecurity (Bowles & Gintis, 1986; O'Connor, 1973; Offe, 1984). Indeed, this kind of conflict is likely to increase with the pressures of globalization as national governments find themselves having to make economic decisions to satisfy, not their citizens, but the demands of global investors and financial institutions, of international trade agreements, and supranational trade and investment regimes.

Beyond this lies the most inescapable pressure of all, the capacity of the environment to sustain life. The drive for economic growth which is inherent in capitalism must sooner or later outstrip the capacity of the environment to sustain it, creating serious problems of resource allocation and distribution that will threaten the very survival of democracy. It might well be that the single most important priority for democratic education in today's world is, in fact, to prepare the young to do what their elders have conspicuously failed to do, to live in ways that respect and preserve the environment that sustains us.

In these circumstances, and given the relative silence of the media and of policy makers on these and related issues, it falls upon the schools to prepare students to participate in the public debate on the future of democracy that we so urgently need. In the recent words of one of the foremost students of democracy, Robert Dahl (1998), "one of the imperative needs of democratic countries is to improve citizens' capacities to engage intelligently in political life" (p. 187). Dahl was talking about much more than schools, but obviously schools have their part to play. As the Principal of the Winnipeg Normal School said in 1932: "The only hope for curing the ills of the world is that young people may picture a better one and strive to realize it. To frame this picture and to cultivate this ambition is the greatest duty of the school" (McIntyre, 1932, p. 45). This is the spirit that should guide education for democracy, especially in the Canadian context, though it is light years removed from the thinking of those who want to turn our schools into servants of the global marketplace.

References

Adamson, W. L. (1980). *Hegemony and revolution: A study of Antonio Gramsci's political and cultural theory.* Berkeley: University of California Press.

Anderson, B. (1991). *Imagined communities: Reflections on the origin and spread of nationalism.* London: Verso.

Anyon, J. (1980). Social class and the hidden curriculum of work. *Journal of Education, 162,* 67-92.

Apple, M. W. (1979). *Ideology and curriculum.* London: Routledge & Kegan Paul.

Apple, M. W. & Beane, J. A. (Eds.). (1995). *Democratic schools.* Alexandria: Association for Supervision and Curriculum Development.

Arnstine, D. (1995). *Democracy and the arts of schooling.* Albany: State University of New York Press.

Barber, B. R. (1984). *Strong democracy: Participatory politics for a new age.* Berkeley: University of California Press.

Barber, B. R. (1996). Foundationalism and democracy. In S. Benhabib (Ed.), *Democracy and difference: Contesting the boundaries of the political* (pp. 348-359). Princeton: Princeton University Press.

Barber, B. R. (1998). *A place for us: How to make civil society and democracy strong.* New York: Hill & Wang.

Belenky, M. F., Clinchy. B. M., Goldberger, N. R., Rule. J. M. (1986). *Women's ways of knowing.* New York: Basic Books.

Bowles, S. & Gintis, H. (1986). *Democracy and capitalism: Property, community, and the contradictions of modern social thought.* New York: Basic Books.

Briskin, L. (1994). Feminist pedagogy: Teaching and learning liberation. In L. Erwin & D. MacLennan (Eds.), *Sociology of education in Canada: Critical perspectives on theory, research and practice* (pp. 443-470). Toronto: Copp Clark Longman.

Budge, I. (1996). *The challenge of direct democracy.* Cambridge: Polity Press.

Butts, R. F. (1989). *The civic mission in educational reform.* Stanford: Hoover Institution Press.

Cairns, A. (1995). *Reconfigurations: Canadian citizenship and constitutional change.* Toronto: McClelland & Stewart.

Callan, E. (1997). *Creating citizens: Political education and liberal democracy.* Oxford: Clarendon Press.

Carlson, D. W. & Apple, M. W. (Eds.). (1998). *Power/knowledge/pedagogy: The meaning of democratic education in unsettling times.* Boulder: Westview.

Caspary, W. R. (2000). *Dewey on democracy.* Ithaca: Cornell University Press.

Chubb, J. E. & Moe, T. M. (1990). *Politics, markets, and America's schools.* Washington: The Brookings Institution.

Crick, B. & Porter, A. (Eds.). (1978). *Political education and political literacy.* London: Longman.

Curtis, B., Livingstone, D. & Smaller, H. (1992). *Stacking the deck: The streaming of working class kids in Ontario schools.* Toronto: Lorimer.

Dagger, R. (1997). *Civic virtues: Rights, citizenship, and republican liberalism.* New York: Oxford University Press.

Dahl, R. A. (1998). *On democracy.* New Haven: Yale University Press.

Dahl, R. (1999). Can international organizations be democratic? A skeptic's view. In I. Shapiro & C. Hacker-Cordón (Eds.), *Democracy's edges* (pp. 19-36). Cambridge: Cambridge University Press.

Davis, B. (2000). *Skills mania: Snake oil in our schools?* Toronto: Between the Lines

Dewey, J. (1888).The ethics of democracy. In *John Dewey: Early works*, Vol. 1: 1882-1888 (pp. 227-249). Carbondale: Southern Illinois University Press, 1969.

Dewey, J. (1916). *Democracy and education.* New York: Macmillan.

Dewey, J (1937). The challenge of democracy to education. In *John Dewey: Later works*, Vol. 11: 1935-7 (pp. 181-190). Carbondale: Southern Illinois University Press, 1987.

Dryzek, J. (1990). *Discursive democracy.* Cambridge: Cambridge University Press.

Dryzek, J. (1996). *Democracy in capitalist times: Ideals, limits, and struggles.* New York: Oxford University Press.

Elster, J. (1994). *Deliberative democracy.* Cambridge: Cambridge University Press.

Entwistle, H. (1978). *Class, culture and education.* London: Methuen.

Femia, J. (1993). *Marxism and democracy.* Oxford: Clarendon Press.

Fishkin, J. (1991). *Democracy and deliberation: New directions for democratic reform.* New Haven: Yale University Press.

Freire, P. (1970). *Pedagogy of the oppressed.* New York: Continuum.

Galston, W. (1991). *Liberal purposes: Goods, diversity and values in the liberal state.* Cambridge: Cambridge University Press.

Galston, W. A. (1999). Diversity, toleration, and deliberative democracy: Religious minorities and public schooling. In S. Macedo (Ed.). *Deliberative politics: Essays on democracy and disagreement* (pp. 39-48). Princeton: Princeton University Press.

Gilligan, C. (1982). *In a different voice: Psychological theory and women's development.* Cambridge: Harvard University Press.

Gilligan, C., Lyons, N. P. & Hammer, T. J. (1989). *Making connections: The relational worlds of adolescent girls at Emma Willard High School.* Cambridge: Harvard University Press.

Giroux, H. A. (1988). *Schooling and the struggle for public life: Critical pedagogy in the modern age.* Minneapolis: University of Minnesota Press.

Giroux, H. A. & McLaren, P. (1989). *Critical pedagogy, the state, and cultural struggle.* Albany: State University of New York Press.

Goodman, J. (1992). *Elementary schooling for critical democracy.* Albany: State University of New York Press.

Gould, C. (1988). *Rethinking democracy: Freedom and social co-operation in politics, economy and society.* Cambridge: Cambridge University Press.

Graff, G. (1992). *Beyond the culture wars: How teaching the conflicts can revitalize American education.* New York: Norton.

Graves, F. L., Dugas, T., Beauchamp, P. (1999). Identity and national attachments in contemporary Canada. In H. Lazar & T. McIntosh (Eds.), *How Canadians connect* (pp. 307-354). Kingston: Queen's University School of Policy Studies & McGill-Queen's University Press.

Gutmann, A. (1987). *Democratic education.* Princeton: Princeton University Press.

Gutmann, A. & Thompson, D.(1996). *Democracy and disagreement.* Cambridge: Harvard University Press.

Heater, D. B. (1990). *Citizenship: The civic ideal in world history, politics and education.* London: Longman.

Hekman, S. J. (1995). *Moral voices, moral selves: Carol Gilligan's feminist moral theory.* Cambridge: Polity.

Held, D. (Ed.). (1993). *Prospects for democracy.* Stanford: Stanford University Press.

Hess, R. D. & Torney, J. V. (1967). *The development of political attitudes in children.* Chicago: Aldine.

Hirst, P. (1994). *Associative democracy.* Cambridge: Polity.

Ignatieff, M. (2000). *The rights revolution.* Toronto: Anansi.

Jacoby, R. (1999). *The end of utopia: Politics and culture in an age of apathy.* New York: Basic Books.

Kelly, A. V. (1995). *Education and democracy: Principles and practices.* London: Chapman.

Kymlicka. W. (1998). *Finding our way: Rethinking ethnocultural relations in Canada.* Toronto: Oxford University Press.

Lawton, D. (1975). *Class, culture, and the curriculum.* London: Routledge & Kegan Paul.

Lazar, H. & McIntosh, T. (Eds.). (1999). *How Canadians connect.* Kingston: Queen's University School of Policy Studies & McGill-Queen's University Press.

Maciejko, B. (1986). Public schools and the workers' struggle, Winnipeg 1914-1921. In N. Sheehan, J. D. Wilson & D. Jones (Eds.), *Schools in the west: Essays in Canadian educational history* (pp. 213-237). Calgary: Detselig.

Manitoba Department of Education. (1913). *Annual report of the Department of Education, 1913.* Winnipeg: Manitoba Department of Education.

Martin, J. (1987). Reforming teacher education, rethinking liberal education. *Teachers College Record, 88,* 406-9.

Marx, K. & Engels, F. (1848/1985). *The communist manifesto.* London: Penguin Books 1985 edition.

Massialas, B. G. & Cox, C. B. (1966). *Inquiry in social studies.* New York: McGraw-Hill.

McDonnell, L. M., Timpane, P. M., Benjamin, R. (Eds.). (2000). *Rediscovering the democratic purposes of education.* Lawrence: University of Kansas Press.

McEwan, B. (1994). Deliberately developing democratic teachers in a year. In J. M. Novak (Ed.), *Democratic teacher education: Programs, processes, problems, and prospects* (pp. 103-123). Albany: State University of New York Press.

McIntyre, W. A. (1932). The school preparing for life. *Western School Journal,* XXXVII: 43-45.

McLaren, P. (1994). Critical pedagogy: Constructing an arch of social dreaming and a doorway to hope. In L. Erwin & D. MacLennan (Eds.). *Sociology of education in Canada: Critical perspectives on theory, research and practice* (pp. 137-160). Toronto: Copp Clark Longman.

Mouffe, C. (1993). *The return of the political.* London: Verso, 1993.

Murphy, J. (1996). *The privatization of schooling: Problems and possibilities.* Berkeley: Sage.

Nathan, J. (1996). *Charter schools: Creating hope and opportunity for American education.* San Francisco: Jossey-Bass.

Nussbaum, M. (1997). *Cultivating humanity: A classical defense of reform in liberal education.* Cambridge: Harvard University Press.

Oakes, J. (1985). *Keeping track: How schools structure inequality.* New Haven: Yale University Press.

O'Connor, J. (1973). *The fiscal crisis of the state.* New York: St. Martin's Press.

Offe, C. (1984). *Contradictions of the welfare state.* Cambridge: M.I.T. Press.

Okin, S. M. (1992). Women, equality and citizenship. *Queen's Quarterly, 99,* 56-71.

Oppenheim, A. & Torney, J. V. (1975). *Civic education in ten countries.* New York: Wiley.

Orrill, R. (Ed.). (1997). *Education and democracy: Re-imagining liberal learning in America.* New York: College Entrance Board.

Osborne, K. (1988). *Educating citizens: A democratic socialist agenda for Canadian education.* Toronto: Our Schools Ourselves.

Osborne, K. (1991). *Teaching for democratic citizenship.* Toronto: Our Schools Ourselves/Lorimer.

Osborne, K. (1992). The emerging agenda for Canadian high schools. *Journal of Curriculum Studies, 24* (4), 371-379.

Osborne, K. (1996). 'Education is the best national insurance': Citizenship education in Canadian schools, past and present. *Canadian and International Education, 25* (2), 31-58.

Osborne, K. (1999). *Education: A guide to the Canadian school debate or who wants what and why?* Toronto: Penguin.

Parker, W. C. (Ed.). (1996). *Educating the democratic mind.* Albany: State University of New York Press.

Pateman, C. (1970). *Participation and democratic theory.* Cambridge: Cambridge University Press.

Phillips, A. (1989). *Engendering democracy.* University Park: University of Pennsylvania Press.

Phillips, A. (1993). *Democracy and difference.* University Park: University of Pennsylvania Press.

Proctor, R. E. (1999). *Defining the humanities: How rediscovering a tradition can improve our schools with a curriculum for today's students.* Bloomington: Indiana University Press.

Putman, J. H. & Weir, G. M. (1925). *Survey of the school system.* Vancouver: King's Printer.

Putnam, R. D. (2000). *Bowling alone: The collapse and revival of American community.* New York: Simon & Schuster.

Radwanski, G. (1987). *The relevance of education and the issue of drop-outs.* Toronto: Ontario Ministry of Education.

Robertson, H. (1998). *No more teachers, no more books.* Toronto: McClelland & Stewart.

Royal Commission on Learning. (1994). *For the love of learning.* Toronto: Queen's Printer.

Royal Commission on Aboriginal Peoples. (1996). Report. Ottawa: Minister of Supply and Services.

Ryan, A. (1997). *Liberal anxieties and liberal education.* New York: Hill & Wang.

Saul, J. R. (1998). *Reflections of a Siamese twin: Canada at the end of the twentieth century.* Toronto: Viking.

Schniedewind, N. (1983). Feminist values: Guidelines for teaching methodology in women's studies. In C. Bunch & S. Pollack (Eds.), *Learning our way: Essays in feminist education* (pp. 261-271). Trumansburg: Crossing Press.

Schor, I. & P. Freire. (1987). *A pedagogy for liberation.* South Hadley: Bergin & Garvey.

Sears, A. (1994). Social studies as citizenship education in English Canada. *Theory and Research in Social Education, 22* (1), 6-43.

Sehr, D. (1997). *Education for public democracy*. Albany: State University of New York Press.

Simon, B. (1978). Problems in contemporary educational theory: A Marxist approach. *Journal of Philosophy of Education, 12*, 29-39.

Simon, R. (1985). Critical pedagogy. In *International encyclopaedia of education*. Oxford: Pergamon, 1119-1120.

Steiner, D. M. (1994). *Rethinking democratic education: The politics of reform*. Baltimore: Johns Hopkins University Press.

Tanguay, A. B. (1999). Canada's political parties in the 1990s: The fraying of the ties that bind. In H. Lazar & T. McIntosh (Eds.), *How Canadians connect* (pp. 217-244). Kingston: Queen's University School of Policy Studies & McGill-Queen's University Press.

Voet, R. (1998). *Feminism and citizenship*. London: Sage Publications.

Westbrook, R. B. (1991). *John Dewey and American democracy*. Ithaca: Cornell University Press.

Whitaker, R. (1999). The changing Canadian state. In H. Lazar & T. McIntosh (Eds.), *How Canadians connect* (pp. 38-59). Kingston: Queen's University School of Policy Studies & McGill-Queen's University Press.

Whitty, G. (1985). *Sociology and school knowledge: Curriculum theory, research and politics*. London: Methuen.

Willis, P. (1976). *Learning to labour: How working class kids get working class jobs*. Farnborough (U.K.): Saxon House.

Young, M. (1958). *The rise of the meritocracy: An essay on equality and education*. London: Thames & Hudson.

Chapter 2
Beyond Common Educational Standards: Toward a Curriculum of Life
John P. Portelli and Ann B. Vibert

Introduction

In the last decade or so there has been a fervent public interest in educational issues, practices, and beliefs. Public debates in Canadian media have focused on such issues as mainstreaming, whole language vs. phonics, separate schools, multiculturalism and antiracism in schools, accountability, standardized testing, teacher testing, and concerns about educational standards. The call for common national standards, the arguments to evaluate more thoroughly students' achievements, as well as the complaints about the lowering of standards in schools, demonstrate the need to seriously examine the issue of standards which has become so predominant in educational debate.

In this chapter we first clarify the notion of standards. We claim that common yet serious misinterpretations arise from confusions about the concept of standards in popular discourse. Second, we offer a critical examination of the assumptions underlying popular discourse about standards; and finally, we offer alternative perspectives on educational standards and justification for these perspectives. These alternative perspectives rest on the conception of the "curriculum of life" – a curriculum that is grounded in the immediate daily world of students as well as in the larger social, political contexts of their lives. We will argue that it would be more worthwhile to direct the efforts spent on establishing and monitoring common standards on support needed to enact a curriculum of life. Such a re-direction would provide better opportunities for creating equity in schools.

We want to make it very clear at the outset that although our focus is on the issue of standards, we do not see this issue as discrete from other current and important educational, social, and ultimately, political debates, including, for example, social justice and issues of difference. In other words, we believe that the issue of standards, like any other educational issue, is not merely an educational issue but also one that is ethical and political in nature. Ultimately, there are no purely educational concerns.[1]

One of the major popular concerns is the claim that we don't have high standards in education (Ontario Ministry of Education, 2000; Nikiforuk, 1993). There seems to be a widespread public concern that educational standards in Canada are slipping in comparison to the "good old days" when education, it is claimed, was more rigorous. Another equally pervasive concern is the fear that we do not have a *common* set of standards throughout the country, which is an echo of the larger plea for common, global, universal standards (Eisner, 1995). The argument seems to be that if we had common, universal standards then our quality of education would not be deteriorating, and students historically marginalized as "at-risk" would have a better chance at completing schooling. Hence the sense of urgency for schools to develop mission statements with which everyone can agree or pretend to agree. This argument is also presented as a plea for practicality: if we do not have a common set of standards, then we cannot proceed or operate well in practice; it is not practical to operate with different criteria. Moreover, having diverse criteria does not make the standards clear.

What are Standards?

Before we move to some critical analysis of these concerns about educational standards, it is crucial to make some clarifying remarks about the nature of standards. The term "standards" has different meanings and is used in different contexts. For example, we refer to "the standard point or complaint made," namely, the typical or popular point made. But then we also say "these are the standards that we use," namely, the criteria that we use to evaluate something, or in a sense, the policies that direct our actions. We also have the Canadian Standards Association (CSA) that develops and monitors standards for commodities and production of materials. The CSA makes sure that the standards are met and that they are at least of acceptable quality. We also use standard in another context when we refer to standard as a flag or emblem, as in "standard-bearer" in the case of the military. The term is also used as a verb when, for example, we try to "standardize equipment" or even "standardize replies." In these instances, what we mean is to try to conform to an established or uniform position or specifications. Surely, in the educational context, we do not mean to use all these different meanings at the same time. But the confusion about the issue of standards arises partly because of the lack of clarity.

In an educational context, as Eisner (1993) warns us, we need to distinguish between "standard as a measurement" and "standard as a value." An example of the first meaning would be the metre: we have conveniently agreed that a meter is 100 centimetres and that we use it as a tool to measure. In this context not many controversies arise. But there is another meaning to the word standard, such as when we say we have high educational standards. The second meaning involves values and criteria, not just an agreed-upon measurement, as in the metric example. Moreover, these criteria are value-laden and will probably involve differences simply because people consider different things to be worthwhile.

It is crucial not to confuse these two very different meanings of standards, but, unfortunately, the notion of *standard as a measurement* and of *standard as a value* are confused in the public discourse about standardized testing in Canada. The assumption is that standardized tests (the measurement) will improve educational standards (the value). Literacy and reading, for example, are treated as if they were objective facts measurable by a yardstick and not contested, value-laden ground. We thus move to a discussion about the popular concerns raised about educational standards in order to raise the values issues that need to be clarified and discussed.

Falling Standards

The first concern is that there is a lack of high standards. There is no doubt that this is a very loaded and serious charge, for no one really wants to promote mediocrity. But are educational standards really low? Of course, the reply will depend on the criteria and underlying values that one is using to assess the quality of education. If two people are using different and possibly conflicting criteria, then it should be no surprise that the evaluations and outcomes will be very different. The claim that standards are low is debatable. A quick glance at a high school curriculum, for example, certainly contradicts the view that the standards have decreased from "the good old days" of educational rigor; the academic high school curriculum of today is decidedly advanced over our curricula 25 years ago both in terms of the quantity and quality of curriculum content, particularly in mathematics and science. On this point, Sobol (1997) contends, "Of course there was no Golden Age – just the memory of our golden youth. All times are the best of times and the worst of times, because the present is always the only time we have" (p. 631). Barlow and Robertson (1994) have argued convincingly that the popular discrediting of public education in Canada is part of a larger hidden agenda. They demonstrate how recent media reports have carefully selected and distorted evaluative data in order to support a view of a failing public education – a tactic designed in part to garner support for cuts to education, they argue. For example, Barlow and Robertson clearly show, by using Stats Can figures, that contrary to popular mythology, the drop-out rate today is lower than that in 1956 and 1971, and that the Economic Council of Canada information on illiteracy is mischievously distorted and inflated. The same point is made by Shannon (1996) and Berliner and Biddle (1995) for the U.S. context.

We are not suggesting here that there are no compelling problems facing public education in Canada. Quite the opposite, in fact. We are suggesting that the issues facing education presently are far more complex than the standards movement would allow. It may be that the cacophony about standards serves as a convenient distraction from far larger social, educational, and political issues facing us. As Apple (1996) puts it with regard to the issue of establishing a national curriculum in the U.S., the national curriculum (and in our context the establishing of common standards) could be seen as "a mechanism for the political control of knowledge" (p. 35). Moreover, as Kohn (1999) has convincingly argued, the "Tougher Standards Movement" has not given rise to higher quality, since in practice, this has amounted to "a little bit of everything and a thoughtful treatment of nothing" (p. 59). Kohn also points out that the plea for rigor or tougher standards has in fact resulted in narrowness for "such objectives as wanting students to learn how to write persuasively or solve problems effectively are dismissed as 'mushy'" (p. 48). The emphasis has been on "long lists of facts and skills that students must acquire" (p. 49). From our perspective, this perpetuates the predominance of a dangerous and limited conception of knowledge – one that focuses exclusively on the given rather than the critical and controversial.

Lack of Common, Universal Standards

As mentioned earlier, there seem to be three reasons for the view that holds that there should be common, universal standards: (a) common standards will secure high quality; (b) they will address equity and access issues for students historically marginalized as "at-risk"; (c) they will make practice more efficient and less confusing. We have to be very cautious about these seductive arguments.

Although there is no necessary nor intrinsic connection between common standards and high quality, some (Adler, 1982; Hirsch,

1987) have proceeded from assuming such a connection to arguing that common standards therefore address equity and access issues. In the American contexts, for instance, Hirsch (1987) has argued that lack of a shared, common cultural curriculum – a curriculum he defines in quite traditional, euro-centric terms – has contributed to inequities of access to educational capital for many of America's marginalized students. But Hirsch's argument hinges on a number of questionable assumptions concerning both curricula in American schools and teaching/learning processes. Specifically, Hirsch assumes that the reasons American students do not know "what every American needs to know" is because they haven't been taught it; in other words, he mistakenly assumes a one-to-one correspondence between the formal and actual curriculum (Portelli, 1993).[2] While we would certainly acknowledge that students marginalized as "at-risk" in America experience a second-rate curriculum (See, for example, Anyon, 1981; Apple, 1992; Haberman, 1991), the *content* of that curriculum is, by many accounts, precisely the sort of content for which Hirsch argues (Connell, 1994; Haberman, 1991; Shannon, 1992). The problem, as Hirsch sees it, of students failing to master what he believes every American needs to know would appear not to be so much rooted in their not having been taught it as in their not having learned it.

Oversimplification of the workings of standards in this manner has given rise to movements like "outcomes-based education," which assumes agreement on issues upon which there may be little real agreement. We may agree that public schools ought to support people's ability to read critically, write clearly, and to think for themselves; however, we may mean very different things by these phrases. Agreement on "outcomes" desired does not guarantee that the outcomes will be achieved. Unfortunately, popular education documents have fallen victim to these kinds of problems. The most obvious case is that of the language used in these documents, including slogans like excellence, co-operative learning, critical thinking, high quality, and good and productive citizens. This kind of rhetoric gives the impression of universality or homogeneity and hides the possibility of differences (Shannon, 1995). The language of forced consensus gives the illusion that there are no differences or that there ought to be no differences, while in fact, there are disagreements and differences among educational "experts" on what amounts to quality education (see Popkewitz, 1991, pp. 191-4).

The argument based on practicality is also deceptive, for even if we were to agree on a commonly held set of standards, in reality we still have to face the diversity and multiplicity that the application and interpretation of standards require. Standards are by nature subject to interpretation. For example, as teachers, even when we espouse identical standards for writing, rarely do we evaluate the same writing identically. In practice, standards are always negotiated. In this sense, claims to common standards are artificial and enforced. Standards, given their interpretive nature, are not naturally given, unquestionable facts (Shannon, 1995).

As an illustration of the points we have been making, we will offer some quotes from teachers who have been involved in national and provincial assessment scoring.[3] These quotes are taken from interviews we have conducted with teachers on issues of assessment, including alternative assessments. The first two quotes are from two teachers who participated in the marking of an alternative literacy assessment in a Canadian province. The markers were given a common set of standards, and they had sessions to clarify the standards and make sure they were interpreting the standards in a uniform manner. Notwithstanding all these precautions, disagreements in application arose:

> *We were given the direction to focus on the piece and not the children. That was very difficult to do....The male evaluators, in all fairness, did not get as tied up in knots over the messy handwriting....The administrators...female administrators seemed to be extremely compassionate,...so excited about looking at children's work....Male administrators were into the numbers game...as if the statistics suddenly became very important....People were trying their very best at being objective and fair as possible, but in many instances when conflicts arose you could see that the lines were definitely developed.*

> *...probably the greatest areas of conflict arose when people seemed to get caught up on grammar....From my perspective I was looking for the content. My argument was that depending on the technology in the schools, a child could work that on the computer and apply a spell check, and it would be perfect. I also felt that some teachers got caught up with handwriting. I have a tendency to look way past that. If it was a neat polished pretty piece some teachers tended automatically to give it a five....There were times when we could not agree on controversial pieces.*

The third quote is from a high school English teacher who was a marker of the School Achievement Indicators Project (SAIP) English assessment. Once again this quote provides evidence that although the markers were working with a commonly agreed-upon criteria, disagreements ensued in the application of the criteria.

> *There were a number of pieces that speak to this,…a piece called 'super guy': It was hard to tell if the piece was ironic or if it was written by a student who had a very poor command of English.…Without bringing the student before us it was very difficult to tell.…So people were divided on this one right down the line.…I read it as being ironic and definitely a 'four.'…Other people said 'what are you saying?' This is two.…Another difference was how people rated VOICE.…A lot of people coming from Nova Scotia voice was a very big thing for us.…If I could hear the individual in the piece my mark went up.…[By voice I mean] who that person was;…the writing was really alive.…Other people from other places in Canada if there was an obvious misspelling in the first sentence then immediately [they dismissed it].…People from Alberta and Ontario are very strong on spelling;…people from Nova Scotia and British Columbia were strong on voice and some of the people from Quebec were strong on voice.*

The call for common, universal standards is problematic on other counts too. Whose standards are we going to follow? Who decides what is going to amount to common standards? If we were to arrive at a set of common standards that would mean that some people's standards may be left out and, if so, for what reasons? Whose standards count the most and why? Who benefits from common standards? These are vital questions that the movement for common standards does not address, for these questions are deemed to be the kind of questions that lead to inefficiency. In reality, however, these are the crucial questions that challenge the inequities of the status quo.

A similar critique to the one we are raising is made by Apple in relation to the call to revert to a "common culture." According to Apple (1996), "such an approach hardly scratches the surface of the political and educational issues involved. A common culture can never be the general extension to everyone of what a minority mean and believe. Rather, and crucially, it requires…the creation of the conditions necessary for all people to participate in the creation and re-creation of meanings and values" (p. 39). We are claiming it is exactly such conditions which are missing in the consideration and plea for common standards. Moreover, forceful emphasis on common standards contradicts popular notions of democracy which, by definition, rule out emphasis on conformity. This is ironic as only 12 years ago the popular western criticism of the Soviet block and China was that these people did not allow diversity. We used to complain about their emphasis on uniformity (same clothes, same jackets, same ties, same hairstyle) which was associated with communism and totalitarianism. The West was seen as the bastion of democracy precisely because of its encouragement of diversity.[4] So now we need to ask: how can we explain the contemporary emphasis on uniformity (as exemplified in the harsh call for common, universal standards) and still claim that we embrace democracy?

In response to our rhetorical question one may retort that insisting on common standards will ensure that all teachers will have high expectations for all students irrespective of their cultural and/or socio-economic background.[5] In other words, one may argue that common standards will ensure that no students will be viewed from a "deficit mentality" (Valencia, 1997). We may be reminded that promoting high expectations for all and diminishing a negative deficit mentality are consistent with the democratic principle of equity. While we definitely agree that having high expectations for all and eliminating deficit mentality are worthwhile educational and democratic aims, the counter argument to our stance fails to demonstrate the unique and necessary connection between common standards and maintaining high expectations for all or reducing a deficit mentality. Will it be really profitable if we focus on high expectations while the standards that guide our practices are not suitable ones? What matters is not that we have common standards but that we have appropriate and fair standards. Moreover, it has been argued that higher and common standards are "used as selection devices to privilege some over others" (Kohn, 1999, p. 102). In other words, what is promoted officially as a way of securing quality for all, in fact, by implication, amounts to a hidden way of sorting out people. Linda McNeil's recent empirical study has established that "standardization creates inequities, widening the gap between the quality of education for poor and minority youth and that of more privileged students" (2000, p. 3).

Contrary to the evidence of major work on issues of race, class, gender, and sexuality by sociologists of education in this century (Anyon, 1981, 1997; Bourdieu, 1973, 1974; Persell, 1979; Rist, 1970; Simon, 1992; Weis, 1990; Willis, 1977), the erroneous view that having common, essential standards will translate into being able to apply them commonly assumes meritocracy or the belief that people advance on the basis of their inherent abilities. It assumes that if we have common standards, then we can apply them fairly and in the same way to all contexts. There are at least two problems with this.

First, there is a difference between *having* a meritocracy and *assuming* a meritocracy. The fact that we assume it is not the same as having it. Second, even if we had a meritocracy, evaluating fairly may need to or imply holding different standards (Martin, 1985). As even Plato argued a long time ago, fairness is not always identical to sameness. To be fair, sometimes we need to account for and acknowledge differences which do not necessarily lead to a common standard or a common solution. In other words, there is a difference between equity and equality (Martin, 1985, especially Ch. 2). As Shannon (1995) argues:

> *Set in this context, equality does not seem to be the ideal toward which we should strive; in fact, it leaves previous inequalities intact while at the same time frustrating any attempts to alter those inequalities by characterizing them as attacks on the ideal of equality. Requirements that we ignore the past and treat unequals equally mean that we can never approach true equality – that is, fairness among human beings. (p. 230)*

Where Do We Stand?

In a nutshell we are arguing that the public discourse around defining and maintaining common standards is ill-conceived, misleading, and fundamentally dishonest. Let us be very clear. We are not saying that we do not care about the quality of education. Criticizing common standards does not imply a lack of concern about quality or standards themselves. As Eisner (1995) puts it: "To give up the idea that there needs to be one standard for all students in each field of study is not to give up the aspiration to seek high levels of educational quality in both pedagogical practices and educational outcomes" (p. 760). We are concerned about quality and what it involves, for example, taking difference seriously. We urge teachers, parents, and guardians to ask the questions concerning quality that are left out by the common standards movement: Whose standards? How are these standards to be arrived at? Who is included and who is excluded from defining these standards (Apple, 1996; Christensen, 1995; Kelly, 1993; Swartz, 1996)? Why is there a real resistance to looking at these kinds of questions? Who benefits from not raising and discussing these questions?

The popular view pushed by the corporate and neo-conservative world rests on the fallacy that unless standards are clear and commonly held then we have no standards. The assumption is that unless we have commonly agreed upon standards set up and advertised, there will be no real change; mediocrity will flourish. We are arguing that it's not the agreement on standards but the discussion of them that will help bring about change. As Shannon (1995) recommends:

> ...*we should begin with the clarification of our starting points for thinking about literacy and assessment that the standards processes seem to paper over. Just what do various groups have in mind when they use terms such as interests of the students, fair, and equitable? We must display these differences in public. It is not our dirty laundry; rather, it is our reasoned way to air the issues. (p.232)*

The media and corporate discourse about standards seems to be based on a belief that standards are very easy to define, that we have common agreement on them and that all we need to do to improve public education is to measure students against these standards, as though measurement itself somehow improves learning (Barlow & Robertson, 1994; Shannon, 1995, 1996). As Margaret Meek Spencer (1993) reminds us, the pig will not gain weight the more often we weigh it. We need to feed the pig as well as consider the quality of the food! Our conclusion is that we need to stop the rhetoric and the unnecessary diagnosing and measuring. There is massive evidence that shows that those who are well-off have a bigger chance of surviving the system (Anyon, 1981, 1997; Apple, 1979, 1996; Curtis, Livingstone & Smaller, 1992; McLaren, 1998; Shannon, 1992; Willis, 1977). Funds need to be spent on supporting teachers' work and improving the quality and climate in schools rather than on unnecessary and expensive standardized testing.

Contrary to popular belief, we are arguing that educational standards are not absolute, fixed, and naturally-given facts. They are socially constructed. Even Richard Weaver (1970), a conservative rhetorician, objected to the way we continuously treat rhetorical, socially contested issues as though they were physical facts about which there can be no disagreement. In other words, we are not dealing with so-called scientific laws that are expected to apply universally by definition. We cannot expect that kind of exactitude when we are dealing with the human predicament. We need to ask who constructed these standards, for what reasons, and whose values are included and excluded from them. The public discussion on standards will continue to reproduce inequities and injustices unless these questions are dealt with seriously and differences are recognized.

This last point may give the impression that we are urging an "anything goes mentality." We are not. We do, however, maintain that insistence on commonality and uniformity will discredit important differences, which is ultimately contrary to one of the basic val-

ues or principles of the democratic spirit, namely, the acknowledgement of differences. In a democracy, for example, people should not be concerned that we have different accents, that we express ourselves differently. The urge for uniformity, on the other hand, can be seen as a fear of dealing with differences, of losing power, of change, ambiguity, and uncertainty. Yet, to be honest, we have to ask another question: Are all differences of equal worth? Is the view that people as human beings ought to be respected, of equal worth to a view that promotes hatred towards certain people? We need to distinguish between (a) accepting that there are different values and (b) holding that all these different values have equal worth. Democracy implies the acceptance that there are different values; it does not imply that all values are of equal worth. Acknowledging difference does not rule out the possibility of recognizing and valuing basic human rights.

Ultimately, our view rests on the belief that the either-or mentality is problematic (Dewey, 1938). We object to the view that maintains that either all values are absolute, or anything goes; or that we either take an extreme conservative position or an extreme liberal position. There are other positions that go beyond this simplistic either-or way of thinking, and account more fully for questions of educational equality in a pluralistic society.

Exactly 100 years ago, John Dewey, the American philosopher of education, wrote:

> We are apt to look at the school from an individualistic standpoint, as something between teacher and pupil, or between teacher and parent. That which interests us most is naturally the progress made by the individual child of our acquaintance, his [her] normal physical development, his [her] advance in ability to read, write, and figure, his [her] growth in the knowledge of geography and history, improvement in manners, habits of promptness, order, and industry – it is from such standards as these that we judge the work of the school. And rightly so. Yet the range of the outlook needs to be enlarged. What the best and wisest parent wants for his [her] child, that must the community want for all of its children. Any other ideal for our schools is narrow and unlovely; acted upon, it destroys our democracy….Only by being true to the full growth of all the individuals who make it up, can society by any chance be true to itself. (1900, p. 6)

It would be very hard, if not impossible, for anyone to disagree that attempting to achieve the "full growth of all the individuals" who make up society is worthwhile and needed. The questions about which disagreements arise include those dealing with how we are going to achieve this and which standards should we be aiming at. In response to the latter, Dewey offers an answer in the above quote: "what the best and wisest parent wants." We believe that this simple answer is rather dangerous. First, we are not in agreement who is the best and wisest parent. Second, it assumes that there is only one best possible reply. In other words, it does not allow for the possibility to have different, yet equally valuable ways and standards. Although we do agree on several things, it is a fact of life, that human beings have different values which will be reflected in different standards.

What are some of our options when we are faced with different standards? We could try to create situations in which one set of standards will dominate or be imposed on all irrespective of contexts and needs and values. Or, we could try to understand differences that exist and allow for a different set of standards to operate at the same time, admitting that there are differences, but acknowledging that standards, although different, may be equally valuable. We argue that the latter is the option that is most conducive to sustaining, developing, and reconstructing democracy (for democracy, by nature, is never stable). Of course, acknowledging and respecting differences does not mean that everything is acceptable. The Keegstra case in Alberta clearly demonstrates this (Hare, 1996).[6] However, in a democracy decisions about what is acceptable require serious and engaged discussions from the citizenry – not just the few. Conditions need to be created that encourage discussion rather than restrict it by threats or authoritarian decisions (some of which may be very subtle, yet very dangerous).

What Does All of This Have to Do With Teaching?

The debate about standards – the attempt to define and enforce appropriate academic standards in Canadian schools – is for teachers in classrooms simultaneously critically important and something of an irrelevant luxury. How the debate comes out, whatever "outcomes" we decide upon, will have immediate and substantial consequences for curricula, determining issues like whether an educated Canadian can continue to be defined solely by her or his knowledge of western European traditions, or whether we might justifiably expect an educated Canadian to know something of the cultural traditions of, for instance, aboriginal peoples. In that sense, the debate has everything to do with classroom teaching, however absent teachers' voices have been from that debate (at least at public levels). But, in another important sense, the exercise of defining common standards is very far removed from the "dailyness" of teaching of actual people in actual classrooms. As one teacher put it, "They can define whatever outcomes they like; unless those outcomes are possible and sensible and purposeful for the real children in my real grade three classroom, the whole exercise will remain just an exercise."

We have argued that the rhetoric within the standards movement is misleading in a number of ways, including the assumption (based on little evidence) that "standards are slipping" in Canadian schools, the assumptions that standards can be easily and justly defined and interpreted, and the slipshod logic that confuses measuring quality with improving quality. From the point of view of teaching, however, the standards debate poses a further problem in that it serves as a distraction from conversations in teaching and schooling which we, as a society, urgently need to engage ourselves – a conversation and support for a curriculum of life.

Let us illustrate this with an example. In one of the schools in which we worked, a grade four child who was a beginning reader was coded by his school as having a reading disorder. Talking to the child, his teacher discovered that for his entire school career the child had spent no more than six months in any one classroom because his father, a construction worker, had been moving all over the country in search of work. In the context of working with the child, the teacher learned that the child's "reading problem" had little to do with reading or academic ability at all, and everything to do with a level of anxiety and disruption in his life that made learning to read difficult and, apparently, irrelevant. Like many educational problems, this child's learning problem was a consequence of a much larger social problem (under-employment and the creation of surplus labor markets) manifested in schooling.

Hence, the act of teaching in Canada's increasingly diverse and increasingly under-funded classrooms graphically illustrates the manner in which education is embedded in complex social and political realities. From this vantage point, the debate about standards – the campaign to define a set of common standards that can only serve to further sanction the official knowledge of the already privileged – is entirely beside the point. Moreover, the debate, perhaps deliberately, distracts us from asking the kinds of pressing questions that teaching presently raises, questions like: Why is it that we appear unable to create just and viable schooling for *all* Canada's peoples? Are teachers being prepared and supported to be able to respond to the many different and conflicting perspectives they encounter in their students? Do they have the time and the support they need to address and come to terms with the kinds of changes happening in their classrooms? The standards debate, by reducing these complexities to a simple matter of defining common standards and measuring student achievement against them, conveniently allows us to blame the individual (the student and/or the teacher) and ignore the larger social and political realities in which teachers, students, and schools are immersed! As Maxine Greene (1995) warns us:

> ...a return to a single standard of achievement and a one dimensional definition of the common will not only result in severe injustices to the children of the poor and the dislocated, the children at risk, but will also thin out our cultural life and make it increasingly difficult to bring into existence and keep alive an authentically common world. (pp. 172-173)

Alternative Vision

What, then, are the alternatives we propose? Our critique of the pervasive current discourse about educational standards in Canada clearly implies an alternative vision for educational policy. Let us, then, be explicit about the alternatives for which we have argued above. As a conclusion, we will identify four alternatives.

1. We have claimed that the public discourse of slipping standards in education in this country is misleading and misinformed. The alternative we are proposing here is an open and balanced *public* debate – a debate acknowledging educational standards as necessarily provisional, dynamic, located, interpretive, and informed by issues of politics and power. Such debate is, after all, far from new within the confines of academic and educational literature. That the central political debate is missing from our public discourse on standards in education is, at the very best, curious.

   We are suggesting that a number of questions need to be asked, publicly, of the slipping standards claim – questions like, "Is this true?" "To what extent is this true?" "What standards are slipping and whose standards are they?" "What new standards are emerging?" "Why is this happening?"

2. We have argued that broad-based standardized testing confuses and over-simplifies a number of issues of quality in education, thereby perpetuating the status quo. We have suggested that the public discourse around standardized testing and test scores

fails to acknowledge thoroughly documented social inequities reproduced through such testing; and, further, that this discourse confuses "standard" as a value with "standard" as a measurement, resulting in the rather magical notion that we can improve quality by measuring it. We have also argued that such an approach to assessment fails to acknowledge central features of standards themselves – namely, that in practice, standards are irredeemably local and interpretive.

The alternative we are suggesting here is, of course, the development of local assessments – or, perhaps more accurately, the development of educational policy acknowledging the reality of local assessment (Eisner, 2000). We need to re-deploy the enormous resources spent in developing national and regional assessments ("bigger and better mousetraps," as Jerome Harste [1992] has called them) in helping teachers to develop and engage in thoughtful local assessment that acknowledges and accounts for the realities of social difference.

3. The flurry of activity to define and measure common standards seems to us to have overlooked the obvious and essential step. If we are genuinely interested in improving the quality of education for all in Canada, surely we need to do more than define what we want and test whether we are getting it. We need to put resources into actually improving the decaying conditions in the nation's classrooms. Teachers are besieged; they lack classroom resources, they lack time for professional development, they lack social and educational support networks, they lack support for real initiative and innovation, their class sizes are rising everywhere just as diversity multiplies and social supports for children and families erode. In short, they struggle just to do their jobs in the face of enormous cutbacks and escalating demands. We are arguing that the time, money, and resources spent on defining common standards and measuring our achievement of them would be much better spent on supporting teachers, classrooms, and schools – IF we were serious about changing schooling and improving education.

4. The general tendency of common standards and standardized testing movements is, for complex reasons, towards the production and reproduction of a mechanistic, technocratic vision of curriculum – a vision which ultimately is based on a conception of education which "may be appropriate for totalitarian societies but is incompatible with democratic ideals" (Eisner, 1995, p.

763). As Beyer and Pagano (1998) argue, such a vision of curriculum is only appropriate to industrial models of education which, as they remind us, "have been thoroughly criticized over the last three decades, and teachers, curriculum designers and principals have increasingly eschewed such models..." (p. 381). Defining common standards and testing against them simply leaves the flesh and blood reality of actual classrooms outside the issue. We are told that violence, for instance, is increasing in schools, and we don't deny this claim. Teachers and schools, however, where violence is an issue may be discouraged from making it central to the curriculum if official sanction is placed on, for instance, students' ability to commute fractions by the end of grade six. The standards movement in its present form appears to mitigate against what we call the curriculum of life.

By "curriculum of life" we mean a central, organizing stance that seems to inform pedagogy. Curriculum of life is not solely an aspect of curriculum, of the teachers' pedagogy, or of school and classroom management. In fact, the normally accepted meaning of the term "management" contradicts the spirit of a curriculum of life. Students and curriculum in this approach are not "managed," but "engaged"; that is, the aim is to actively involve them in the life of the school. Curriculum of life is an approach to pedagogy which informs and gives coherence to often disparate aspects of school life. It is implicit in curriculum, in school organization and policy, in discipline, in school/community relations, in classroom and school-wide pedagogy, in school culture. In other words, the curriculum of life is a conception of curriculum that breaks down the walls between the school and the world. Social studies, language arts, mathematics, science, and art become "disciplines" in the original sense of the word; that is, they are disciplined ways of thinking through important questions and concerns. The curriculum of life is rooted in the school and community world to which the students belong, addressing questions of who we are and how we live well together; it extends into the larger world of possibilities beyond school and community bounds; and it addresses directly questions about the larger social and political contexts in which these worlds are embedded.

The curriculum of life is grounded in the immediate daily worlds of students as well as in the larger social and political contexts of their lives. As such, students' worlds and lives are not addressed as factors that need to be excused, pitied, mediated, or fixed in order to get on with the curriculum, but as the vital ground of or for learning. This is an approach to curriculum that presupposes genuine respect for children's minds and experience – without romanticizing either. The connection between the curriculum of life and students is essentially an ethical one, for as Freire (1998) argues: "It's impossible to talk of respect for students for the dignity that is in the process of coming to be, for the identities that arise in the process of construction, without taking into consideration the conditions in which they are living and the importance of the knowledge derived from life experience, which they bring with them to school" (p. 62).

Teachers are telling us that the curriculum of life – the actual, immediate and urgent experiences, issues, and questions of children in schools – is becoming more and more the irresistible content of the classroom. By failing to recognize this situation, the common standards movement cuts educators off from the very questions they most need to engage in with each other, just at a time when they have no choice but to engage these questions in their daily life practice in classrooms. Maxine Greene (1984) has captured the gist of our thinking here:

> *We need…spaces for expression, spaces for freedom, yes, and a public space. By that I mean, as Hannah Arendt did, a space where living persons can come together in speech and action, each one free to articulate a distinctive perspective.…It must be a space of dialogue, a space where a web of relationships can be woven, and where a common world can be brought into being and continually renewed. (pp. 295-6)*

Notes

[1] For an elaboration of this point, see: Freire (1996), Giroux (1994), Portelli (1996), and Shor (1992).

[2] As teachers all know there is a big difference between lesson plans and actual practice. Likewise, just saying in a document is no guarantee that the proposed will actually take place. For example, several education documents have told us that diversity will be respected and supported. However, for example in Halifax, when the first cuts in education were made, ESL teachers were among the first to be reduced and, in some instances, even eliminated.

[3] These quotes are from a research on alternative literacy assessment conducted by the authors in 1996.

[4] In reality one could argue that in the West we actually encourage individualism rather than genuine diversity; that is, while individual differences are accepted, that is not the case with social differences such as race and gender. One has to be careful not to conflate a sort of apolitical individualism with democracy.

[5] This argument seems to be implicit in Diane Ravitch's (2000) recent work.

[6] Jim Keegstra was a public school teacher in Alberta from 1968 to 1983 when his teaching license was revoked by the Alberta Minister of Education and he was expelled from the Alberta Teachers' Association. In 1985 he was convicted on the charge of promoting hatred against Jews through his teaching.

Acknowledgements: We thank Amanda Datnow and R. Patrick Solomon for their comments and suggestions on an earlier draft of this chapter.

References

Adler, M. (1982). *The Paideia Proposal*. New York, NY: McMillan.

Anyon, J. (1981). Social class and school knowledge. *Curriculum Inquiry, 11* (1), 3-42.

Anyon, J. (1997). *Ghetto schooling: A political economy of urban educational reform.* New York: Teachers College Press.

Apple, M. W. (1979). *Ideology and curriculum*. London: Routledge & Kegan Paul.

Apple, M. W. (1992). *Teachers in text*. Cambridge, MA: Harvard University Press.

Apple, M. W. (1996). *Cultural politics and education*. New York: Teachers College Press.

Barlow, M. & Robertson, H. J. (1994). *Class warfare: The assault on Canada's schools.* Toronto: Key Porter Books.

Berliner, D. & Biddle, B. (1995). *The manufactured crisis: Myths, fraud and the attack on America's public schools*. Reading, MA: Addison-Wesley.

Beyer, L. E. & Pagano, J. A. (1998). Democratic evaluation: Aesthetic, ethical stories in schools. In L. E. Beyer and M. Apple (Eds.), *The curriculum: Problems, politics and possibilities* (2nd Ed.) (pp. 380-396). Albany: SUNY Press.

Bourdieu, P. (1973). Cultural reproduction, and social reproduction. In R. Brown (Ed.), *Knowledge, education, and cultural change* (pp. 71-112). London: Tavistock.

Bourdieu, P. (1974). The school as a conservation force: Scholastic and cultural inequalities. In J. Eggleston (Ed.), *Contemporary research in the sociology of education* (pp. 32-46). London: Methuen.

Christensen, L. (1995) Whose standard? Teaching standard English in our schools. In D. Levine, R. Lowe, B. Peterson & R. Tenerio (Eds.), *Rethinking schools: An agenda for change* (pp. 128 - 135). New York: The New Press.

Connell, R. W. (1994). Poverty and education. *Harvard Educational Review, 64* (2), 125-149.

Curtis, B., Livingstone, D. & Smaller, H. (1992). *Stacking the deck: The streaming of working class kids in Ontario schools*. Toronto, ON: Our Schools/Our Selves.

Dewey, J. (1900/1974). *The school and society*. Chicago, IL: The University of Chicago Press.

Dewey, J. (1938). *Experience and education*. New York: MacMillan.

Eisner, E. W. (1993). Why standards may not improve schools? *Educational Leadership*, Feb., 22-3.

Eisner, E. W. (1995). Standards for American schools: Help or hindrance? *Phi Delta Kappan, 76* (10), 758-765.

Eisner, E. W. (2000). Those who ignore the past ...? 12 'easy' lessons for the next millennium. *Journal of Curriculum Studies, 32* (2), 343-357.

Freire, P. (1996). Reading the world and reading the word: An interview with Paulo Freire. In W. Hare and J. P. Portelli (Eds.), *Philosophy of education: Introductory readings* (2nd, revised.) (pp. 185-192). Calgary, AB: Detselig Ent. Ltd.

Freire, P. (1998). *Pedagogy of freedom: Ethics, democracy, and civic courage.* Lanham: Rowman & Littlefield Publishers.

Giroux, H. A. (1994). Teachers, public life, and curriculum reform. *Peabody Journal of Education, 69* (3), 35-47.

Greene, M. (1984). 'Excellence,' meanings, and multiplicity. *Teachers College Record, 86* (2), 283-297.

Greene, M. (1995). *Releasing the imagination: Essays on education, the arts, and social change.* San Francisco: Jossey-Bass Publishers.

Haberman, M. (1991). The pedagogy of poverty versus good teaching. *Phi Delta Kappan, 73* (4), 290-294.

Hare, W. (1996). Propaganda in the classroom: The Keegstra case. In W. Hare and J. P. Portelli (Eds.), *Philosophy of education: Introductory readings* (2nd, revised.) (pp. 149-164). Calgary, AB: Detselig Ent. Ltd.

Harste, J. (1992). *Evaluation and Standards.* Keynote Address, Nova Scotia Reading Association Annual Conference. Halifax, NS: Mount St. Vincent University.

Hirsch Jr., E. D. (1987). *Cultural literacy: What every American needs to know.* Boston: Houghton Mifflin.

Kelly, U. (1993). Teaching English: Who's subject to what? In D. Bogdan and S. Straw (Eds.), *Constructive reading: Teaching beyond communication* (pp. 205-213). Portsmouth, NH: Boynton Cook.

Kohn, A. (1999). *The schools our children deserve: Moving beyond traditional classrooms and "tougher standards."* Boston, MA: Houghton Mifflin.

Martin, J. R. (1985). *Reclaiming a conversation: The ideal of the educated woman.* New Haven: Yale University Press.

McLaren, P. (1998). *Life in schools: An introduction to critical pedagogy in the foundations of education.* (3rd Ed.). New York, NY: Longman.

McNeil, L. M. (2000). *Contradictions of school reform: Educational costs of standardized testing.* New York, NY: Routledge.

Nikiforuk, A. (1993). *School's out: The catastrophe in public education and what we can do about it.* Toronto: MacFarlane Walter & Ross.

Ontario Ministry of Education and Training. (2000). *Learning for life.* Toronto, ON: Ministry of Education.

Persell, C. (1979). *Education and inequality.* New York, NY: Longman.

Popkewitz, T. (1991). *A political sociology of educational reform: Power/knowledge in teaching, teacher education, and research.* New York, NY: Teachers College Press.

Portelli, J. P. (1993). Dare we expose the hidden curriculum? In J. P. Portelli and S. Bailin (Eds.), *Reason and values* (pp. 171-197). Calgary, AB: Detselig Ent.

Portelli, J. P. (1996). The challenge of teaching for critical thinking. In W. Hare and J. P. Portelli (Eds.), *Philosophy of education: Introductory readings* (2nd, revised.) (pp. 55-72). Calgary, AB: Detselig Ent. Ltd.

Ravitch, D. (2000). *Left back: A century of failed school reform.* New York, NY: Simon & Schuster.

Rist, R. C. (1970). Student social class and teacher expectations: The self-fulfilling prophecy in ghetto education. *Harvard Educational Review, 40* (3), 411-451.

Shannon, P. (1992). Reading instruction and social class. In P. Shannon (Ed.), *Becoming political: Readings and writings in the politics of literacy education* (pp. 128-138). Portsmouth, NH: Heinemann.

Shannon, P. (1995). Can reading standards really help? *The Clearing House,* March/April, 229-232.

Shannon, P. (1996). Mad as hell. *Language Arts, 73* (5), 1996, 14-19.

Shor, I. (1992). *Empowering education: Critical teaching for social change.* Chicago: The University of Chicago Press.

Simon, R. (1992). *Teaching against the grain: Texts for a pedagogy of possibility.* Toronto, ON: OISE Press.

Sobol, T. (1997). Beyond standards: The rest of the agenda. *Teachers College Record, 98* (4), 629-636.

Spencer, M. M. (1993). Memorial lecture for Patricia S. Barnes. Mount Saint Vincent University, Halifax, N.S. (March 27).

Swartz, E. (1996). Emancipatory pedagogy: A post-critical response to 'standard' school knowledge. *Journal of Curriculum Studies, 38* (4), 397-418.

Valencia, R. R. (Ed.) (1997). *The evolution of deficit thinking: Educational thought and practice.* London: The Falmer Press.

Weaver, R. (1970). *Language is sermonic.* Baton Rouge: Louisiana State University.

Weis, L. (1990). *Working class without work: High school students in a de-industrializing society.* New York, NY: Routledge.

Willis, P. E. (1977). *Learning to labour: How working class kids get working class jobs.* Westmead, England: Saxon House.

Chapter 3
Texts, Tyranny, and Transformation: Educational Restructuring in Ontario[1]

Alison I. Griffith

Introduction

"Restructuring," "down-sizing," "privatization," "down-load-ing"; all are popular ways of describing substantial changes in tra-ditional social institutions in Canada, including mass compulsory schooling. These terms signify changes in the global production and distribution of capital that are transforming the sphere of reproduc-tion, including families and schools, in dramatic ways (Brody, 1994; Smith, 1998). In this chapter, I look at the processes that are trans-forming Kindergarten to Grade 12 education in Ontario. I am inter-ested in the textually coordinated activities through which restruc-turing, marketization, and globalization become the everyday work of parents, teachers, and administrators *within and across* the institu-tions of social reproduction. In particular, this article explores the "technical and administrative matters" (Dehli, 1996) of restructuring that reorganize and reshape the everyday work of local school administrators.

In this chapter,[2] I contend that the restructuring of education in Ontario denotes a shift in education from education for democracy or citizenship to education for a global labor market (Ohmann, 1997; Smith, 1998). This shift is coordinated through the texts of educa-tional restructuring that were introduced by successive provincial governments – governments whose educational philosophies are otherwise diametrically opposed. The major vehicle for Ontario's educational reorganization is standardization – of curriculum, report cards, and testing. Currently, the primary education policy coordinating the shift is *Bill 160: The Education Improvement Act* (1997) which (intentionally or otherwise) supports a retreat from the possibilities of emancipatory or critical leadership to the tyranny of bureaucratic-managerial leadership.[3] Textually-mediated relations – the texts of restructuring – that link government policy to the every-day work of principals, teachers, students, and parents are central to this transformation.

Global Economies and Educational Change

Since the beginning of mass compulsory schooling, education has been the focus of reform through evaluations (Curtis, 1992; Madaus, Scriven & Stufflebeam, 1989), curriculum reviews (Bloom, 1987), changes in teacher education (Bullough & Gitlin, 1995), and traditional and non-traditional policy initiatives (Griffith, 1992). Indeed, it could be claimed that school restructuring is as old as public education. I would argue, however, that the restructuring that we see in today's schools has a qualitatively different character than in previous historical periods. In much of the current literature, educational changes are described as "marketization," "globalization," and "restructuring" (Dehli, 1996a). While these terms focus our understanding of post-modern educational change in slightly different ways, they all point to a transformation of compulsory schooling that transcends local and national boundaries in unprecedented ways. Brodie (1994), among others, suggests that institutional restructuring is embedded in the restructuring of capital – what Smith designates "a new regime of (capital) accumulation" (Smith, 1998, p. 13). Weiner (2000) notes that popular models of educational reform often ignore the relational issues of schooling that are not easily transformed into accountability processes generated out of the administrative and technical interests of educational administration. Dehli (1996a) notes that there are generally recognized features of (particularly Kindergarten to senior matriculation) school restructuring which include:

> ...reductions in overall state funding for education; contradictory and uneven moves to decentralize school governance, while simultaneously centralizing curriculum planning and assessment procedures by tying them to fiscal controls and accounting practices; shifts from collective bargaining to individual (and competitive) negotiations with teachers and other educational workers about contracts, wages and working conditions; and moves to commercialize and privatize many education services and to introduce forms of parental 'choice'. (p. 364-5)

Kenway echoes Dehli's assessment, noting: "Schools are subject to the de- and re-centralizing agendas of governments in most Western countries. On the decentralizing agenda is school management, funding on a per capita basis and the inter-school competition which arises from both. On the re-centralizing side are curriculum and, ironically, market ideologies" (Kenway 1998, p. 7). Feminist researchers exploring restructuring note that educational restructuring is embedded in transformations of global capitalism that include a re-instantiation of gender, race/ethnicity, class, sexual orientation, and social class inequalities (for example, Barlow & Robertson, 1994; Brody, 1994; David, 1998; Dehli, 1996a, 1996b; Kenway, 1998; Smith, 1998; see also Levin, 1998).

From different perspectives, they note two issues that are particularly salient for this research. First, educational restructuring initiatives are being driven from outside the school walls by the business possibilities inherent in the marketization of schooling, by changes in the labor market, by the fear of the business and professional elite for the future of their children, by the exporting of social problems into the social mandate of schooling, and by the (at-times deliberate) political misreading of educational research and evaluation. Second, educational restructuring is reorganizing the relationships between schools and those social institutions (such as families) that are intimately tied to schooling. Schooling, historically, has depended on the unpaid and invisible work of mothers to achieve its social mandate (Griffith & Smith, 1990; Smith & Griffith, 1990; Griffith, 1995; Griffith & Waggoner, 1998).

Dehli (1996a) argues that the trends identified as "globalization" and "marketization" provide new subject-positions for parents and educators, available to them and taken up in relation to traditional forms of social privilege. David (1998), in her discussion of the relationship between mothering work and school choice, shows that educational restructuring shifts more work and responsibility for managing children's education from school to family settings. Smith (1998) brings into view the struggle to reframe the public discourse of education: "...the drive for privatization [of social programs, including education] unloads what had been taken for granted as proper functions of the state on to an idealized version of the family" (p. 17-18). At the same time, as the process of capital accumulation is transformed, the idealized family form becomes harder to maintain. More mothers are employed outside the home and the traditional mothering work on which schooling depends becomes less available to families who cannot keep the mothers' labor focussed on the work of coordinating and managing their children's participation in schooling (Smith & Griffith, 1990).

Throughout the feminist literature on restructuring, researchers note the re-instantiation of class privilege in the intersection of school restructuring, the transformation of capital and the intensification of the school's reliance on the invisible work of mothering in families. These authors note the intimate relationship between the development of a global economy and the changes in education. Smith (1998) describes a new public discourse that abandons the promise of equity through schooling, that changes the relation between families and schools (see also Dehli, 1996; Barlow & Robertson, 1994). Indeed, educational restructuring and change, for example in the processes of privatization (Kenway, 1998) and school choice (Dehli, 1996; David, 1998), ripple through the whole fabric of the society from the kitchen to the corporate boardroom.

Educational change and restructuring is subject to and shapes the social organization of society in each historical period. In Ontario, this is a time of transition from one regime of capital accumulation and educational system to another. The transition is evidenced by uneven and contested restructuring in schools, changes in the relationship between home and school, changes in the labor market as capital shifts from a regional to a global context, and the struggle to construct a new discourse of schooling in the public media. In other words, this transition intersects and coordinates the everyday practices of people across many different social institutions, both public and private. Research on restructuring, therefore, is particularly suited to the methodology of institutional ethnography.

Texts, Institutions, and Action

Institutional ethnographic (IE) research is a methodology for exploring the socially-organized processes – including the textually-mediated processes – that shape our everyday/everynight experience (Smith, 1987). IE research begins in local experience. In contrast to other experientially-grounded research methodologies (for example, ethnomethodology, symbolic interaction, semiotics, and so on), the focus on local experience is the entry-point for an investigation of the ways that extra-local relations construct our everyday world of experience. For example, in my everyday/everynight world of experience, I send my children to school, teach classes, walk the dog, and make sure everything is in place for the principal's credentialling course. As I engage in these mundane experiences, I activate and participate in a range of objectified, institutional relations that neither begin nor end in the moment of my engagement – the textually organized relations that coordinate public schooling, private property, higher education, the labor market, and so on. The disjuncture between the local and the extra-local organization of everyday experience – the personal experience that is coordinated with and coordinates the objectified institutional social relations – is the fertile ground of inquiry for IE research.

Smith argues that, in contemporary society, the "social relations of objectified knowledge" are primarily textual. Texts are ubiquitous but rarely explicated in sociology (Smith, 1990a, 1990b) or education (Corson, 2000). Texts have a material presence (books, papers, computer software, television, and other media), yet, by definition, are structured to stand outside the time and space of their creation or use. Texts appear as the 'same' text at each moment of their use, although our time-embedded interpretation of them may differ. Factual texts (as opposed to fictional texts) are constructed as part of an ongoing conversation between texts – a discourse of linked regimes of truth (Foucault, 1972) – and to act and be activated in the everyday/everynight world of lived experience (Smith, 1990).

As institutional ethnographers, we begin in the everyday/everynight world of experience and trace the "social relations of objectified knowledge" that gives our daily lives their particular shape (Smith, 1990, p. 202). The nexus between local experience and the extra-local relations of ruling (Smith, 1987) is often (although certainly not always) coordinated textually.

IE and Education

Education is through and through a textually-mediated process. As such, IE is a particularly interesting methodology for exploring the social relations of education that extend beyond the walls of schools, governments, and families (Bechely, 1999). For example, Stock (2000) has explored the constitutive and co-ordinative character of the primary school report card. She describes the report card as an instance of the textual coordination of teachers' everyday interaction with children in the classroom. As she notes, enrolling a child in kindergarten or any other school level requires a number of documents (texts). Parents must collect and bring with them to the local school their children's birth certificates, inoculation and vaccination certificates, records of residence, and so on. These documents are recorded on the Ontario School Record (OSR) – the textual identity of the student. Once enrolled, a child's progress through the grades is reported on (now standardized) report cards. These report cards become the primary text that coordinates the child's school career – the "Action Central" for scripting the textual representation of the child (Stock 2000, p. v).

> *When the report card text enters the child's record [the Ontario School Record], it can be seen to have constructed what we might call the "scripted child," the child who is now known in relation to his or her documentary record. A new kind of identity is formed for her or him*

that is tied to the documentary records. How he or she has been for a particular teacher in a particular year and how her or his experience has been translated into report card discourse is projected into the child's future. (p. 166)

The report card text not only projects the '"scripted child's" school future, it also coordinates the readings of the OSR texts by the principal, parents, other teachers, and professionals such as social workers or school psychologists assigned to work with schools (Griffith, 1984). The report card coordinates the text-reader conversations (Smith, 1998) within and outside the walls of the classroom. While parents may (and often do) contest particular aspects of the report card – i.e., there may be a struggle over the content – once the report card text is placed in the OSR, it is embedded in the textual record that shapes the next text-reader conversation. The report card is embedded in an organizational process (the extra-local) that extends beyond momentary, local interpretations of teachers, parents, and school administrators. Whether sending children to school, helping with homework, teaching a class, or writing up report cards, the process is coordinated textually.

In this chapter, I focus on the texts – the objectified knowledge – that shape the practices of restructuring in the school. As a way of tracing the institutional actions of the texts of restructuring, my analysis traces the geography of the text-reader conversations to discover the texts of restructuring in action. Exploring this feature of textual relations – coordinating actions and framing knowledge across institutional boundaries – brings into view the local moments of articulation to the extra-local relations of restructuring.

The Texts of Restructuring

In Ontario today, the texts of restructuring are primarily, although not exclusively, government initiatives for re-designing K-12 education. As many researchers and commentators have noted, educational restructuring initiatives were begun prior to the current neo-conservative government, but the pace of their implementation has increased substantially over the past five years. One of the most notorious and wide-reaching restructuring texts is *Bill 160, the Education Quality Improvement Act* (1997). This legislative text is supported by related texts – government initiatives focused on particular aspects of the process to restructure public education, including subsequent and related legislation, curriculum development, and increased accountability measures such as teacher testing. "...*Bill 160* amends the *Education Act* to provide for significant reforms in education governance, finance, labor relations and school instruction; every Part of the *Education Act* is affected" (Righton, 1997, p. 1). For example, under *Bill 160*, principals and vice-principals were removed from the teachers' federations. They now negotiate contracts directly with their Boards of Education, placing school administrators and classroom teachers in new, possibly oppositional relationships within schools.

Several authors have drawn attention to the retreat from the democratic organization of schooling that is embedded in *Bill 160*. According to Hargreaves and in keeping with the restructuring trends identified above, the current texts of restructuring in Ontario: "...centralize significant areas of decision-making and authority, they redefine who is a classroom teacher and who is not, they reconfigure the official relationships between teachers and administrators, and they substantially restructure the work of secondary school teaching itself" (Hargreaves, 1998, p. 3). A collection of essays titled *From Reform to Renewal: Beyond Bill 160*, published (1998) soon after the *Act* became law, pointed to the erosion of democratic education in Ontario. *Bill 160* is characterized as an inadequately-conceived reform strategy (Fullan & Hannay, 1998); as destructive to the profession of teaching (Hargreaves, 1998); as a reform which ignores equity issues (Goldstein, 1998); as an unreasoning response to educational concerns (Livingstone, 1998); and as a reform that will intensify inequity through the myth of school choice (Dehli, 1998).

As well, *Bill 160* has been reviewed by and for K-12 educators across Ontario. For example, assessments of the implications of *Bill 160* for principals, vice principals, and superintendents were done by the Ontario Principals' Council (Memorandum, March 4, 1998), the Ontario Public Supervisory Officials' Association (October 21, 1997), and the Simcoe County Board of Education (Memorandum, March 11, 1998). Lawyer Shibley Righton reviewed the Act for the Education and Public Law Group, with reference to issues of concern to school and central office administrators, before *Bill 160* was voted into law in the Legislature (November 19, 1997). There was extensive media coverage; news stories focusing on particular aspects of the *Act*, newspaper columns (Landsberg, 1998), and editorials devoted to analyzing the Bill and its impact on K-12 education, for example, *Toronto Star* (1998). Despite province-wide unrest that included much public protest, *Bill 160* became educational policy in Ontario.

After the *Bill* was made law, the resistance to the government's restructuring policies continued. During the fall of 1998, many Boards of Education locked out their teaching staff and, in other Boards, teachers engaged in a variety of job actions, the prominent issue being teaching loads and teachers' jobs. The struggle to reframe the public discourse of education continued. A news item reported on CBC Radio Two quoted Premier Harris apologizing to the business elite for Ontario students who were described as "...products of a mediocre system" (September 24, 1998, 9:00 a.m.). During the summer and fall of 2000, threats of confrontation from both government and the teachers' unions continued.

Currently, the textually-mediated conversations continue. Standardized tests, standardized report cards, standardized staffing formulas are constructed to exert central office control over most aspects of local school life. The transformation from local to centralized control was premised on claims for a more efficient and effective educational system – one that would transform a "mediocre system" into a world-class system. However, the Tracking Project authors tell a different story.

> *The downward trends we saw developing last year in libraries, English as a Second Language programs and school administration continue. More schools are going without full time principals, and there continue to be long waiting lists for Special Education services. Some students are now riding on buses for three hours a day, a number that may increase as more schools close. One very serious concern is that increased reliance on parent volunteers and fundraising will create grave inequities in the education system. (Tracking Report, 2000)*

Several teachers unions have voted to strike, are working to rule, or are withholding services. These actions are being taken against particular Boards of Education, but the confrontational stage was set by budgetary, staffing, and curricular changes made by the current neo-conservative government. Restructuring and resistance to centrally-mandated change initiatives are the defining feature of education in Ontario today.

In an institution as dispersed and bureaucratic as K-12 education, the textually-mediated processes of *Bill 160* co-ordinate restructuring (and resistance). They shape the possible and probable interactions of educators and administrators at every level, of elected officials in local and provincial government, of the media across Ontario, of political action groups, and of students, clerical and physical plant workers, and parents in the day-to-day routines of schools. The texts of restructuring are not contained by the walls of a school, a system, or the institution of K-12 schooling. The texts of restructuring link people across institutions into a conversation shaped in textual terms. For example, during the teachers' job action against the legislation, picketers (teachers, clerical and administrative staff, community supporters, and parents) discussed the media stories in the newspapers and on television, read the information flyers produced by their unions, and discussed the implications of *Bill 160* as they knew it (field notes, 1997). Educational restructuring in Ontario, then, is a textually-mediated discourse that coordinates interactions between administrators, classroom teachers, students, and parents.

I have argued (Griffith, 1984, 1992) that educational policies are active texts within and across institutions (see also Smith, 1990a). The struggle to develop and implement policy is more than a struggle between people with different visions of education. School change requires and intends particular administrative routines, actual practices done by people in different parts of education. Legislation and policies that work – i.e., that are administratively actionable – must be able to co-ordinate the work practices of a range of people in diverse work settings. So, too, the texts of restructuring must co-ordinate the work of the central Board of Education, teachers, education assistants, and principals in schools, and parents and children as they move between the family and the school. Dehli (1996) provides an insight into this co-ordinative process with reference to restructuring, "Appearing often as fairly mundane, neutral and helpful strategies to improve efficiency and accountability of government and education, many marketization initiatives are seen as technical and administrative matters...." (p. 368). The phenomenon we call restructuring occurs at the intersection between texts made to act, and people in positions of responsibility who are able to enact them. At each level of the institution of public schooling, restructuring appears as a series of technical, administrative practices driven by *Bill 160*. As Smith notes, "People enter and participate in them [fields of socially organized activity], reading/watching/operating/writing/drawing texts; they are at work and their work is regulated textually; whatever form of agency is accessible to them is accessible textually as courses of action in a text-mediated mode" (Smith, 1996, p. 174). Textually-organized, mundane, technical, and administrative matters are, I suggest, some of the essential practices through which educational restructuring is accomplished in schools.

The Technical and Administrative Matters of Staffing Classrooms

One of the social positions from which educators engage with the texts of restructuring is that of the principal of a school. At this level, restructuring often takes the form of administrative and technical matters for which the principal is responsible. In May 1998, I attended a meeting of principals teaching in the York University Principals' Qualification Program. Prior to the meeting's start the conversations between the principals were intense words flying fast and furious across the room.

"Are you doing 6 over 7 or 6.5 over 7?"

"My Board is still negotiating with the Unions."

"I have a meeting tomorrow morning with OPSEU [one of the unions representing teachers] and the Superintendent. I hope we can reach an agreement as we have less than a month of school left this year."

"Well, our Board has settled on 6.5 over 7."

The principals were from four different high schools in three different Boards of Education. They were discussing the ways the staffing formulas of *Bill 160* were organizing their end of term work in order that the new staffing could be implemented the next school year. *Bill 160* puts more emphasis on teacher time in the classroom and discounts other activities that have traditionally counted as student contact time. The changes in staffing formulas were being negotiated in many Boards of Education in Ontario. Indeed, the staffing formulas precipitated the rotating strikes, negotiations, and lockouts of that school year.

The new staffing formula, and the political struggle in which it is embedded, shaped the process, provided the boundaries to the negotiations, and placed the participants in particular relationships to each other. At each moment of the difficult and extensive meetings between different people (government policy-makers, superintendents in different Boards of Education, principals from individual schools, clerical workers, union representatives) at different sites across the institution of K-12 schooling, the deliberations were oriented to implementing the much-contested staffing formulas. Textually, the staffing formula appears as the same staffing formula to all participants in the administrative conversation – the Ministry of Education, Boards of Education and the upper-level administrators, and to the principals – regardless of time, place of discussion, or participants in the discussion. Nonetheless, the 'same' staffing formula was being negotiated differently between each Board of Education and teachers' union. This was the basis of the conversation overheard and noted above.

For each principal, the 'same' staffing formula has different local implications. Student, parent, and community populations differ widely across Ontario. The work of principals is, in part, an administrative display that they have been able to bring the unique character of their school into correspondence with the requirements of a centralized bureaucracy. However, the work of the principal also extends beyond the technical matters of administering a school, for example in their relationships with teachers, students, and parents. Thus, the texts of restructuring must be activated within a community with traditionally organized ways of working together.

Technical and administrative changes such as staffing formulas have (deliberately) far-reaching consequences for collegial and teacher-student relationships within schools. The staffing formulas organize the principal's work of distributing teaching staff across grade levels, across levels of student enrollment, of assigning required and elective course instructors in their areas of teaching expertise. The textually mediated staffing formula of *Bill 160* organizes the principals' staffing practices as a technical and administrative matter of compliance.

However, staffing is now conducted between subject-positions that have changed. As noted previously, principals and vice-principals have been removed from the teachers' bargaining units. Principals now have a different relationship with staff. As principals implement the new staffing formulas, they do so from outside the cadre of professional teachers, and within a social institution that has polarized over the past three years.

The changed relationship between principals and their staff, and the impact of this change on school leadership, are outside the administrative frame of the staffing formula but not outside the everyday experiences of the school's community. A secondary school principal I interviewed (September 1998) told of the difficulty the staffing formulas created for him. An experienced principal, he had moved to a new school that September. He saw his work as building relationships with staff, working with staff, students, and parents to re-shape the school as an equitable and diverse community. He noted that the new staffing formulas, combined with the new regulations for student contact hours, limit the staff's ability to "discover the vision for the school" as well as to "create the school that fits the vision." The new staffing formula means that teachers do not have time to meet or to work collaboratively on curriculum and school management. Students have more compulsory subjects to complete in a shorter period, parents (read mothers) are busier than in previous years, and the family is more dependent on the school for the educational needs of their children.

This principal noted that the staffing formula and other restructuring initiatives affect the use of time in the school. Time has always been a rare commodity for educational and administrative staff in schools. In particular, the collaborative and relational interactions of emancipatory or critical leadership require that the school community have time to work on committees (curricular, pedagogical, administrative, extra-curricular), school management issues, and so on. However, time outside the classroom is much less available. As teachers are required to spend more time in the classroom, as students are required to take more courses in less time, as families must provide more support to the student, the time within which to do the work of schooling becomes intensified.

The new staffing formulas erode the possibilities for collaborative, relational leadership in the local school. Indeed, the removal of principals and vice-principals from the teachers' unions, and the new staffing formulas with their emphasis on instructional time as the indicator of teaching and learning, support a traditional, bureaucratic division between teaching and administration. The possibilities for emancipatory leadership or bureaucratic-managerial leadership (Corson, 2000; Foster, 1989) are played out in the decisions that must be made by the principal as she/he coordinates the local context with the extra-local, administrative, and technical matters of educational restructuring. Emancipatory or critical leadership is eroded by the technical and administrative control of teachers' time in the classroom and principals' accountability for implementing unwanted changes. The technical and administrative requirements of staffing formulas ripple out through the school, re-affirming a top-down model of educational administration.

Concluding Comments

The historical promise of compulsory schooling has been that all children deserve the best education a society can offer. Indeed, this promise drives the literature on educational change. For example, authors as diverse as Sergiovanni (1992), Fullan and Hargreaves (1997), and Regan (1995) argue that collaborative educational leadership supports increased professionalism for teachers and addresses equity concerns within the school community. This promise also shapes credentialling programs for local school administrators, such as York University's Principals' Qualification Program, that teach leadership practices supportive of collaborative or relational leadership.

Yet, as we have seen above, Ontario school administrators who favor critical or emancipatory leadership are increasingly unable to frame their work within these models. Those administrators who have managed to hold on to the principles of emancipatory or collaborative leadership have had to learn to administer creatively and some of the schools in Ontario are wonderful examples of administering 'against the grain'. However, as control of educators' work is further centralized, and as experienced teachers and principals leave the school system, the retreat into managerial forms of leadership will intensify. As the feminist research into restructuring and globalization (cited above) notes, the current wave of educational restructuring is more likely to re-instantiate the traditional inequities of schooling than it is to re-affirm the promise of education. As this chapter shows, the technical and administrative matters of restructuring are the local experiential moments of tyranny and transformation. Leadership that links the textually-mediated administrative task to emancipatory action, then, must be a central topic in the teaching and learning of democratic education.

Notes

[1] This paper was first presented at the conference, Restructuring and transformation of institutional processes in Canada: Applications of institutional ethnography. York University, Toronto, Ont. Canada. October 30 - November 1, 1998.

[2] This chapter draws from my ongoing research on educational restructuring in Ontario. Data sources include: 1) documents from the various levels of school administration, including the Ministry of Education and the newly restructured Boards of Education in the Metropolitan Toronto area; 2) interviews with experienced principals from seven Boards of Education; 3) newspaper articles collected from Toronto newspapers; and 4) participant observation data collected by graduate students enrolled in my qualitative research course that was taught during the Ontario teachers' job action, Fall, 1997.

[3] These distinctions were drawn from the work of Foster (1989) and Corson (2000) who identify the work of a leader as essentially emancipatory.

References

Barlow, M. & Robertson, H. (1994). *Class warfare: The assault on Canada's schools.* Toronto: Key Porter.

Bechely, L. Andre. (1999). *To know otherwise: A study of the social organization of parents' work for public school choice.* Doctoral dissertation. Los Angeles: University of California.

Bloom, A. (1987). *The closing of the American mind.* New York: Simon & Schuster.

Brody, J. (1994). Shifting the boundaries: Gender and the politics of restructuring. In I. Bakker (Ed.), *The strategic silence: Gender and economic policy* (pp. 46-70). London/Ottawa: Zed Books/The North-South Institute.

Bullough, R. & Gitlin, A. (1995). *Becoming a student of teaching: Methodologies for exploring self and school context.* New York: Garland Publishers.

Corson, D. (2000). Emancipatory leadership. *International Journal for Leadership in Education, 3* (2), 93-120.

Curtis, B. (1992). *True government by choice men? Inspection, education and state formation in Canada West.* Toronto: University of Toronto Press.

David, M. (1998). *International feminist perspectives on mothering and schooling.* Symposium on globalization of education: Feminist perspectives on schooling, family and the state. American Education Research Association Meetings, San Diego, April 13-17.

Dehli, K. (1996a). Between 'market' and 'state'? Engendering education change in the 1990s. *Discourse: Studies in the Cultural Politics of Education, 17* (3), 363-376.

Dehli, K. (1996b). Travelling tales: Education reform and parental 'choice' in postmodern times. *Journal of Education Policy, 11* (1), 75-88.

Dehli, K. (1998). Shopping for schools: The future of education in Ontario? From reform to renewal: Beyond Bill 160 [Special Issue]. *Orbit magazine, 29* (1), 29-33.

Foster, W. (1989). Chapter 2: Toward a critical practice of leadership. In J. Smyth (Ed.), *Critical perspectives on educational leadership.* London: Falmer Press.

Foucault, M. (1972). *The archeology of knowledge.* New York: Harper Colophon.

Fullan, M. & Hannay, L. (1998). Assessing strategies – good reform, bad reform. From reform to renewal: Beyond Bill 160 [Special Issue]. *Orbit magazine, 29* (1), 7-9.

Fullan, M. & Hargreaves, A. (1997). *What's worth fighting for in the principalship?* (2nd Edition). Toronto: Ontario Public School Teachers' Federation; New York: Teachers' College Press.

Goldstein, T. (1998). Working toward equity. From reform to renewal: Beyond Bill 160 [Special Issue]. *Orbit magazine, 29* (1), 14-16.

Government of Ontario. (1997). *The Education Quality Improvement Act (Bill 160).*

Griffith, A. (1984). *Ideology, education and single parent families: The normative ordering of families through schooling.* Doctoral dissertation. Toronto: University of Toronto.

Griffith, A. (1992). Educational policy as text and action. *Educational Policy, 6* (4), 415-428.

Griffith, A. (1995) Connecting mothering and schooling: The discursive organization of children's development. In A. Manicom & M. Campbell (Eds.), *Studies in the social organization of knowledge.* Toronto: University of Toronto Press.

Griffith, A. & Waggoner, K. (1998). Parent involvement in education: Ideology and experience. In A. Griffith & S. Schecter (Eds.), Mothering, educating and schooling [Special Issue]. *Journal for a Just and Caring Education, 4* (1), January, 65-77.

Griffith, A. & Smith, D. (1990). "What did you do in school today?" Mothering, schooling and social class. *Perspectives on Social Problems, 2,* 324.

Hargreaves, A. (1998). Introduction. From reform to renewal: Beyond *Bill 160* [Special Issue]. *Orbit magazine, 29* (1), 3.

Kenway, J. (1998). *Local/global labour markets and the restructuring of gender, schooling and work.* Symposium on globalization of education: Feminist perspectives on schooling, family and the state. American Education Research Association Meetings, San Diego, April 13-17.

Landsberg, M. (1998, February 7). *The Toronto Star.*

Levin, H. (1998). Educational performance standards and the economy. *Educational Researcher, 27* (4), 4-10.

Livingstone, D. (1998). Public opinion. From reform to renewal: Beyond Bill 160 [Special Issue]. *Orbit magazine, 29* (1), 17-22.

Madaus, G., Scriven, M. & Stufflebeam, D. (1989). *Evaluation models: Viewpoints on educational and human service evaluation.* Boston: Kluwer-Nijoff Publishing.

Memorandum. (1997, October 21). The Ontario Public Supervisory Officials' Association.

Memorandum. (1998, March 4). Ontario Principals' Council.

Memorandum. (1998, March 11). Simcoe County Board of Education.

News broadcast. (1998, September 24, 9:00am), CBC Radio Two.

Ohmann, R. (1997). English and the Cold War. In Chomsky, N. et al. (Eds.), *The cold war and the university: Toward an intellectual history of the postwar years.* New York: New Press.

Regan, H. (1995). In the image of the double helix: A reconstruction of schooling. In D. Dunlap & P. Schmuck (Eds.), *Women leading education* (pp. 407-423). New York: SUNY Press.

Righton, S. (November 19, 1997). *Bill 160: The education quality improvement act, 1997 Highlights and amendments of concern to superintendents, principals and vice principals.* Toronto: Education and Public Law Group.

Sergiovanni, T. (1992). *Moral leadership: Getting to the heart of school improvement.* San Francisco: Jossey-Bass.

Smith, D. (1987). *The everyday world as problematic: A feminist sociology*. Boston: Northeastern University Press.

Smith, D. (1990a). *The conceptual practices of power: A feminist sociology of knowledge*. Boston: Northeastern University Press.

Smith, D. (1990b). *Texts, facts and femininity: Exploring the relations of ruling*. London: Routledge.

Smith, D. (1996). The relations of ruling: A feminist inquiry. *Studies in Cultures, Organizations and Societies, 2*, 171-190.

Smith, D. (1998). The underside of schooling: Restructuring, privatization, and women's unpaid work. In A. Griffith & S. Schecter (Eds.), Mothering, educating and schooling [Special Issue], *Journal for a Just and Caring Education, 4* (1), 11-29.

Smith, D. & Griffith, A. (1990). Coordinating the uncoordinated: Mothering, schooling and the family wage. *Perspectives on Social Problems, 2*, 25-43.

Stock, A. (2000). *An ethnography of assessment in elementary schools*. Doctoral dissertation. Toronto: University of Toronto.

Toronto Star. (1998, March 19). A28.

Tracking Report 2000: The effects of funding and policy changes in Ontario's elementary schools (2000). HYPERLINK http://www.peopleforeducation.com/tracking.html

Weiner, G. (2000). *School effectiveness for whom? Audit and high stake epistemologies and methodologies*. Paper presented to the School of Education, University of the West of England, Bristol, UK. (November 2).

Chapter 4
Limited Vision:
The Ontario Curriculum and
Outcomes-Based Learning

Carol Anne Wien and Curt Dudley-Marling

Introduction

A common response to criticism of public education in Canada and the United States has been to establish higher standards through the development of common curricular outcomes across a school district, province, state, or nation (Barlow & Robertson, 1994; Berliner & Biddle, 1995; Brown, 1991). The Department of Education in Alberta, for example, has reformulated its programs into "results-based curricula" that focus on observable and measurable learning outcomes, shifting the curriculum from "what is taught to what is learned by each student" (Barlow & Robertson, 1994, p. 213). The Ontario Ministry of Education and Training recently released *The Ontario Curriculum, Grades 1-8* (Ontario Ministry of Education and Training, 1997) to replace *The Common Curriculum, Grades 1-9* (Ontario Ministry of Education, 1995), introduced only two years ago by the previous New Democratic Party government. Ontario's Conservative government, which has been extremely critical of the province's education system, declared that its new curriculum is more rigorous, systematic, and consistent than the curriculum it replaced. The preamble to *The Ontario Curriculum, Grades 1-8* (1997) states: "The required knowledge and skills for each grade set high standards and identify what parents and the public can expect children to learn in the schools of Ontario" (p. I). The document goes on to say:

> The provision of detail will eliminate the need for school boards to write their own expectations, will ensure consistency in curriculum across the province, and will facilitate province-wide testing. Province-wide consistency will be helpful to students who change schools, and will help parents in all regions to have a clear understanding of their child's progress. (p. 2)

Like Alberta's new curriculum, *The Ontario Curriculum, Grades 1-8* emphasizes learner outcomes. It is logical to evaluate what is learned by students as opposed to what is taught by teachers, but implicit in approaches to education that rely on standardized, measurable outcomes is a vision of education rarely made explicit by educational policy makers.

Moving to Outcomes-Based Learning in Ontario

In 1995, Ontario's NDP government released *The Common Curriculum*, which, at first glance, seemed to arise out of the progressive educational philosophy that has influenced the Ontario Ministry of Education and, to a lesser extent, the schools of Ontario for close to 30 years – as seen, for example, in *The Formative Years* (Ontario Ministry of Education, 1975) and *Ontario Schools: Intermediate and Senior Divisions Programs and Diploma Requirements* (Ontario Ministry of Education, 1984). Arguably, the broad intention of *The Common Curriculum* as a policy framework was holistic, favoring the integration of curriculum, but leaving the means of reaching the "ten essential outcomes" up to individual boards and schools. *The Common Curriculum* stated that "All teaching should be based on a view of life as an integrated whole, in which people, things, events, processes and ideas are interrelated" (p. 19). Additionally, the stance of *The Common Curriculum* emphasized student ownership of learning and a "shift in curriculum emphasis to more integrated programming and active, inquiry-oriented learning" (p. 7).

It is just such a stance, and the ability of some schools to implement it, that led many American educators to praise Ontario schools (Brown, 1991; Goodman, 1986; Weaver, 1988). For example, Ken Goodman (1986) saw Ontario as a place particularly congenial to the kinds of progressive reading practices he has advocated for over 30 years. Similarly, Brown (1991) praised Ontario for "thoughtful schools" that encouraged flexible problem solving skills. He described Ontario schools as "symbolically rich places, where vivid and interesting conversations are taking place" and students and adults were "visibly engaged in inquiry, discovery, learning, collaborative problem solving, and critical thinking" (p. 233).

There was, however, a second stance in *The Common Curriculum* that marked a radical departure from the progressive pedagogical tradition that had influenced Ontario educational policy since the late 1960s (Hall-Dennis Report, 1968). This departure was signalled by the recurrence of a single phrase throughout the second half of *The Common Curriculum* document: "students will." Thus we read, "By the end of Grade 3 students will..."; "by the end of Grade 6 students will..."; by the end of Grade 9 students will..." Not students should, might, could, can, or may, or even "it is expected that students will," and not some or most or many, but "students will." We take this to mean *all* students. Arguably, what such language did was set up an authoritarian series of commands for teachers and school boards in particular. What happens if students cannot or do not reach these arbitrary markers of learning? What is assumed by the expectation that all students will, for example, by the end of Grade 3: "use the major reading strategies of prediction, confirmation, and self-correction to read for meaning in all contexts" (p. 33)? Statements like these set out a production schedule, a set time frame, that all students must follow. Such time schedules ignore the reality teachers face in classrooms – children who could learn much more than the stated outcomes as well as those who cannot learn it on the government's schedule, whether for developmental reasons or for other reasons, such as the necessity of learning English or French as a second language.

To some degree, the 1997 Ontario curriculum preserves the integrative stance of *The Common Curriculum*, if not its progressive language. The introduction to the document states:

> *Teachers will…emphasize the importance of language skills in the course of instruction in other subjects. In a well-developed program, teachers of all subjects help students acquire language skills. Teachers will therefore plan programs that will enable students to broaden their knowledge and skills by combining the study of language with the study of other subjects. (p. 4)*

Nevertheless, the channelling of an integrative philosophy through the device of lists of outcomes or expectations sets up a rigid, static system. It also implies a production schedule operating in a lock-step fashion. The specification of expectations as "observable" and 'measurable" certainly means the use of tests to determine whether outcomes have been achieved. In fact, the government itself makes the point that one advantage of provincial standards is that they facilitate province-wide testing. There may be efforts to avoid standardized, norm-referenced tests, but the pressure to produce comparisons will ultimately make norm-referenced testing irresistible. Whatever the form of testing, evidence from the United States indicates that *the test* becomes the curriculum (see, for example, Brown, 1991; Shannon, 1988). Teachers will teach what is on the test or what they believe will be on the test.

The Ontario Curriculum, Grades 1-8, like *The Common Curriculum* it replaces and other models of outcomes-based education, sets out an authoritarian and static vision with ideological links to the back-to-basics reform that has been part of American education since the mastery learning and competency-based movements of the 1970s (Carroll, 1963; Spady, 1994). The implementation of outcomes-based learning as fragmented lists of discrete items paralyzes broader, more integrative directions in education. The outcomes-based learning direction sets up a quintessentially narrow and controlling vision of teachers and teaching, of learners and learning, and of both diversity and ecology.

The Vision of the Learner and of Learning in the Ontario Curriculum

The Ontario curriculum presents an integrated view of learning in which the learner is engaged in enquiry. In reading, for example, the document's authors indicate that:

Although the lists of expectations [outcomes] might suggest that the skills involved in reading are discrete skills, they are in fact aspects of one integrated process that is best applied in a context that students see as meaningful and that encourages them to think creatively and critically about what they are reading. (1997, p. 26)

This suggests an active learner who participates in negotiating what is learned and how this is learned, and who has both some ownership of the learning undertaken ("best applied in a context that students see as meaningful") and some agency as a learner ("encourages them to think creatively and critically"). Arguably, this is a democratic vision, supported by theories of social constructivism (Duckworth, 1995; Jones & Nimmo, 1995; Vygotsky, 1978) which insist that the location of power be shared among participants. However, once the new Ontario curriculum begins to specify lists of what "students will" do at specific stages of their education, the vision of the learner shifts from active participant to passive recipient, the assumption being that the learner is a receptacle for storing what has been learned. To see the learner as a storehouse is an instrumental view in which power is one-sided, removed from the learner. When teachers and school boards must respond to "students will," it is likely that the aggressive force of such societal prescriptions will override inquiry-based learning, student ownership of learning, and participation in negotiating both content and means. The "learner as a receptacle" stance also contradicts the constructivist view that learners seek meaning in their lives.

Because the lists of observable expectations override the role of learners in their learning, the new Ontario curriculum obscures major consequences of schooling: to put it in the language of the document, the lists overlook a very large category of "outcomes." Teachers may think that because they select an outcome and use an activity (or test) to reach it, this outcome will be achieved; however, unless teachers examine the connections between outcomes and learners, selected outcomes may be logically connected to activities or tests but not to learning. The Ontario curriculum assumes that the designer of outcomes knows precisely the links between a specific outcome and the learning events required to reach it. These links, however, are not self-evident. Kindergarten teachers, for instance, frequently plan lessons around the teaching of colors (a week on orange, or red) and they believe they have successfully taught colors when the children provide some evidence that they *know* the colors at week's end. This content has the force of long tradition, but most children *know* color names in their mother tongue well before they come to school. In other words, this is a trivial curriculum, unworthy of the time spent on it when more complex possibilities engage children more seriously. Teachers may also falsely believe that knowing the color is the sole "learning outcome." Specifying only instrumental outcomes may lead teachers to miss other consequences of their teaching practice.

Nowhere does *The Ontario Curriculum, Grades 1-8* (or any other outcome-based learning document of which we are aware) deal with unintended outcomes of schooling. What goes on in schools, however, is an outcome of the curriculum, whether recognized or not. Disaffected or withdrawn students, students who hate school and can hardly bear to attend, students who think they are failures, that they are not good enough, that they can do nothing right, and teachers who are stressed beyond bearability are all potential outcomes of schooling. As Prescott (1974) noted, outcomes omit the daily life of classrooms: outcomes and the tests that measure them efface learner responses and teaching practices. Britzman (1991) points out that socialization is not simply what happens to people as they move through sets of experiences. It is also necessary to think about "what they make happen because of what happens to them" (p. 56). In other words, the Ontario curriculum does not describe learning that is dialogic, nor does it acknowledge the complex negotiations that occur among people as part of the consequences of learning. Relationships among learners and teachers are not linear, leading to single specified outcomes, but responsive to feedback. A vision and description of curriculum should take into account these complex and recursive processes in education.

Much of what the Ontario curriculum describes as expectations, Polanyi (1958) called tacit knowledge, the substrata of what persons or groups know and can do in their complex culture. To let sub-skills dominate at the expense of content in context or of identity, authenticity, careful motivation, and the provision for some creativity in education, means too few teachers will focus on the leading edge of learners' thought, reflection, judgement, deep feeling, and intellectual engagement. There is too much emphasis on efficiency and narrowly defined skills. Such documents obscure the numbing effect of a fragmented curriculum and the consequences for motivation of both teachers and students.

The imposition of outcomes on Ontario schools is a colonization of the learner by an ideology of instrumentalism and of corporate values of efficiency. The American model of schooling has historically been one of assimilation of varied immigrant groups (i.e., the "melting pot") to the dominant (corporate) discourse of power. Part of the Canadian identity has been, at least until recently, resistance to the straightforward imposition of American values and procedures on our institutions. The failure of outcomes processes in American schools has been well documented since the late 1970s (Apple, 1979, 1988; Giroux & Penna, 1981; Phillips, 1994; Shannon, 1988). The startling point is that educational institutions in Ontario are adopting an approach that is fundamentally flawed because it is essentially undemocratic and exclusionary, and the expected Canadian resistance to American processes has not been much in evidence.

The vision of the learner that ultimately emerges from the Ontario curriculum, because of the force of "students will," is a vision of a machine. Dehumanizing and demoralizing for everyone, it is also ultimately immoral, because a machine has no responsibility.

These documents, describing endless expectations, fail to acknowledge that education affects the structure of the psyche or that learning is experienced subjectively. If education does not deal seriously with learners' deep commitments and desires to be particular kinds of people, and the contents of the unconscious in terms of imagined possibilities for being, then all of us are servants to a vision of education less than fully human, less than who we might become, for it results in loss of agency, loss of power, loss of deep feeling and motivation to produce, loss of a sense of place where one belongs. This vision of education annihilates affect and *supports* alienation and a fractured identity by creating a circumscribed notion of meaning that makes no place for human feeling.

The Vision of Teachers and Teaching

The Ontario curriculum fundamentally alters the role of teachers from participants in negotiating the content and means of education to efficiency experts. The lists of expectations and performance criteria that inevitably accompany the "students will" component of the documents contributes to what Apple (1988) terms the "de-skilling of teachers," reducing teachers to mere technicians carrying out instruction determined by someone else. In the United States, for instance, many teachers are told *what* to teach (i.e., learning outcomes), *how* to teach (e.g., many teachers there are required to use basal readers), and *when* to teach (e.g., they are ordered to teach reading and writing at particular times during the day [Amspaugh, 1993]). Shannon (1988) suggests that some teachers in the United States may even be told *who* to teach – the brightest students who will contribute to higher test scores for the school.

A standardized curriculum and more frequent testing also effect more efficient surveillance and control of teachers' and students' behavior. Together they comprise an authoritarian, undemocratic vision of schools in which previous generations have predetermined all that is worth knowing, and hold authority to prescribe the necessary knowledge for succeeding generations of learners. Given the rate of change in contemporary society, rates of global immigration and interleaving of cultural groups, given current disruption from social and economic conditions, and rates of technological change, not only is this patently untrue, but it suggests an authoritarian stance that attempts to restrict future generations to current knowledge. But knowledge is not static, nor is there one version of what counts as knowledge.

How does de-skilling occur in the work lives of teachers? It arises through the management of lists: teachers are forced to become experts in managing a bureaucracy of paperwork. Keeping lists shuts down thoughtful reflection about what is occurring in classrooms and focuses teachers' practice on particular kinds of documentation and the management of paper. One teacher reported in an interview exploring the impact of outcomes documents:

> *It's just that it makes me weep. I feel I'm drowning in paper. It's incredibly overwhelmingly time consuming in terms of paper. I'm wondering how I'm ever going to get all this stuff I've got now in heaps and piles, folders and files in there in the right place. Checked off. I've got to do it for every child, for every criterion.*

She estimated she had 750 performance criteria, each to be documented with three pieces of paper. "You're supposed to have 2,250 pieces of paper in each child's portfolio – that's supposed to help parents?" Such obfuscation could not be any board's real intention, but this was the reality understood by this teacher. She continued, "I'm finding that it is expedient to just teach a lesson and give a sheet, and then I've got it – the evidence I need." Such a reductionist direction is a recipe for the destruction of creative thinking and critical reflection by teachers and students.

Other consequences for teachers include a return to the lock-step problem. A lock-step curriculum is one in which content is fixed in a sequence specified across time. Whereas the new Ontario curriculum documents speak of integration of curriculum, what teachers informally describe, as they try to reconstruct curriculum across divisions with divisional planning, is not integration but a return to the lock-step curriculum of a fixed production schedule – and this despite Spady's (1994) insistence that outcomes require variable time for student achievement. In other words, to avoid repetition, so the argument goes, teachers decide *when* specific content will occur, and teachers become unable to use this content at other times. This is the *train* curriculum, each content topic like a separate boxcar: children catch it or miss it, depending on the time when it is offered. If the child doesn't get it when it is slotted into the production schedule of fixed times, too bad, because the curriculum moves on to something else. Because of the pressure to contain more and more content, the time slots get shorter and shorter, with more transitions between them, until teacher and students are harassed by constant rushing to the next topic (Wien, 1996), the inability to sustain learning on any topic, and students' growing belief that none of it matters very much – it will all change in a few minutes anyway.

The Vision of Diversity and of Ecology

Provincial and federal policies seek to create a multicultural Canada that makes a place for the diverse voices of its citizens. The coercion towards a standard curriculum in Ontario has a very different impact. School curriculum cannot be culturally neutral (James, 1994) and pretending that the Ontario curriculum is culturally neutral makes it impossible to create schools that are truly congenial to the range of human differences present in our schools. Nor can a standardized curriculum ever be a fair curriculum, for underlying the expectation that "all students will" is the assumption that all students have an equal opportunity to achieve. Nonetheless, serious cultural, economic, and linguistic differences are represented in Ontario's schools. Holmes (1980) suggests that standard or common curricula ensure equity by providing "a level playing field." But such a belief assumes that all students come to school with the same advantages, the same cultural capital. The evidence, however, indicates that this is not so (see Delpit, 1988; Gee, 1990; Griffith, 1995). Gee (1990) observes, for example, that the literacy practices in the homes of white, middle-class parents ensure that most of their children will successfully learn to read and write with ease simply because the literacy practices in their homes so closely resemble what is valued at school. When students from different cultural or linguistic groups fail to learn to read as well or as quickly as their mainstream counterparts (really, fail to learn the middle-class discourse of power) we tend to blame their different experiences with the materials of literacy, what Ayers (1993) calls "cultural deprivation theory recycled for the '90's." The reality is that students from different cultural and linguistic backgrounds tend to come to school with different sets of literacy experiences from their peers, not with deficient literacy experiences (Teale, 1986). To succeed in schools, these students are frequently required to efface their own cultural background and experience (Bowman & Stott, 1994; Heath, 1983).

If knowledge and skills should be common to all students, how does a society decide which (or whose) knowledge and skills will be privileged? Cultural values are embedded in ways of doing things, and an instrumental focus privileges corporate values. Why should education be restricted to the values of the corporate elite? The recent Ontario documents convey no doubt about whose knowledge is important, nor do they acknowledge that this could be a site of debate. *The Ontario Curriculum, Grades 1-8* privileges the knowledge of those already privileged. Difference is to be accommodated by different materials (books that represent a range of peoples, for instance) and different teaching methods. But the *how* of schooling, its organizational structures (time schedules, work processes), can disenfranchise both individuals and groups just as surely as the content of schooling, its curriculum (Dyson, 1993). The Ontario curriculum documents do not acknowledge or deal with this in any way. To accommodate diversity – and Ontario schools are remarkable for their diversity – through materials and methods alone pretends that all students come to school with the same background and experience and that all backgrounds are treated equally by school curricula. Outcomes, in lists of great numbers, undercut efforts to be culturally sensitive, for, whether intentionally or not, they coerce teachers into emphasizing the dominant culture of power.

A school in a community is part of a complex ecological system of social and biotic relations. What happens in one part of an interrelated system affects what occurs in other parts. The stance in the Ontario curriculum which demands that a set of "students will" does not permit users of the document to acknowledge that classrooms and schools and individual learners are all complex ecological systems located in broader ecological communities. Ecological systems are feedback systems, cybernetic systems (Bateson, 1989) in which the productivity of one part influences the productivity of another. Energies are released and repressed in classrooms as in individual human bodies. Three students at the back of a high school classroom, chairs tilted on back legs, size 11 sneakers filling up the spaces around them, and sniggering – whether at *Pygmalion* or chemistry equations – affect what the teacher can do and the thinking, affect, and energy of everyone in the class, whether they join or resist. A child with special needs in kindergarten who rushes from the sandbox, cup in hand, into the bathroom and scoops a drink of water from the toilet affects what the teacher is able to do with 22 other children in that room. What the learner does requires the teacher's response, no matter the list.

Outcomes, thus, cannot be fixed in a single direction (although intentions or goals can) for such a description of supposed learning outcomes or expectations vastly oversimplifies and denies (or silences) the multiple agendas and the field of choices from which teachers select the particulars of what to attend to at any given moment. A multitude of consequences occurs beyond those single points called "learning outcomes" and they are all outcomes of the learning situation, whether or not the document notices them. In other words, documents like *The Ontario Curriculum, Grades 1-8* describe but a tiny part of the whole and do not sufficiently recognize schools as ecologically interrelated to their surroundings or as feedback systems.

As well, outcomes-based documents for education treat human activity as the most important fact of culture. Relations to the environment are mentioned, but sustained attention to the condition of the earth in urban settings, to the destruction of habitats and environments in the face of expanding urbanization, to the restoration of habitat in schoolyard and strip block, and daily attention to its state are insufficiently emphasized in the Ontario curriculum. University students who come to the Toronto area from northern Ontario, for instance, are often appalled by the state of the trees – half dead with bare branches – but then few schoolyards have trees at all to learn to watch and to care for. First Nations groups in particular traditionally bear a trained and sustained sensitivity to the natural environment around them. Their perspective has the power to shift our attention from an approach that is increasingly corporate, based on the myths of progress and economic success (Bowers, 1993), to an approach that tries to sustain and care for the earth. As Bateson (1989) argues, we *could* become caretakers of the earth: "We must transform our attitude toward all productive work and toward the planet into expressions of homemaking, where we create and sustain the possibility of life" (p. 136).

Outcomes-based learning approaches teach students and teachers first that someone else controls and dominates what they do: the fundamental value – taken-for-granted as an assumption of one's culture – is domination of others and of the earth, and this is exactly what requires a counterfoil, if a model of taking care of the earth and its peoples is to begin to be sustained.

An Alternative Vision: Education as a Spiral, Coil, or Mobius Strip

An example of an alternative image of the child is suggested by the schools of the municipality of Reggio Emilia, Italy. This system of 33 schools for young children assumes an image of children as magnificent, powerful, capable beings whose thinking and understanding of the world is intellectually profound, philosophical, and complex (Cadwell, 1997; Malaguzzi, 1993; Rinaldi, 1997). The role of the school and community is to support children's discoveries of what they can hypothesize, investigate, and verify through experiences with their "hundred languages": each "language" offers a vehicle for thinking, for feeling, and for understanding the world and includes literacy in a wide range of media, from graphic (drawing, painting, clay work, and wire sculpture) to computers. The extraordinary work of ordinary young children in Reggio Emilia over the past 30 years is highlighted in an exhibit, "The Hundred Languages of Children," that has been travelling world museums since 1980.

To write about the Reggio approach as a contrasting vision to outcomes-based learning is to offer an interpretation. Reggio educators argue that there are many perspectives and all perspectives are subjective, belonging to a participating subject (Rinaldi, 1997). Six key principles show the contrast between this philosophy and that of outcomes-based learning, and demonstrate how the metaphor behind this approach is organic and holistic, embodying the interconnections among elements. A single example for each principle illustrates one instance of how such a principle is embedded in their practice, but this practice is more sophisticated and complex than either of the authors has experienced in over 30 years of teaching in North America.

Relationality. Using systems theory as a foundation, no person or object is seen in isolation, nor is any learning a discrete bit, but each is seen always in relation to other possibilities or parts of the community. Nothing is done in isolation: the search is always for complex contexts, more elaborated relations. As an example, 5-year-olds explored measurement in the context of needing to tell the carpenter exactly how to make a new table just the same as one already in the class. In the process, the children tried all sorts of body parts (head, arms, legs) as non-standard units of measurement, made progress with a shoe, and eventually invented their own metre sticks (Reggio Children, 1997).

Progettazione. This term, literally "pedagogy of listening" (Rinaldi, 1997), does not translate adequately into English. It could also be called a pedagogy of going beyond the obvious, the trivial, the known, to uncover children's thinking around a topic. It is project work with a small group of children that may endure many months on a single topic, "long stories" in which teachers offer a subtle and precise scaffolding in planning activities that emerge out of teacher understanding of what children are thinking about.

Documentation. This curriculum planning is based on detailed documentation of children's processes so that the children's thinking becomes visible. Such documentation includes photographs of work in progress, permanent displays in the schools, audio taping and transcribing conversations of the children, and poring over these to decide on plans and future challenges. The elaborate documentation processes are constructed at three levels – for the children as they work, for the teachers as they work, and for the history of the schools and community – and demonstrate teaching as research rather than as transmission. The children can revisit the first project on making a portrait of the stone lions in the piazza, from 1979, while having their own experiences with these stone lions. This documentation is deeply engrossing to teachers, children, parents, and visitors (over

9000 foreign visitors have been received since *Newsweek* named the Diana School the best in the world for its age level in 1991).

Transparency. Being able, always, to see beyond to other possibilities is a principle embedded both in ways of thinking about teaching and in the design of the physical environment. Reggio schools, for example, have an indoor courtyard so there is always a relation between indoors and outdoors. Classrooms have carefully placed windows between them so children can see what others beyond their space are doing. Teachers use transcripts of children's talk to make transparent the children's thinking about a problem and to invent events for taking it further: one project underway at the Diana School in 1997 was an investigation of children's theories of immortality.

Collaboration. Long-term projects with small groups of children serve as vehicles for exploring thought and furthering children's development as a community and within the community. Two teachers work together on a project, with assistance from the *atelierista* (a specialist in using materials – such as a visual artist, musician, potter, or designer). Parents and others in the community frequently participate in school events – from transcribing audio tapes to attending parties. When the children were making an "amusement park for the birds" with fountains and a lake in their playground, the municipality was convinced to install more water pipes, and the workers installed them as part of the curriculum. Adults "lend" children their knowledge when necessary but encourage children to design, plan, and create from their own investigation and understanding of the world.

Reciprocity. The sense of connectedness among participants and respect for children's capability are evident both in slowing down to unhurried time and in their image of "tossing a ball" or throwing a provocation to the children and waiting to see what the children make of it, how they "toss" an idea back. Their documentation on clay development, for instance, shows two girls attempting to make horses, and their difficulties getting the clay horses to stand up. The teachers then challenged a group of children to make chairs out of clay, thus confronting the problem of stability when working with clay (Reggio Children, 1996). The teachers' plans emerge in response to children's actions: each side influences the moves the other makes to generate a negotiated or emergent curriculum in which power (to control what to do) is shared.

A practice of education with such principles suggests the metaphor of the spiral or coil or mobius strip (see Bateson, 1994). In these metaphors the interconnectedness of all things is present, as *The Ontario Curriculum, Grades 1-8* (1997) suggested in its opening statements. Such metaphors suggest an ecological awareness and a recognition of multiple perspectives. In contrast, the body of the curriculum document uses an outdated metaphor to describe learning. It takes for granted that the metaphor is factual, a truth, when it is instead a mental image. Bowers (1993) pointed out that such images are deep cultural analogs, scripts for thinking based on powerful taken-for-granted assumptions. *The Ontario Curriculum* describes learning as "a list of parts," as in assembling a machine. The list to make the machine is used as the central metaphor for learning. We argue that this is the wrong metaphor if the integrative, holistic, enquiry-oriented stance that the document supports is to be possible. The metaphors of a coil or spiral or mobius strip are closer to the intention of the integrative stance. Each of these metaphors for learning acknowledges that learning is a recursive process, folding back on earlier layers with new meanings, new resonance, building on that and recurring yet again: as Bateson (1994) said, "learning flourishes on the subtleties of recycled attention" (p. 112). Each of these metaphors acknowledges the interconnectedness of all things, as the 1995 document stated: "All teaching should be based on a view of life as an integrated whole in which people, things, events, processes, and ideas are interrelated" (p. 19). The problem with *The Ontario Curriculum* is that the central metaphor it takes for granted as appropriate to describe learning – the list of parts to assemble a machine – is outdated, narrowly focussed, and paralyzes the integrative, enquiry-oriented direction.

If teachers and school boards were able to use *The Ontario Curriculum* more as a reference document, like dictionaries, encyclopaedia, or indexes to maps, then the contents make more sense. It would then provide outsiders to education with a partial explication of what those implementing education are trying to do. It could also be understood as descriptive rather than prescriptive and as a map to a terrain that can never be exhaustively described. Education cannot be exhaustively described because it constantly changes: it is always uncertain, ambiguous, contested, and conflicted. However, to treat the documents as moral codes prescribing what shall be done is to prevent the integrative, holistic, enquiry-orientation from ever being possible, because the finite energies and time of teachers are dominated by documenting lists of discrete (and often trivial) outcomes.

Most significantly, documents of outcomes-based learning are based on the image of the child as deficient, needy. In contrast, the Reggio image of the child is of a magnificent being capable of great power and productivity. The difference in "outcomes" is clear to any observer of the "Hundred Languages of Children" exhibit: the high standards, depth of thought, inventiveness, and maturity of the children's work far surpass those of children in most systems of education. Curriculum documents that merely proliferate lists, and regulate teachers in documenting discrete items on these lists, betray both students and teachers because they stunt students' education and development. Such reductive responses de-spirit both teachers and students, because they must spend their lives thinking in terms of discrete learning outcomes and the tests that measure them. If we can today see that what was done to the children of aboriginal groups in residential schools resulted in a kind of cultural genocide (Richardson, 1993; Royal Commission on Aboriginal Peoples, 1996), through the forced silencing of aboriginal languages, customs, and culture, then *The Ontario Curriculum, Grades 1-8*, which will silence the cultures and languages of diverse groups in schools, could someday be regarded as an implement of cultural repression. This is so counter to the documents' stated policy intentions and to the Canadian value of multiculturalism that implementation of the curriculum requires careful consideration of the consequences for large groups of people in the province.

In closing, we note that there are teachers, schools, and school boards that create wonderful results in classrooms and communities despite the current chaos and uncertainty in education. They manage to excite students and send them off on provocative journeys of learning. Programs in teacher research, in enquiry into language, mathematics, science, and social studies education, in integration of the Arts and of artists into the schools, in design and technology – to mention but a handful – demonstrate exciting results and radiant students and teachers. But the Ontario curriculum does not assist them in so doing, because it paralyzes the integrative, holistic stance that permits such endeavors. We argue that there are many routes to a set of goals in education, and that to have commitment to a route both teachers and students must participate in thinking, feeling, and meaning making, not simply as machines or clerics carrying out the orders of others, but as full participants in a democratic process that educates its members for full citizenship and responsibility in adult life.

References

Amspaugh, L. (1993). Does anybody care? *Phi Delta Kappan, 74,* 14-17.

Apple, M. (1979). *Ideology and curriculum.* London: Routledge & Kegan Paul.

Apple, M. (1988). *Teachers and text.* London: Routledge & Kegan Paul.

Ayers, W. (1993). *To teach: The journey of a teacher.* New York: Teachers College Press.

Barlow, M. & Robertson, H. J. (1994). *Class warfare: The assault on Canada's schools.* Toronto: Key Porter Books.

Bateson, M. C. (1989). *Composing a life.* New York: Atlantic Monthly Press.

Bateson, M. C. (1994). *Peripheral visions: Learning along the way.* New York: Harper Collins.

Berliner, D. C. & Diddle, H. I. (1995). *The manufactured crisis: Myths, fraud, and the attack on America's public schools.* Reading, MA: Addison-Wesley.

Bowers, C. A. (1993). *Critical essays on education, modernity, and the recovery of the ecological imperative.* New York: Teachers College Press.

Bowman, B. & Stott, F. (1994). Understanding development in a cultural context: The challenge for teachers. In B. L. Mallory & R. S. New (Eds.), *Diversity and developmentally appropriate practices: Challenges for early childhood education* (pp. 119-133). New York: Teachers College Press.

Britzman, D. (1991). *Practice makes practice: A critical study of learning to teach.* Albany: State University of New York Press.

Brown, R. G. (1991). *Schools of thought: How the politics of literacy shapes thinking in the classroom.* San Francisco: Jossey-Bass.

Cadwell, L. B. (1997). *Bringing Reggio Emilia home: An innovative approach to early childhood education.* New York: Teachers College Press.

Carroll, J. B. (1963). A model of school learning. *Teachers College Record, 64* (December), 723-733.

Delpit, L. (1988). The silenced dialogue: Power and pedagogy in educating other people's children. *Harvard Educational Review, 58,* 280-298.

Duckworth, E. (1995). *"The having of wonderful ideas" and other essays on teaching and learning* (2nd ed.). New York: Teachers College Press.

Dyson, A. H. (1993). *Social worlds of children learning to write: In an urban school.* New York: Teachers College Press.

Gee, J. P. (1990). *Sociolinguistics and literacies: Ideology in discourse.* Philadelphia: The Falmer Press.

Giroux, H. & Penna, A. (1981). Social education in the classroom: The dynamics of the hidden curriculum. In H. Giroux, A. Penna & W. Pinar (Eds.), *Curriculum and instruction* (pp. 209-230). Berkeley, CA: McCutchan.

Goodman, K. (1986). *What's whole in whole language?* Richmond Hill, ON: Scholastic-TAB.

Griffith, A. (1995). Mothering. In A. Manicom & M. Campbell (Eds.), *Knowledge, experience, and ruling relations* (pp. 108-121). Toronto: University of Toronto Press.

Hall-Dennis Report. (1968). *Living and learning: The report of the provincial committee on aims and objectives in the schools of Ontario.* Toronto: Ontario Ministry of Education.

Heath, S. B. (1983). *Ways with words: Language, life, and work in communities and classrooms.* Cambridge: Cambridge University Press.

Holmes, M. (1980). Forward to the basics: A radical conservative reconstruction. *Curriculum Inquiry, 10,* 383-417.

James, C. E. (1994). "I don't want to talk about it": Silencing students in today's classroom. *Orbit, 25*(2), 26-29.

Jones, E. & Nimmo, J. (1995). *Emergent curriculum.* Washington, DC: National Association for the Education of Young Children.

Malaguzzi, L. (1993). History, ideas, and basic philosophy. In C. Edwards, L. Gandini & G. Forman (Eds.), *The hundred languages of children: The Reggio Emilia approach to early childhood education* (pp 41-89). Norwood, NJ: Ablex.

Ontario Ministry of Education. (1975). *The formative years.* Toronto: Ontario Ministry of Education.

Ontario Ministry of Education. (1984). *Ontario Schools: Intermediate and senior divisions programs and diploma requirements.* Toronto: Ontario Ministry of Education.

Ontario Ministry of Education. (1995). *The Common Curriculum, Grades 1 to 9.* Toronto: Ontario Ministry of Education.

Ontario Ministry of Education and Training (1997). The Ontario Curriculum, Grades I -8 [Online version]. Available at: http://www.edu.gov.on.ca/eng/documentlcurricul/curricul.html

Phillips, C. B. (1994). The movement of American children through sociocultural contexts: A case of conflict resolution. In B. L. Mallory & R. S. New (Eds.), *Diversity and developmentally appropriate practices: Challenges for early childhood education* (pp. 137-154). New York: Teachers College Press.

Polanyi, M. (1958). *Personal knowledge.* Chicago: University of Chicago Press.

Prescott, E. (1974). Approaches to quality in early childhood programs. *Childhood Education, 50,* 124-131.

Reggio Children. (1996). *The hundred languages of children* (Catalogue to the exhibit) (Rev. ed.). Reggio Emilia, Italy: Municipality of Reggio Emilia.

Reggio Children. (1997). *Shoe and the metre: Children and measurement – first approaches to the discovery, function, and use of measurement.* Reggio Emilia, Italy: Municipality of Reggio Emilia in collaboration with the Italian Ministry of Education.

Richardson, B. (1993). *People of Terra Nullius: Betrayal and rebirth in aboriginal Canada*. Toronto: Douglas & McIntrye.

Rinaldi, C. (1997). *Lectures. May study tour for North Americans*. Reggio Emilia, Italy.

Royal commission on Aboriginal Peoples. (1996). *Final Report, Volume 1*. Ottawa, Ontario: Government of Canada.

Shannon, P. (1988). *Broken promises: Reading instruction in 20th century America*. Granby, MA: Bergin & Garvey.

Spady, W. G. (1994). *Outcomes-based education: Critical issues and answers*. Arlington, VA: American Association of School Administrators.

Teale, W. H. (1986). Home background and young children's literacy development. In W. H. Teale & E. Sulzby (Eds.), *Emergent literacy: Writing and reading* (pp. 173-206). Norwood, NG: Ablex.

Vygotsky, L. V. (1978). *Mind in society: The development of higher psychological processes*. Cambridge, MA: Harvard University Press.

Weaver, C. (1988). *Reading process and practice: From socio-psycholinguistics to whole language*. Portsmouth, NH: Heinemann.

Wien, C. A. (1996). Time, work, and developmentally appropriate practice. *Early Childhood Research Quarterly, 11*, 377-403.

Chapter 5
A Wolf in Sheep's Clothing: A Critique of the Atlantic Provinces Education Foundation Program

David MacKinnon

Introduction

My purpose in this chapter is twofold: (1) to provide an overview of the outcomes-based Atlantic Provinces Education Foundation Program (APEF); and (2) to offer a critique which illuminates both its problematic aspects and its possibilities. In so doing I draw upon a selection of literature on outcomes-based education, on informal discussions I have had with both past and current officials of the Nova Scotia Department of Education,[1] and on an analysis of documents that are the products of the APEF initiative. The latter includes the brief pamphlet that frames the initiative, *The Atlantic Canada framework for essential graduation learnings in schools* (Atlantic Provinces Education Foundation, n.d.), and the published foundation documents in mathematics, science, social studies, and English language arts.[2] Given space limitations this chapter will not undertake an analysis of the curriculum guides that have been developed in identified foundation areas.[3] Rather, the analysis will focus on the nature of the initiative, the structure it imposes on curriculum through its focus on outcomes, the assumptions that underlie its language, and selected examples of general and key-stage learning outcomes.

The details of the critique are left to later sections of this chapter. In broad strokes, however, the analysis uncovers the contradictions that are disrobed when an initiative reduces what matters in education to a series of *common* observable and measurable student behaviors, while at the same time claiming a constructivist and student-centred orientation to learning that exhorts teachers to attend carefully to issues of equity and diversity. Many of the principles addressed in the foundation documents are worthy and would serve admirably to initiate public debate about a rich and democratic education. But such an education, as Fink (1997) notes, must be lived as well as taught. An initiative that is likely to diminish teacher professional judgement and narrow the range of educational possibilities within schools, and that defines "students' needs" without engaging them in their identification, is not, at its core, democratic.

Context

The public education system in Nova Scotia has experienced significant turbulence and change over the past two decades. In 1982, the number of school boards in Nova Scotia was reduced from 85 to 21 (Nova Scotia Department of Education, 1981), and in 1996 further amalgamation occurred as part of the government's Expenditure Control Program (Nova Scotia Education and Culture, 1997, p. 1), resulting in the creation of seven regional school boards. Since 1980/1981, there has been a loss of over 25 000 students and over 1100 teachers (Nova Scotia Department of Education, 1998-1999). Loss of teaching positions has not been solely a function of dwindling enrolments. Fiscal restraint and re-allocation of monies has seen board funding cut substantially, resulting in reductions in the number of teaching positions and an increase in the number of part-time term teaching positions.

Numbers rarely reveal impact. Morale within the teaching force has taken a severe pummelling, actual class sizes have increased substantially, support for professional development is a shadow of what it used to be, and the newest and saddest ritual in public education in Nova Scotia is the collective holding of breath as budget time approaches each spring. Teachers, children, and parents have taken to the streets to protest reductions in the numbers of teachers, threats of school closings, program cuts, and the increased frequency of environmental problems for teachers and students associated with aging and crumbling buildings. Within this same time frame, schools faced other substantive issues. Nova Scotia adopted an inclusion policy for special needs children in the province, resulting in the sorts of anxieties and frustrations that accompany any significant change, and the substantial re-learning that inclusive practice requires of teachers (MacKinnon & Brown, 1994). As if this was not enough, the rapid infusion of technology into schools and curricula within the last few years has added a new and significant learning challenge to teachers' must-do list. Now, with the APEF initiative and the emergence of standardized examinations, and the feared impact of this on teacher autonomy and professionalism, teachers are once again beset with huge challenges to the way they do their work. This layering of change upon change has created substantial instability – to put it mildly – in the teaching force and serious questions about the shape of the future for public education in Nova Scotia.

Atlantic Provinces Education Foundation Program

Origin and Framework

The APEF is an outgrowth of the Maritime Provinces Education Foundation, established in 1982 "for the purpose of enhancing regional content in school materials and to provide a structure for inter-provincial cooperation" (Atlantic Provinces Education Foundation, n.d., p. 4). Newfoundland and Labrador joined the partnership in 1995. The organization serves as a vehicle for dialogue and collaboration among Atlantic ministers of education on topics of common interest.

The language used to define their collaborative work on this initiative is clearly housed in an outcomes-based approach to schooling, and, as the following excerpt makes clear, only thinly veils a commitment to develop standardized approaches to assessment:

> *The Atlantic provinces' departments of education agree that the challenges facing their public school systems are strikingly similar. They agree that students' needs can be well met if there are clearly articulated statements of what students are expected to know and be able to do by the time they graduate from high school, if the curriculum reflects these expectations, and if the provinces can accurately assess students' achievement of them. (Atlantic Provinces Education Foundation, n.d., p. 4)*

This framework document[4] establishes six areas in which students are expected to demonstrate knowledge and skills. These are referred to as *essential graduation learnings* (Table 1). In each case a broadly stated graduation outcome is articulated in behavioral terms, and serves as a basis for developing curriculum outcomes.

In addition to defining the essential graduation learnings in the six domains, the framework document speaks to the implication these outcomes have for assessment. In particular, it makes clear that standards are needed in order to assess the level of student achievement, and that the Atlantic provinces are collaborating to develop assessments and/or examinations for grades 3, 6, 9, and 12. At the present time, assessments are undertaken at grades 6 and 9, and standardized exams are administrated in grade 12 in biology, chemistry, physics, and English language arts, accounting in each case for 30% of a student's mark in the graduation year. A standardized exam will soon be available for grade 12 mathematics. In recognizing the diversity of student populations, the document suggests that various assessment methods will be used, mentioning Braille, flexible timing, and tape recorders or scribes as possibilities. It is a clear assumption of this document that all students, regardless of individual circumstance, will be able to achieve the essential graduation learnings through the general and key-stage curriculum outcomes, albeit at different levels of achievement.

Table 1	
Atlantic Provinces Education Foundation: Essential Graduation Learnings	
Domain	**Essential Graduation Learning**
1. Aesthetic Expression	Graduates will be able to respond with critical awareness to various forms of the arts and be able to express themselves through the arts.
2. Citizenship	Graduates will be able to assess social, cultural, economic and environmental interdependence in a local and global context.
3. Communication	Graduates will be able to use the listening, viewing, speaking, reading and writing modes of language(s), and mathematical and scientific concepts and symbols, to think, learn and communicate effectively.
4. Personal development	Graduates will be able to continue to learn and to pursue an active, healthy lifestyle.
5. Problem solving	Graduates will be able to use the strategies and processes needed to solve a wide variety of problems, including those requiring language, and mathematical and scientific concepts.
6. Technological competence	Graduates will be able to use a variety of technologies, demonstrate an understanding of technological applications, and apply appropriate technologies for solving problems.
Based on: Atlantic Provinces Educational Foundation (n.d.), pp. 8-11	

The Subject Area Foundation Documents

There are presently foundation documents for English language arts, social studies, science, and mathematics. Each document has sections that speak to vision, the identification of general and key-stage curriculum outcomes, and the context in which teaching and learning takes place. The latter includes principles underlying the particular curriculum area, the learning environment, equity and diversity, and assessment.

In the next few pages I offer a brief overview, with examples of general and key-stage outcomes, of each of the foundation documents, as a way of providing readers with a sense for their content and orientation.

English language arts. The English language arts foundation document begins with the following vision statement:

> *The Atlantic Canada English language arts curriculum is shaped by a vision of enabling and encouraging students to become reflective, literate individuals who use language successfully for learning and communicating in personal and public contexts. (Nova Scotia Education and Culture, n.d.a, p. v)*

In its introduction, the document makes clear that the curriculum is defined in outcomes terms, that its key focus is literacy, that it is designed to encourage active student participation, that it emphasizes personal, social, and cultural contexts of language, and that it provides a basis for determining student achievement (p. 2). Like all the foundation documents, it differentiates between general curriculum outcomes and key-stage curriculum outcomes:

> *General curriculum outcomes are statements which identify what students are expected to know and be able to do upon completion of study in a curriculum area. Key-stage curriculum outcomes are statements which identify what students are expected to know and be able to do by the ends of grades 3, 6, 9, and 12 as a result of their cumulative learning experiences in a curriculum area. (p. 3)*

The middle section of the document identifies ten general curriculum outcomes. Each of these is divided into key-stage outcomes for grades 3, 6, 9, and 12. Readers are encouraged to examine Appendix A for an identification of the ten general outcome statements. I have selected an example of one key-stage outcome to reveal the manner in which the expectations progress at each of the four key stages (Table 2).

Each of the ten general outcome statements in the document is presented in a manner similar to those in Table 2: a broad outcome statement broken into specific key-stage outcomes.

The "contexts" section of the document describes the nature of an appropriate English language arts learning environment. Such an environment is identified as having seven key elements: (1) a balance among various modes of classroom activities, including teacher

	Table 2
	English language arts key-stage outcome progression (example)
Key-stage	**Outcome statement** *Students will be able to respond personally to a range of texts*
End of grade 3	Students will be expected to make personal connections to texts and describe, share and discuss their reactions and emotions.
End of grade 6	Students will have achieved the outcomes for entry-grade 3 and also be expected to explain why a particular text matters to them and demonstrate an increasing ability to make connections among texts.
End of grade 9	Students will have achieved the outcomes for entry-grade 6 and will also be expected to respond to some of the material they read or view by questioning, connecting, evaluating and extending (move beyond initial understanding to more thoughtful interpretations).
End of grade 12	Students will have achieved the outcomes for entry-grade 9 and will also be expected to make informed personal responses to increasingly challenging print and media texts and reflect on their responses.
Based on: Nova Scotia Education and Culture, n.d.a, pp. 26-27	

talk and student talk, and oral and written activities; (2) experiences that challenge learners; (3) the classroom as a centre of inquiry; (4) the use of a wide variety of resources, including print, media, and computer networking; (5) full use of technology; (6) a variety of interactive learning activities, including pairs and small group work; and (7) meaningful and positive homework experiences (pp. 38-41). It also comments on the creation of an inclusive environment and a plethora of assessment techniques.

Social studies. The vision statement at the beginning of the social studies foundation document speaks to citizenship and globalization:

> *The Atlantic Canada social studies curriculum will enable and encourage students to examine issues, respond critically and creatively, and make informed decisions as individuals and as citizens of*

Canada and of an increasingly interdependent world. (Nova Scotia Education and Culture, 1999, p. v)

The introduction to the document provides a brief statement about the nature of social studies, referring to it as a "multidisciplinary lens through which students examine issues affecting their lives from personal, academic, pluralistic, and global perspectives" (Nova Scotia Education and Culture, 1999, p. 2). As with other foundation documents, a section is included which links the six areas of essential graduation learnings – aesthetic expression, citizenship, communication, personal development, problem solving, and technological competence – with the type of work that students will undertake through social studies.

The middle portion of the document specifies six general curriculum outcomes, each of which is identified in Appendix B. As in

| *Table 3* |
| *Social Studies key-stage outcome progression (example)* |

Key-stage	**Outcome statement(s)** *Students will be expected to demonstrate the ability to make responsible economic decisions as individuals and as members of society*
End of grade 3	Students will be expected to distinguish between needs and wants.
End of grade 6	Students will have achieved the outcomes for entry-grade 3 and will also be expected to give examples that show how scarcity and opportunity cost govern the economic decisions made by individuals and governments.
End of grade 9	Students will have achieved the outcomes for entry-grade 6 and will also be expected to explain how economic decisions are made by individuals, organizations and governments, based on scarcity and opportunity cost.
End of grade 12	Students will have achieved the outcomes for entry-grade 9 and will also be expected to analyze how economic decisions are made by individuals, organizations and governments, based on scarcity and opportunity cost.
Based on: Nova Scotia Education and Culture, 1999, pp. 20-21	

the English language arts section, I have elected to extract an example of a key-stage social studies outcome and demonstrate the manner in which it changes through the four stages (Table 3).

Following the identification of key-stage outcomes, the foundation document describes the appropriate teaching and learning contexts in which social studies takes place. Social studies is described as being "empowering" and "effective" if it meets six conditions: meaningful, significant, challenging, active, integrative, and issues-based (p. 29). Collectively, these generally speak to a teaching and learning environment that is stimulating, student-centred, cross-disciplinary, and socially responsible. In addition, the context section of the document encourages a classroom environment that is resource-based, and promotes a commitment to issues of equity and diversity. "Resource-based" is described as learning that "involves students, teachers, and teacher librarians in the effective use of a wide range of print, non-print, and human resources" (p. 30).

Science. The foundation document in science, like the others, begins with a vision statement for scientific literacy:

> *The Atlantic provinces' science curriculum is guided by the vision that all students, regardless of gender or cultural background, will have an opportunity to develop scientific literacy. Scientific literacy is an evolving combination of the science-related attitudes, skills, and knowledge students need to develop inquiry, problem-solving, and decision-making attitudes, to become lifelong learners, and to maintain a sense of wonder about the world around them (Nova Scotia Education and Culture, 1998, p. v).*

The introduction to the document elaborates upon the central tenet of the vision statement: scientific literacy. Scientific literacy is considered a result of scientific inquiry, problem solving, and decision making, what the document identifies as the "why," "how," and "should" questions (p. 3). The general outcomes for the science curriculum are focused on the development of skills, knowledge, and attitudes, and the relationships among science, technology, society, and the environment (p. 11).

These outcomes serve as the basis for the elaboration of general curriculum outcomes (Appendix C). Each of these is then divided into key-stage curriculum outcomes for grades 3, 6, 9, and 12. Table 4 offers an example of the progression of key-stage science curriculum outcomes.

	Table 4 Science key-stage outcome progression (example)
Key Stage	**Outcome statement(s)** *Students will develop an understanding of the nature of science and technology, of the relationships between science and technology, and of the social and environmental contexts of science and technology.*
End of grade 3	Students will be expected to investigate objects and events in the immediate environment, and use appropriate language to develop understanding and to communicate results.
End of grade 6	Students will have achieved the outcomes for entry-grade 3 and will also be expected to demonstrate that science and technology use specific processes to investigate the natural and constructed world or to seek solutions to practical problems.
End of grade 9	Students will have achieved the outcomes for entry-grade 6 and will also be expected to describe various processes used in science and technology that enable people to understand natural phenomena and develop technological solutions.
End of grade 12	Students will have achieved the outcomes for entry-grade 9 and will also be expected to describe and explain disciplinary and interdisciplinary processes used to enable us to understand natural phenomena and develop technological solutions.
Based on: Nova Scotia Education and Culture, 1998, pp. 19-20.	

The contexts section of the science foundation document has four main emphases, referred to as "principles of learning and teaching science." The first of these concerns the relationships among science, technology, society, and the environment, an important focus throughout the science curriculum. The second is an elaboration of the principles of constructivism, with a number of academic references to key scholars in the field. The third describes the linkages among the science disciplines, with an emphasis on the concepts of change, diversity, energy, equilibrium, matter, models, and systems.

The final emphasis, as in the other foundation documents, is on resource-based learning.

The contexts section also includes a discussion of appropriate learning environments, while addressing in particular the need for instructional variation, the use of investigative techniques, and the importance of homework. In addition, the section speaks to the importance of equity and diversity, with emphasis on special needs children, gender, and multiculturalism.

Mathematics. The vision statement which frames this foundation document connects mathematics literacy and the ability to function in a technological society:

> *The Atlantic Canada mathematic curriculum is shaped by a vision which fosters the development of mathematically literate students who can extend and apply their learning and who are effective participants in an increasingly technological world. (Nova Scotia Education and Culture, n.d.b, p. v)*

The brief introductory section of the foundation document makes clear that the principles which informed the mathematics foundation curriculum are linked to a 1989 publication by the National Council of Teachers of Mathematics, *Curriculum and evaluation standards for school mathematics.* This document is cited on numerous occasions within the introductory discussion of curriculum outcomes (pp. 7-10). Particular emphasis is given to the unifying ideas of problem solving, communication, reasoning, and connections.

The APEF document identifies seven general curriculum outcomes (Appendix D), each broken into a series of key-stage outcomes for grades 3, 6, 9, and 12. Table 5 provides an example of the development of key-stage curriculum outcomes specific to patterns and relationships.

In the "contexts for teaching and learning" section of the foundation document, six basic principles are identified. These all relate to the circumstances that best facilitate the learning of mathematics: varied instructional approaches, support for risk-taking, the establishment of clear expectations, and a recognition that students have different learning styles (pp. 27-28).

	Table 5 *Mathematics key-stage outcome progression (example)*
Key-stage	**Outcome statement(s)** *Students will explore, recognize, represent and apply patterns and relationships, both informally and formally.*
End of grade 3	Students will be expected to recognize, describe, extend and create patterns and sequences in a variety of mathematical and real-world contexts (e.g., geometric, numeric and measurement)
End of grade 6	Students will have achieved the outcomes for entry-grade 3 and will also be expected to describe, extend and create a wide variety of patterns and relationships to model and solve problems involving real-world situations and mathematical concepts.
End of grade 9	Students will have achieved the outcomes for entry-grade 6 and will also be expected to analyze, generalize and create patterns and relationships to model and solve real-world and mathematical problem situations.
End of grade 12	Students will have achieved the outcomes for entry-grade 9 and will also be expected to model real-world problems using functions, equations, inequalities and discrete structures.
Based on: Nova Scotia Education and Culture, n.d.b, pp. 16-17.	

Summary

In the previous section, I provided an overview of the program's framework and a cursory description, using selected examples, of the outcomes-based curriculum for English language arts, social studies, science, and mathematics, the only areas currently with published foundation documents.

The APEF program is both rational and behavioristic. Rational, as it is used here, refers to technical or instrumental rationality, i.e., actions that lead to the efficient accomplishment of specified goals (Scott, 1987, p. 31). Behavioristic refers to educational activities that are limited to things observable and measurable, an outgrowth of the behavioral objectives movement of the 1960s (Eisner, 1996, p. 334). Rational and behavioristic elements are manifest in the APEF program insofar as curriculum development has been guided by a clear hierarchy of outcomes – essential graduation learnings; general curriculum outcomes; key-stage outcomes for grades 3, 6, 9, and 12; subject area curriculum guides – with all outcome statements written in terms of student performance. These outcomes serve as standards for student achievement, although all of the foundation documents suggest that the degree to which a given student achieves a particular outcome can and will vary significantly. While no description was offered of specific subject area curriculum guides, the ones I have examined in the foundation areas are rationally informed by the foundation documents.

Critique

This critique has two subsections, the first focusing on aspects of the Atlantic Provinces Education Foundation program that are considered to be problematic, the second on aspects of the program that offer possibilities for public education. In the "Problematic" subsection, four central aspects of the APEF initiative are identified for discussion. All of these, while specific to APEF, are also troubling aspects of outcomes-based education in general. In the "Possibilities" subsection, I identify three aspects of the initiative that, with modifications, hold promise for the realization of a more equitable and democratic educational practice.

All of the points raised are offered for critical analysis and public discourse, and not as a condemnation of, or support for, this particular initiative. The APEF initiative is part of an outcomes-based "wave" currently washing over much of North America. It stems from criticism of public education and concerns related to system accountability dating back to the 1970s (Capper & Jamison, 1993; King & Evans, 1991; Wolf & Reardon, 1996). Interestingly, there is nothing particularly "Atlantic" about the initiative. None of the graduation learnings or the general and key-stage curriculum outcomes addresses anything that is unique to Atlantic Canadians. As such, APEF is housed within a larger educational and political discourse on the purposes and outputs of public education, a debate largely informed by economic rationalism (Bagnall, 1994, p. 20).

Problematic

Assumptions of outcomes-based education. Bagnall (1994) suggests that outcomes-based education is premised on a number of assumptions, two of which are of particular interest here: the universality of outcomes precision, and the flexibility of the framework.

Regarding the former, Bagnall argues that any educational outcome is of practical value only if it is perceived that a change in learner behavior can be attributed to the educational event itself. Consequently, outcomes must be clearly specifiable, reliably observable, reliably quantifiable, and essentially unchanging (p. 22). Since a key component of accountability is a demonstration of accomplishment, any curriculum design constructed with accountability as a cardinal principle must be stated in language that renders the outputs measurable. This necessarily begets a narrowing of possible outputs, and thus a narrowing of the educational enterprise itself. The latter can happen in spite of the best intentions of curriculum designers. As Spady (cited in McNeir, 1993, p. 3) notes, "Once established, broad exit outcomes guide every aspect of the instructional system."

As demonstrated previously, all curriculum outcomes identified in the APEF foundation documents have been stated in behavioral language and are linked to various forms of assessment, standardized and otherwise. For example, the foundation document in science states, "The assessment of student learning must be aligned with curriculum outcomes and the types of learning opportunities made available to students" (Nova Scotia Education and Culture, 1998, p. 43). Similarly, the social studies document states, "Instruction and evaluation are centred around outcomes. Not only are outcomes used in providing *structured* teaching and learning, but they also provide a framework for assessment and evaluation" (Nova Scotia Education and Culture, 1999, p. 36) (emphasis added). While there is no indication in the foundation documents that the general and key-stage outcomes must frame all of what a teacher does and a student learns, the likelihood of them having major influence is substantial.

Bagnall (1994) also speaks to the flexibility of an outcomes-based curriculum, "Outcomes-driven education is also premised on the belief that the educational institution will tend to be optimally flexible, in response to the shifting *wants of the learners*" (p. 25) (emphasis added). It is too early to tell whether the APEF program will demonstrate resilience, but there are three inherent aspects of the undertaking that challenge flexibility.

The first is that the initiative was never based on the *wants* of the learners. Students were not involved in any meaningful way in its conception or design. Given that they are its intended focus, this seems especially curious. In an article on the value of an outcomes-based education, King and Evans (1991) make a comment that is revealing: "OBE forces *us* to express what *we* value in education, to commit educational resources to bringing that to life for students, and – in contrast to present practice – *to continue until we have succeeded*" (p. 74) (emphasis added). The thrust is to "bring to life for the students" that which "we" value. The language is not dissimilar to the following quote from the framework document (Atlantic Provinces Education Foundation, n.d.): "They [Atlantic provinces' departments of education] agree that students' needs can be well met if there are clearly articulated statements of what students are expected to know and be able to do by the time they graduate from high school…" (p. 4). Based on my reading of the documents, and on informal discussions with individuals who have been part of the APEF process, there is no indication whatsoever that students have played a contributory role in deciding what their needs are. The "we" is a privileged "other."

The second challenge to flexibility is that the initiative's design is by its very nature one of organizational rationalization. Organizational rationality "refers to the extent to which a series of actions is organized in such a way as to lead to predetermined goals with maximum efficiency" (Scott, 1987, p. 31). While this seems infinitely reasonable, as all organizations exist for some purpose, the way to accomplish these goals varies considerably, depending in part on the complexity of goal attainment and the stability of the environment in which the organization exists (Mintzberg, 1989). In brief, goal attainment in education is complex, primarily because the way to accomplish educational goals – the technology of teaching – is not known with precision; there are many ways to teach effectively. Furthermore, the environment in which schools exist is not stable; that is, we cannot predict that the goals we seek to accomplish now will be relevant ten or more years into the future. For these reasons, a very tightly rationalized, mechanistic system is likely to be unresponsive to change (Blackmore & Kenway, 1995; Morgan, 1997).

A tightly rationalized system also assumes a strong correlation between the formal curriculum and what is actually taught. As this increasingly becomes the case – and it will if teachers believe it to be so – teachers' professional autonomy will be eroded and their role as active curriculum agents will be diminished (Apple, 1993, pp. 122-123).

To say that the APEF program is an example of tight rationalization may be an overstatement, but it is reasonable to suggest that it is a move in that direction. The fact that outcomes are specified at four stages of schooling, and not just at the end, further entrenches a sense of rigidity. As Bagnall (1994, p. 25) suggests, "outcomes-driven education…is inherently inflexible once the educational goals have been set for a programme."

The third problem for flexibility is that the APEF initiative is a cooperative effort among four government departments of education. Since the foundation documents are identical for each province, modifying them would presumably require unanimous consent, which by its very nature requires more time and negotiation than do initiatives specific to one province.

"*All roads lead to Rome.*" In an analysis of outcomes-based learning in Ontario, Wien and Dudley-Marling (1998) highlight a contradiction in the language of the curriculum documents that could just as easily have been written about the APEF initiative. They suggest that while the language of the Ontario documents is holistic and integrative, implying active student involvement and ownership, the requirement that "students will…" shifts the emphasis from "active participant to passive recipient" (p. 408).

Each one of the APEF foundation documents, using varied language, describes learners as active constructors of knowledge and full participants in the educational enterprise:

- The foundation document in English language arts lists the following as one of the principles underlying the curriculum: "Language learning is an active process of constructing meaning, drawing on all sources and ways of knowing" (Nova Scotia Education and Culture, n.d.a, p. 37).

- In an explication of resource-based learning, the social studies foundation document states, "In a resource-based learning environment, students and teachers make decisions about appropriate sources of information, tools for learning and how to access them" (Nova Scotia Education and Culture, 1999, p. 30).

- In the mathematics foundation document, mathematics is identified as a "constructive rather than a passive activity," and that "students should be encouraged to represent their own understandings in various ways" (Nova Scotia Education and Culture, n.d.b, p. 27).

These statements, and numerous others within the documents, position the learner as an active participant in the construction of knowledge and meaningful learning activities. To then insert behavioral outcomes, at four specific stages, gives the contradictory message that regardless of their active engagement in the educational process, students must ultimately dance to someone else's tune. This double message is most explicitly revealed in the science foundation document, coincidentally the only document which devotes a section to constructivism: "Science is often seen as an appropriate subject for the application of constructivist principles, since the hypothesizing and testing of cognitive structures that are fundamental to cognitive growth in the constructivist scheme mirror the work of scientists" (Nova Scotia Education and Culture, 1998). Yet, two sentences later:

> *However, science itself is a way of looking at and explaining the world. Thus, the acquisition of concepts to help explain a phenomenon is too broad an aim. The concepts that the learner develops should be consistent with those concepts that scientists already hold for that particular phenomenon (p. 31).*

My way of making sense of this is to suggest that the foundation documents argue for substantial variability of process, but for a degree of uniformity in outcome.

The caveat to this, and the reason I use the phrase "degree of uniformity" in the sentence above, is that all of the foundation documents clearly state that while all students are expected to achieve the specified outcomes, the level of achievement can vary substantially. This might be somewhat reassuring were it not for the existence of standardized exams at the grade 12 level.

Standards and standardization. The APEF framework document devotes three pages to a discussion of the implications of the foundation program for student assessment. A central concept in that discussion is "standards." The subsection on achievement standards opens as follows:

> *Curriculum outcome statements make clear the achievements students are expected to demonstrate at key stages in their schooling; they do not, however, describe the range of these achievements. For teachers, students and parents to assess the level at which work is done, either during the course of a year or at the end of a year, or both, standards are needed. (Atlantic Provinces Education Foundation, n.d., p. 18)*

It then qualifies the use of the term "standards," indicating that it "is used to describe different levels of student achievement" (p. 18). It also suggests that assessment can take many forms, citing portfolios, performances, essays, and projects as examples (p. 20). Furthermore, assessment will be confined to curriculum outcomes, and essential graduation learnings will not be measured directly (p. 23).

This suggests a degree of flexibility in terms of student achievement. Curriculum guides recommend assessment strategies for teachers, but tests and examinations are teacher-created, though presumably informed by the general and key-stage curriculum outcomes. Given the breadth of the outcomes, this does not appear particularly onerous. Furthermore, each of the foundation documents includes a section on equity and diversity, and within it teachers are instructed to include assessment strategies that account for such things as gender, ability, and cultural background.

However, the inclusion of standardized tests in several subjects in grade 12 counters the professed commitment to accepting different levels of student achievement. In fairness, these exams presently account for only 30% of a student's mark in selected courses, leaving the majority of the evaluation to other forms of teacher-created assessment strategies. Nonetheless, this introduces an element of standardization to the evaluation process that can only be interpreted as an attempt to impose baseline evaluation standards on all students in these subjects. The danger with this is the possibility of the test becoming the curriculum (Wien & Dudley-Marling, 1998, p. 408), although there is disagreement on the likelihood of this happening (Rudman, 1995, p. 308). Furthermore, there is no reason to believe that the percentage of a student's mark derived from a standardized exam will remain at a given level. By the very act of introducing these evaluation instruments, the door is opened to their use in other subjects and at other grade levels, with the possibility that their import could grow to constitute a larger percentage of a student's mark.

Without exception. The last point to be made about the APEF program and other outcomes-based initiatives is the assertion that all students, regardless of personal or social circumstances, can achieve them (Capper & Jamison, 1993, p. 429). As previously mentioned, the foundation documents assert that different levels of achievement are acceptable. Regardless, the creation of curriculum outcomes can only be seen as a hegemonic process in which selected members of one generation or group decide what the next generation needs to know. As Robertson (1998) states:

> *The language we use to talk about the process of education determines how we think about education's purposes and value – there are no neutral words. To speak of learning as a journey is not just metaphor-*

ically different from referring to it as executing measurable outcomes. Yet outcomes – specified, allegedly concrete statements of what all students should know and be able to do at specific points along the journey – have taken over as the focus of education reform in North America and beyond. (p. 33)

Wien and Dudley-Marling (1998) refer to outcomes as a "colonization of the learner by an ideology of instrumentalism and of corporate values of efficiency" (p. 410). Despite the clear and impressive attempts of the document writers and others involved in the process to be holistic, sensitive to difference, and student-centred, the APEF initiative stands as an example of hegemonic process.

Possibilities

All educational initiatives garner support and criticism. In this brief subsection, I switch lenses to identify aspects of the APEF initiative that, in my estimation, open the door to constructive possibilities for schooling.

Guidelines. There is a substantial literature on effective teaching methods and effective schools. Some authors suggest that enough is known to allow for the construction of curriculum outcomes as a vehicle to drive school programs (Valesky, Markus, Willis & Nelson, 1993, p. 5). While others agree that there is a significant research base, what constitutes effective teaching varies with context (Borich, 2000, p. 26; Good & Brophy, 1997, p. 17).

Assessment of student learning is an integral component of school process. Any organization, and particularly a public organization, is logically asked to account for its outcomes. However, the problem in the case of education, as Wagner (1989, p. 25) notes, is the determinate quality of the results. Regardless of the acceptability of the established outcomes, and the precision with which they can be known, they cannot assess all that is of value in education. Unlike King & Evans (1991), who argue that the outcomes process forces us to identify what we value in education (p. 74), I contend that those virtues that can be stated in behavioral and measurable terms constitute only a slice of the pie. As a result, outcomes-based education should inform the educational process, not define or guide it. In Bagnall's (1994) terms, it "should be seen only as contributing" (p. 31).

What does this mean? Effectively, it means that an outcomes process should seek to identify, through the input of all constituents, those things we value in education, regardless of how precisely they can be measured. In my conversations with present and former officials in the Nova Scotia Department of Education, every individual strongly agreed that there is much of value in education that is not expressed in the APEF outcomes-based curriculum. Yet, the bottom line is that the framework and foundation documents essentially define public education in the Atlantic Provinces.

Broadening. Following from the argument above, I suggest that the APEF initiative be seen as a work in progress, not an end in itself. To my knowledge, students, as a constituent group, had no meaningful input into the process. Beyond this, a negotiation process that involves representatives from four provinces, by its nature, results in a loss of local voice. Furthermore, the number of teachers directly involved in the initiative (seated around the table) decreased over time due to financial restraints. The framework document is vague in terms of the degree of meaningful input from constituents outside of the departments of education and the teaching profession, referring only to "ongoing communication and consultation with appropriate stakeholders according to provincial practices" (Atlantic Provinces Education Foundation, n.d., p. 15). A democratic process needs to be transparent, and inclusive of all stakeholders. The APEF program is a narrow beginning to what could be a more democratic and meaningful process.

Opportunity to learn. Yackulic and Noonan (2000) propose that the development of educational outcomes should be informed by research on a student's opportunity to learn. This refers to factors that influence student achievement, commonly agreed upon to be personality factors, classroom variables, and policy and resource allocation factors (p. 83). While I am resistant to analyses that seek solely to explain variation in student achievement based on a form of "deficit" thinking, I see much potential in an initiative that embeds within its policy directives an understanding of the conditions of marginalization and the sorts of school practices that move in the direction of equity. A focus on opportunities for children to learn would envelop such a discourse.

There are contradictory messages in the APEF documents in this regard. All of the foundation documents include a section on equity and diversity, each of which exhorts teachers to construct their curriculum and teaching practice in inclusive ways. Yet, the mechanistic, rationalistic identification and achievement of outcomes runs counter to the language of holism and integration, in so far as it assumes the acceptability of common standards for diverse students as long as curriculum and classroom practice is inclusive. This contradition is magnified by the introduction of standardized assessment practices.

However, the foundation documents also encourage forms of non-standardized assessment, including portfolios, work samples, teacher-made tests, learning journals, and peer and self-assessment. Depending on their construction and the way they are used, many of these fall under the umbrella of authentic assessment, in that they are based on "real world" tasks and thus presumably more meaningful to students (Darling-Hammond & Ancess, 1996, p. 54). If the standardized assessment practices were removed, and teachers supported in developing inclusive classroom practices, including diverse forms of assessment, the thrust of the APEF initiative would be somewhat more palatable and less contradictory.

Closure

It is very clear that the four Atlantic departments of education have devoted considerable time and resources to the creation of the APEF program. It is equally obvious that the basic thrust of this initiative has merit: switching the evaluative focus in schools from teacher performance to student accomplishment. What is troubling is the manner in which this is done.

I have attempted to demonstrate that an outcomes-based approach to education provides an inadequate foundation for public education. Behavioral outcomes, by definition, are confined to that which is observable and measurable. In spite of the increasing popularity of curriculum outcomes, projects like the APEF initiative are necessarily incomplete, and perhaps unwittingly misguided. While they create a rationalized structure for the operation of public schools, they render invisible aspects of education that cannot be reduced to testable outputs. Instead of public debates on the value and purpose of education, and the subsequent creation of documents and other forms of representation which honor the substance of these debates, the APEF initiative is a reductionist and anti-democratic exercise aimed largely at increasing system accountability. This is not meant to trivialize the substantial work of those involved in the initiative, or to suggest that educational systems should not be held accountable. Rather, it is my belief that observable outcomes are only part of a complex undertaking, and to emphasize them to the exclusion of other, equally worthy educational goals, is to assign them an undeserved position of privilege. Despite the best efforts of committed educators, identified outcomes will, to the detriment of everyone, likely come to represent what is considered important in schooling.

Two more foundation documents are in press, and others will follow until all subject areas have been brought into the fold. Atlantic Canada will then have a powerful statement of what matters in the education of its children. More standardized tests will be developed to assess the achievement of the outcomes and these will grow in importance.

Yet, there is value in the foundation documents. Discussions concerning the diversity of classroom environments, inclusive teaching practices, and authentic assessment are a welcomed departure from the more circumscribed practices of the past. Also, increased attention to varied learning styles and the constructed nature of knowledge reveal hope for a pedagogy that is meaningful for all students. If the foundation documents could serve as a stepping stone to a richer and deeper discourse, they would have merit. As an end in themselves, they fall sadly short.

Notes

[1] All discussions with present or former employees, who are or have been involved with the Foundations Program of the Nova Scotia Department of Education, were informal. By agreement, no one has been quoted directly. However, their input was invaluable in contextualizing the framework and foundation documents and in broadening my understanding of the initiative. Their role was one of information; my analysis of the initiative, with which they may disagree, is mine alone.

[2] At the time of writing, two additional foundation documents are in press: one on technology and one on arts. I did not have the opportunity to examine either.

[3] By "foundation area," I refer only to those content areas that have thus far been developed under the APEF umbrella, and have resulted in the creation of foundation documents that are identical for each of the Atlantic Provinces, each of which then serve as a framework for the development of subject area curriculum guides. This includes mathematics, social studies, English language arts, and science. Foundation documents are currently in press for technology and arts, but no shared curriculum guides have yet been produced.

[4] The framework document, *The Atlantic Canada framework for essential graduation learnings in schools*, is at the apex of a hierarchy of documents that have been produced through this initiative. As mentioned in the text, my analysis concentrated exclusively on the top two levels of the hierarchy, and did not include course-specific curriculum guides. Schematically, the hierarchy is as shown below:

> The Atlantic Canada Framework for Essential
> Graduation Learnings in Schools

Foundation document **Science**	Foundation document **Mathematics**	Foundation document **Social Studies**	Foundation document **English language arts**
Science curriculum guides	Mathematics curriculum guides	Social Studies curriculum guides	English language arts curriculum guides

References

Apple, M. W. (1993). *Official knowledge: Democratic education in a conservative age.* New York: Routledge.

Atlantic Provinces Education Foundation. (n.d.). *The Atlantic Canada framework for essential graduation learnings in schools.* Halifax, NS: Atlantic Provinces Education Foundation.

Bagnall, R. G. (1994). Performance indicators and outcomes as measures of educational quality: A cautionary critique. *International Journal of Lifelong Education, 13* (1), 19-32.

Blackmore, J. & Kenway, J. (1995). Changing schools, teachers, and curriculum: But what about the girls? In D. Corson (Ed.), *Discourse and power in educational organizations* (pp. 233-256). Cresskill, NJ: Hampton Press.

Borich, G. D. (2000). *Effective teaching methods* (4th ed.). Upper Saddle River, NJ: Prentice-Hall.

Capper, C. A. & Jamison, M. T. (1993). Outcomes-based education re-examined: From structural functionalism to post-structuralism. *Educational Policy, 7* (4), 427-446.

Darling-Hammond, L. & Ancess, J. (1996). Authentic assessment and school development. In J. B. Baron & D. P. Wolf (Eds.), *Performance-based student assessment: Challenges and possibilities* (pp. 52-83). Chicago, IL: Ninety-fifth yearbook of the National Society for the Study of Education.

Eisner, E. W. (1996). Standards for schools: Help or hindrance? In W. Hare and J. P. Portelli (Eds.), *Philosophy of education: Introductory readings* (pp. 333-344). Calgary, AB: Detselig.

Fink, J. (1997). *Critical pedagogy: Notes from the real world.* Don Mills, ON: Longman.

Good, T. L. & Brophy, J. E. (1997). *Looking in classrooms* (7th ed.). Don Mills, ON: Longman.

King, J. A. & Evans, K. M. (1991). Can we achieve outcome-based education? *Educational Leadership, 49* (2), 73-75.

MacKinnon, J. D. & Brown, M. E. (1994). Inclusion in secondary schools: An analysis of school structure based on teachers' images of change. *Educational Administration Quarterly, 30* (2), 126-152.

McNeir, G. (1993). *Outcomes-based education.* (ERIC Document Reproduction Service No. 379 765).

Mintzberg, H. (1989). *Mintzberg on management.* New York: The Free Press.

Morgan, G. (1997). *Images of organization* (New Ed.). Thousand Oaks, CA: Sage.

Nova Scotia Department of Education (1981). *Report of the Commission on Public Education Finance.* Halifax, NS.

Nova Scotia Department of Education (1998-1999). Research and statistics [On-line]. Available: http://stats.ednet.ns/statsum/edstats.htm.

Nova Scotia Education and Culture. (n.d.a). *Foundation for the Atlantic Canada English language arts curriculum.* Halifax, NS: Atlantic Provinces Education Foundation.

Nova Scotia Education and Culture. (n.d.b). *Foundation for the Atlantic Canada mathematics curriculum.* Halifax, NS: Atlantic Provinces Education Foundation.

Nova Scotia Education and Culture. (1997). *School board amalgamation: Co-ordinators' reports.* Halifax, NS.

Nova Scotia Education and Culture. (1998). *Foundation for the Atlantic Canada science curriculum.* Halifax, NS: Atlantic Provinces Education Foundation.

Nova Scotia Education and Culture. (1999). *Foundation for the Atlantic Canada social studies curriculum.* Halifax, NS: Atlantic Provinces Education Foundation.

Robertson, H.-J. (1998). *No more teachers, no more books.* Toronto, ON: McClelland & Stewart.

Rudman, H. C. (1995). The standardized test flap: An effort to sort out fact from fiction, truth from deliberate hyperbole. In L. W. Roberts & R. A. Clifton (Eds.), *Contemporary Canadian educational issues,* (pp. 305-322). Toronto, ON: Nelson Canada.

Scott, W. R. (1987). *Organizations: Rational, natural, and open systems* (2nd ed.). Englewood Cliffs, NJ: Prentice-Hall.

Valesky, T. C., Markus, F. W., Willis, J. & Nelson, J. O. (1993). *Total quality management as a philosophical and organizational framework to achieve outcomes-*

based education and effective schools. Paper displayed at the Annual Meeting of the Mid-South Educational Research Association, New Orleans, LA. (ERIC Document Reproduction Service No. 365 703)

Wagner, R. B. (1989). *Accountability in education.* New York: Routledge.

Wien, C. A. & Dudley-Marling, C. (1998). Limited vision: The Ontario curriculum and outcomes-based learning. *Canadian Journal of Education, 23* (4), 405-420.

Wolf, D. P. & Reardon, S. F. (1996). Access to excellence through new forms of student assessment. In J. B. Baron & D. P. Wolf (Eds.), *Performance-based student assessment: Challenges and possibilities* (pp. 1-31). Chicago: Ninety-fifth yearbook of The National Society for the Study of Education.

Yackulic, R. A. & Noonan, B. W. (2000). Measurement of the full scope of learning. In Y. Lenoir, W. Hunter, D. Hodgkinson, P. de Broucker, & A. Dolbec (Eds.), *A pan-Canadian education research agenda.* Ottawa, ON: Canadian Society for the Study of Education.

Appendix A	
Atlantic Canada Education Foundation: English language arts outcome statement	
Broad focus	**General curriculum outcomes**
Speaking and listening	1. Students will speak and listen to explore, extend and reflect on their thoughts, ideas, feelings and experiences. 2. Students will be able to communicate information and ideas effectively and clearly, and to respond personally and critically. 3. Students will be able to interact with sensitivity and respect, considering the situation, audience and purpose.
Reading and viewing	1. Students will be able to select, read and view with understanding a range of literature, information, media and visual texts. 2. Students will be able to interpret, select and combine information using a variety of strategies, resources and technologies. 3. Students will be able to respond personally to a range of texts. 4. Students will be able to respond critically to a range of texts, applying their understanding of language, form and genre.
Writing and other ways of representing	1. Students will be able to use writing and other ways of representing to explore, clarify and reflect on their thoughts, feelings, experiences and learning; and to use their imagination. 2. Students will be able to create texts collaboratively and independently, using a variety of forms for a range of audiences and purposes. 3. Students will be able to use a range of strategies to develop effective writing and other ways of representing and to enhance their clarity, precision and effectiveness.
Based on: Nova Scotia Education and Culture, n.d.a, pp. 16-35.	

Appendix B Atlantic Canada Education Foundation: Social Studies outcome statements	
Broad focus	**General curriculum outcomes**
Citizenship, power and governance	Students will be expected to demonstrate an understanding of the rights and responsibilities of citizenship and the origins, functions and sources of power, authority and governance.
Culture and diversity	Students will be expected to demonstrate an understanding of culture, diversity and world view, recognizing the similarities and differences reflected in various personal, cultural, racial and ethnic perspectives.
Individuals, societies and economic decisions	Students will be expected to demonstrate an ability to make responsible economic decisions as individuals and as members of society.
Interdependence	Students will be expected to demonstrate an understanding of the interdependent relationship among individuals, societies and the environment – locally, nationally and globally – and the implications for a sustainable future.
People, place and environment	Students will be expected to demonstrate an understanding of the interactions among people, places and the environment.
Time, continuity and change	Students will be expected to demonstrate an understanding of the past and how it affects the present and the future.
Based on: Nova Scotia Education and Culture, 1999, pp. 16-27.	

Appendix C **Atlantic Canada Education Foundation:** Science outcome statements	
Broad focus	**General curriculum outcomes**
Science, technology, society and the environment	Students will develop an understanding of the nature of science and technology, of the relationships between science and technology, and of the social and environmental contexts of science and technology.
Skills	Students will develop the skills required for scientific and technological inquiry, for solving problems, for communicating scientific ideas and results, for working collaboratively and for making informed decisions.
Knowledge	Students will construct knowledge and understanding of concepts in life science, physical science and Earth and space science, and apply these understandings to interpret, integrate and extend their knowledge.
Attitudes	Students will be encouraged to develop attitudes that support the responsible acquisition and application of scientific and technological knowledge to the mutual benefit of self, society and the environment.
Based on: Nova Scotia Education and Culture, 1998, pp. 19-28.	

Appendix D Atlantic Canada Education Foundation: Mathematics outcome statements	
Broad focus	**General curriculum outcomes**
Number sense	Students will demonstrate number sense and apply number theory.
Operation sense	Students will demonstrate operation sense and apply operations principles and procedures in both numeric and algebraic situations.
Patterns and relationships	Students will explore, recognize, represent and apply patterns and relationships, both formally and informally.
Measurement	Students will demonstrate an understanding of and apply concepts and skills associated with measurement.
Spatial sense	Students will demonstrate spatial sense and apply geometric concepts, properties and relationships.
Collection, display and analysis	Students will solve problems involving the collection, display and analysis of data.
Uncertainty	Students will represent and solve problems involving uncertainty.
Based on: Nova Scotia Education and Culture, n.d.b, pp. 12-25.	

Chapter 6
"No-one has ever grown taller as a result of being measured" Revisited[1]
More Educational Measurement Lessons for Canadians

Sharon Murphy

In the early 1990s, Canadian education appeared perched on the edge of a precipice. Up until the mid-1990s, Canadian education had been regarded as relatively progressive by many educators in the United States (e.g., Brown, 1991). In terms of assessment, schools were described as using anecdotal reporting as supplemental to or as the basis for documenting student progress. Although, even in the early 1990s, standardized assessment measures[2] were in use in varied forms across Canada, in general such measures were not high-stakes measure — that is, the consequences of such measures did not have a significant impact on students, teachers, schools, or others involved in education. In general, and in keeping with the advice offered in most basic textbooks or technical manuals on assessment, standardized measures were considered one piece of information in relation to the very complex task of documenting student learning.[3]

However, in the early 1990s in Canada, the call for high-stakes standardized testing was part of an overall movement from conservative quarters to reform the educational system. For example, the editors (e.g., Thorsell, 1992; 1991) and columnists (e.g., Nikiforuk, 1991; 1992) of the *Globe and Mail* newspaper appeared to speak with a unified voice calling for national standardized testing. Even the newspaper's education reporter covered stories on testing with the zeal of the converted, not critically analysing *why* testing might be called for in a time of shrinking financial resources, but, instead, writing with an underlying assumption that standardized testing would be good for the educational system (e.g., Lewington, 1993a; 1993b; 1991).

Given the context of the early 90s, I drew upon the history of large scale standardized testing in the United States to provide some lessons that Canadians might reflect upon in their thinking about standardized testing (see, Murphy, 1994). Now, several years later, Canadian education is in a new context with respect to standardized testing. Under the auspices of the Council of Ministers of Education of Canada, all provinces take part in the School Achievement Indicators Program (SAIP) which periodically assesses a sample of students in curricular areas such as science, reading, writing, and mathematics (http://www.cmec.ca/saip).[4] In addition, there has been widespread participation in the International Mathematics and Science Studies and the Organization for Economic Co-operation and Development's (OECD) Program for International Student Assessment (PISA) (http://www.eqao.com/home_page/nat_int/5e.html) involving 28 OECD countries in the assessment of reading, mathematics, and science. Added to these national and international assessments are provincial standardized tests routinely administered by many provinces. In some provinces, such as Ontario, the law *requires* that students take the tests, schools must prepare action plans to respond to the results for their school, and graduation from high school is dependent upon the completion of a literacy exit examination (http://www.eqao.com/home_page/1Ce.html). The stakes are becoming very high indeed. The context has shifted significantly since the early 1990s and out of this new context, I believe, arise several more educational measurement lessons for Canadians.

Lesson 1. Neither standards nor standardized testing mean excellence or are a guarantee of excellence.

In discussions about standardized testing, the terms *standards* and *standardized* testing are often equated. In fact, the introduction of either or both of these is often imagined to be a remedy for the ills of schooling and a guarantee of improved schooling (e.g., Nikiforuk, 1997). Underlying such discussions are worries about curricular diversity in schools. The solution proposed is for all students to study the same curricula and be assessed in the same manner. Eliminating variability and assessing an imagined unitary curriculum somehow seems to be an assurance of excellence. Yet, the foundations of each of these assumptions is at best weak and at worst frivolous.

Consider, for a moment, the term standards. Generally speaking, standards refer to levels of adequacy. In Canada, we are fortunate to have an organization that protects consumer interests called the Canadian Standards Association.[5] This association examines products and rates them on their safety for consumer use. Products are rated as either safe – they meet the standard – or they are not safe.

So for example, electrical products manufactured in Canada are CSA approved; yet, we know that there is considerable variability in the quality and safety of such products. CSA does not evaluate every product, but a sample of products, in order to assign its ratings. Even within the same product line, some products are known to perform more satisfactorily than others. Some parts malfunction, causing product recalls as a safety measure. So, standards are neither a guarantee of uniformity nor of excellence.

Even when several different categories of ratings (e.g., ranging from *adequate standard* to *excellent standard*) for products are used, there is still variability among the products within these categories in terms of the quality of goods. So, for instance, one could imagine that even for one type of "excellently rated" product sold by a manufacturer, there would be variation from product to product as to the degree to which the product exceeded the standard.[6] Once again, the uniformity that might be imagined as being promised by the rating does not hold.

In addition, what counts as adequate changes across time. If the CSA had rated the knob and tube wiring of the early 1900s, it probably would have deemed it adequate at the time, but today many insurance companies insist on the rewiring of homes with such wiring. Such changes occur because our values and our society have changed. We demand safer and safer products and we demand more of them in much more varied conditions than previously. So, as our values and uses change so do our expectations of adequacy.

The lessons we can learn from the CSA are: (a) that standards are social constructs – they shift and change across time, and (b) that the judgement of standards involves approximate estimation, and not infallible precision. Standards for the CSA are about adequacy and, even though they suggest adequacy, they are not a guarantee of adequacy.

If this view of standards is applied to education, then a somewhat different conversation about standards results. Like CSA standards, the adequacy standards in education are social constructions that shift over time. This shifting across time is not inherently good or bad but is a result of changing values in society. In the same way that the CSA standards do not differentiate among the subtleties of individual consumer goods being rated, educational standards do not capture the fullness of learning and may not even capture the adequacy.

While the term standards may not have the definitiveness that some imagine, the relationship between *standards* and *standardized tests* is even more tenuous. The word "standardized" in standardized testing refers to two aspects of the testing process (see, Anastasi & Urbina, 1997): (a) how the text is administered – the ideal is to administer the test in similar conditions with similar instructions so as to eliminate this element as a competing explanation for performance, and (b) how the test is constructed – usually, standardized tests are scored by comparing the performance of persons taking the test to the performance of a comparator group who initially took the test.[7] As this description suggests, standardized tests, as traditionally conceptualized, are not referenced in relation to standards.

All of this being said, provincial ministries of education in Canada have attempted to make the connection between standards and standardized testing by creating large scale assessments that are relatively uniform in their administration (meeting one of the two aspects of standardized assessment according to Anastasi & Urbina, 1997) and that usually have a multiple choice component allowing for comparability of scores from year to year (having the effect of norms, though technically not operating as such).[8] Such tests usually do not include enough items to reliably indicate anything about sub-skills and, therefore, claims that suggest that teachers can use the tests diagnostically are ill-founded.[9]

For non-multiple-choice elements, a type of pseudo-norming occurs through the use of rubrics. Rubrics involve the creation of descriptors that identify clusters of performance. Although student performance is not force-fit into the normal curve, it is usually assigned by a panel of judges a categorical label such as poor, low average, average, high average, excellent. Finally, some provinces, such as Ontario, have attempted to transform standards into standardized assessment by mapping their curricular grid onto assessments (http://www.eqao.com/home_page/nat_int/5e.html). However, the manner in which such mapping is done is not described in public literature released on the testing procedures, so its integrity is difficult to assess. Furthermore, there is some doubt that the week-long assessments intended to mimic actual classroom activities in provinces like Ontario (see, http://www.eqao.com/eqao/home_page/information/1C2e.html) are actually accomplishing this goal since some of the responses of school districts suggest otherwise (see, for example, the Durham District School Board's action plan prepared in response to the district's performance, http://www.eqao.com/eqao/home_page/Durham/01.htm).

Lesson 2. Test results that are reported numerically, despite the cautions of the test developers, take on a life of their own.

To their credit, and in keeping with the *Code of Fair Testing Practices in Education* (1988),[10] many jurisdictions caution against the reporting of test results independent of the particular contexts in which they were gathered. For example, the Education Quality and Accountability Office (EQAO) in Ontario says "rankings tell us nothing about why scores are high or low, they invite simplistic and misleading comparisons which ignore the particular circumstances that affect achievement in each school, and they distract people from addressing the critical issue of how to improve learning for all students" (http://www.eqao.com/eqao/home_page/information/1C3e.html). Of course, this is somewhat like placing a warning of "Harmful to your health" on a package of cigarettes – everyone knows how the cigarettes will be used.

That being said, the picture that is created of Canadian schools after test results are released is rapidly mimicking that of its southern counterpart, the United States, where testing of such different sorts has been in existence for such a long time that Hanson (1993) describes it as a testing culture, and where public schooling has rapidly deteriorated in recent times. What happens when statistics permeate cultures is the "making up of people" because, as Hacking (1990) claims, "enumeration requires categorization, and that defining new classes of people for the purposes of statistics has consequences for the ways in which we conceive of others and think of our own possibilities and potentialities" (p. 6). In other words, it isn't enough that patterns of behavior on standardized tests are enumerated, but when they are, they must be named as average, above average, or below average and, somehow, whole nations, provinces, schools, and individual students are considered average, below average, or above average, rather than the small sample of behavior that generated the statistics in the first place.

Furthermore, as Poovey (1998) argues, because numbers are associated with precision, they "*seem* to guarantee accuracy" (p. 30). The result is that a series of questions or tasks somehow seems to precisely represent the whole educational system for a grade, a school, a province, or a nation. Yet, if one thinks about how the relatively small cluster of items on a test represents grade three-ed-ness, for instance, few people would agree that the representation is sufficient. Indeed, Haladyna (1994), whose scholarship is aimed towards improving multiple-choice tests, reports that critics have "noted that item [question] writing [in multiple-choice tests] is not a scholarly area" (p. 188), and admits himself that item writing has "a checkered past…it fails to qualify as a science" (p. 190). So not only is there the problem of the inappropriate extrapolation of category labels from the numbers produced in standardized testing, but there are the additional problems of how the test represents the domain being assessed and the historical difficulties in elaborating a science of item writing for multiple-choice tests.

Because the social artifacts that are tasks of any testing event get transformed into numbers (with their associations of precision) and these in turn get transformed into categorical labels, the results are headlines that read like the following:

> *Boos and hisses for our classrooms. (Giles, September 7, 1996, p. D2)*

> *World education league: Who's on top? Some countries seem to educate their children much better than others. (Economist, 1997, p. 21)*

> *Ontario schools get failing grade despite changes. (McCann, 1999, p. A15)*

To make such attributions based on the type of data generated from standardized tests is not only misleading but is ethically bankrupt because it feeds into a false sense of the failure of our social systems. Of course, those doing the attributing are in the media, and this leads to the next lesson Canadians can learn from testing.

Lesson 3. Invariably, the media will misuse information from standardized testing to manufacture news and, in doing so, contribute to making the consequences of such testing much weightier than they should be.

Since the early 1990s, newspapers from the *Halifax Chronicle Herald* to the *Vancouver Sun* have not only run headlines announcing the results of test scores, they have often milked the results of tests so that they can print at least three news stories that tell, in effect, the same thing – what the results of the most recent provincial, national, or international tests have been. As the following headlines illustrate,[11] these media outlets, like their counterparts to the south in the United States (Kaplan, 1998), turn educational matters into gladia-

toresque infotainment by creating mythic rivalries pitting one jurisdiction over another:

Catholic students tops in the city. (Dawson, May 16, 1996, p. A1)

Toronto matches province in three Rs. (Chamberlain, December 2, 1998, p. B5)

Alberta beats U.S. in world wide test. (Dawson, 1998a, p. B4)

Of course, left unstated in most of these types of articles is the fact that ranking (that is placing first, second, third or forty-fifth, for that matter) should not be the focus of the reporting because the minuscule differences that separate rankings, while statistically sig-nificant, may not be practically significant. For instance, if the aver-age on a test for one jurisdiction is 49.5 and for another it is 49.45, one places first and the other second but the meaningful practical difference between these two scores is negligible. Rankings take on even less meaning once something called the standard error of meas-urement is placed around each score. The standard error of meas-urement is the "range of fluctuation likely to occur in a single indi-vidual's score as a result of irrelevant, chance factors" (Anastasi, 1982, p. 102). Often this is several points wide. So for example, if the standard error of measurement for a test is ± 2.00 with a 95% confi-dence level, then the score of 49.5 should really be reported by stat-ing that the score would fall between 47.5 and 51.5 about 95 times out of 100. If the standard error of measurement is applied to the score of 49.45, then it should be reported as ranging from 47.45 to 51.25 about 95 times out of 100. As this example illustrates, there would be such tremendous similarity in scores that, even though the difference between scores might be statistically different, for all intents and purposes the performances underlying these scores are quite similar. Of course none of this type of information makes good copy, and hence never even makes it to the computer keyboards of reporters and columnists, let alone the newsroom floor.

News stories that emphasize rankings, combined with a general negative tone in the press toward education, undoubtedly con-tribute to how parents think about the importance of tests and, in general, exacerbate parental worries about the education of their children. In the province of Alberta, for example, the Alberta Teachers' Association linked school transfers to parents who were chasing after schools with higher standardized test results (Dempster, May 19, 1996). In the province of Ontario, reporters write of parents who once believed in the public school system who are mortgaging their homes to enrol their children in private schools (Dennis, 1993b). Nationally, lead-ins to stories on home schooling are commentaries about the loss of confidence in the public school system (*This Morning*, CBC Radio, August 24, 2000).

Ironically, while newspapers and other media outlets run sensationalist headlines that create an climate of misinformation about the quality of education,[12] there are reports that concerns are being raised within journalism's own ranks, in the United States at least, about the decline in the quality of journalism. For example, in a poll of publishers and editors in the United States that was conducted by *Editor and Publisher*, "some 47.9 percent agreed that press coverage was 'shallow and inadequate.' About 55.7 percent thought coverage was too cynical. A huge 65.8 percent agreed that newspapers cover politics and personalities at the expense of policy" (Hamil, 1998, p. 17).

The question can rightly be raised as to what is fuelling both the move to standardized testing and the style of reporting of stories on education and other areas of public interest. As Lesson 4 suggests, different aspects of globalization appear partially responsible.

Lesson 4. In a time of globalization, business interests and business ways of thinking have infused public policy and contributed to the move toward standardized testing.

The move to globalization of business has been the hallmark of the past 25 years. Increasingly, companies have merged to create large multinational corporations that hold an allegiance to no one social polity as represented by governments. Instead, these corporations operate in their shareholders' best monetary interests[13] and seek out economical (i.e., cheap) ways to bring more product to market and increase profit margins. Because of their sheer economic pan-world size, such companies enjoy influence with governments and their agencies (Drohan, 2000; Gessell, 1998; Robertson, 1996). With respect to education, businesses have tended to exercise their influence in two ways: (a) based on their egocentric business view of the world, they want to change the model of education from a social one to a business one, and (b) based on their business sense, they want to decrease the financial obligations (taxes) they have and, as a result, large government subsidized programs like education become targets for "downsizing."

Business has not been shy about introducing a corporate mentality to education (see, Robertson, 1998). Sometimes the moves seem indirect, such as the Investors Group (http://www.cmec.ca/saip/writ94en.html) or the Spar Aerospace sponsorship of the SAIP program (http://www.cmec.ca/saip/indexe.stm). Others are subtle hints. For example, in 1992, Cedric Ritchie, Scotiabank Chair, in one address reflected nostalgically on his own schooling and ascribed a motivating quality to tests (School testing, 1992). Yet, other times the intentions are revealed fairly explicitly, as in 1993, when a *Toronto Life* story headline read – "Class action: What if schools were run like mini-corporations with the principal as CEO and the parents and teachers as a board of directors" (Dennis, 1993a, p. 33), or when the Conference Board of Canada produced a list of employability skills (Galt, 1992), or when the Economic Council of Canada recommended that closer links be forged between the world of work and school (Lewington, 1992).[14]

In any case, underlying the models is the tracking of progress statistically, like the stock market,[15] with not much consideration of social context[16] in which individual schools operate and without much attentiveness to the broader social functions of schools. The result is the replacement of the ethic of pedagogical care with one of production. Based on their business sense, business influences appear blind to the possibility that "widgets" need things like food, shelter, and care. They seem naively oblivious to the fact that if a widget hasn't had breakfast in the morning or the widget's parents have marital difficulties, then that widget just won't take shape in the way that the factory owner had planned and no amount of counting will change that. However, in the news media, the business mentality toward education seems to be dominating, and, as such, represents a substantial shift in societal views of the roles of schools. In short, *in loco parentis* seems in danger of being replaced by *in loco "entrepreneurist."*

All of this being said, one might ask why business leaders, despite being immersed in the rhetoric and practices of business, seem to be so short-sighted in relation to education. Two somewhat contradictory but related explanations can be brought to bear. The first is that in the recession-based economics of much of the 1990s, both business and government attempted to create explanations that could account for the malaise of the economy. Unemployment was not blamed on the layoffs or "downsizing" of corporations as a result of aggressive expansion or false expectations for the market (i.e., their own bad decisions) but on the inadequacies of the education system (for a discussion, see, Barlow & Robertson, 1994; Robertson, 1998). With transplanted Americans as CEOs of some large Canadian businesses, it was not a far stretch for them to draw upon their own culture to support standardized tests as a solution, even if numerous studies (see Murphy, 1997; Murphy et al., 1998) raised serious questions about the use of standardized tests in the United States.

Secondly, in keeping with a relatively focussed agenda, large corporations have long cried for taxation cuts from all levels of Canadian government. Considerable fodder for fuelling moves directed towards the disassembling of the publicly funded system and the concomitant tax reduction come from the creation of a loss of public confidence in the school system through the reporting of standardized test rankings, where by definition *only* one nation or province can be first, and where the situational variables[17] confronting each school system are not considered. In Canada, charter schools, though meeting with mixed success, have found their way into the province of Alberta and discussions about them have occurred in other jurisdictions. Some feel that charter schools may be the proverbial 'foot-in-the-door' of the privatization of schooling (Talaga, 1999). Privatization would mean that not only would taxes on businesses be reduced, but the school system would become much more stratified in terms of social class than it already is. This stratification would ghettoize the cash-strapped public system, making it the system for the lower classes, who would become the employment pool for unskilled service and labor workers. The affluent private system would generate the lower numbers of highly skilled knowledge workers that business needs for the next century (Barlow & Robertson, 1994; Robertson, 1998).

Lesson 5. The consequences of standardized testing can have a negative impact on the quality of education students are receiving and the effects can be particularly detrimental to children whose race, culture, or first language is not that of the majority.

Standardized tests could be considered not much more than a waste of school time if they did not carry with them consequences. Indeed, in most contemporary theorizing about the validity of standardized tests, the consequences of testing are significant determinants in validating the test. Validity theorist Samuel Messick (1988) suggests that there are two components to assessing the validity of test use and interpretation: evidential and consequential. Appraisals of a test's construct validity (how well it represents the construct being assessed), relevance, and utility make up the evidential basis of validation of a test; the value implications and social consequences of a test make up the consequential basis for validating a test. These validation appraisals are about the warrantability of the test – whether the test justifiably can be used to support the decisions and impacts that result from it. Claims of "objectivity" and "freedom from bias" are but advertising hoopla in the absence of systematic analysis of the validity of tests.

In the preparation of validity arguments for assessments, Ministries of Education appear to have paid particular attention to the evidentiary portion of their validity argument and have not attended as well, if at all, to the consequential portion of their argument. Such patterns are in keeping with validation practices in the United States (Murphy et al., 1998). So, for example, the EQAO validation process refers to the development of tables of specifications which attempted to match the curriculum to the test, the use of expert panels who assessed the assessment instruments for "clarity and arrangement of assessment directions and questions, appropriate reading level (vocabulary and sentence length and structures), arrangement of assessment items, and the number of opportunities to demonstrate performance at each level." Reference is also made to "extensive field testing" but no statistical information is provided (http://www.eqao.com/eqao/home_page/information/1C5e.html). Such issues all relate to whether the test assesses the construct of interest and whether competing explanations for a student's performance can be eliminated from the test – all elements of evidential validation. In terms of consequential validation, no descriptions are provided in the validity question-and-answer portion of the EQAO website. One can infer some concern about consequential validity in that the test developers definitively state that the results of the Grades 3 and 6 tests are not to be used as part of student grades (appropriately making this test low-stakes) and that rankings should not be focussed upon in interpreting results.

In analysing the validity arguments provided by EQAO, even their efforts at evidential validation have fallen short. For example, Robertson (1998) reports that:

> *Ontario's Grade 3 tests were partly based on the Robert Munsch story* <u>*Moira's Birthday*</u>*, a choice that caused some discussion at the testing-orientation meetings. Teachers who risked complaining that many of their multicultural students had never celebrated birthdays or eaten pizza at a party had their names and schools pointedly recorded by*

Ministry of Education officials. An alternate story turned out to be about horseback riding – that familiar inner-city recreation. (p. 71)

This example suggests that performance on the tests created may not have been due to reading ability but to the background knowledge and culture of students. Indeed, Robertson's (1998) example illustrates the inherent difficulty in creating standardized tests – once knowledge is represented so too is culture, and to attempt to create a culturally neutral test is close to impossible. Nevertheless, as noted earlier, the Ontario government is proceeding with plans to implement a high-stakes literacy exit examination for high school students. The consequences of not doing well in such an examination will be the failure to obtain a high school diploma.

As the culture of testing permeates the fabric of Canadian schools, the consequences of testing begin to spread throughout the whole of the education system. The question must be raised as to their consequential validity – whether the flawed instruments that are standardized tests should have such a significant role in defining what happens in the education of students in classrooms.

For example, one of the most common consequences of standardized testing in the United States is curricular narrowing resulting from teaching-to-the-test (see, Murphy, 1997; Murphy et al., 1998). Curricular narrowing means that anything not covered by the test (e.g., broad based education, problem solving, and inquiry) is replaced with a focus on fostering high performances on test items through practice. The strain of producing high test scores in high-stakes test environments is such that in the United States, there are reports of teachers cheating to ensure their students do well (e.g., Goodnough, 1999). In the province of Ontario, action plans submitted by school boards, that are posted on the EQAO website, indicate that curricular narrowing is already occurring as a direct result of provincial assessments. For example, one plan states that the "format and instruments of the assessment differ from those more typically found in Durham classrooms" and that one of the means to solving this problem is to provide "practice with the format of the assessment, [so that] students will become more adept at working independently and at extending and explaining their answers." The plan goes on to indicate that such practice will extend downwards into first and second grade and that the school district has entered into an agreement to adapt units developed by a consortium of Catholic boards for the same purpose (http://www.eqao.com/eqao/home_page/Durham/03.htm). Peel District school board also discusses the development of similar practice tasks (http://www.eqao.com/eqao/home_page/Peel/03.htm). The net effect of such curricular changes is that teachers and students are spending valuable curricular time rehearsing for tests rather than engaging directly with the curriculum. Furthermore, this effect is also being downloaded into first and second grade classrooms not directly involved in the assessment, thereby magnifying this effect even more.

The solution for bringing some sanity back into educational assessment in Canada lies with politicians. Unfortunately, as the next lesson illustrates, politicians represent both the weakest and the strongest link in the standardized assessment process because their own self-interests can get in the way of social good.

Lesson 6. The inappropriate implementation and interpretation of standardized testing has allowed politicians to misguide the public, a consequence of which is the destabilization of the education system.

With the increasing global conservatism of the 1990s and the economic recession that marked the middle of that period, many world governments felt pressure from large money lenders and fiscal rating agencies to reduce their deficits. Indeed, deficit reduction and eliminating the national debt became the mantra of most Western leaders, who realized that they could lose control of the economics of governing and, in doing so, would lose control of other elements such as social policy. Politicians in Canada looked inward, isolating many sectors of the public service including education and health care.

At about the same time that Canadian governments entered this period of fiscal conservativism, they began to look for relatively cheap and seemingly defensible ways to demonstrate their accountability to a public weary of the rhetoric of downsizing. In at least one province, film footage was leaked of the Minister of Education talking of creating a crisis in education in order to begin a "reform" process (Brennan, 1995; Krueger, 1995; Lewington, 1995; Ryan, 1995). As in the United States, standardized testing provided Canadian politicians with a cheap way to *appear* to be doing something about education. For instance, even though the administration of a single test (not including teacher time administering the test or costs of incidental school supplies) might be several million dollars (http://www.cmec.ca/saip/writ94en.html), such figures are small in comparison to what direct improvements would cost (e.g., lowering the number of students in any one class, providing stronger supplemental instruction for students with special needs or whose first language is not English, or providing a greater variety of literature to school libraries). As provinces such as Alberta and Ontario cut back on the number of teachers or the amount of funding to schools and school districts (Grossman, 1998; Hudson, 1998; Landsberg, 1999; Zurowski, 1987), they complemented the cutbacks with the standardized testing. The strategy was simple and effective – criticism could be deflected away from cuts to programs and targeted toward test results that were themselves a kind of documentary of the effects of the curricular, staffing, and resource changes confronting many schools. The implementation of standardized testing allowed politicians to point to a specific action they had implemented that echoed the conservative wish for simpler times when learning could be "measured," children were silent, and the government could be seen as doing good.

Politicians have not been reluctant to use press releases to serve their own agenda. So, for example, when most students perform at an acceptable level, this is deemed to be inadequate performance rather than be taken for what it seems to suggest – that most students seem to be doing okay or even pretty well (Robertson, 1998). At other times, when situations warrant, politicians made more of test results than is warranted – claiming their province is number one – when it is likely that their own Ministry officials briefed them as to the inherent problems in the statistics associated with standardized tests (e.g., Dawson, 1998a).

However, according to Robertson (1998), the reporting of standardized test results is not open merely to the typical criticisms of making unwarranted inferences. She reports on one incident where a Minister of Education eagerly announced his province ranked first in a test only to be taken aside by a Deputy Minister and reminded that the data had been massaged so that another province came first. In essence, if Robertson's (1998) unnamed source accurately described the situation, absolutely no confidence can be placed in test results that have been so manipulated. Perhaps the most that could be said of such results is that they are credible assessments of political game playing.

Folded in with the political use of standardized test results is the manner in which politicians and the press position educators who have not remained silent with the advent of standardized testing.

When teachers criticize tests, teachers are positioned as self-interested rather than as professionals interested in the welfare of the students they teach. An example that characterizes the tone of the critique is best represented in the following headline: "What are they afraid of? BC teachers reject testing, for their students and for themselves" (*British Columbia Report*, 1999, p. 46). So, standardized testing appears to be used to police teachers and, in doing so, it contributes to the deprofessionalization of teaching. This deprofessionalization permeates numerous documents produced by assessment offices that are responsible to governments. Witness, for example, the following information taken from the EQAO website in Ontario:

> *What needs do EQAO's assessments serve? ...*
>
> *Teachers and principals need informed and timely feedback on how their students are performing and on ways to improve teaching and learning in the classroom.*
>
> *Parents need clarification of the content taught and standards expected in Ontario schools. In addition to specific information about their children's performance and progress.*
>
> *Taxpayers need to know that students' knowledge and skills are assessed provincially, nationally and internationally. In addition, they need to know about the state of Ontario's schools through data on student achievement, school climate, partnerships with parents and other factors. (http://www.eqao.com/home_page/information/1C2e.html)*

This document suggests that teachers do not know how students in their own classes are doing. Of course, if they do not know this, then they obviously cannot communicate it to parents. Why parents and teachers are differentiated from taxpayers is an ideological manoeuvre designed to separate these constituencies. Why they need to know *that* assessment occurs, rather than know the outcome of it, seems to unwittingly reveal that the point is not the assessment but the appearance of surveillance, of being in charge, that counts. One wonders whether the data on "school climate, partnerships with parents and other factors" is even collected since it receives so little attention from anyone, but such incidentals do not take away from the general implication of inadequacy accorded teachers in this set of statements. To add to the general pummelling of teachers and the support for standardized tests, several jurisdictions are in the process of developing standardized tests for teachers (Schofield, 1999; What are they..., 1999) even though such tests have been found to be quite limited in their validity when research has been conducted on them (Dybdahl, Shaw & Edwards, 1997).

Besides the obvious motive of sleight-of-hand self-preservation on the part of politicians, one factor behind such tactics may be the dismantling of the publicly funded school system in favor of charter schools (Talaga, 1999). Such moves are again echoes of United States educational policies. But regardless of the motivations, the consequences have been the demoralization of the teaching force, the abandonment of teaching as a profession by many, and the consequent likelihood that Canada will enter the millennium with more inexperienced teachers to shepherd its educational "clients" forward than it has in some time (Brown, 2000; Goar, 2000a; Goar, 2000b; Mallan, 2000).

Coda: Resistance May Not Be Futile

The lessons chronicled above provide a somewhat bleak picture of Canadian education at the outset of the millennium. Yet, some signs of hope have appeared from the culture that *is* all about ranking and testing – the United States – and from within Canada itself. At least some of the media and the public at large appear to have either heeded the critiques of standardized testing or have done their own analysis to figure out that standardized tests just might not be the answer to enhancing the quality of education. Recently, *Newsweek* (McGinn, 1999a; 1999b) and *U.S. News and World Report* (Lord, 2000; Wildavsky, 1999) each presented stories that seriously questioned the role and consequences of standardized testing. In addition, resistance to standardized testing is appearing in pockets throughout the United States, either through the actions of individuals or of groups (see, Ohanian, in press). In Canada, the *Toronto Star* (Chamberlain, 1999), the *Globe and Mail* (Galt, 1992), and the *Calgary Herald* (Dawson, 1998b) filed similar stories in which the parents or others were raising concerns.

Whether such discussion is sufficient to topple the powerful semiotic hold standardized testing has over the public imagination is doubtful, but at least such critical debate and resistance offer occasions to introduce alternative assessment strategies that could demonstrate accountability while avoiding some of the documented drawbacks of standardized tests.

Endnotes

[1] DES cited in Murphy & Torrance, 1988, p. 105.

2 In this article, the terms standardized measures or standardized assessment will be used to refer to assessment measures administered to groups of children and will not be used to refer to assessment measures administered to individuals on a one-to-one basis in a clinical form. An example of the latter assessment measures would be the Weschler series of intelligence tests which are administered by trained personnel to individual children on a one-to-one basis in a setting removed from the classroom.

3 See Murphy, Shannon, Johnston, and Hansen (1998) for examples from the technical manuals for published standardized reading tests in wide use in the United States. Typically, basic textbooks on assessment and the introductory portion of technical manuals for a specific type of standardized assessment caution users with a statement something like the following: "When selecting a test for a specific purpose, the test user has a clear responsibility to ascertain that the test has validation evidence appropriate to the intended use in the local situation"(Crocker & Algina, 1986, p. 218). Such advice is a complicated way of saying "Don't make more of this test than is warranted."

4 In the early days of the proposal, there was dissension among the ranks of the Ministers of Education as to whether all provinces would participate. For example, then Minister of Education Marion Boyd indicated that the province of Ontario would be opting out of the assessment (Boyd, 1991; Lewington, 1991). This decision stirred some debate (e.g., Nikiforuk, 1991; Valpy, 1991) but eventually the province relented (Exam uniformity, 1991).

5 For information about the Canadian Standards Association, see http://www.csa.ca/english/home/index.htm.

6 The same is true for any category system. Categories may enable us to aggregate like-items but the aggregation of a group of items under that label is not a guarantee of identicality but of similarity. One example might be color labels. Even though there is a primary color red, in our everyday life we do not cease categorizing the color on a fabric red because it does not match the primary color. We may even invoke a prototypical idea of redness in our minds but will name the color red even though it has bluish or yellowish elements in it.

7 The group who initially took the test is often selected using specific criteria (e.g., stratified sampling in which samples are taken from representative regions or population groups where the test developers imagine the test will be used). Their scores are ranked in order from highest to lowest and then fitted to a normal distribution.

8 Multiple-choice assessments are recognized by cognitive psychologists and some who work in the educational measurement field as the least cognitively complex form of testing there is. For example, Bennett (1993) and Snow (1993) each present taxonomies of assessment that position multiple-choice assessment towards the bottom of their scales.

9 The more samples you have of a behavior, the better your claims that your sample reliably represents the characteristic behavior of a person. So, for instance, especially in multiple-choice tests, if you use one question to sam-

ple children's knowledge of plot devices in a story, the child has a one in four (if there are four options to choose from) chance of guessing the answer to item (question). So, getting the item correct may not reveal anything about the child's knowledge. If there are two items on the same skill, then it seems obvious that the chances of getting a correct answer by guessing have become more challenging, and, conversely, if the answer is correct, you can have more confidence that the correctness came as a result of knowledge. If there are four, the results are even more reliable. Haladyna (1994) suggests that "a 50-item test can produce highly reliable scores" (p. 27) but he does not provide recommendations as to how many items are needed to assure reliability of assessment in each sub-skill area.

10 The code was not created by critics of testing, but by those who use testing in their daily work. The Joint Committee creating this code was initiated by the American Educational Research Association, the American Psychological Association, and the National Council on Measurement in Education. In addition to these three groups, the American Association for Counseling and Development/Association for Measurement and Evaluation in Counseling and Development, and the American Speech-Language-Hearing Association are also sponsors of this document.

11 The production of such headlines is not only widespread but relatively constant across the past several years. This sampling of headlines is taken from a listing of over 140 headlines indexed in the CBCA database from April 1994 to February 2000 that focus exclusively on announcing the results of standardized tests. News services indexed that reported these headlines include: the *Calgary Herald*, *Canadian Press Newswire*, the *Globe and Mail*, the *Montreal Gazette*, the *National Post*, the *Toronto Star*, *Western Report*, and the *Vancouver Sun*.

12 An analysis of the misinformation on education circulating in the press can be found in Barlow and Robertson (1994) and Robertson (1998) for the Canadian context, and Berliner and Biddle (1995) for the United States.

13 I deliberately use the phrase "best monetary interests," since the world of the 21st century had many people holding mutual funds, stocks, and bonds that reap the benefits of the deals made by multinational corporations. The scale of globalization (its largeness and seeming unreachability for the average individual) seems to allow investors to blithely and paradoxically complain about the erosion of social programs and the loss of cultural identity, while RRSP accounts full of stocks, bonds, and mutual funds grow fatter each day.

14 This latter point suggests that business is interested in seeing an end to a liberal arts education and views schools as training grounds for their businesses. Of course, if workplace training resided in these imagined schools many workers would find themselves in an employment ghetto, but businesses would find the workers they needed for low-skilled jobs.

15 See Poovey (1998) for a critical history of bookkeeping. Such a history raises some of the same kinds of questions I have raised about testing in relation to business and commerce.

[16] In the United States, in particular, some have argued that standardized testing and the rhetoric of standards would be fine if it were accompanied by delivery standards – that is by standards that assured a minimal level of infrastructure and support to allow for optimal delivery of instruction (Porter, 1995). Of course, such standards, to be effective, would have to be administered relatively – for instance, old rural or inner city schools in need of refurbishing might need more support than new suburban schools, poor neighborhoods might need more than more affluent neighborhoods. Because of the nuanced decision-making that is required in such contexts and because of the superficial appearance of inequities in funding, such models are difficult to implement since they demand an understanding of the social fabric as a whole and not just one's own desires.

[17] Individual schools can vary in terms of their ability to cope with and respond to the myriad demands placed on them. So, for instance, in one school children may come to school well fed, may have sufficient resources to pay for materials for extracurricular activities and field trips that enrich learning, may have computers in the home that complement school activities, and may have adults in the home who can provide support (from themselves or others) when students encounter difficulty. In other instances, children may need breakfast support programs, may be lacking in those extra funds for enrichment and home activities, and may find that because of employment demands, their parents cannot provide the kinds of support the school expects. In the latter case, schools often attempt to support their students as best they can. In order for children in each of these schools to attain comparable education (and comparable outcomes on assessments), they need to have comparable resources. To report assessment results without considering the very different situational demands schools face is like reporting stock market results in one economy that has experienced a drought and in another that has had a good growing season while ignoring the facts of the drought or the good growing season.

References

Anastasi, A. (1982). *Psychological testing* (5th ed.). New York: Macmillan.

Anastasi, A. & Urbina, S. (1997). *Psychological testing* (7th ed.). Upper Saddle River, NJ: Prentice Hall.

Barlow, M. & Robertson, H. (1994). *Class warfare: The assault on Canada's schools.* Toronto: Key Porter.

Bennett, R. E. (1993). On the meanings of constructed response. In R. E. Bennett & W. C. Ward (Eds.), *Construction versus choice in cognitive measurement: Issues in constructed response, performance testing, and portfolio assessment* (pp. 1-27). Hillsdale, NJ: Lawrence Erlbaum.

Berliner, D. C. & Biddle, B. J. (1995). *The manufactured crisis: Myths, fraud, and the attack on America's public schools.* New York: Addison-Wesley.

Brennan, R. (1995, September 13). Minister plotted 'to invent a crisis': Snobelen video spurs angry calls for him to resign. *Toronto Star*, A3.

Brown, L. (2000, May 14). Why would anyone want to be a school principal? *Toronto Star*. On line archives: http://www.thestar.com/back_issues/ED20000514/news/20000514NEW08_CI-PRINCIP.html

Brown, R. G. (1991). *Schools of thought: How the politics of literacy shape thinking in the classroom*. San Francisco: Jossey-Bass.

Boyd, M. (1991, May 18). Standard test results useless. *Toronto Star*, D3.

Chamberlain, A. (1998, December 2). Toronto matches province in three Rs. *Toronto Star*, B5.

Chamberlain, A. (1999, May 10). Grades 3, 6 begin Ontario-wide tests: Some parents boycotting them. *Toronto Star*, A2.

Code of Fair Testing Practices in Education. (1988). Washington, D.C.: Joint Committee on Testing Practices, American Psychological Association.

Crocker, L. & Algina, J. (1986). *Introduction to classical and modern test theory*. New York: Holt, Rinehart, and Winston.

Dawson, C. (1996, May 16). Catholic students rate tops in the city. *Calgary Herald*, A1 & A2.

Dawson, C. (1998a, February 25). Alberta beats U.S. in world wide test. *Calgary Herald*, B4.

Dawson, C. (1998b, April 17). Parents eye boycott of exams. *Calgary Herald*, B1 & B2.

Dempster, L. (1996, May 19). ATA charge parents switch schools. *Calgary Herald*, A1.

Dennis, W. (1993a). Class action: What if schools were run like mini-corporations, with the principal as CEO and the parents and teachers as a board of directors? *Toronto Life*, 27 (7), 33-35.

Dennis, W. (1993b). Learning the hard way: Why parents who once believed in the public school system are mortgaging their homes to buy their kids a future. *Toronto Life*, 27 (13), 37-39.

Drohan, M. (2000, February 15). Why Axworthy stopped talking tough: Corporate lobbying and some hard realities caused him to soften his tone. *Globe and Mail*, A1 & A9.

Dybdahl, C. S., Shaw, D. G. & Edwards, D. (1997). Teacher testing: Reason or rhetoric. *Journal of Research and Development in Education, 30* (4), 248-254.

Exam uniformity OK'd. (1991, December 10). *The Calgary Herald*, B10.

Galt, V. (1998, May 22). Grade 3 test prompts parental boycott: Five-day province-wide exam unfair to children who don't speak English at home, families say. *Globe and Mail*, A1 & A10.

Galt, V. (1992, May 8). Employers eager to advise students: Council wants schools to teach skills. *Globe and Mail*, A5.

Gessell, P. (1998, January 3). Corporate influence: How it's burgeoning in Canadian culture. *Vancouver Sun*, D1 & D4.

Giles, H. (1996, September 7). Boos and hisses for our classrooms. *Globe and Mail*, D2.

Goar, C. (2000a, March 25). Is this what voters wanted? *Toronto Star*. On line archives: http://www.thestar.com/back_issues/ED20000325/opinion/20000325NAR07_OP-GOAR25.html

Goar, C. (2000b, June 24). Ontario's quiet brain drain. *Toronto Star*. On line archives: http://www.thestar.com/back_issues/ED20000624/opinion/20000624NAR07_OP-GOAR24.html

Goodnough, A. (1999, December 9). New York city teachers nabbed in school-test cheating scandal: Results determine ranking. *National Post*, B1 & B2.

Grossman, D. (1998, May 22). Game over for sports? Students, teachers fume as funding cuts jeopardize programs. *Toronto Star*, B8.

Hacking, I. (1990). *The taming of chance*. Cambridge: Cambridge University Press.

Haladyna, T. M. (1994). *Developing and validating multiple-choice test items*. Hillsdale, NJ: Erlbaum.

Hamill, P. (1998). *News is a verb: Journalism at the end of the twentieth century*. New York: Ballantine.

Hanson, F. A. (1993). *Testing testing: Social consequences of the examined life*. Berkeley: University of California Press.

Hudson, K. (1998, May 9). Deaf students protest funding cuts. *Toronto Star*, A10.

Kaplan, George R. (1992). *Images of education: The mass media's version of America's schools*. Arlington, VA: National School Public Relations Association.

Krueger, L. (1995, September 15). What crisis? John Snobelen explains. *Globe and Mail*, A16.

Landsberg, M. (1999, May 9). Tories taking students down a rough road. *Toronto Star*, A2.

Lewington, J. (1991, September 28). Changes expected in national testing plan: Proposal must be altered to meet objections by Ontario, educators told. *The Globe and Mail*, A6.

Lewington, J. (1992, April 30). Shake up schools, council urges: Performance of primary, secondary and technical schools unsatisfactory, report says. *Globe and Mail*, A1 & A2.

Lewington, J. (1993a, February 8). Costs blamed for delay in national testing. *The Globe and Mail*, A5.

Lewington, J. (1993b, February 20). Ways sought to weight schools: Ontario wants to make education system accountable. *The Globe and Mail*, A5.

Lewington, J. (1995, September 14). Snobelen apologizes for inventing crisis: Harris raps Education Minister's knuckles. *Globe and Mail*, A8.

Lord, M. (2000, April 3). High-stakes testing: It's backlash time. Students, parents, schools just say no to tests. *U.S. News and World Report*, 54.

Mallan, C. (2000, June 10). National ads discourage teachers from Ontario: Provinces new after-school rules may fuel shortage. *Toronto Star*. On-line archives: http://www.thestar.com/back_issues/ED20000610/news/20000610NEW20_NA-TEACHX10.html

McCann, W. (1999, October 28). Ontario schools get failing grades despite changes. *Halifax Chronicle Herald*, A15.

McGinn, D. (1999, September 6). The big score: High-stakes tests are rapidly becoming a rite of passage in districts around the country. But do they really improve learning? *Newsweek*, 46-51.

McGinn, D. (1999, September 6). 'Tests are an easy way out': Two educators urge parents to look beyond numbers. *Newsweek*, 50-51.

Messick, S. (1988). The once and future issues of validity: Assessing the meaning and consequences of measurement. In H. Wainer & H. I. Braun (Eds.), *Test validity* (pp. 33-45). Hillsdale, NJ: Lawrence Erlbaum.

Murphy, R. & Torrance, H. (1988). *The changing face of educational assessment*. Philadelphia: Open University Press.

Murphy, S. (1994). No one ever grew taller by being measured: Six educational measurement lessons for Canadians. In L. Erwin and D. MacLennan (Eds.), *Sociology of Education in Canada* (pp. 238-252). Toronto: Copp Clark.

Murphy, S. (1997). Literacy assessment and the politics of identities. *Reading and Writing Quarterly, 13*, 261-278.

Murphy, S., with Shannon, P., Johnston, P. & Hansen, J. (1998). *Fragile evidence: A critique of reading assessment*. Mahwah, NJ: Lawrence Erlbaum.

Nikiforuk, A. (1991, September 20). Andrew Nikiforuk reports on a mouse that has education's elephants on the rampage – limited national testing. *The Globe and Mail*, A16.

Nikiforuk, A. (1992, May 1). Not testing children because they might fail is patronizing garbage, writes Andrew Nikiforuk. *The Globe and Mail*, A24.

Nikiforuk, A. (1997). Lessons in learning: Rigorous standards, national goals and a clear curriculum are the keys to any first-rate school system. *Canadian Business, 70* (16), 22 & 24.

Ohanian, S. (in press). You say stakeholder; I say robber baron. *Language Arts*.

Poovey, M. (1998). *A history of the modern fact: Problems of knowledge in the sciences of wealth and society*. Chicago: University of Chicago Press.

Porter, A. (1995). The uses and misuses of opportunity-to-learn standards. *Educational Researcher, 24* (1), 21-27.

Robertson, H. (1998). *No more teachers, no more books: The commercialization of Canada's schools*. Toronto: McClelland Stewart.

Robertson, H. (1996). Whose business is education? *Canadian Dimension, 30* (6), 31-33.

Ryan, P. (1995). The day Mr. Snobelen let the cat out of the bag: When Ontario's Education Minister begged pardon last month for his talk of 'inventing a crisis,' he seemed to be apologizing to other crisis-makers for revealing one of the tricks of the trade. *Globe and Mail*, A19.

Schofield, J. (1999, October 11). Putting teachers to the test: In a bid to make education more accountable, testing has moved to the head of the class. *Maclean's* (Toronto Edition), 112 (41), 64.

School testing. (1992, September 11). *The Globe and Mail*, B4.

Snow, R. E. (1993). Construct validity and constructed-response sets. In R. E. Bennett & W. C. Ward (Eds.), *Construction versus choice in cognitive measurement: Issues in constructed response, performance testing, and portfolio assessment* (pp. 45-60). Hillsdale, NJ: Lawrence Erlbaum.

Talaga, T. (1999, June 19). C is for choice: Alberta was the first province to introduce parent-run charter schools. Many educators are convinced Ontario will be next, and they aren't happy about it. *Toronto Star*, J1 & J3.

Thorsell, W. (1991, December 27). The ABC's of education testing [Editorial]. *The Globe and Mail*, A12.

Thorsell, W. (1992, November 7). How national testing would work [Editorial]. *The Globe and Mail*, D6.

Wildavsky, B. (1999, September 27). Achievement testing gets its day in court: A key Texas case goes to trial as minority groups seek to stop a school reform trend. *U. S. News and World Report*, 30 & 32.

What are they afraid of? BC teachers reject testing, for their students and for themselves. (1999, May 17). *British Columbia Report, 10* (4), 46.

World education league: Who's on top? (1997, March 29/April 4). Some countries seem to educate their children much better than others. *Economist, 342*, 21-23.

Valpy, M. (1991, September 25). Minister's stance on testing reasonable. *The Globe and Mail*, A12.

Zurowski, M. (1987, February 20). Education funding cuts prompt teachers' anger. *Calgary Herald*, B2.

Chapter 7
Education, Business, and the 'Knowledge Economy'

Alison Taylor

Introduction

[I]n the critical years from the mid 1960s to the late 1970s, business leaders were increasingly distant from schools....During the past six to eight years, [they] have been gradually re-establishing connections with public education. It seems clear that changes in the labour supply have been the most significant spur to this renewed interest...Business leaders have come to understand that the emerging labour market supply problem is essentially an educational problem. (Canadian Chamber of Commerce, 1990, pp. 9-10)

There is much evidence of this increased interest in formal education by national and provincial level corporate-sponsored groups in the 1980s and 90s. A survey of member companies by the Business Council on National Issues (BCNI, 1997, pp. 32-33) found that 40% of respondents increased their support to education between 1990 and 1995 because of its perceived role in "building a creative and competitive workforce for the future." Documents discussing K-12 education have been produced by the Conference Board of Canada (e.g., Bloom, 1991; Bloom & Kitagawa, 1999), Business Council on National Issues (Finlayson, 1985), the Corporate Higher-Education Forum (Henchey, 1990), the Canadian Chamber of Commerce (CCC, 1990), and the Fraser Institute. In my home province of Alberta, reports have been produced by the Alberta Chamber of Resources (e.g., ACR, 1990), and the Alberta Chamber of Commerce (ACC, 1995). Most of these documents construct education as a means for developing a highly skilled workforce and thus securing national economic prosperity. To ensure this, they recommend tightening relationships between schools and the workplace.

This chapter explores the implications of increasing corporate involvement in schools. While businesses are also interested in educational organizations as a market for products and services and a site for producing free market supporters, I focus on their interest in schools' role in producing a labor force that is functional for the changing workplace (Carnoy & Levin, 1985). Therefore, while privatization and marketization are part of the current picture in education, they are not the central focus of this discussion. Instead, the changing relationship between the State and other "stakeholders"[1] in relation to labor market changes is key. After documenting corporate interest in schooling and the receptivity of governments to the recommendations of business-sponsored groups, I look at why this alignment has developed and consider the implications for democratic processes.

Cataloguing Corporate Involvement

The national group that has done the most work in the area of K-12 education to date is the Conference Board of Canada (CB). The CB is a corporate-sponsored research institution (with a sister organization in the U.S.) that aims to enhance the performance of Canadian organizations within the global economy. It formed a National Business and Education Centre in 1990 to address the issue of preparing Canada's youth to meet future workplace needs. Around the same time, the CB established a National Council on Education (NCE) comprised of senior executives and educators, and a Corporate Council on Education (CCE) comprised only of corporate executives of member companies. The latter group oversaw the development of the employability skills profile (ESP) in 1992, a document that has been widely distributed and cited since its release. The ESP is a one-page document that outlines the academic, personal management and teamwork skills, attitudes, and behaviors that employers require of employees. They are described as "the skills every person requires to ensure personal success, to improve corporate productivity and profit and, by extension, to further national competitiveness" (Bloom & Kitigawa, 1999, p. 16). A recent CB report talks about the impact of the ESP as follows:

> Millions of copies later, the ESP continues to guide change within business, education, and government institutions....Employers, employees, educators and students know that the development of employability skills is essential to Canada's continued competitiveness and growth in highly competitive global markets. (Bloom & Kitigawa, Executive Summary)

The CB's perception of the impact of the ESP is not greatly exaggerated if we look at Alberta as an example. Alberta Education's 1996 "Framework for Enhancing Business Involvement in Education" (FEBI) makes several references to the need for students to develop "employability skills" as defined by the CB. Not only were teachers and school boards encouraged to require students to develop employability skills portfolios to document their skill development, but the province agreed to review its provincial learning expectations to determine the "degree to which curriculum address-es employability skills" (Alberta Education, 1996). More recently, a representative of Alberta Learning – the "super department" that arose from the amalgamation of Alberta Education and Advanced Career Development in 1999 – suggested that the department was developing a set of "essential competencies" for students as a way of concretizing the CB's employability skills (Interview, March 16, 2000). In addition, school boards and local CB members have taken up the challenge of operationalizing employability skills. As a per-sonal example, the assistant principal began the parent orientation at my daughter's elementary school in Calgary in 1996 by talking about the CB's ESP and its relevance for students and teachers. In 1994, a CB member in Calgary worked with six school boards in the area to develop an employability skills portfolio pilot project (Taylor, 1998). Bloom (1994) presents 14 case studies from across Canada that highlight educational partnerships, projects, and programs aimed at enhancing students' employability skills.

While the dissemination of the ESP has been one of the CB's "success stories," the group has also worked to promote other ele-ments of its vision for education. In 1990, it began to hold annual business-education conferences in different provinces, involving government, business, and education delegates. These conferences promoted the need for business, government, and educators to work together to better prepare students for the 21st century. They also provided a forum for disseminating CB documents such as the ESP and a national Vision for Education. Conferences and documents promoted partnerships with business, choice,[2] national standards, increased focus on outcomes and accountability, decentralized deci-sion-making, more attention to problems of drop-outs and illiteracy, increased technology and innovation in schools, and greater atten-tion to math and science (Taylor, 2001).

Several of these themes are repeated and/or amplified in the reports of other business groups. For example, although CB events provided a forum for choice proponents, the topic has not been a primary focus for most members. However, the free market Fraser Institute[3] has promoted school choice for several years. The group sponsored a 1988 report which recommended that vouchers (for public or public and private schools) be used to grant parents greater flexibility in choosing schools, and that performance-based reward structures be implemented in education (Easton, 1988, p. 108). The failings of the public education system and the solutions of charter schools, vouchers, tax credits, and school assessments are reiterated in a 1999 report called "The Case for School Choice."[4] The Fraser Institute has focused on making schools more efficient and effective by running them more like businesses.

While other business groups may share this view, they have focused more on the role of schools in producing a world-class workforce. For example, the Canadian Chamber of Commerce promotes school-business partnerships as a way of giving employers more control over the preparation of workers (CCC, 1990). Further, the idea that the "future belongs to the knowledge worker," and that education must "adopt new modes of operation and learning that will keep pace with the change in society" was central to a 1995 report on school-to-work transition by the Alberta Chamber of Commerce (ACC, p. 3). This document refers to the important work done by the CB on employability skills, and to the work of the ACR on school-business partnerships. It also reflects the interests of members and the provincial labor market in its suggestion that "society does not need and cannot accommodate everyone with a university education" (p. 5). The greatest demand was projected to be for "highly skilled technicians and specialized trade workers" (p. 5). Therefore, educators were encouraged to expand work education programs such as apprenticeships, cooperative education, and workplace experience.

The ACR has similarly raised concerns about projected labor shortages in the skilled trades since the early 1990s. A 1990 report by the ACR and the Construction Owners Association of Alberta emphasized inadequate labor supply by region in relation to the demand generated by several resource projects. Key issues arising from the report were the shortage of workers, particularly in the trades, inadequacies in secondary and post-secondary education and training, and inadequate communication among stakeholders (employers, educators, and government) (1990, p. 67). Authors envisioned new roles and relationships among stakeholders. The report recommended that industry "take the lead in establishing a special partnership arrangement at the provincial level to address employment issues" (p. 71). Since this report, the ACR has played a key role in the educational policy community. In 1991, it co-sponsored a report with Alberta Education that highlighted problems with Alberta schools in comparison with those in Japan, Germany, and Hungary. Again, the ACR was motivated by concerns about "the low level of interest in science and technology and skilled trade careers among Alberta youth" (ACR and Alberta Education, 1991, p. i). It took the lead in addressing this perceived problem through *Careers, the Next Generation,* a pilot project begun in 1994 to address school-to-work transition for non-college bound youth and to promote trades careers (ACR, 1995). In 1997, the establishment of the CNG Foundation, with majority funding from the province, institutionalized this industry-driven provincial partnership. The formation of such a foundation had been recommended in the FEBI report (Alberta Education, 1996). These examples suggest that employers, particularly large resource sector employers, have been quite influential in educational policy in the province since the early 1990s.

There are some differences among business groups that are related to the different types of companies that they represent. For example, the CB represents multinational corporations across Canada for the most part, as does the BCNI. Within the Alberta context, the ACC represents companies of varying sizes, and the ACR reflects the specific interests of resource-sector companies. At the same time, there are overlaps in memberships, with chief executives from the CB also playing active roles in the ACR and ACC, for example. Perhaps for this reason, there are more similarities than differences between the CB and ACR agendas for education. Both groups assume that students are not adequately prepared for work in the "knowledge economy." Both promote the need for closer ties between schools and the workplace, and recommend that employers take the lead in articulating their labor force needs. Both promote the need for developing a common vision that business, government and educators can work toward. Solutions include greater involvement of business in education at provincial, school board, and school levels in terms of policy-making and practice. While ACR concerns focus on the projected shortages of skilled trades workers and the CB tends to emphasize the preparation of knowledge workers more generally, several business leaders argue that skilled trade workers *are* knowledge workers in the new economy. Therefore, while business is not homogeneous, a surprising degree of corporate consensus has developed in the 1980s and 90s around education.

Allies in Education Policy

There has also been considerable alignment between the visions for education promoted by corporate groups like the CB and governments since the early 1990s (Taylor, 2001). For example, the visions for education expressed in the federal government's report

"Learning Well...Living Well" (LWLW, Government of Canada, 1991) and in the Economic Council report "A Lot to Learn" (1992) are quite similar to those proposed by business groups. LWLW begins by suggesting that "Canada's learning performance is simply not good enough" and is causing Canada to lose ground to industrial competitors (S3, S2). It envisions a high skill information economy where the achievement of economic goals brings social benefits. In keeping with the views of groups like the BCNI, LWLW also emphasizes that changes in education require stakeholders to work together to bring about changes in public awareness and attitudes rather than increased investment.

Specific recommendations from a follow-up report include developing performance indicators for system and student achievement; strengthening linkages between "schools, other learning institutions, and the world of work" (Government of Canada, 1993, p. 40); promoting math, science, and technology studies; and encouraging the adoption of computer technology in schools. The Economic Council report also recommended increased attention to standards and accountability in education. Specific recommendations aimed at strengthening linkages between school and work included overhauling the apprenticeship system, institutionalizing school-business and wider community partnerships, and supporting co-operative education programs.

Within Alberta, government reports have also echoed the concerns of corporate representatives about education. The partnership between the ACR and Alberta Education that led to the "International Comparisons" report (1991) is one of several examples of the department's partnerships with industry. It is also tied to the broader government vision expressed through the Toward 2000 Together consultations in the early 1990s. In resulting reports, the vision of the private sector as the engine of growth and the role of government in developing an infrastructure that is conducive to business are prominent themes (Advisory Committee, 1993). Alberta Education was engaged in a parallel visioning process at this time and its 1991 "Vision for the Nineties" report repeats the slogan of *education for economic prosperity.* Priority areas in K-12 schooling included improving standards and results, emphasizing basic skills, improving programs and opportunities in science, encouraging school-work linkages, and improving fiscal equity across boards (Alberta Education, 1991). The restructuring introduced in Alberta Education's "three-year business plan for education" in 1994 addressed these areas. The province's standardized testing program was expanded in earlier grades, funding was centralized, the K-12 budget was cut by 12.4 percent, school councils were mandated, Charter schools were introduced and plans to improve business involvement and technology integration were made. Roles and responsibilities were redefined as follows:

> *The province will define acceptable and excellent standards of student achievement. Business will be a key player in defining the specific learning requirements of industry. Schools, school jurisdictions and the province will audit and report on the full range of student learning. (Alberta Education, 1994, p. 6)*

Five implementation teams were established to implement different aspects of the business plan. For example, the "Framework for Enhancing Business Involvement in Education" (FEBI) (Alberta Education, 1996) reflects the work of one of these teams. This report recommended that:

- A provincial Career Education Foundation be established to promote and co-ordinate business-education partnerships and workplace learning opportunities. Government, business, and labor could work through this foundation to enhance the image of trade, service, and technical careers.

- Schools should encourage all senior high school students to participate in workplace learning. Students should also be given information about alternative career paths such as apprenticeships in high school. Junior and senior high schools were encouraged to have students develop annual career plans and employability skills portfolios.

- A private/public sector committee should review K-12 curricula to ensure that all students acquire a general understanding of how business operates and the role of business in society.

- Business people should become more involved in policy making at all levels. Their role in communicating to educators their short and long-term labor needs and the associated employability skills was seen as especially valuable.

As I discuss later, these recommendations arguably reflect the interests of business members who were involved in the FEBI process.

The influence of large multinational corporations on public policy has increased dramatically since the mid-1970s, according to Workman (1996, p. 22). The Fraser and C.D. Howe Institutes and the

BCNI have pushed for public sector constraint. Furthermore, public sector restructuring along the lines of Osborne and Gaebler (1993) has been popular with business representatives who believe that "the era of big governments" is past (BCNI, 1997). In education also, efforts to tighten the links between school and work reflect, for the most part, the interests of business leaders. Given this alignment, we might ask two questions: why has this agenda met with so little resistance from education "stakeholders," and what are the implications for democratic processes?

Situating Corporate Involvement

There are several reasons why the discourse of "education for economic prosperity" has met with little resistance from educators. First, the futurist tone of *knowledge economy discourse* makes it difficult to challenge, and the promise of jobs in high performing, democratic workplaces is attractive to all stakeholders. Second, given high youth unemployment rates and economic uncertainty, the discourse of progressive vocationalism (cf. Ball, 1990) is seductive for parents, students, and teachers who are concerned about the life chances of non-college bound youth. Finally, the pragmatic realities of decreased educational funding make the idea of increased external support through partnerships attractive to educators. The result is a belief that "the more educators understand and support the efforts of [progressive] businesses, the better off education will be" (Boutwell, 1997, p. 7). Each of these reasons is discussed further below.

The business-sponsored reports on K-12 education discussed earlier collectively promote the vision of a knowledge economy with the promise of more fulfilling jobs for workers in high performance organizations. This vision provides hope for middle class professional parents who have become increasingly concerned about their children's job prospects in an uncertain economy (cf. Ehrenreich, 1989). The idea of preparing students for more democratic workplaces is also likely to enlist some progressive educators. For example, Boutwell (1997) argues that the requirements of the knowledge economy lead to a confluence between two historically opposing groups. He calls the first group "utilitarians," who have historically attempted to direct education toward specific, pragmatic ends, and the second, "educationalists," progressive educators who are more concerned with the development and growth of individual children without reference to society's needs. The idea that the objectives of educators and business people have been converging in recent years is also expressed in an OECD report, which states:

[I]ncreasingly, the most important skills needed at work, and those that firms want to encourage schools to teach, are more general. Thinking flexibly, communicating well, working well in teams, using initiative – these and other "generic" skills in the workforce are becoming crucial to firms' competitiveness. (1992, p. 11)

The knowledge economy vision is appealing not only for professional parents, but also for non-college bound students and the parents and teachers who care about them, since old jobs are reportedly being "retooled" for this new economy. For example, in Alberta, trades workers are to be part of the knowledge worker group. As a corporate member of the FEBI advisory committee states:

Trades people traditionally have been the people who are seen as, you know the old expression, "they leave their brains at the door and they bring their hands to work" and do what they're told. Well that's slowly, and in some places not so slowly changing. For these major [resource] projects we've got workforces of 2 or 3,000 people and we've got to be able to get them motivated to think about what they're doing. …We have to bring people into these businesses who can do what has to be done differently, who can add value to what's being done that hasn't been there before, and to continue to create wealth for the country. (Interview, December 1, 1999)

The notion of breaking down academic and vocational barriers and providing a more progressive work education experience is undoubtedly appealing to practical arts teachers, as well as to progressive educators more generally. Further, for students who lack the interest or grades required to go to university (and their parents) this discourse provides the hope that has been lacking in recent years with high youth unemployment and the growth in "Mcjobs."

The futurist character of knowledge economy discourse also makes it difficult to challenge. For the reasons discussed above, people want to believe in the knowledge economy and it has "become an article of faith in public discourse" (Livingstone, 1999, p. 134). But let us consider whether that faith is warranted. Knowledge economy theory generally assumes that "workers increasingly require more skill, become more involved in planning their own work, and increasingly constitute a professional class" (Livingstone, p. 137). However, empirical investigation of Canadian trends indicates that there has been only gradual skill upgrading, that most work organizations (including "high performance" ones) continue to operate on principles of hierarchical control, and that the professional class is increasing very slowly (pp. 137, 62). Trends of unemployment and underemployment lead writers to conclude that paid work reform should be considered "at least as seriously as educational reform has been" (Lowe, 2000, p. 84).

Despite this evidence, even educators who share scepticism about the changes in the workplace that have been brought about by the knowledge economy to date argue that it provides a desirable vision for the restructuring of education. For example, although Boutwell (1997) agrees that the employment promises of the knowledge economy have not materialized, he believes that pressures on employers to develop into high performing work organizations (HPWOs) will make them more receptive to ideas around workplace democracy. Similarly, Brown and Lauder (1992) emphasize the promises of post-Fordism in their call for changes to the current Fordist education system. Therefore, educators believe that they can harness the promises of the new economy to their own agendas for education. Perhaps in this way schools can be leaders of change.

Boutwell's (1997) argument assumes representatives from business, government, and education can work together in harmony to pursue the knowledge economy vision. However, not all writers share this faith. For example, in contrast to the functionalist assumptions that underlie the discourse of education for economic prosperity, Carnoy and Levin (1985) propose a way of making sense of the world that is rooted in social conflict theory. Like Boutwell (1997), they identify two competing forces in education; but unlike Boutwell, they see the conflict between these forces as fundamental to public education because of its contradictory location within capitalist democracy. One force aims to reproduce the inequalities required for social efficiency under monopoly capitalism (similar to Boutwell's "utilitarians"), and the other aims to equalize opportunities in pursuit of democratic and constitutional ideals (1985, p. 24). Carnoy and Levin describe the dominance of one force or the other in different historical periods and do not see reforms in the 1980s (which lean toward tightening links between schools and inequitable workplaces) as a departure from that pattern. Livingstone (1999) also sees recent economic changes as an acceleration of dynamics rather than a radical break from the past. In this scenario, the ACC (1995, p. 7) suggestion that "cultural differences and conflicts within business and education are more a result of isolation and misunderstanding than any real or substantive differences in value systems or societal goals" is overly optimistic. Rather, class conflict between workers and owners continues, and the interests of business representatives in the main and those of progressive educators are unlikely to converge as long as schools continue to pursue democratic values.

The preceding discussion suggests that theoretical assumptions about the relationship between education and the economy and social change shape responses to the discourse of education for economic prosperity. However, there are also very pragmatic reasons why this discourse has met with little resistance from educators. The notion of partnerships with business, for example, is very attractive to schools that have suffered cutbacks in recent years. Pressures on teachers stemming from a reduction in supports therefore adds to their concerns about preparing young people for the 21st century and increases their interest in listening to potential business sponsors. Teachers and schools are more receptive to corporate curriculum products, corporate management models, and partnerships.

In the United States, over half of schools were reported to have some sort of alliance with a business corporation (Davis & Botkin, 1994). A survey of BCNI members found that the average company receives 2000 requests for assistance each year. Businesses have also become more strategic, shifting their priorities from arts and culture to education and other areas where they anticipate a greater payoff (BCNI, 1997). In this climate, business and education interests again appear to converge, despite the cynical reminder that business groups were key in promoting government policies that led to public sector downsizing in the first place. For educators who have seen their position within the government's policy community slip in recent years, alliances with strong partners are also strategic. As Boutwell (1997) notes in the U.S. context, enlightened business groups like the CB are collaborating with educators on reforms, and have more clout than other allies (such as parents) at state and federal levels.

Implications for the Democratic Process

In the functionalist view of the school-workplace relation, it is the workplace that takes centre stage. Youth are to be molded by schools to some set of predetermined standards derived from workplace norms. Education is a means to an end, rather than an end in itself. (Carnoy & Levin, 1985, p. 19)

In this section I discuss the extent to which the quotation above reflects current reality, and to the extent that it does, recommend ways of strengthening the democratic and egalitarian side of education. The comment that the workplace takes centre stage in a functionalist view of school-workplace relations resonates with the idea that education must be reformed to meet the knowledge economy vision promoted by business and government leaders. However, what is not sufficiently acknowledged is that there is a long way to go before this vision will be realized. As a result, educators are urged to focus on students' employability skills rather than the extent to which these skills are actually utilized in most organizations, to improve students' work ethic instead of considering the extent to which their attitudes reflect limited opportunity within "command and control" workplaces. As Lowe (2000 p. 118) suggests, there is a "field of dreams" quality to discussion.

Empirical evidence should cause educators to be concerned about first, the likelihood of realizing the HPWO vision, and second, the faith placed in business leaders to bring about democratic workplace reforms. HPWOs are described as able to adapt to change, have few formal levels of hierarchy, are responsive to their environments, are concerned about stakeholders, and value human resources (Lowe, 2000, p. 132). However, the claim that these organizations are becoming the norm in the new economy does not match current reality, particularly in terms of valuing human resources by empowering, developing, and rewarding employees. For example, Lowe (p. 124) reports that a recent survey of CEOs found that "employees" did not make the list of their top nine priorities. The first two were "customers" and "cost competitiveness." Further, while one in three companies surveyed by Statistics Canada in 1998 had been involved in re-engineering in the three years prior to the survey, only 7.2 percent of establishments had introduced democratic workplace innovations, and the most common of these was an employee suggestion program (Lowe, 2000). Livingstone (1999) also points to a 1994 Ontario survey which suggests that while popular demand for a greater say in the running of firms has become more widespread across class positions, corporate executives are most resistant to the more democratic forms of workplace change. At the same time, underemployment has increased over the past 25 years. For example, Canadian surveys suggest that around 20 percent of the employed workforce has a higher credential than their job requires for entry, and between 40 and 60 percent of employees do not use their skills and knowledge in the performance of their jobs (Livingstone, 1999). A survey of BCNI members found that "short term stock price performance, rather than long term growth, has become the dominant concern of institutions as a group" (BCNI,

1997, p. 37). These findings should cause educators to pause and consider how much faith they should place in business leaders to bring about democratic workplace change. Instead, Lowe (2000) emphasizes the important role for government in promoting internal workplace changes, while Livingstone (1999) asserts that "no democratic movement [in the workplace] can be successful without widespread support in the general population" (p. 257).

The preceding discussion suggests that macro-level discourse around economic changes needs to be challenged by educators. For example, the comment that business should be a "key player in defining the specific learning requirements of industry" (Alberta Education, 1994, p. 6) begs a number of questions. Which business employers are to define the learning requirements? While "progressive" private sector employers such as Syncrude have been key players in educational policy discussions, the preceding discussion suggests that they are unlikely to represent most employers. Further, it is clear that even enlightened employers find it difficult to transcend their private interests in the definition of learning requirements. For example, the ACR has been a key player in the push to revitalize vocational/career education in the province in the past ten years in order to meet projected labor shortages. However, what happens when the boom is over? What assurances do the new trades workers have of continued employment?

Further, how much attention is given to equity in the new vocationalism by government and employers? Given that very few apprenticeships have attracted young women in the past, does this mean that, in effect, male students are being prepared for the 21st century of work? To what extent are work education programs reproducing the gendered occupational structures of the workplace? Also, to what extent are programs focusing on improving the chances of non-college bound youth versus lowering the aspirations of "academic" students? Given the evidence that high school systems stream students in keeping with their parents' class position and occupation (Curtis, Livingstone & Smaller, 1992), this is a relevant question. Finally, what kind of learning is actually required for most workplaces? How many organizations reflect the HPWO model and how many are more inequitable and anti-democratic than schools? Educators and other members of the public need to ask such questions.

In addition to challenging the knowledge economy vision, educators can work toward democratizing reforms in schools that will potentially affect change in the workplace. Educators can take seriously Dewey's notion that the purpose of work education is not to adapt workers to an existing industrial regime but rather to alter the existing industrial system and ultimately transform it by developing capacities that allow workers greater control over their fates (Dewey, 1977). Toward this goal, Simon, Dippo, and Schenke (1991) provide a framework for a critical pedagogy of work education in schools. By recognizing the socially and politically constructed features of work, this model challenges the limiting of possibilities that can occur when training is the exclusive emphasis of work education. Another model is provided by Rindge School of Technical Arts in Massachusetts. Recognizing that vocational education has been part of a divisive system of tracking, this school aims to provide vocational students with "the same basic and advanced academic skills and critical thinking skills that all students should learn for further education or for work" (Rosenstock & Steinberg, 1999, p. 56). Reforms at the school in the 1990s focused on developing a democratic culture and involving the students in community development projects that enable them to understand local needs and recognize their abilities to have an impact in the community. These and other examples suggest that establishing links between schools and the community can be a key part of teaching for democratic citizenship (Osborne, 1991). However, this requires that partnerships be developed with a range of community organizations, not just with private sector corporations.

The notion of *partnership* between business and education and the more general notion of *multi-stakeholder consultation* need to be examined because these trends have important implications for democratic processes and outcomes. Multi-stakeholder consultation is part of the new public management practices introduced by governments in Canada and beyond in recent years. The goal is to engage different stakeholders in dialogue in order to develop consensus around public policy issues. However, if we acknowledge discrepancies between the power and resources of different stakeholders, it is clear that a great deal of attention must be given to inclusion and process. Young (1999, p. 155) writes:

> [I]t is important to make a principle of inclusion explicit because contemporary liberal democracies often do so badly on this score. Passive or active exclusions are an important means of preserving power and privilege without impeding the operation of formal democracy. In principle, inclusion ensures that every potentially affected agent has the opportunity to influence deliberative processes and outcomes. In a

mass, mediated, and representative democracy, in practice inclusion means that all the structural social groups, perspectives, interest groups, at least somewhat widely held opinions, and culturally affiliated people have effective opportunity to have their views on issues represented and that others are held to account in the face of their perspectives.

Other aspects of the public policy processes are also critical to strong democracy. Barber (1984) argues that:

The test of legitimacy is whether an individual value has been changed in some significant way to accommodate larger – that is, more common or public – concerns. If a value emerges from the process entirely unchanged by that process, then either it remains a private value masquerading as a public norm or it denotes a prior consensus that has been revealed by the political process. (p. 137)

An important part of this process involves naming values, identifying issues, setting agendas, and delineating options (Barber, 1984).

These comments are useful to consider in light of the process of developing the FEBI in Alberta, a process not unlike other consultation processes undertaken by federal and provincial governments in recent years. In terms of inclusion, the key stakeholders were seen as education, business, and government. The FEBI advisory group included eight representatives from private sector industry/business groups, four from education (representing teachers, school boards, superintendents, and parents) and six from government (four bureaucrats from three departments and two politicians). There were 15 men and three women. Only one labor representative was invited to participate in the FEBI process, and when that person did not come, no replacement was sought. The predominance of private sector employers and lack of input from organized labor and community groups demonstrates a failure to be formally inclusive.

The process was no doubt affected by the composition of the advisory group and starting assumptions of bureaucrats. Examples suggest that private values came to masquerade as public norms (cf. Barber, 1984). First, although business was defined in the FEBI report as including "private, for profit and not-for-profit organizations," the advisory group focused almost exclusively on private sector employers (Alberta Education, 1996, p. 2). Second, the FEBI mandate focused on supply side issues, in other words, adapting schools to a knowledge economy vision (BIAG & MLA Team, 1996). Although interviews with education members of the advisory group suggest that they challenged aspects of this vision, there is no evidence of this in reports. Third, interviews with advisory group members suggest that there was little discussion of values, no votes were taken and the goal was to develop consensus. The fact that business representatives were predominant no doubt made this easier.[5] Finally, documents and presentations demonstrating "successful" models of business involvement in schools were provided throughout the FEBI process. We can expect that models provided by the CB, ACR, the Calgary Educational Partnership Foundation,[6] and Junior Achievement would have reduced the interest of concerned members in challenging values and assumptions that had become dominant in the process.

The identification of issues and agenda-setting was therefore largely accomplished by government and business representatives. This had an impact not only on the process of developing the FEBI but also on outcomes. The FEBI recommendation that the province develop a Career Education Foundation was implemented in 1997 with the establishment of the *Careers...the Next Generation Foundation*. This industry-driven foundation was a logical extension of the initial ACR partnership mentioned earlier. Another FEBI recommendation was that business representatives have more input into educational policy processes at all levels. Immediately following this report, the government added business representatives to its Programs Assessment and Advisory Committee (PAAC). School boards are also involving business representatives on committees to a greater extent.

The preceding discussion suggests that weak democratic processes lead to weak democratic outcomes. However, it also provides a direction for concerned individuals and groups. First, it is necessary to recognize that achieving democracy in schools and in workplaces will involve struggle. The idea that there has been a convergence of interests between business and education is overly simplistic. Yes, vocational discourses have been retooled for the "knowledge economy" vision, but traditional "Taylorist" forms of organization and social relations persist. Furthermore, capitalist logic jeopardizes democracy by promoting political power as a derivative of economic power, privatizing interests through the market, and encouraging the development of monopoly (Barber, 1984, pp. 253-255). For schools, the challenge is therefore to ensure that democracy is strengthened rather than weakened. From this perspective, their role is to prepare students to be fully participating citizens with a strong sense of their democratic rights and responsibilities.

Second, it is critical for schools to keep the goal of promoting equity for all students in sight as they enter relationships with corporate partners. The pressure is to reproduce in schools the frequently inequitable practices of corporations. Recognizing this, schools must be vigilant about partnership activities, asking, for example, how many students are involved, which students are involved, and how are they selected. If partnerships are pursued, it makes sense to involve a range of organizations within the community. Student participants in work experience and co-operative education programs should be encouraged to critically reflect on their experiences (Simon, Dippo & Schenke, 1991).

Third, given the emphasis of governments on multi-stakeholder consultation, a broader variety of groups must demand access to discussions about educational reform. Organized labor, feminist, antiracist, and other social justice groups need to respond to the increased involvement of business groups in the educational policy community. While recognizing that groups have varied levels of resources, strengthened alliances among these groups can reduce the prospect of corporate domination in the policy process. Partnerships involving private sector players must also be publicly accountable. Again, one way of increasing accountability is to broaden the range of partners who are included.

The past decade has seen increased pressures on educators resulting from budget cuts, increased standardized testing, and competitive pressures within and outside of the public system. In this time of vulnerability, increased business involvement appears to offer solutions. But as the preceding analysis indicates, educators and other members of the public need to recognize the contradictions between business rhetoric and reality and make a commitment to the struggles that lie ahead if we are truly interested in developing a people-centred vision for society.

Endnotes

[1] The use of the term "stakeholder" may itself reflect increased corporate influence in the public sphere. An OECD report on school-business partnerships suggests that the interest in involving more "stockholders" (i.e., the "range of organizations and individuals who influence and get involved with education") can be observed in most OECD countries (1992, p.9).

[2] For example, the 1991 conference included a presentation by John Chubb, who with Terry Moe co-authored the book "Politics, Markets and America's

Schools" (1990). Also, Charter school advocate Joe Freedman was included as a parent representative on a panel at the 1993 conference.

3 According to its website, the Vancouver-based Fraser Institute was "founded in 1974 to redirect public attention to the role markets can play in providing for the economic and social well-being of Canadians" (i.e., Milton Friedman style economics). It has 2500 individual, corporate, and foundations supporters in Canada and beyond (39 percent of supporters are corporate members). The Institute's goal is to "have an impact in stretching the frontiers of the Canadian public policy debate" (see website: www.fraserinstitute.ca/about_us/). In addition to the documents mentioned, the Institute published its second annual report card on Alberta's high schools in 2000.

4 This report, written by Claudia Rebanks Hepburn, is available at the following website: <www.fraserinstitute.ca/publications/critical_issues/1999/school_choice/section_01.htm>

5 For example, a representative from the Alberta Federation of Labour who was later interviewed about the FEBI report disagreed with several assumptions and recommendations (Interview, February 1, 2000).

6 The Calgary Educational Partnership Foundation is a non-profit organization established in 1991 to increase the active involvement of the business community in the activities of the Calgary and area school boards.

References

Advisory Committee. (1993). *Toward 2000 together: An economic strategy by Albertans for Alberta*. Edmonton: Government of Alberta.

Alberta Chamber of Commerce Education Committee. (1995). *School to work transition*. Edmonton: Alberta Chamber of Commerce.

Alberta Chamber of Resources. (1995). *Careers . . . the next generation: 1994-95 Project Report*. Edmonton.

Alberta Chamber of Resources and Construction Owners Association of Alberta. (1990). *Alberta resource developments in the 1990s: A response to potential skill shortages*. Edmonton.

Alberta Chamber of Resources and Alberta Education. (1991). *International comparisons in education – Curriculum, values and lessons*. Edmonton: Alberta Chamber of Resources.

Alberta Education. (1991). *Vision for the nineties: A plan of action*. Edmonton.

Alberta Education. (1994). *Meeting the challenge: Three-year business plan*. Edmonton.

Alberta Education. (1996). *Framework for enhancing business involvement in education*. Edmonton.

Ball, S. (1990). *Politics and policy making in education*. London: Routledge.

Barber, B. (1984). *Strong democracy: Participatory politics for a new age*. Berkeley: University of California Press.

Bloom, M. (1991). *Reaching for success: Business and education working together,* Conference Report of the Second National Conference on Business-Education Partnership (Report 77-91-E/F). Ottawa: The Conference Board of Canada.

Bloom, M. (1994). *Enhancing employability skills: Innovative partnerships, projects and programs* (Report 118-94). Ottawa: Conference Board of Canada.

Bloom, M. & Kitigawa, K. (1999). *Understanding employability skills* (Report 257-99). Ottawa: Conference Board of Canada.

Boutwell, C. (1997). *Shell game: Corporate America's agenda for schools.* Bloomington: Phi Delta Kappa Educational Foundation.

Brown, P. & Lauder, H. (1992). Education, economy and society: An introduction to a new agenda. In P. Brown & H. Lauder (Eds.), *Education for economic survival* (pp. 1-44). London: Routledge.

Business Council on National Issues. (1997). *Jobs, growth and community.* Ottawa.

Business Involvement Advisory Group and MLA Team. (1996). *Creating independent and interdependent learners: Business and education working together.* Edmonton.

Canadian Chamber of Commerce. (1990). *Business-education partnerships: Your planning process guide.* Toronto: Canadian Chamber of Commerce.

Carnoy, M. & Levin, H. (1985). *Schooling and work in the democratic state.* Stanford: Stanford University Press.

Chubb, J. & Moe, T. (1990). *Politics, markets and America's schools.* Washington: The Brookings Institute.

Curtis, B., Livingstone, D. & Smaller, H. (1992). *Stacking the deck: The streaming of working class kids in Ontario schools.* Toronto: Our Schools/Our Selves.

Davis, S. & Botkin, J. (1994). *The monster under the bed: How business is mastering the opportunity of knowledge for profit.* New York: Simon & Schuster.

Dewey, J. (Spring 1977). Education vs. trade training: Dr. Dewey's reply. *Curriculum Inquiry, 7:* 38.

Easton, S. (1988). *Education in Canada.* Vancouver: Fraser Institute.

Economic Council of Canada. (1992). *A lot to learn: Education and training in Canada.* Ottawa: Minister of Supply and Services.

Ehrenreich, B. (1989). *Fear of falling.* New York: Harper Collins.

Finlayson, J. (1985). *Youth unemployment in Canada: The problem and some possible responses.* Ottawa: Business Council on National Issues.

Government of Canada. (1991). *Learning well...living well.* Ottawa: Minister of Supply and Services.

Government of Canada. (1993). *The prosperity action plan: A progress report.* Ottawa.

Henchey, N. (1990). *Designing Canada's future: Learning for the 21st century.* Montreal: Corporate-Higher Education Forum.

Livingstone, D. W. (1999). *The education-jobs gap.* Toronto: Garamond.

Lowe, G. (2000). *The quality of work: A people-centred agenda.* Toronto: Oxford University Press.

OECD & Centre for Educational Research and Innovation. (1992). *Schools and business: A new partnership.* Paris: OECD.

Osborne, D. & Gaebler, T. (1993). *Reinventing government.* New York: Plume.

Osborne, K. (1991). *Teaching for democratic citizenship.* Toronto: Our Schools/Our Selves.

Rosenstock, L. & Steinberg, A. (1999). Beyond the shop: Reinventing vocational education. In M. Apple & M. Beane (Eds.), *Democratic schools: Lessons from the chalk face* (pp. 48-67). Buckingham: Open University Press.

Simon, R., Dippo, D. & Schenke, A. (1991). *Learning work: A critical pedagogy of work education.* Toronto: OISE Press.

Taylor, A. (1998). Employability skills: From corporate "wish list" to government policy. *Journal of Curriculum Studies, 30*(2), 143-164.

Taylor, A. (2001). *The politics of educational reform in Alberta.* Toronto: University of Toronto Press.

Workman, W. T. (1996). *Banking on deception.* Halifax: Fernwood.

Young, I. (1999). Justice, inclusion, and deliberative democracy. In S. Macedo (Ed.), *Deliberative politics: Essays on democracy and disagreement* (pp. 151-158). Oxford: Oxford University Press.

Chapter 8
School Reforms in Ontario: The "Marketization of Education" and the Resulting Silence on Equity

George J. Sefa Dei and Leeno L. Karumanchery

Introduction

In Canada the belief in principles of fairness, justice, and equity conflict but coexist with attitudes that reflect racism and discrimination against minority groups. One of the consequences of these conflicting value sets is the perceived lack of official support for policies that might ameliorate the low status of racial minorities. These policies and practices require changes to the existing socio-political and economic order, usually through state intervention. However, this type of state intervention is often in conflict with the ideals of a liberal democracy: the belief that people are rewarded solely on the basis of merit and that no individual or group is singled out for discriminatory or preferential treatment (Henry & Tator, 1994). Although appearing consistent with liberal democratic values, the deeply ingrained ideology of *meritocracy* belies the truth of oppression and social advantage. Within this conceptual frame, skin color is seen as irrelevant in determining status, and those who experience racism, and suffer the material or nonmaterial consequences of those encounters, are somehow responsible for their state of being. In pathologizing minority youth and their families, these discourses function as one of the bases of merit-based models of education reform.

The educational system reinforces social differences through the implementation and use of dominant Euro-centric notions of what is valid and invalid knowledge. In a multi-ethnic society it is both legitimate and important that we question the appropriateness of promoting and maintaining an educational system that is geared to the needs of the majority. Educational reforms carry the potential to reshape how resources are shared and/or redistributed so as to work toward the optimum use of human talents and skills. How can we move beyond a Euro-Canadian cultural, economic, and political grid truly to engage multi-ethnic student populations? How can we ensure that efforts at positive, solution-oriented reform truly work to benefit and advance the state of education today and in the future?

As noted by Fine (1991), and Fullan and Hannay (1998), good intentions are not enough, and we cannot ensure that such efforts will result in any specifically desired effect. However, we can assess the relative merit and potential of these strategies in relation to those successful practices that have been employed in the past. Schorr (1997) sought to establish such a framework through a large-scale review of existing educational policy programs that had met with a certain degree of success. By focusing on those attributes that stood consistently throughout successful programs, Schorr developed seven guidelines for successful educational reform. He asserts that successful programs: (a) are comprehensive, flexible, responsive, and persevering; (b) view children not as single entities, but in relation to their families; (c) engage families as members of a neighborhood or larger community; (d) have a clear mission and a long-term, preventive orientation that does not hamper their ability to evolve over time; (e) are managed in an exemplary manner by competent and committed individuals with identifiable skills; (f) are staffed by trained individuals who can provide a high-quality, supportive, and responsive service; and (g) function in a cooperative environment built on trust, mutual respect, and strong interpersonal relationships (Fullan & Hannay, 1998). The current educational system is not designed along these lines, and in turn it is not designed to meet the needs of all students. However, in recognizing the importance of including all students in the processes and experience of schooling, it is crucial that we extend Schorr's framework to include equity issues as integral to a successful educational program. It has been painfully obvious for a long time that equality of access does not result in equality of outcome. This problem arises because access alone does not mean that students who occupy the margins of society will mysteriously find their culture, race, and ethnicity reflected in the center of their school experience. As students, teachers, and parents engage schools with their raced, classed, gendered, and sexualized bodies, it is essential that we augment Schorr's frame with an integrative antiracist guideline that links identity to schooling; stressing that race, class, gender, sexuality, and other forms of difference are crucial variables in education.

From an integrative antiracist perspective (Dei, 1996), it is recognized that all social oppressions intersect with each other and that a discussion of one such oppression – racism – necessarily entails a discussion of class, gender, and sexual inequality in schooling as well. Race and gender in particular provide a context for power and domination in society. Some educators have come to recognize the connection between equity, identity, and academic success (Alladin, 1996; Brathwaite & James, 1996). However, although this knowledge has seen the birth of more than a few initiatives designed to change the landscape of schooling, global trends would suggest that equity issues are in jeopardy of being cut back or stopped altogether.

Hatcher (1998) argues that New Labour government's modernist policies of "School Improvement" in the United Kingdom promote approaches to schooling reform that do not take the unequal effects of race, class, and gender into consideration. These types of reforms display four main characteristics: an abstract universalism that downplays the specificities of local school situations; a decontextualization that devalues the importance of students' experiences, histories, cultures, and identities as they relate to the learning process; a consensualism that avoids dealing with conflict and controversy; and a managerialism that privileges a top-down approach to the administration of schooling. In the failure to address the structural, political, and historical dimensions of change and the promotion of a deracialized approach to schooling, these features of market-based reform illustrate some of the problems inherent in "corporate managerialist models of education" (p. 268).

Today, fiscally conservative governments have forced many communities to face reforms that effectively undermine public schooling. In Africa, Asia, and the Caribbean, national governments faced with budget deficits, economic recessions, and other monetary woes are abandoning equity commitments. They are "favouring privatization, reduced government expenditures, user charges and difficult choices between sub-sectors in education" (Jones, 1997, p. 373). Literature from the United States and the UK demonstrates that the intrusion of market forms and relations into schooling is not a uniquely "Southern" phenomenon and that these market discourses are reshaping educational systems across international borders. Hatcher (1998) writes on events in Britain where the current discourse and practice of "school effectiveness and improvement" has sidelined equality and social justice concerns. In these contexts, race and equity issues remain peripheral to educational policy developments despite continuing "profound inequities...affecting students from ethnic minority backgrounds" (p. 287).

Whether one interrogates educational reforms in the developing world, or in European, Asian, and North American contexts, the supreme reign of the global marketplace is evident, and the enormity of the related reforms cannot be overlooked. The focus on market-driven reform policies has serious consequences for teaching, learning, and the administration of education as we move into the next millennium. There are implications for how we come to understand social justice and the role or relation of antiracist education for equity in schooling. Although it is important to stress that equity cuts have become a central feature of schooling reform around the globe, this article focuses on a local view: a Canadian perspective. Recent events in Ontario education provide clear examples of the problems inherent when school reforms are conceived and undertaken without a proper, well-informed consideration for the centering of equity issues. In this article, we[1] adopt an antiracist analysis of Ontario's educational reform initiatives, pointing to the consequences for equity and access in education. We highlight contrasting reforms that might be undertaken under the banner of an antiracist, inclusive framework that establishes the need to address questions of equity, representation and difference as cornerstones of educational change (Dei, 1996).

In this article we are left with no choice but to move beyond the safe and seductive zone of "innocent discourse" and adopt a tone of advocacy (as an alternative). We begin by arguing that there are several paths to equity in education, and that these paths may connect at some points. Yet in the zeal to connect equity in its broad sense, it is important to separate discourse from policy. For example, there is a problem in creating a single undifferentiated category of *other* when devising specific policy measures to address educational inequities and social oppression. We need to highlight the specific needs of various communities as we discursively draw the connections between oppressions and social equity issues. Politically we have chosen to address the issue of equity in education through the lens of race and how it intersects with other forms of difference. In looking at equity and reform we pinpoint race as a major (not the sole) focus. Antiracism has long provided the theoretical framework for our critical work on equity and social oppression, and this article articulates our current thinking in that frame.

We wish to present this article as a theoretical discussion informed by field research. Between 1992 and 1995 Dei, working with other students, completed a three-year study on the experiences of Black or African-Canadian students in Ontario public schools, with a particular focus on the issues of disengagement and dropping out (Dei, Mazzuca, McIsaac & Zine, 1997). This researcher has completed another multiyear effort to identify exemplary practices of inclusive schooling in the same education system (Dei et al., 1996 & 2000). Findings in these extensive empirical investigations (working with graduate students) have strengthened our conviction regarding the urgent need for positive educational change.

In doing this work there is always a danger that theory will be vilified while practice is privileged or that theory will be completely dissociated from practice. This problem demands a refinement and restatement of the philosophical basis for the specific pedagogical, curricular, and instructional changes that we are seeking to promote in schools (Dei, 1999). Our previous and ongoing research allows us to offer a grounded critique of school reforms in Ontario. Specifically, we use existing knowledge to identify the themes around which to look at equity and its place in current school reforms. Toward the end of our discussion we draw on specific research knowledge to suggest possible paths of action in order to bring equity issues to the forefront of educational change in Ontario.

School Reforms Ontario Style

In the summer of 1995 Ontarians elected a Progressive Conservative government. Under the banner of a "common sense revolution," these provincial Tories unveiled an agenda that spoke to a specific economic plan or vision for Ontario. Couched in a language of democracy, self-reliance, and family values, the new government's restructuring campaign began with the cancellation and/or weakening of several laws and policies that endeavored to improve the social condition of society (Dehli, 1996). In systematic fashion, with their majority government, the Tories moved directly in observance with the set guidelines for marketization and attempted to push several far-reaching and controversial Bills through parliament. They pushed against the public sector with *Bill 136*, a measure intended to expand management rights while curtailing those of unions. With *Bill 142*, which among other things would redefine disability criteria and set the stage for profit-minded companies to administer welfare, they moved against what they deemed to be special interest groups (i.e., welfare recipients, unemployed, sick, disabled, and elderly people). In addition to these revisions, the Tories also began an all-out assault on antiracist education and inclusive practice. With *Bill 104*, the provincial Tories proposed the amalgamation of existing school boards from 167 to 66, a cost-cutting measure that would allow for a drastic reduction in democratically elected trustees. Further, *Bill 104* would see the establishment of an Education Improvement Commission, a non-democratically appointed government authority with sweeping powers over school boards and accountable only to the Minister of Education.

Early in their mandate the provincial Tories pledged to work with the business community and corporate capital interests to restructure and downsize the education system to ensure school improvement. The intent of these initiatives was to insert Ontario into the global marketplace, thereby ensuring that schools would be able to produce a cheap and compliant labor force. However, in order for these reforms to be pushed through without a serious public backlash, it was necessary to create a "crisis in schooling." By undermining the reputation of public education, the Conservatives manufactured a province-wide concern over "the declining quality of Ontario education." Once their rhetoric was in place, the Tories were able to move ahead with their restructuring agenda. Within months of the Conservative accession, schools across the province found that many of the programs that had worked toward equity and social justice (i.e., employment equity legislation, affirmative action, ESL, etc.) were either cut back severely or terminated altogether (Dehli, 1996).

These cuts were an enormous blow to the future of antiracist and equity education in Ontario, as they directly opposed initiatives that worked toward ameliorating the problems of representation in schooling. As the undeclared targets of the conservative agenda, racial, gender, and cultural minorities have found themselves taking the brunt of the government's material and ideological attack (Dehli, 1996). As a whole, these bottom-line moves against what the new government considered to be special interests did not go unnoticed. However, despite the scope and radical nature of these initiatives, no move garnered as much attention in the media, in parliament, and in the social consciousness as did the *Education Improvement Act, Bill 160*, a direct attack on teachers' unions and a consolidated move toward the marketization of education in Ontario.

Bill 160

As a measure designed primarily to decentralize state responsibility to schools while centralizing power under the auspices of government control, *Bill 160* covers various aspects of educational policy and practice in Ontario. As documented in the minutes of the Ontario English Catholic Teachers' Association 1996 annual general meeting, the provincial Ministry of Education and Training was charged to implement a series of far-reaching reforms. Such an approach would work against school dynamics and power structures that seek to discourage and/or inhibit collaborative environments in schooling. The revisions affect: bureaucratic powers over taxation; financial cuts to kindergarten, summer school, upgrading, adult education, continuing education, and special education programs; school councils; school boards; the authority of the Minister of Education and Training to sanction the employment of non-certified teachers, and the ability to control teacher prep time and class size; and in relation to the infusing of schooling with market models, it calls for the replacement of up to 90 hours of classroom learning time with work experience.

Framed in the discourse of market and choice, *Bill 160* is an example of the massive grasp for centralized power by the state as it concentrates its authority over public education in the hands of a few cabinet ministers and government advisers. It is also an example of the state's attempt to cut millions of dollars from the education budget. As *Bill 160* moves Ontario education into the global marketplace and resources become linked to enrollment and quantitative performance, public education in Ontario is quickly becoming an endangered or obsolete concept. As many critics have argued, if left unchecked, *Bill 160* will eventually lead to a privatized educational system. The Bill talks about quality and improvement, but has no grounded discussions on equity questions. Following the restructuring agenda, the extensive reforms include restricting the rights of teachers to strike, reducing the number of professional activity days, and reducing the powers of teacher federations. Further, as the reforms push a "more bang for your buck" mentality, *Bill 160* moves to quantify educational quality and improvement by: implementing standardized testing; establishing an Education Quality Accountability Office; reducing the number of elected trustees; and amalgamating the provincial school boards.

With such a large number of extensive changes to the system, the constitutionality of the Bill was taken to task on numerous fronts, and with the passing of the Bill several challenges were undertaken in the Ontario courts. Recently, Justice Peter Cumming ruled that in at least one key respect the Bill is unconstitutional: Section 93 of the Constitution states that the government cannot take away the right of separate school boards to levy their own taxes. This landmark decision forced the provincial government to take a step back and reassess their restructuring timetable. However, as a backlash to the ruling, Cumming's assertion that "the majority does not need protection from the majority" prompted cries of "interest group politics," and it sparked much debate as to whether denominational boards should be afforded separate rights from those of the public boards. In reality a critical analysis of this apparent dichotomy would reveal the interdependent nature of both terms: equality does not preclude difference, and difference does not negate equality. Further confrontations arose in September 1998 when a number of Ontario's publicly funded schools were closed by strikes and/or lockouts. Toronto's Catholic Board locked out all its high school teachers on the first day of the new school year, and during that same period thousands of Toronto District high school teachers staged rotating walkouts.

Amid the countermoves and appeals that will probably keep these questions in the air and unanswered for some time, the Tory government marches onward with their restructuring agenda. *Bill 160* itself is both extensive and comprehensive, and it is not our intent to review it here. Rather, we are specifically interested in using an antiracist perspective to address the theoretical and practical functions of the Bill as it relates to the marketization of Ontario education. Regarding these trends, two central issues are of utmost concern as we explore some of the implications of ongoing educational reforms in the province of Ontario. First is the tendency toward the marketization of education, and second is the continued rhetoric of "excellence" that sees antiracism and equity initiatives as an affront to "quality education."

The Rhetoric of Reform

When the new Tory plan for education reform was implemented, banking theories of education[2] in an economic reductionist[3] framework were used to characterize schooling as a business: a functioning enterprise where parents and employers are seen as consumers and students as clients. A critical analysis of this market mentality reveals a complex that contributes more to the fetishizing[4] and commodification of education than it does to the improvement of it, but the conceptual stance established by the government set the stage for a political and ideological battle with Ontario teachers that used rhetoric to portray the market as necessary and natural while exploiting the public's already existing dissatisfaction with government institutions to paint teachers and their unions as self-serving, inefficient, and bloated (Dehli, 1996). The Conservative media machine hides these realities so neatly in a language of reformation and progress that non-critical analysts failed to see the "forest for the trees."

It is important to note that it is unrealistic and more than a little conspiracy-minded to suggest that these political moves are part of some type of class plot. As suggested by Fullan and Hannay (1998), it would seem more feasible that political perspectives become hampered by "built-in blinders." That is to say, that the overarching desire to be re-elected will often encourage actions that produce short-term or material reforms that the voting public can see and experience. Further, as noted by Micklethwait and Wooldridge (1996), local contexts are too often lost in the political attempt to produce magical solutions to social problems, which also act as magical re-election strategies. The problem here is that such reforms are usually based on common sense understandings of the world and poorly informed research (Fullan & Hannay, 1998). Painting the Harris government as evil and sinister serves little purpose. As governments become more preoccupied with deficits, debt, and the mobility of educational capital, however, they become less interested in the experiences of students.

Regardless of the intentions behind these reforms, education in Ontario today is spoken about in the language of market economy. The usual application of banking analogies in the use of such terminology as *consumers, beneficiaries, products, productivity, motivation,* and *investments* all have powerful affinities in the discourse of the marketplace. Although this type of talk has an intent focus on the administrative and organizational effectiveness of an efficient school system, there is hardly an in-depth interrogation of the institutional structures and processes that deliver education (e.g., teaching, learning, curricular development, and the representation of bodies), particularly with respect to equity concerns. The government heralds standardized curriculum and a regimented educational process in relation to the cost-effectiveness of public schooling. As the discourse of the marketplace gains prominence in educational contexts, students will see themselves categorized and their progress or outcomes monitored and measured in ever-increasing degrees. Some hard questions remain unanswered, however. For example, what does it mean to have a standardized curriculum in a schooling context that universalizes the dominant group's frame of reference and world views? How does the discourse of efficiency and cost-effectiveness efface concerns about difference and equity? How is the focus on teachers' professional competence and the academic proficiencies of students helping to assign educational failures to physical bodies, rather than to the systemic and organizational structures that deliver education? How is the measurement of school effectiveness in purely educational outcomes part of a political discourse intended to rationalize a shift to private schooling?

Interrogating the Rhetoric of Reform

As noted by Fullan and Hannay (1998), *Bill 160* may be interpreted as a prime example of the political search for a magical re-election initiative: a wrong-headed reform that sacrifices the possibility of true educational improvement in favor of short-term goals that might impress voters. On the other hand, the Conservative gaze may be set beyond election politics and toward the economic possibilities that arise parallel to a market-based educational system. Regardless of the motives, one thing is clear: in their adoption of an educational agenda that is constituted in a market mentality, the Ontario Conservatives signal that *Bill 160* and related educational reforms are not about the improvement of education. Rather, these reforms must be seen as part of an agenda designed to increase political power and economic gain. With the passing of the Bill, a series of events have been set in motion that will work toward the marketization of education in Ontario. These developments signal a direct threat to the very ideals of public schooling in Ontario.

As Dehli (1998) asks, with the passage of *Bill 160*, what is the government planning to do with its new powers? What are we to expect from market-driven forms of schooling in Ontario? What happens when the desire for school choice is pitted against concerns for educational access and equity in public education? How do we improve student learning and promote educational innovation in the socio-political contexts of divided groups and communities competing for access to limited resources and reduced educational funding? The success of public education must extend beyond the ability of schools to meet the needs of those students able to take advantage of the system. An excellent school should be defined by its ability to meet the needs of those students least able to take advantage of available educational opportunities. Although we must all be proud of the successes of schools, society must also be willing to accept responsibility for educational failures; they cannot be attributed to schools alone. Too often in public discourse we hear of the need for schools, students, parents, and communities to take responsibility, but what about state and governmental responsibility?

The popular refrain of the Conservative government's "common sense revolution" is that "the system does not work, and it needs fixing," or "the government is broke, and it alone cannot do everything." Much of the "common sense" rhetoric about accountability and the tightening of government purse-strings has focused on the need for parents, teachers, and communities to take responsibility for the education of their youth. Conversely, this discourse creates a false dichotomy between the public and the private spheres by inferring that the government should be able to abandon or seriously curtail its own responsibilities to public education. It is important to note here that the Harris government's seeming preoccupation with money management and the bottom line hides an agenda that is more concerned with the restructuring of education, a move or series of moves that should be seen as a significant product of the "restructuring process of planned decentralization" (Kenway, 1995, p. 2).

Kenway (1995) asserts that as state policy begins to reflect these commercial interests, four main movements will develop as fundamental to the process of restructuring: *devolution, deregulation, dezoning,* and *disaggregation.* Devolution refers to reductions in state funding as well as other efforts overtly to decentralize government responsibility for schools while centralizing curriculum and assessment procedures under the auspices of government control. Deregulation suggests that policy will move to eradicate or weaken existing constraints on the market (e.g., moving systemic control away from elected officials and toward government appointees, opening teaching responsibilities to unqualified staff, "union-busting" of teachers' unions in an attempt to shift from collective bargaining to individual settlements, forcing schools to look for alternative resources through cuts in state funding, etc.). Dezoning removes major structural barriers that constrain the market; with this transition students become free to move between schools, and quality of education becomes a matter of affordability. Disaggregation incorporates market ideals of competition into schooling in lieu of collectivity and cooperation, concepts that are deemed outmoded.

In line with Kenway's (1995) formula, while alluding to a crisis in education the provincial government has consistently underfunded schools and side-stepped state responsibility to implement programs and initiatives that sustain and improve public education.

Admittedly certain changes are called for in the current school system in Ontario. From the perspective of disadvantaged racial minorities, the need for change arises because schools continue to disappoint a good number of our youth in spite of all the good intentions. Although change is inevitable, however, the provincial government has shown that not all change is good, positive, or solution-oriented. Ongoing changes in Ontario's education speak to the power of "big money." So far the rhetoric and practice of the government show that we cannot simply trust it to enact those fundamental changes of utmost concern to minority students and parents. These concerns relate to how schools deal with race, antiracism, equity, power, and social difference in their organizational, curricular, and instructional practices. If there is a rigidity and ineffectiveness in the current school system, it is in part due to the failure of administrators to use their power to address issues that could enhance learning opportunities and educational outcomes for all youth.

What good is it to spend our energies on dismissing the terminology of antiracism and difference when the problem of engaging race, class, gender, and sexuality remains? The rhetoric of school improvement should translate to concrete action. Educational change must ensure that the pursuit of accountability and transparency replaces the bland talk of market logic and cost-effective education. A consequence of the government's educational plan, if left unchecked, will be the creation of a two-tier school system where the privatization of profitable state institutions will reign supreme. Those who can afford to will maintain quality education, while the poor and the disadvantaged will be left with an under-funded public school system. Governments cannot believe that educational systems can simply be downsized to success, and they cannot hope that a shift to a market-driven school system will address the structural problems of delivering education. Rather than parents, students, and local communities being seen as consumers in the educational marketplace, they must be seen as equal partners and stakeholders who can work diligently with educators, school administrators, and policy-makers in a collective endeavor.

The task of transforming Ontario schools rests on conscious and sincere attempts to match the pursuit of academic excellence and quality education with considerations of equity and social justice. The promotion of excellence is inextricably linked with addressing access, equity, and power issues in education. Change that exacerbates educational inequity is neither desired nor positive. Unfortunately, the government's market-based educational reforms do not place the struggles of marginalized youth high on the political agenda. Many in society may not have any discomfort in seeing a predominantly white teaching body deliver education to minority and working-class student populations (Dehli, 1994; Dei et al., 1997; Solomon & Levine-Rasky, 1994). The discomfort can be found in the eyes of the marginalized who do not see themselves reflected in school settings (e.g., teaching and administrative staff, curriculum, and texts).

An effective approach to curricular and institutional reform must take into account the question of bodies and local environments. However, a significant aspect of ongoing Tory reforms is the development of a common curriculum for secondary and elementary school levels. For marginalized groups there are nagging questions: who is writing these new curricula? How do the new curricula address questions of equity and social difference? Whose values, ideas, and knowledge are being represented? In the framework of outcomes-based schooling, one must ask how outcomes are to be achieved by all when the playing field is not level. The government's original idea to dezone schooling and contract out instructional programs and curriculum development to private firms in the U.S. is indeed problematic. This move raises questions of how local contexts, sensitivities, histories, and social politics are to be taken up in the design and structure of curricular and instructional materials for schools. Perhaps more important, the development of curriculum and instructional materials in a market-driven educational system can only ensure that classroom teachers stay close to the prescribed curriculum and tailor teaching and pedagogical practices more closely to test-taking (Whitty, Edwards & Gewirtz, 1993). Parents' input into curriculum design (if any) and teaching matters will be measured by the cost-effectiveness of reform initiatives and how well students could perform on Province-mandated standardized tests.

Recently, Dehli (1998) has argued that the idea of choice in public and private education is not new and that choice has been part of the Ontario public school system for years. For example, the existence of separate and public schools, however limited, French-language schools, gifted programs, and alternative schools has allowed parents to exercise some degree of choice in the education of their youth. These were not choices propelled by a purely market or profit-making incentive and/or cost-effective ideology, however. With the influence of market forces on the value of knowledge, in time "non-exchange value" disciplines such as the arts, social sciences, and the humanities could well become residualized as well (Kenway, 1995).

Market-driven choice and competition serve the whims of the wealthy and most powerful in society, those who would benefit by having access to Ontario schools determined by income, family status, race, and social power. "Local contexts matter a great deal to how choice programs work, who is able to take advantage of them, and how effective they are" (Dehli, 1998, p. 5). Historically, in every market-driven school choice program, equity considerations are hardly paramount and central. The material consequences of dezoning and free choice in the public sector will become evident as the dichotomy between the haves and the have-nots is magnified in educational sites. As noted by Kenway (1995), in selecting students based on money and prestige, schools that cater to the wealthy will enjoy ever-increasing access to resources and opportunities, whereas lower-income schools will find it increasingly difficult to provide the basics of a quality education for their students.

One could argue that *Bill 160* might open space for students and parents to opt for choice in schools in the long run. An example is charter schools as part of the right-wing political agenda for vouchers and privatization of education in the U.S. Admittedly the implementation and establishment of charter schools are not direct features of *Bill 160*, but as noted by Kenway (1995), a definite progression toward dezoning and disaggregation is to be expected here. Minority parents need to be aware that discussions about choice do not provide the space and context for focus schools that address minority youth disengagement from schooling. For example, some African-Canadian parents call for African-centered schools as an alternative form of schooling inside (and not outside) the public school system. Having these schools is not a matter of choice so much as the school constitutes a radical approach to make the public school system respond to the needs of African-Canadian students. As Dei et al. (1997) argue, an African-centered school is a strategic move to address the problem of poverty, race, difference, and its consequences on schooling and education for disadvantaged youth. African-centered schools should offer real and accessible options in a publicly funded educational system for African and other minority families whose children are disengaged from the conventional school system.

Another equity consideration is the impact of educational reforms on redundancies and layoffs of teachers. It is possible that schools can use parents and local educators to teach students about cultures, histories, and indigenous knowledge. The experience of these community educators can be integrated into official school language and discourse such that classroom teaching would be supplemented and schools could deliver a more "complete" education. In the case of a government intent on cost-cutting, "common sense" dictates that the use of replacement teachers would be approached as an opportunity to save. Like many others we are concerned about the use of replacement teachers when there are qualified, unemployed teachers from disadvantaged and minority backgrounds. Furthermore, under present initiatives "redundant" teachers will be laid off, and the principle of "last hired, first let go" will rid the schools of the younger (and for the most part recently hired) progressive teachers, who are disproportionately racial minorities and women.[5]

Similarly, the political rhetoric of average class size must be scrutinized for its equity dimensions. The government has co-opted parents and local communities' genuine concern about class size and its impact on effective teaching to satisfy its political and ideological interests. For example, the official rhetoric was that by September 1998 the average pupil-teacher ratio would be 25:1 at the elementary level and a maximum of 22:1 for high schools. Conventional knowledge asserts that the government has legislated smaller class sizes and that extra teachers will be hired to relieve overcrowded classrooms. Unfortunately this is not the reality. As Tozer (1998) points out, the government "has not placed a maximum on the number of students in any class in Ontario. There is not even a cap on the average class size in each school." In fact, it is the average of each amalgamated school board that the government has capped. In other words, class size will not be uniform throughout the province, in specific schools, or school boards. There is some inconsistency in the official logic: How can class sizes be reduced while teachers are being laid off? A genuine commitment to reducing class sizes would require both funding and material-physical resources, but the government has not made a commitment to re-invest any educational savings to achieve this goal. There should be some concern that the Minister of Education will use the power to set class sizes as a way of bypassing workload issues and addressing staffing situations in schools without necessarily hiring new teachers. At the heart of this concern is the discretionary use of power, which may or may not be informed with knowledge of the practicalities of teaching in schools and classroom settings.

Equity means sharing power. Under current government policy, Bill 160 affirms parental voice in the administration of school. Alongside other government policies, the bill officially wrests power from school boards into the hands of trustees, and it makes school councils mandatory. School councils can *advise* school principals on matters such as curriculum changes, setting budget priorities, responding to province-wide testing results, and establishing the code of student conduct. Bearing this in mind, important questions remain unanswered. What are the rules governing the operation of school councils? Whose interests are being served? Are all parents duly informed about these councils? Are there variations of parental involvement that must take into account local demographics and the dynamics of social difference (e.g., class, race, ethnicity, and gender)? Does volunteering for school councils make for the effective participation of diverse social groups? What are the limits to the work of school councils? Whose interests or agendas are served by the current transfer of power to school councils? As already pointed out, the current discourse of parental voice in schools is skewed to protect certain interests, the status quo. Local communities will need to be vigilant if they are to ensure that school councils do not set the stage for U.S.-style charter schools that receive public money but are run privately (Chamberlain, 1998).

In addition to the government initiatives on school councils, moves have also been made to develop policy around school, family, and community partnerships. As noted by Kenway (1995), these initiatives are developed on the premise that restructuring and marketization will help to place parents and community as important new stakeholders in education. At first glance this would seem to integrate community knowledge and experience into schools. Furthermore, the advisory role of parents would appear to present them with new responsibilities or abilities to monitor and influence schooling with respect to greater accountability. Some concerns with these initiatives remain, however. First, the decision-making potential of these positions has not been clearly set out, and second, as noted by Dehli (1996) and Martell (1995), parental advisors will probably be less accountable than democratically elected trustees.

However, of greatest concern in relation to family and community partnerships is the direction that these initiatives will take without the added influence of antiracist, inclusive practices. At the heart of this concern is the "privileged paralysis" displayed by the public as human rights and other social justice initiatives were cut under the banner of "freeing market conditions." There is a consistent refrain in public discourse that suggests that too much time has already been spent on "marginal" matters such as heritage language courses and race relations. In the present atmosphere, market-based initiatives that encourage parental choice, power-sharing, and coalitions between pro-market progressives will probably continue to oppress and suppress voices that exist on the margins while asserting that it is again time for the majority to gain more power in schooling (Dehli, 1996).

Noting the problems associated with the encroachment of market forces into schooling, a critical analysis reveals that a dangerous or damaging reality exists alongside every possible benefit. In these times when the marketization of education seems almost to be a foregone conclusion, it is crucial that all models of school reform take equity issues into consideration. If the market is to become the new model on which schools are organized, steps must be taken to ensure that marginalized and minority students do not continue to fall through the cracks of the system and that they are afforded a real chance in the structure of the new regime. Of course, in regard to the political and economic motivations behind these reforms, a case could certainly be made to suggest that inclusive measures would be cost-effective in the long run (e.g., keeping students in school will promote the development of an educated work force, etc.), but this is not our project. Inclusive schooling must be seen as an indispensable voice to be developed alongside all educational reforms, not just those based on the market.

As educational reforms carry the potential to reshape definitions of Canadian identity, we must make efforts to ensure that this identity is based on a model that works toward equity and social justice for all. We believe that educational reform policy is best informed through a critical reading of actual classroom practices (e.g., questions of curricula, pedagogy, and instruction). We are interested in how schooling might be moved beyond its present Euro-Canadian cultural, economic, and political grid. To these ends, we begin from an understanding that actual classroom practices must be a starting point for developing policy. Rather than relying on policy and theory to inform our reading of school improvement, we develop our theoretical framework form within a working study of actual schooling practice. This work asserts that if we are truly to engage all our youth and not only those best able to take advantage of the system, we must ensure that all students are centered in their schooling experience. Crucial to that vision is a commitment to ensure that the environment, culture and organizational life of schooling reflects the complex and diverse make-up of student populations. Inclusivity is fundamental to positive and effective school reform, as it not only enhances the learning process, but it also helps students to develop a sense both of self and of community. This is our argument and rationale for inclusivity at a time when market models of education would seek to reduce education to issues of money management and the bottom line.

Discussion

In a democratic society, individual choice may be lauded, but having choice in educational options can mean many things and be implemented in multiple ways. One way is to insist on a form of choice that satisfies narrow, parochial, and self-centered interests. This is the kind of choice that allows only a segment of society to meet its wishes without due regard for the wider public good. Choice in the marketplace is a question of power and resources. An educational agenda that heralds choice in a competitive marketplace has the possibility of ensuring that the most wealthy can meet their wants and desires while the least advantaged struggle with their needs. Often when people of privilege demand choice in schooling, they speak in the context of private schools. On the other hand, when the poor and disadvantaged call for alternative schooling to meet the needs of children, they do so in the context of concern about continuing differential schooling outcomes for youth and a desire for equity and justice.

Of similar interest are how right-leaning governments co-opt the progressive discursive critique of public schools by using racially disadvantaged groups to serve their conservative political interests. For example, when poor, racial minority parents, students, and educators criticize mainstream schools for their inability to meet the needs of all students, a Conservative government may easily identify with such criticism to further its own political agenda. The government may use the opportunity to further its agenda of moving from public to private schooling. In other words, although voices may appear to share similar concerns, political agendas may be radically different. The Harris government is interested in wresting power from schools and school boards in order to define the direction, form, and content of schooling for the population. The question is how do we build a common view of educational justice and help transform the school system?

We affirm the position that race, gender, class, and sexuality are consequential in the schooling experiences of all youth. Race and other forms of difference implicate schooling in powerful ways. Further, race, class, gender, and sexuality are not absolute concepts of difference. These concepts or categories are not separate, bounded identities, mutually exclusive of one another. They are not deterministic of character, behavior, and fixed identity. In rethinking schooling and education in Euro-American contexts, educators may work with these categories in an integrative approach. This may help promote community cohesion and advance the cause of destabilizing or disrupting the real interest-group politics promoted by those who defend the current status quo (E. Price, personal communication, 1998). This is the essence of an integrative, inclusive, and antiracist approach to schooling. Definite political interests have historically shaped and continue to sustain the status quo. Rupturing the system requires a fundamental structural change that can be made through an antiracist and equity agenda.

As argued elsewhere (Dei, 1996; 2000), an antiracist discursive framework interrogates how local communities (e.g., parents, families, students and educators) interact with and in the institutional structures of schooling. Although conventional examinations of these issues are conducted through the lens of power and hierarchy, the antiracist framework challenges the relegation of *other* knowledge, voices, experiences, and histories to unseen, undesirable, and discarded spaces. Moreover, antiracism moves beyond a simple acknowledgment of oppression to an open challenge of White privilege and its accompanying rationale for dominance. It also upholds the power of resistance and agency as embedded in all sites of social oppression. Furthermore, an antiracism discursive framework acknowledges the role of the educational system in the production and reproduction of racial, class, and gender inequality in society. It acknowledges the need to address difference and diversity by developing a system that is responsive to the needs of all its members. It also decries the marginalization of certain voices in society, as well as the failure to incorporate the knowledge and experience of subordinate groups into the educational mainstream.

In contrast to present educational policy, an integrative antiracist agenda deals with disparities of power and long-term systemic or structural change rather than remedial patchwork efforts that seek to appreciate, celebrate, or tolerate difference and diversity. Further, an integrative approach sees social relations as a fundamentally antagonistic, unequal, and contradictory associations between dominant and subordinate groups: an essentially inequitable competition in the sense that groups are positioned differently in terms of domination and subordination. Myriad histories and experiences, as well as social, cultural, and economic conditions produce social diversity. To address inequality and to deal with the dynamics of social difference (race, class, gender, and sexuality), efforts should be directed toward removing structural disadvantage.

Since 1995 we and a number of graduate students at the Ontario Institute for Studies in Education of the University of Toronto (OISE/UT) have been examining methods through which exemplary inclusive practices can be employed to integrate antiracism in educational reform. Through the use of in-depth interviews, focus groups, and workshops, this three-year, SSHRC-funded investigation has obtained site-specific ethnographic information on a variety of initiatives and practices affecting student achievement, as they arose in schools, homes, families, and community-based educational sites. Our research focused on several key factors in student achievement: the ways community and home-based initiatives empower minority youth through the teaching of rights, responsibility, and advocacy; how non-hegemonic cultural capital is produced in the home, and how these elements might be brought into mainstream schooling; and the inclusion of community voices and concerns into the mainstream through school councils and other practices.

With these foci, Dei (with Broomfield et al., 1996) has highlighted certain areas that are highly relevant for attention in the task of inclusive schooling. We believe these are important areas for genuine reform to focus on as part of the search for meaningful educational change. In accordance with the findings of this research, we use five interactive criteria that measure the strength and overall efficacy of inclusive programs and initiatives of educational reform: (a) representation; (b) language integration; (c) school, family, and community partnerships; (d) cooperative education; and (e) equity, values, and access in education. In general, these domains reflect many of the guidelines used by Schorr (1997) to frame successful educational initiatives.

As critical educational researchers, we see these inclusive domains as directly oppositional to the themes of merit, individualism, and competition that are played out in the reforms presently sweeping education in Ontario. Unlike the framers of these reforms, we cannot afford to turn a blind eye to the realities of inequity and social difference as they relate to schooling. Schools are not neutral; they have a crucial role to play in the task of addressing the challenges and opportunities posed and created by diversity and difference. The complexities of modern society call for progressive educational strategies that are multifaceted, complex, and yet interdependent. Schooling reform must be placed in this context because local communities are evolving fast, and traditional pedagogical, educational, and institutional measures are no longer appropriate. We conclude our critique of the present reforms by introducing these inclusive criteria. We use these domains to illustrate the structure and ways well-informed, practical change might develop.

The domain of *representation* both observes and moves beyond Schorr's (1997) call to view children in relation to their families. Entrenched in the domain of representation are several subsets – visual, knowledge, and staff representation – each working to promote a connection between the student and his or her environment; each working to see students not as single entities, devoid of culture and history, but as dynamic, multifaceted actors who are constituted through their experiences. As part of an initiative toward educational reform, these domains must be approached and implemented jointly so as not to deny or dilute their interactive and interrelated natures.

Visual representation refers to the need for students to see themselves represented and reflected in the physical structures of the school and classroom. Educational change that allows all students to promote their culture actively in their school environment strengthens ethnic identity and cohesion by offering a greater and sustained connection with school cultures. *Knowledge representation* promotes learning about other cultures, histories, and experiences through a deep exploration of their origins and a validation of differences. Compared with visual representation, this subdomain goes beyond commitment to, and valuing of, different knowledge and experience. Here diversity is seen as an invaluable asset to be investigated and embodied in the essential make-up of the system. Knowledge representation is one way the experience and cultural knowledge of oppressed people may be validated, either through content (i.e., promoting access to other forms of knowledge and experience) or through cultural form (i.e., the visual representation of diversity through art, culture, etc.). *Staff representation* includes those practices that encourage and actively strive to diversify the teaching and administrative staff in order to deal with power-sharing and employment equity. Educational change should promote equitable hiring practices by recruiting teachers from various ethno-racial backgrounds. The practice serves to validate, endorse, and establish the relationship between the diversity of world views, the multiplicity of school culture, and student success. Educational policy should mandate schools to reflect these myriad forms of representations in their practices. For example, curriculum reform should promote multiple knowledge values, and the hiring practices of schools could seek out a diverse teaching staff that would help serve the needs of a wide student body.

With respect to *language integration*, educational research has shown language maintenance to be a fundamental indicator of ethnic identity, as well as an important resource through which learning outcomes can be enhanced. The domain of language integration functions in Schorr's (1997) assertion that successful strategies must have a long-term, preventive function capable of evolving over time. At the heart of this domain is the motivation to see multiple languages brought into the center of curricula, a move that would establish language maintenance as a fundamental aspect of inclusive practice by acknowledging difference and diversity in student populations. Through the use of ESL programs and other language resources, the educational system needs to validate and promote first-language education along with English skills development. School reforms must promote language development as a starting point to change whereby both identity development and school success might be bolstered.

The integration of *school, family,* and *community partnerships* needs school structure to adapt a more cooperative and collaborative learning model. Integral to such a shift would be the creation of space for family and community involvement in schools. Such a partnership would allow members of the community to influence school practices and the delivery of education through the introduction of experiential knowledge and further alternative community-based resources. This domain occupies a dual perspective in which the family-community-school partnership manifests itself through educational collaboration and community initiative. Schools will benefit from proactive and creative community-based strategies, and community initiatives will be bolstered and supported in return. As suggested by Schorr (1997), acknowledging and engaging students and families as part of a greater community offers numerous advantages toward real inclusion and student success. Real parental and community involvement in decision-making and the incorporation of community-based knowledge in schooling are fundamental to a successful partnership and a move away from the reactive parent-community-school model. The success of reforms depends on how school administrators, teachers, students, parents, and other local community groups see themselves as part of the planning, initiation, implementation, and evaluation process.

Schorr (1997) asserts that it is crucial that a *co-operative environment* be developed between service providers and their students. By co-operative education we mean practices that promote collaborative learning between students themselves and the educational staff. This type of schooling style emphasizes communal work and de-emphasizes individual achievement. Cooperative education necessitates a validation of student knowledge, giving them a sense of partnership in the school and encouragement to succeed. Past research (Gutmann, 1987; Lieberman, 1986) suggests that not only will a child's experience of schooling influence his or her development of self-esteem and sense of personal identity, but that the environment of schooling will also develop or impede his or her feelings about issues of social commitment and responsibility. Educational systems that promote notions of personal success or failure and competition foster an individualistic environment in schooling that develops a student's sense of personal goals and achievement while devaluing the importance of community and social awareness. Gutmann contends that students display an increased engagement in education when their teachers are committed to a co-operative and collaborative approach to schooling. Reforms must enhance co-operative approaches to schooling and education by valuing different knowledges as they arise from different bodies and experiences.

The practice of equity, access, and values in education includes all strategies and practices that address issues of equity and social justice as they enhance student success and community work. Educational change should seek to introduce programs that work with a comprehensive understanding of equity and the qualitative value of justice. Beyond a critical understanding of these issues, of paramount importance is the implementation of equity programs and practices that will directly affect student participation, access to school culture, and inclusion.

Aspects of these domains are found reflected in community-based and alternative schooling initiatives all over North America. For example, Jewish day schools, African immersion schools, and antiracism educational practices all reflect aspects of these domains functioning in a specialized context. Furthermore, in the main-stream, initiatives that promote these necessary inclusive steps can be found in numerous school settings. Programs such as the Ambassador Program promote the integration of ESL students into regular school programs by pairing new students with peers in their class who are of the same racial or ethno-cultural background and who speak the same language; by acquiring books in various lan-guages, initiatives such as the Bilingual Book Project make it feasible for non-English-speaking parents to read to their children in their first language, thereby promoting parental involvement while sup-porting the philosophy that literacy is literacy in any language. Equity needs to be at the forefront of schooling reforms.

We may incorporate these domains into schooling so that all people, and in particular marginalized groups, are seen with respect to the totality of their experiences, histories, and cultures, not just with respect to their victimization and oppression. These domains may be used to challenge openly the status quo by advancing other knowledge and perceptions and moving toward critical and inclu-sive pedagogy and practice. The infusion of these inclusive domains into schooling will encourage the inclusion of previously neglected knowledge into curricula, pedagogy, and administration. It is impor-tant to note here that these methods assert that emphasis in school-ing should no longer be placed on dominant views of oppression and power. Rather, White privilege is to be both acknowledged and critiqued, while oppressed voices from within communities that have hereto existed on the margins of culture are fully reflected in the system (Bellissimo, 1996).

Conclusion

With the radical educational shifts introduced by and through *Bill 160*, new challenges are being created for everyone involved in schooling: students, teachers, parents, community workers, admin-istrators, and educators in pre-service institutions. The challenge is in how we navigate the new political, social, and economic environ-ment of education in Ontario to best serve the needs of a diverse stu-dent body. We propose that the province's new curriculum be used as a linchpin through which we may connect elements of proposed educational reform with an antiracist pedagogical approach.

The operational domains outlined here can be read as philosophies to guide educational transformation and should be incorporated into all phases of educational reform to ensure a meaningful transformation of the educational system at all levels (curriculum, pedagogy, school environment, and organization). In addressing the implications associated with the Ministry of Education and Training's new curriculum for Ontario schools, we cannot and must not ignore the importance of integrating multiple pedagogical, communicative, and instructional practices into the work of schools. In using these inclusive domains to guide educational transformation, we move beyond simplistic notions of racism in the classroom toward real and positive change.

As we move into the next millennium, schooling in North America continues to face the challenge of enhancing educational outcomes for all youth. With respect to the poorly thought-out reforms recently initiated by the conservative government in Ontario, and particularly in the light of Mike Harris' recent re-election, we present our five inclusive domains as a feasible framework by which to reconceptualize the possibilities of school reform. In this regard it is imperative that new educational paradigms be based and constructed on a recognition of the diverse, complex and multilayered nature of human experience.

We propose that the challenges facing school systems and the consequences or implications of pursuing a right-leaning educational agenda can be dealt with only through collective efforts. Communities of today are communities of differences, and the strength of a community lies in its ability to harness its differences and commonalities and work toward transformative action or change. Embarking on this collective struggle requires that as a community we begin to engage in dialogue across our differences and commonalities because political struggles organized along lines of division contain the seeds of their own demise. So as we advance in our quest for inclusive education, we must use not only a language of hope, but also a vision of hope. This vision clearly sees that meaningful educational change cannot relegate equity issues to the background. Equity must be front and center of the agenda to reform school systems to meet the needs of all youth. Dealing with diversity is not simply a challenge – it is an imperative.

Notes

[1]Unless otherwise specified, *we* is used to refer to all who read this manuscript and share in the ideas being espoused.

[2]Banking theories of education (Freire, 1990) assert that students learn in fairly linear and direct fashion. The teacher speaks, the student listens, and then uses the information provided by the teacher to move on to the next stage or concept. The student is seen as an empty vessel into which the teacher pours his or her knowledge. Within this frame, as Dei (1996) also opines, issues of social justice, power, and oppression are left entirely out of the picture.

[3]Economic reductionism is an intellectual strategy that seeks to reduce the diverse phenomena of human social and political life to wholly economic relations.

[4]Fetishism of educational institutions, or rather the imbuing of system with the human qualities of fairness, individuality, and equality that permeates the democratic market ideology.

[5]The knowledge that recent retirement statistics suggest a major teacher shortage is not much comfort to minority educators who continue to face unemployment because they are deemed unqualified.

References

Alladin, I. M. (1996). *Racism in Canadian schools*. Toronto, ON: Harcourt Brace.

Bellissimo, D. (1996). *Inclusive curriculum – A synopsis and annotated bibliography: An examination of best practices of inclusive schooling in Ontario*. Unpublished manuscript.

Brathwaite, K. & James, C. E. (Eds.). (1996). *Educating African Canadians*. Toronto, ON: Lorimer.

Chamberlain, A. (1998, May 18). Do parent councils work? *Toronto Star*.

Dehli, K. (1996). Between "market" and "state"? Engendering education change in the 1990s. *Discourse: Studies in the Cultural Politics of Education, 17*(3), 363-376.

Dehli, K. (1998). *Shopping for schools: The future of education in Ontario*. Unpublished manuscript, Department of Sociology and Equity Studies, Ontario Institute for Studies in Education of the University of Toronto (OISE/UT).

Dehli, K. (with Januario, I.) (1994). *Parent activism and school reform in Toronto*. Toronto, ON: Report to the Ontario Ministry of education and Training.

Dei, G. J. S. (1996). *Anti-racism education: Theory and practice*. Halifax, NS: Fernwood.

Dei, G. J. S. (1999). Knowledge and politics of social change: The implications of anti-racism. *British Journal of Sociology of Education 20* (3), 395-409.

Dei, G. J. S. (2000). Towards an anti-racism discursive framework. In G. J. S. Dei & A. Calliste (eds.), *Power, knowledge and anti-racism education: A critical reader* (pp. 23-40). Halifax, NS: Fernwood Publishing.

Dei, G.J.S. (with Broomfield, P., Castagna, M., James, M., Mazzuca, J. & McIsaac, E.) (1996). *Unpacking what works: A critical examination of "best practices" of inclusive schooling in Ontario.* Project funded under the Transfer Grant from the Ontario Ministry of Education and Training to the Ontario Institute for Studies in Education of the University of Toronto.

Dei, G. J. S., Mazzuca, I., McIsaac, E. & Zine, J. (1997). *Reconstructing "drop-out": A critical ethnography of the dynamics of Black students' disengagement from school.* Toronto, ON: University of Toronto Press.

Dei, G. J. S., James, I. M., James-Wilson, S., Karumanchery, L. & Zine, J. (2000). *Removing the margins: The challenges and possibilities of inclusive schooling.* Toronto, ON: Canadian Scholars' Press.

Fine, M. (1991). *Framing dropouts: Notes on the politics of urban high schools.* New York: SUNY Press.

Freire, P. (1990). *Pedagogy of the oppressed.* New York: Continuum.

Fullan, F. & Hannay, L. (1998). Assessing strategies: Good reform/bad reform. *Orbit, 29*(1), 7-9.

Gutmann, A. (1987). *Democratic education.* Princeton, NJ: Princeton University Press.

Hatcher, R. (1998). Social justice and the politics of school effectiveness and improvement. *British Race, Ethnicity and Education 1*(2), 267-289.

Henry, F. & Tator, C. (1994). The ideology of racism: "Democratic racism." *Canadian Ethnic Studies, 26*(2), 1-14.

Jones, P. W. (1997). The World Bank and the literacy question: Orthodoxy, heresy and ideology. *British International Review of Education, 43*(4), 367-375.

Kenway, I. (1995, September). *The marketization of education: Mapping the contours of a feminist perspective.* Paper presented to the British Education Research Association, Bath.

Lieberman, M. (1986). *Beyond public education.* New York: Praeger.

Martell, G. (1995). *A new education politics: Bob Rae's legacy and the response of the Ontario Secondary School Teachers' Federation.* Toronto, ON: Lorimer.

Micklethwait, I. & Wooldridge, A. (1996). *The witch doctors: Making sense of management gurus.* New York: Times Books, Random House.

Schorr, L. (1997). *Common purpose: Strengthening families and neighborhoods to rebuild America.* New York: Doubleday, Anahur.

Solomon, P. & Levine-Rasky, C. (1994). *Accommodation and resistance: Educators' responses to multicultural education. Report to the Canadian Heritage.* North York, ON: York University.

Tozer, C. (1998, May 18). Misleading parents on class sizes. *Toronto Star.*

Whitty, G., Edwards, T. & Gewirtz, S. (1993). *Specialization and choice in urban education: The city technology college experiment.* London and New York: Routledge.

Chapter 9
The Struggle for Equity, Diversity, and Social Justice in Teacher Education

R. Patrick Solomon and Andrew M.A. Allen

Introduction

[M]ost teacher education programs have been, and continue to be, entirely removed from a vision and a set of practices dedicated to the fostering of critical democracy and social justice. (Giroux & McLaren, 1986, p. 227)

Giroux and McLaren's damning critique of teacher education links teacher preparation to the school's function in reproducing the inequities pervasive in contemporary post-industrial societies. Their critique is still timely in the frenzy of school reform movements, and lays a foundation for teacher educators to re-examine ways to prepare the next generation of teachers to work for equity, democracy, and social justice in increasingly diverse North American societies. The ongoing efforts by government and "reform entrepreneurs" to centralize the control of public education have made schools politically charged and hotly contested terrains. Such a politicization of schooling, with vested interest groups contesting curriculum and pedagogy, student evaluation, extra-curricular supervision, teachers' workload, and teacher testing and evaluation, has serious implications for teacher education.

Over the past few decades, progressive teacher educators such as Lisa Delpit, Christine Sleeter, Kenneth Zeichner, Deborah Britzman, Henry Giroux, and Peter McLaren have explored the pedagogy and politics of preparing teachers for a democratic society; a society that claims to value and practise equity, social justice, and diversity. Urban classrooms across North America now reflect a range of social and cultural differences that include race, ethnicity, religion, social class, sexual orientation, and exceptionalities. The biggest challenge facing teacher educators today becomes: how do we prepare teachers to work equitably and democratically with diversity? More specifically, what are the challenges of doing field-based pre-service teacher education where pedagogy and politics are often in conflict?

Theoretical and Conceptual Issues

A review of the literature points to the role of the teacher and its centrality in promoting and maintaining equity and social justice in a democratic society. In their article, "Education, teacher development and the struggle for democracy," Hartnett and Carr (1995) assert that teachers need to be critically reflective in their professional roles because:

> *Society is dependent upon the quality of their [teachers'] judgements, values, knowledge and sensitivities, in particular in social contexts, to negotiate acceptable solutions to issues of authority in education; to sustain the development of democratic values in the wider society; and to creating a social environment in which children can deliberate about, and reflect critically upon, the nature of the good life and the good society. They are a critical pivot between the state, parental power, institutional power and the development of democratic values and attitudes in each new generation. (p. 43)*

Yet, Giroux and McLaren (1986) argue that traditional teacher education programs do little to foster critical democracy and social justice in schools and the larger society. Instead, they play the role of service institutions preparing students with the technical expertise and the appropriate discipline to fit into the machinery of corporate structures. Schools do not engage in transformative or emancipatory acts, they claim. Giroux and McLaren therefore urge teacher educators to move beyond reproducing society and its norms, values, and ways of operating, and "adopt a more critical role of challenging the social order so as to develop and advocate its democratic imperatives" (p. 224).

Too often, Giroux and McLaren argue, teacher candidates in the theoretical dimension of their programs develop preconceptions of schools as one-dimensional in their rules and regularities, void of the social, cultural, and political contexts of institutional life. When they enter their practicum or fieldwork site, candidates are rudely awakened by the contradictions, ambiguities, and constant struggles for dominance among competing interest groups. For prospective teachers to get deeper insights into these factors that impact contemporary schooling, Giroux and McLaren suggest that teacher education scholarship must address the social construction of schooling; teachers must be educated to become "transformative intellectuals" so that they may "treat students as critical agents, question how knowledge is produced and distributed, utilize dialogue, and make knowledge meaningful, critical, and ultimately emancipatory" (p. 215). Those are the essentials of democratic schooling and critical citizenship.

But in a society that is becoming increasingly diverse, especially in its racial, ethnic, cultural, social class, and sexual orientation, the challenges of preparing a democratic environment for students grow even greater. To provide democratic conditions for their students, Hartnett and Carr suggest that teachers need to start grappling with complex moral and political issues at the initial stages of learning to teach. An essential starting point should be to examine the limitations of their own education and experiences, and question the way these may negatively affect other groups in society. Again, Hartnett and Carr (1995) were very specific in the ways that minority groups' cultural values and differences are often perceived as deficits and translated into school failure. But such self-interrogation has proven problematic for some teachers because their conservative belief system and world views are often in conflict with more progressive views on diversity and social difference (Ahlquist, 1992; Sleeter, 1992a; Tatum, 1992). According to Britzman (1991), pre-service teachers are embodied in such social categories as race, class, and gender in ways so crucial to their identities that interrogating such markers becomes problematic for them.

Despite these obstacles to self- and professional development, Liston and Zeichner (1990) and Zeichner (1993) support the view that teacher educators must continue to provide the opportunity for prospective teachers to deconstruct those beliefs that hinder the delivery of democratic education. Zeichner (1996, p. 210) concludes, "In societies that profess to be democratic, teacher educators are morally obligated to attend to the social-reconstructionist dimension of teaching practice despite any practice difficulties in doing so." But the achievement of democratic values in teacher education and teaching faces many challenges as pre-service teachers move from university-based theorizing to field-based, practicum classrooms.

First, state dictatorial intervention into public schooling in many Western democracies has imposed a new social order. Their new policies on the schooling process have dictated the restructuring of the curriculum, pedagogy, and the assessment of student learning. With such an imposition, the conditions of teachers' work have become rather restrictive. Hartnett and Carr (1995) observe:

> [T]hese governments have reduced the capacity of classroom teachers to play an active role in the creation of a more open system of schooling and a properly democratic society, and move them towards the role

of operatives in a system which is managed centrally by politicians and their officials. (p. 46)

Such an undemocratic reduction of the teacher's role to merely operational or technical, devoid of social or political contexts, has been well documented in the research literature (Apple & Weis, 1983; Hartnett & Carr, 1995; Davis, 2000; McLaren, 1998; McNeil, 2000). This technicist conception of schooling provides limited opportunities for teachers to integrate into their curriculum and pedagogy their own insights, perspectives, and lived experiences. This restricted role in the schooling process is perceived to subvert the development of demo-cratic forms of education. For teacher candidates, learning to teach in such restrictive environments is essentially dis-empowering. Further, the discontinuity of equity and social justice principles from theory to classroom practice is often frustrating (Grant & Zozakiewicz, 1995; Menter, 1989; Solomon, 2000).

Second, the social and political contexts of field-based teacher education severely restrict the extent to which teacher candidates can engage in reflective, critical, and enquiring practice. Menter's (1989) and Grant and Zozakiewicz's (1995) studies of candidates in practicum schools are insightful in exposing how the maintenance of the "status quo" within school cultures impedes the practice of democracy. Menter's analysis of the traditional apprenticeship approach to teacher education provides the picture of the triad: the candidate, the co-operating teacher, and the practicum supervisor (from the teacher education faculty) locked in a relationship charac-terized by "stasis." The culture of the school and its power relations socialize members of this triad into ways of behaving so that con-flicts and confrontations are minimized or avoided altogether. Menter observes, "All members of the triad seek to minimize, coun-teract or negate any influence or innovation which might upset the stability of the triad" (p. 470).

In such contexts, teaching innovations such as antiracism and antisexism that address equity, social justice, and democratic issues were perceived as tension-generating and were likely to upset the social relationships between candidates and their conservative men-tor teachers. Consequently, progressive pedagogical strategies learned in teacher education theory are often not translated into classroom practice. The avoidance of controversial issues, and an uncritical reflection on school and societal practices exposed a rather undemocratic learning environment for these candidates, as well as the students with whom they work.

The third factor that relates to the field-based development of teacher candidates is the extent to which their co-operating or mentor teachers at practicum sites are aware of, and are committed to equity and social justice. Research conducted in the U.K. (Nehaul, 1996; Troyna, 1994; Troyna & Williams, 1986), the U.S.A. (Cross, 1999; Sleeter, 1992b), and Canada (Henry, Tator, Mattis & Rees, 1995; Klassen & Carr, 1997; Solomon & Levine-Rasky, 1996) have demonstrated a range of teacher attitudes, perspectives, and classroom practices when working with social difference and diversity as they relate to race, ethnicity, culture, language, and immigrant status. In Troyna and Williams' (1986) British study, for example, teachers and other critics of progressive education perceived the introduction of antiracism policies into schools as a destruction of the traditional "color-blind" education; policies that threatened the autonomy of teachers and students (p. 97). In the Canadian context, Solomon and Levine-Rasky's (1996) research on teacher perspectives of multicultural and antiracism education uncovered a wide variation in attitudes, perspectives, and practices. Attitudes favored a more benevolent, harmonious brand of multiculturalism rather than a critical integration of culture into the mainstream curriculum. Moreover, teachers tended to reject the study of race, racism, and antiracism because they perceived it to be confrontational and antagonistic; it "stirs up the pot" (p. 29).

The research on educators' responses to other forms of social difference has revealed similar sentiments. For example, there was a strong tendency for teachers and the institutional culture of the school to resist the inclusion of students with disability in the regular classroom (Bunch, Lupart & Brown, 1997; Bunch & Valeo, 1997). Bunch points out that while it was no longer politically expedient for educators to separate other social groups on the basis of race, gender, language, or culture, students with disabilities are still being arbitrarily and artificially separated on the basis of learning differences (Bunch, 1999, p. 1).

Finally, a dimension of social difference that has generated much tension and anxiety among educators in contemporary schooling is that of sexual orientation. Epstein's (1998) work, *Parent night will never be the same: Lesbian families challenge the public school system*, addresses the issues of homophobia and heterosexism. Sears' (1994) extensive studies of educators and lesbian, gay, and bisexual families in the United States address the broader issues of social justice and democratic schooling for all. Here, he argues:

> *[T]he hidden curriculum of school fosters conformity and passivity while seldom encouraging critical thinking, ethical behavior, and civic courage....Within this environment, controversial ideas and individual differences are seldom welcomed. The discussion of homosexuality, the treatment of lesbian, gay and bisexual students, and the restrictive definition of family are some of the most glaring examples. (p. 150)*

This review brings together three strands in the research literature with the potential to have significant impact on teacher education for equity and social justice. State imposition of a standardized curriculum, the conservative social and political culture of schools, and teachers' individual perspectives and attitudes toward social difference all appear to conspire against the preparation of teachers for a democratic society. In the sections that follow we describe the research setting and present teacher candidates' lived experiences in these learning environments. The final section offers suggestions for creating a more equitable and democratic learning environment for the teachers of tomorrow.

Research Setting and Methodology

The study was conducted in the year 2000 with participants of a pre-service teacher education program at an urban Ontario university. This program was developed in 1994 to promote equity, social justice, and diversity issues in teacher education and teaching. More specifically, the program's objectives were to:

- provide an environment in which teacher candidates [TCs] of various social identities (race, ethnicity, gender, sexual orientation, exceptionality, social class, etc.) have extended opportunities to develop teaching competencies and build professional relationships in a collaborative manner;

- integrate issues of equity, social justice, and diversity into the curriculum and pedagogy of teacher education scholarship and the classrooms of practicum schools; and

- develop collaboration among practicum school staff, representatives of community organizations, teacher candidates, and their teacher educators, forming a community of learners.

Candidates admitted to the one-year, post-baccalaureate B.Ed. program that prepares teachers for the primary-junior classroom (kindergarten to grade 6) reflected, to some extent, the diversity in the larger urban population. The candidates of color in the cohort being studied were primarily of African and Asian heritages, with those of African descent coming from the Caribbean, parts of the

U.S., and Canada. Those of Asian descent originated from South Asia (India and Pakistan), East Asia (Japan, China, Korea), and Southeast Asia (Philippines, Vietnam). White candidates were of British, French, Italian, and other Eastern European heritages. While most candidates were Canadian-born, a number of candidates were immigrants and were schooled to varying degrees in their country of origin before migrating to Canada.

The teacher education program was comprised of the following courses: Models and Foundations of Education, Human Development and Socialization, Communication and the Education Process, and a more practical introduction to the curriculum and schooling process. Issues of equity and social justice were integrated into all aspects of the program, from theoretical formulations in the university coursework to its practical applications in field-based practica. The following is a description of practica as stated in the Faculty of Education Preservice Teacher Education Handbook, 1999-2000:

> *These practica serve several purposes. In addition to providing direct experience and an opportunity to apply newly acquired skills and knowledge, the practica serve as a major source of curriculum in the sense that they bring candidates face to face with concrete situations. These situations are frequently used as the basis for seminars held at the university, which are associated with the practicum. The underlying assumptions of this approach are that teaching can be considered as a form of problem solving and that candidates learn best through ongoing experiences which allow them to understand and master their environment.(p. 36)*

Candidates spent over 60% of their teacher education in practicum settings. For the first semester they spent the opening week observing the teaching-learning process. This was followed by two days per week of learning to teach in their practicum schools culminating in a teaching block of two weeks. In the second semester this process was repeated with an additional three-week teaching block. This second experience was usually in another division in another school setting.

The supervision, mentorship, and evaluation of candidates in their practicum setting were the responsibilities of a team of collaborating professionals. The candidate was assigned to a host teacher [HT] (often known as an associate, co-operating, or mentor teacher in other programs) whose role, among other duties, was to be a mentor, providing ongoing modelling of effective teaching. (In this chapter the terms "host teacher" and "mentor teacher" will be used interchangeably.) More importantly for this study, the HT's role was also "to assist candidates to integrate theory and practice" (Faculty Handbook, p. 40). The Adjunct Professor [AP] was an experienced member of the teaching staff at the practicum site and served as a liaison with the University, provided in-school support for candidates, conducted seminars, and evaluated candidates' teaching. The Course Directors [CDs] from the University were ultimately responsible for the candidates' placement, support, and evaluation. They also facilitated the practicum seminars that brought together issues of theory and practice.

Data for this study came from: individuals and focus group interviews with teacher candidates who volunteered for the study; electronic mail responses to research questions placed in the program's on-line conference folder (this was for the convenience of those who could not attend the face-to-face interviews); and a practicum supervisor's documented observations in practicum schools. Following the final teaching experience, candidates were invited to discuss in a focus group or by electronic mail, ways in which their school's understanding and implementation of the new Ontario curriculum (written and unwritten) may have impacted their learning to teach for equity and diversity. The interviews were audio taped, transcribed, and triangulated with electronic responses and practicum supervisors' observation notes. The triangulation of data is an analytical process to determine the extent to which data collected by different approaches in different settings reveal similar (or different) insights. From the categories generated from these data sources, we were able to develop some salient themes. In making generalizations about the data, we grounded our findings in excerpts from interviews, electronic responses, and field notes from a supervisor's observations. In the findings that follow, all candidate names and practicum schools are pseudonyms.

Findings

From an analysis of the data emerged three interrelated themes: teacher candidates' perception of the discontinuity of educational and social theory from the teacher education curriculum to practicum classrooms; the culture and power relations within schools and the "stasis" or "silences" they create in candidates' practicum classrooms; and the strategies candidates employ to create spaces for themselves to engage in a pedagogy of equity, diversity, and social justice. An underlying theme of these findings is the state imposition of a standardized curriculum, and teachers' contradictory political and pedagogical responses to its implementation. Candidates' own interpretation of the situation based on their prior experiences within schools and their newly acquired theoretical knowledge of equity, diversity, and social justice created some healthy tensions that have the potential to democratize the schooling process. Issues emerging from the study raise some important questions about teacher education and ways it may be transformed to meet the needs of a democratic society.

Theory-practice Relationship

The teacher candidates in this study expressed strong views about the discontinuity they experienced in relating the theory of their university curriculum to the expectations in their practicum classroom. Such theory and practicum seminar courses encouraged and prepared candidates to confront and contest the inequities they encounter in school settings and the society at large. This study of schooling in its social context analyzed the interaction of social, political, and economic structures that marginalize groups deemed socially different because of their race, ethnicity, social class, sexual orientation, gender, and exceptionality. This curriculum then provided the environment for candidates to develop a critical reflective practice that is inclusive and has the potential to transform classrooms, making them more equitable for marginalized groups.

While many schools and their teachers provided an equity-conscious learning environment for candidates to implement an equity and social justice agenda, this study focused on the more undemocratic practices in the schooling process. The candidates were often assigned to practice teach in classrooms where participating mentors and school staff members held conservative political views, and were openly unsupportive of interrogating school curriculum and pedagogy. One candidate explained:

> There is a gap between theory and practice. I felt that what we learned in theory and practice were both terrific, but somehow they were never connected. I never used theory in my practicum classroom; when I tried to use it I was discouraged because I wasn't sticking to the [new] curriculum.

As this teacher candidate has indicated, she experienced ambivalence in accepting that learning to teach in her practicum school meant a strict adherence to the formal curriculum and the established teaching norms of that institution. She reported further that in her classroom placement, her host teacher often expressed the perception that equity and diversity issues were a distraction from the standardized curriculum and were of little practical value to the realities of the classroom. At times, as the excerpt below revealed, candidates felt that school staff actively discouraged them from going beyond what was outlined in the formal curriculum, and they received negative feedback to the more critical approaches to their teaching:

> I was ridiculed for focusing on [equity issues]. That's the problem I had in my school. They were saying, "I think you're focusing way too much on equity and are not so much on the curriculum." That's why I had to step back. I was thinking, "Okay, I'm not going in the right direction for that [host] teacher." Everything was for that teacher and what she was expecting....I didn't feel comfortable as a student in the Urban Diversity Program to take these [equity] issues into practice because I didn't feel we were supported [by the host teacher].

The gap between educational theory taken up in teacher education and its application in "real schools" has been an ongoing source of contention for theoreticians and teacher practitioners alike (Entwistle, 1996; Zeichner, 1996). Entwistle is quite insightful in identifying some practitioners' misconceptions about theory developed in privileged utopian contexts that bear little resemblance to the real classrooms in which they work (p. 20). He therefore urges teachers to think about theory more in terms of a guide or framework to reflect upon their practice. Such reflections may lead to more insightful, morally sensitive approaches to teaching. We support the notion that reflective teaching provides the opportunity for practitioners to relate educational theory to their own classroom context and open up spaces of empowerment to creatively modify theory to reflect their experiences, or develop new and more critical theories that more accurately reflect their reality. Zeichner's (1996) work on the reflective practitioner confirms that they are more responsive to working with ideas and concepts that are generated within their contexts, and emerge from their experiences, expertise and practices.

As teacher educators, we contend that beginning teachers need some form of theoretical lenses to frame, understand, and guide pedagogical practices. The preparation to work for equity, diversity, and social justice in democratic classrooms must therefore expose them to critical social theory. We believe that providing learning environments that nurture a dialogic relationship between theory and practice is an essential starting point in progressive teacher education. A crucial dimension of the field-based component of learning to teach in this program was the practicum seminar. Here, candidates were scheduled the time and space to reflect upon and discuss the theory-practice relationship as they experienced it in their practicum classrooms. As Entwistle (1996, p. 27) concludes, "The continuous process of interrogating our practice with theory and refining our theory in the crucible of practice is the condition of our growth as both theorists and practitioners."

In general, candidates surmised, some school staff members were sceptical about the Faculty of Education curriculum focus. Teachers' claims of curricular overload and perception of university theorizing of equity and diversity issues as "the fantasy world" with little or no application to the "real world" of the lean [standardized] classroom curriculum contradicted the theoretical component of the teacher education program. They felt that these "soft" curriculum issues were no longer relevant in the current climate of school reform and were taught at the university by "professors" who were completely detached from actual classroom practice. Adjunct professors and host teachers were perceived by their candidates to be in conflict with teacher education program objectives and created this sense of discontinuity of educational ideas and philosophy. In a group discussion, candidates reconstructed their mentors' beliefs and attitudes toward the teacher education curriculum in statements such as "This [classroom teaching] is the real world; that [teacher education for equity and diversity] is fantasy." "That doesn't work in the real world." One candidate concludes: "It felt as though we were going to the university in a fantasy world and then we went to the real world [practicum schools] to teach, leaving all the theory behind." The discontinuity from university theorizing about the teaching-learning process to practical application in classrooms limited the extent to which candidates could implement a transformative equity and social justice agenda.

Delpit (1995) draws on John Dewey's emphasis of the relationship between theory and practice in teacher education and urges educators to create a learning environment where the diversity of teachers' voices, experiences, and prior knowledge is made to inform their classroom practice. The failure to link these experiences to theoretical constructs will likely result in "intellectual subserviency," that is, making teachers targets and operatives for the state, business, and other vested interest groups in education.

The findings of the study indicate that teacher educators who provided the opportunity for candidates to link prior knowledge and experience to pedagogical theories were often perceived by teacher practitioners as "theory bound" and who "have not really been out there [in the field], but only go by what they learn from books," a sentiment documented in Delpit's research (1995, p. 125).[1] Giroux and McLaren (1986) insist that teacher education curriculum use critical social theory to interrogate the educational traditions and practices pervasive in schools. It is only with such examination that we can uncover whose interests are being served by schools and what groups are being marginalized. The unresolved issue for teacher educators becomes: how do they resolve the ambiguities created by working in settings where the standardized curriculum displaces education for democracy and social justice? We will revisit this issue later.

Teaching Practice "Stasis"

Within the social system of the school, the power relations in classrooms are maintained through pressure to conform to the social and pedagogical structures. For example, the imposition of a standardized curriculum on teachers leads to a structure of relationship between the mentor teacher and teacher candidate that ensured "safe passage" of this formal curriculum to students. Mentors caught in this dilemma often sent ambivalent and contradictory messages: "Experiment with teaching, but stick to the prescribed curriculum." These comments indicate that mentors were cognizant of the importance of experimentation in learning to teach, but such freedom was subverted by the constraints of curriculum expectations.

For most teacher candidates, it took quite some time before they realized that they had to stick with the stated and unstated expectations and follow established teaching practices. They eventually internalized the fact that surviving the practicum meant imitating the host teacher and adhering to the school ethos. Consequently, teacher candidates developed a duality in the way they approached both the theoretical and practical components of the program:

> *Winston: I felt like I was trying to do something different from what the HT had set up in both my first and second terms. Finally I learned, I say it perhaps with tongue in cheek, but also kind of with a little bit of regret, that my role was not to confront or try and teach differently from the host teachers. My role, in order to survive was to follow what she had set up. So I realized this with great relief.*

Diedre: I think that host teachers and host schools are so focused on teaching everything laid out in the [new] curriculum, that they lose focus of the more serious issues, like gender inequities and the many different "isms" that we were taught to address during our year at the University. I do, however, believe that teachers need training on how to address these issues and integrate them into their lessons. I also believe that educators need to be reminded that the curriculum is just a guide which cannot stand alone. Maybe, then, they would begin to understand us [teacher candidates].

For candidates then, learning to teach was no longer negotiated; it had become a relationship where the veteran teacher directed and the apprentice followed without questioning authority. For instance, some host teachers would sometimes mediate the relationship between teacher candidates and the students. They often interrupted the candidate's lesson to ensure the pre-established norms of the classroom were preserved as this excerpt indicate:

I learned to read her [the HT]. I am not sure when I started doing this. Sometimes she would resort to "premeditated interruptions." She would intervene when the students were loud or energetic, or any situation like this. She would ring her bell. So that was interrupting my connection to the students.

Candidates became acutely aware of the power relationship in the classroom and quickly learned that their role was to be submissive and to imitate the host teacher. In Edward's case, for instance, he was expected to demonstrate his commitment to being in the classroom to teach despite any circumstances:

I just got to the point where the dynamics of teaching in someone else's classroom and having to dance to their tune and having double meaning coming at me all the time were disturbing. I got to the point where I literally indicated to her that I didn't really want to teach one day. But she retorted, "No, you have to teach today; you just get in there." She really pushed me. Which in some ways may have been the right thing to do. But then later, I phoned her because I was sick with a fever. And I called her to say I would not be coming in the next day. And she said, "Well, I won't be coming in either; I'm home sick. So you should show up, you should go in. You got to get back up on the horse."

The host teacher's seemingly undemocratic approach in dealing with the situation left Edward feeling disempowered and subordinated. The curriculum governed the relationship between mentor and candidate. This pressure to please mentors and evaluators resulted in "doing what the mentor does." Candidates were stripped of creativity, their lived experiences and perspectives marginalized. The candidate's classroom role became submissive:

> *I am trying to build a relationship with a person I don't know. I am placed in their classroom. It is HER (emphasis) classroom. I was constantly trying to please her. I felt a pressure to please. Another factor was that psychologically she was quite older than I was and I felt it was a kind of motherly relationship. I expected a motherly relationship where she would guide me. When I didn't get that I felt in a way rejected. The curriculum governs that relationship. On one hand you have a relationship and you have the curriculum; and on the other, you have the school-university relationship. I felt a lot of pressure to please.*

The experiences of these candidates in their practicum settings draw attention to institutional expectations and the structure of relationships among groups in these settings. Candidates yearned for a relationship with their mentors that would open doors and provide opportunities for critical, reflective practice; relationships that would create an equitable work environment for themselves, and a democratic learning environment for their students. On the contrary, they were faced with a social structure in which candidates remained marginal to the power hierarchy, and were expected to conform to, rather than interrogate the structure. Any attempt to challenge the institutional culture and practices of the school ran the risk of alienating and further disempowering them. Alienation from school staff and colleagues, closing down of the communication process, withdrawal of support and unfavorable evaluations of teaching performances were some of the potential consequences that candidates could ill afford.

To safeguard against such responses, some candidates retreated into "silence." Grant and Zozakiewicz (1995) describe such silences as "the lack of critical discussion regarding multicultural education, as it relates to social justice issues" (p. 267). Here, the authors define more elaborately the multicultural education philosophy:

> *The philosophy encompasses democratic principles such as equality, justice and equity. Cultural pluralism and the recognition and affirmation of cultural groups (i.e., race, ethnicity, gender, class, ability, sexual orientation) are key components of multicultural education. Other key components are the promotion of social justice and the development of social structural equality.*

In the next section we analyze candidates' perceptions of their mentors' often contradictory reactions to the imposed curriculum within the context of a school culture that was more conservative than reconstructionist. More important for this study is candidates' exploration of strategies that overcome the "stasis" and "silences" that limit critical, reflective practice.

From Restrictive to Liberatory Pedagogy

Teacher candidates' engagement with the pedagogy of equity and social justice depended, to a large extent, on their mentor's classroom politics and commitment to diversity. Teachers' pedagogical stance, as candidates perceived it, appeared to be located in the extent to which they have bought into the standardized curriculum, their conservatism as teachers and their level of commitment to democratic ideals. In this section, we analyze the ways candidates observed and responded to a conservative element among their mentors, as well as a more radical faction that resisted standardization in often contradictory ways. Finally, candidates disclosed their mentors' expectations of them within this new curriculum framework and revealed ways in which they created "teachable moments" for an inclusive curriculum.

In the following excerpts taken from interviews, candidates struggled to make sense of some mentor teachers' seemingly passive acceptance of a curriculum and pedagogy candidates perceived as unresponsive to equity and diversity issues.

> *Winston: When the New Democratic government was in power, it was well documented that you had to have an equity policy for school boards. But now the Conservative government has no equity policy, or at least in the curriculum, there is nothing about equity,[2] some teachers are quite happy about that because they did not want to do it in the first place. So maybe it is easier now because here is the curriculum and there is nothing about equity, and "I don't want to have to teach about it anyway." A lot of the teachers I met certainly fall into that category.*

> *Edward: I think it has to do with the perception of the teaching profession as being sort of a conservative establishment that socializes the status quo. Therefore, the people who were being drawn into education are the people who feel that it is okay, or that that [standardization and control] is right.*

Here, candidates speculated that teachers may be intrinsically a conservative group of professionals committed to status quo maintenance rather than being advocates of change. The notion of teachers as conservatives is supported in the teacher education literature

(Lortie, 1975; Sleeter, 1992a & b; Solomon & Levine-Rasky, 1996). Such a group may be predisposed to reproducing the social order rather than disrupting it. It was therefore unproblematic for this group to wait out progressive government policies (i.e., *Antiracism and Ethnocultural Equity in School Boards: Guidelines for Policy Development and Implementation,* Ontario Ministry of Education and Training [1993]) and continue "business as usual" upon the return of reductionist educational policies.

Yet, there were other teachers who did not conform to standardization and state control of the curriculum. Their reactions may well have been a political response to an education system that tries to reduce student learning to a narrowly prescribed set of expectations and outcomes. Candidates quickly learned from their mentors how the politics of resistance and superficial accountability were played out in classrooms. They recounted teachers' superficial approaches to the coverage of curriculum materials that did not reflect the experiences of the diversity of students in their classes. A specific example here is resistance to state-generated test exemplars that universalize the experiences of middle class students while marginalizing those of "the other." On the other hand, these teachers emphasized an inclusive curriculum that mainstreamed the experiences, values, and perspectives of non-dominant group students.

From these candidates' perceptions of the situation, teachers' emphasis appeared to be placed on fulfilling curriculum requirements in a very superficial way. Teachers adapted a range of formal and informal checklists to "mark off" curriculum areas taken up in class. The quantification of learning is seen to be all-important in the reporting process, be it on report cards to parents, or as an indicator to policy-makers.

These forms of teacher response to curriculum standardization and state control of schooling are also reported elsewhere in the research literature. Linda McNeil's (2000) book, *Contradictions of School Reform: Educational Costs of Standardized Testing,* is an insightful documentation of the ways teachers have responded to policymakers' attempts at standardization and accountability. Very vividly, McNeil described how teachers employed a "double-entry" strategy to comply with the official proficiency-based curriculum while continuing to teach to the "real" curriculum. This "real" curriculum being the more substantive information, the acquisition of skills, the complex content students require to function in an evolving American society. Here, McNeil provides more insights into teachers' responses and their potential impact on the teaching-learning process:

> It caused them to have to play games in front of their students, appearing to conform while attempting to teach. It trivialized the curriculum by transforming the content of school into testable pieces scarcely recognizable as components of academic subjects. (p. 215)

Other forms of teacher non-compliance documented by McNeil include non-proficiency based evaluations that better represented student learning, posting fictitious scores from proficiency-based assessment tools on their classroom doors (mainly for show) to give administration the impression that they were following district policy; and where possible, they deleted and omitted courses or units of study that could not be adapted to "the artificial simplification of the proficiencies" (p. 209).

A rather important conclusion drawn by McNeil is the "perverse effect" of legislative and controlled learning on the tradition of democracy in the public school system. Once government controls are in place, democratic governance and external critique will eventually be reduced to zero. One of the teacher candidates in our study was quite insightful in drawing conclusions similar to McNeil's about the long-term "de-democratizing" effect of the imposed curriculum:

> So pretty soon, if a teacher tries to raise issues in the class there is a possibility there that the government will then say, "You cannot cover things that are not in the curriculum. You must cover the curriculum."

Finally, how did teacher candidates respond to the various, often contradictory messages about equity and social justice that they received in their practicum schools? Initially, they were frustrated by the restrictive environment in which they tried to integrate issues of social difference into the curriculum. The following extended excerpt from a university practicum supervisor's field notes provides some insights into the experiences of one candidate:

> A fairly contentious situation has developed with a TC and her mentor teacher over the teaching of critical social issues in the class. Marion is a white female TC who has been successful so far in the program. Her new placement at Sunnyvale school has been working out well. The mentor teacher was pleased with her work and had "absolutely no complaints" when I first visited the class. However, when Marion began taking up difficult issues around race and power with the students, the teacher became uncomfortable. Marion reported that at one time, the students wanted to know why it was that the

> *two teachers in the room [she and her mentor teacher] were white and that they, the students, were all of racial minority backgrounds. They began inquiring about power and started to draw parallels between the school system and society. She said that the mentor teacher was visibly upset with the lesson at that point. After that lesson, the mentor teacher reported to the Adjunct Professor that Marion was not pulling her weight and that she had concerns about Marion's program without giving specifics. Marion talked about the experience with her study groups in our [practicum] seminars back at the university. She said that it became difficult to work with her mentor teacher [when she] started challenging her openly in front of the children. The mentor became distant and unsupportive. The relationship in the classroom became hostile and uncomfortable. Marion surmised: "She [mentor teacher] at first thought I was just like her. Initially, she said I reminded her of herself when she first started teaching. But when I started teaching about equity and she saw the things that I was doing, the type of things I wanted to discuss with the students, she must have thought, 'No, you are nothing like me.'"*

The excerpt above raises interesting issues about what constitutes acceptable curriculum discourse and how the exploration by candidates of inequities within school and society generate tension and sour relationship with mentors and potentially jeopardize their future in the teaching profession. The research of Menter (1989) in Britain and Grant and Zozakiewicz (1995) in the U.S. reveals the institution's desire to avoid discussions of contentious issues such as race and gender and maintain "silences" that will not interrogate the status quo. Candidates are discouraged from critiquing social reality as oppressive, unjust, and inequitable for some minority groups. The preferred curriculum is one that is disassociated from the lived experiences of marginalized students; a curriculum that Cross (1999) describes as "linear, mechanistic, static, singular, prescriptive, and preset" (p. 38). Issues of race, power, and privilege that predetermine and dominate the lives of minorities are expected to be "off limits" for exploration. Critical analyses of privilege, especially white privilege in Canadian society, are strategically restricted. Teachers and others in the position of power are reluctant to unpack the invisible knapsack in a racialized society (McIntosh, 1990). Instead, they unproblematically present success in school and society as meritocratic; as achievement based on ability and hard work. Such school culture poses difficult choices for equity-conscious candidates. Do they teach for social justice and risk ostracism from mentors; or do they honor the "silence" on inequities during their practicum and "wait until they get their own classrooms?" These are the issues of field-based practicum that teacher educators must address.

Despite the restrictions in moving beyond the narrowly defined curriculum, candidates committed to social justice issues were strategic in doing the necessary research and integrating this knowledge into their teaching. In the following excerpt, a candidate describes how he used the prescriptive "Columbus discovery stories" to talk about the inequities of colonization and the destruction of Aboriginal/ First Nations cultures in Canada:

> *If you stick to the [curriculum] expectations you definitely won't get the equity issues coming out, and that is the easiest thing to do. But, I am doing a little research on Christopher Columbus; I am looking in the library for different books that are written for elementary kids. None of them or very few deal with the issues of the destruction of the cultures that were here [in North America] before the colonialists landed. If the teacher is not aware of this history, they cannot bring it up. Teacher candidates in our program are aware of it and will bring it up.*

Underlying this excerpt is the responsibility that teachers, and particularly dominant group teachers and TCs like himself, have in challenging racism and helping to create schools that are more equitable and democratic for their students. Howard (1999) argues that the inner work of multicultural teaching must lead to the outer work of social transformation and that this approach must be a crucial aspect in the preparation of white teachers learning to teach in diverse settings. Because the candidates' backgrounds, experiences, socialization patterns, worldviews, etc. often leave them ill-prepared to teach in multicultural settings, teacher education programs must first encourage and promote deep introspection for TCs towards personal and professional transformation. As a result, teachers and TCs ought to become committed to larger social change and transformation, begin to question social dominance and oppression, and redress historical inaccuracies in the curriculum (Howard, 1999).

Other candidates resort to convenient occasions and "teachable moments" to integrate sensitive issues such as those of sexual orientation and homophobia into their pedagogy:

> *There seems to be a big gap between what we were learning in the faculty and what we were teaching in practicum schools about things such as homophobia and heterosexism. These are the most sensitive for some teachers. They are not used to it [these issues] as yet, although one of our teacher candidates in our school brought in the video: It's*

Elementary [3] *and we did watch it at lunchtime. It had a pretty good response from those who came to watch it. However, the consensus was that this kind of issue could not be discussed in the classroom. But, I did discuss it with my students when my HT was out of the classroom. She was away for two or three days. But, only when it came up; I didn't do it out of the blue; I just did it when the students were using [homophobic] language.*

It is ironic that candidates were often perceived as experts at social difference issues and called upon by school personnel to deal with homophobic name-calling incidents on the playground. A candidate reports, "When a student called another, 'Gay,' the teacher directed, 'You are the Urban Diversity expert; you deal with it.'"

To conclude this section, it is rather interesting that some of the pre-service teachers in this study employed similar strategies to those of their veteran colleagues in McNeil's (2000) study, in resisting curriculum standardization and restricting the schooling process to quantifiable learning of dominant group knowledge forms. Both groups of teachers, at different stages of their professional careers, have sent a strong message of equity in their pedagogy; a pedagogy that is inclusive and responsive to the needs, perspectives, and dreams of diverse peoples in Canadian society. The challenge for teacher education becomes: how do we create a learning environment where teacher candidates, their mentor teachers, and teacher educators form a learning community that will promote social justice and democracy for the next generation of Canadians? This is indeed a complex task, but one that needs our urgent attention. In the next section we offer some suggestions.

Implications for Teacher Education

The findings of the study reveal some of the challenges faced by teacher educators in preparing future teachers to work for democratic living in a diverse society. A review of the candidates' lived experiences in practicum schools highlight a volatile mix of political, pedagogical, and institutional factors that appear to conspire against learning to teach for democracy and social justice.

Even before entering the practice environment candidates must overcome their own conservative beliefs and often narrow perspectives on inequities in school and society. As they move into the field with their new visions of schooling for equity and social justice, they encounter an institutional culture that maintains a rigid structure of relationship among such groups as administrators, teachers, students, and parents represented there. Candidates find themselves disempowered at the bottom of a school hierarchy that avoids the exploration of such social differences as race, class, ethnicity, gender, exceptionality, and sexual orientation. Such school cultures restrict the flow of theoretical exploration of social difference from the teacher education curriculum to the practicum classroom.

The introduction of a standardized school curriculum and the centralization of its management in state bureaucracies further compromised candidates' initiative to bring new perspectives, insights, and resources to student learning. They become relegated, as are their veteran mentors, to the role of mere operatives, simply implementing pre-packaged curriculum. Teacher resistance to their prescribed mechanistic role in the schooling process has resulted in schools as politically-charged work environments, riddled with contestations and tensions. This is the political and social-cultural arena in which candidates learn to teach. As one candidate aptly pointed out:

> *I think the one thing that the Urban Diversity program really helped us focus on was being agents of change....We were put in a program that pushed against the grain. In many ways, I think that was wonderful. But I must say in some ways there were times when I thought to myself, "If your focus is to get candidates practising the equity things you teach in the university courses, they have to be placed in a school that is supportive of the Urban Diversity program objectives. If the school is not supportive, you cannot expect the TCs to go in and practise equity. They can't be expected to work against a brick wall at such a vulnerable time in their careers.*

The section that follows grapples with the thorny issue of structuring transformative field experience with safe spaces for candidates to teach for social justice and democracy.

Transformative Potential of Professional Development Schools

Over the years, professional development schools (PDS) have gained popularity in many school jurisdictions as an environment where teacher candidates, mentor teachers, and teacher educators from university faculties work together as a community of learners. The creation and function of these teaching-learning environments have been well documented in the research literature (Cochran-Smith & Lytle, 1993; Darling-Hammond, 1998; Lieberman & Miller, 1990; Stoddart, 1993; Zeichner, 1996).[4] There is usually a commitment on the part of partners in PDS collaboration to make teacher development a priority and to provide a learning environment that nurtures both pre-service and in-service teachers.

How may the organization and structure, the content, and ped- agogy of professional development schools eliminate the obstacles faced by teacher candidates in traditional field placements? First, PDS structure should be able to identify among its teachers a critical mass that is committed to teacher development. This mass should move beyond those mentors to whose classrooms candidates are assigned, to the larger teaching and support staff. Indeed, the administrative leadership within the school must tacitly demon- strate its support for this initiative. A critical mass of mentor teach- ers is key to the success of the PDS since we argue for candidate placement with teams of teachers rather than in single classroom placements (Duquette, 1996; Zeichner, 1996). Duquette argues for candidates' "enrichment through exposure to different perspec- tives" (p. 75). By the same token, PDS should be structured to accom- modate a critical mass of candidates. Such a mass has the potential to be self-sustaining and to serve as political and emotional support for each other in a school culture that is potentially marginalizing. A critical mass of candidates will also create a synergy within the school and serve as partners and additional personnel resources for school research projects, community outreach programs, and other school change initiatives (Quinn & McKay, 1998).

This leads to the critique of traditional forms of learning to teach and the exploration of alternative approaches. Zeichner's (1996) review of the "educative practicum" raised concerns about the tra- ditional approaches to the practicum and common obstacles belying them. First, he critiques the apprenticeship approach where the novice teacher is assigned to the veterans. This model is based on the implicit assumption that "good teaching is caught and not taught; that good things happen more by accidental fortune than by delib- erate design" (p. 218). Candidates learning to teach by this model are often in a "sink or swim" situation, argues Zeichner, and there are fundamental limitations since candidates are not exposed to other teachers' styles and perspectives. Our study reveals a more damning indictment of this model: candidates placed with undemocratic, authoritarian, power-driven veteran teachers are severely restricted in learning to teach for democracy and social justice. In fact, they often find themselves in counter-productive conflict situations with their mentors.

In the other models of learning to teach: "the applied-science practicum" and "the inquiry-oriented practicum," Zeichner provided some insightful contrasts. In the "applied-science" approach knowledge gained in academic courses are applied to practicum classrooms; "the practicum becomes essentially a time to demonstrate things learned previously" (p. 221). On the contrary, in the "inquiry-oriented" approach, new knowledge and theories about the teaching-learning process are generated through action research in schools and communities, and collaborative practicum seminar discussions evolving from practice. Teacher reflection that evolved from the latter approach is critiqued by Zeichner because, too often, what candidates reflect upon how they reflect may not help them develop as teachers.

We propose, therefore, a PDS setting that capitalizes on the strengths and avoids the pitfalls identified by Zeichner, especially those reported by candidates in this study. For example, dimensions of the inquiry-oriented practicum provide candidates the opportunity to carry out research projects in their classroom, school, or community. Here, candidates will require the support of their university supervisors to explore issues related to equity, social justice, and social difference, since school personnel may not be proactive in supporting research agendas that raise sensitive issues about schooling and inequality. Such inquiry-related approaches to pre-service teaching could evolve from candidates' initial urban community study that explores ways in which such factors as socio-economic and ethnocultural dimensions of urban communities impact the schooling process and learning outcomes. Narode, Rennie-Hill, and Peterson's (1994) urban community study by pre-service teachers raised many insightful questions about the differential schooling of distinct racial groups in the community.

Candidates' own action research questions could take up other forms of social difference such as ethnicity, social class, immigrant status, language, and religion in an effort to find out how schools respond to those differences. Following such inquiry, candidates and their mentors could collaborate in developing proactive strategies for working equitably with marginalized groups. Beyond the structuring of a collaborative learning environment for both pre-service and in-service teachers is the content to be explored. Exploring sensitive issues of equity and social justice means exposure to "difficult knowledge" in a school culture that would rather avoid them. The framing of the discussion of difficult knowledge could take place in

School and Society or Social Issues courses removed from university classrooms and provided in professional development schools. Such a forum allows for a realistic and immediate interface of critical social theory and lived experiences of classroom teachers. This kind of discourse allows for critique of theory's applicability in school settings, and the probability of theory modification to accommodate realistic situations in "real" schools. Peggy McIntosh's (1990) model of Seeking Educational Equity and Diversity (SEED) has been utilized successfully in the critical inquiry into classroom practices and has helped teachers develop strategies for infusing equity and social justice issues into their pedagogy (Norquay, 1996; Solomon & Rezai-Rashti, 1997).[5]

Finally, the transformative potential of professional development schools cannot be fully realized until teacher candidates, their mentors in these schools, and their teacher educators become politically strategic in re-inserting equity and democracy into the schooling process. Here, McNeil (2000, p. 265) warns about the "perverse effects" of legislative teaching and learning:

> *The effects within schools and school systems may not be nearly so "perverse" as the effects within our system of democracy, as these attempts to legislate and control learning reduce the public possibilities for retaining democratic governance of school once the controls are in place. One reason for this is that an accountability-based control system, as a closed system, structures out possibilities for external critique.*

Teacher development programs therefore need to operate at two levels. First, it must build into its scholarship the notion of democratic citizenship and the role of teachers in sustaining democratic living in a diverse society. As Giroux and McLaren (1986) argue, teachers as "transformative intellectuals" must be politically and morally charged to be on guard for the "specific histories, experiences, and knowledge that students use to define their identities" (p. 228). Teacher education curriculum should be as much about cultural politics as it is about pedagogy. It should explore every aspect of the relationship between culture, politics, economics, and contemporary schooling.

The second level is that of democratic practice and comes out of Giroux and McLaren's notion that "schooling is an ongoing struggle for democracy" (p. 216). As we have seen much too often, educators settle for consensus and compromise in an effort to avoid conflict and confrontation. It is therefore imperative that teachers and their candidates negotiate spaces in curriculum to teach students ways of maintaining the democratic tradition in education. Democratic ideals cannot be maintained through compromise.

Notes

[1] Staffing for the program is based on a combination of Faculty of Education professors and leading professionals from area boards of education who are seconded to the Faculty. A survey of the tenure stream faculty at the University revealed that the assumption is unfounded. A large majority of faculty have taught at various levels in schools and have practical experiences there. In addition, teacher practitioners are seconded on an ongoing basis from active teaching in local schools to work with candidates in the pre-service and in-service programs.

[2] A review of the *Ontario Common Curriculum: Policies and Outcomes Grades 1-9* (1990) reveals that, contrary to popular belief, issues of equity and social justice, and the recognition that the curriculum must reflect the needs and interests of students "regardless of gender, racial and ethnocultural background, social class, sexual orientation or ability" (p. 11) are outlined in this document. But those values all but disappeared from the new curriculum guidelines that replaced them.

[3] *It's Elementary* (video) "is a window into what really happens when teachers address lesbian and gay issues with their students in age-appropriate ways. With moving footage shot in six public and independent schools across the US, the film takes viewers inside first through eighth grade classrooms to find out what young students have to say about a topic that often leaves adults tongue-tied. Rarely do adults have the chance to hear what children already know about gay people, and about the concerns and questions on their minds. And rarely is there an opportunity to see how addressing anti-gay prejudice in the classroom is connected to preventing violence, supporting families, and promoting social equality. *It's Elementary* gives you that chance for the first time. This inspiring film – both the full-length documentary and the shorter educational training version – is a unique resource for educators, parents, and other adults for encouraging constructive dialogue about one of the most controversial issues facing schools today." (From: Chasnaff & Cohen's (1997) description of the video in promotional materials).

[4] Professional Development Schools are variously labelled (e.g., professional practice schools, partnership schools, etc.) to reflect the clinical or laboratory environment that is closely supervised. The concept comes from the medical model of teaching hospitals. These models often develop out of strong partnerships between school jurisdictions and faculties of education (teacher education initiatives) and are often a part of school improvement project initiatives.

[5] A rather strategic move was made by Solomon and Rezai-Rashti (1997) to reduce the impact of school culture and to provide a neutral territory for the exploration of equity issues. Co-operating teachers and their teacher candidates were moved to a neutral P.D. site for a series of half-day workshops offered from September to May. Content of the workshops included: gen-

der identity, race and cultural identity, social class, inclusion by ability, etc. The provision of a neutral, non-evaluative professional development environment empowered candidates to engage their veteran teachers and teacher educators in an egalitarian way.

Acknowledgements: We thank Naomi Norquay and John Portelli for their critical comments on our earlier draft of this chapter; Sherri Nishimura Wong for her help in preparing the manuscript; and the teacher candidates for sharing with us their lived experiences within schools.

References

Ahlquist, R. (1992). Manifestations of inequality: Overcoming resistance in a multicultural foundations course. In Carl Grant (Ed.), *Research and multicultural education: From the margins to the mainstream* (pp. 89-105). London: Falmer.

Apple, M. & Weis, L. (Eds.) (1983). *Ideology and practice in schooling*. Philadelphia: Temple University.

Britzman, D. P. (1991). Decentering discourses in teacher education: Or the unleashing of unpopular things. *Journal of Education, 173*(3), 60-81.

Bunch, G. (1999). *Inclusion: How to: Essential classroom strategies*. Toronto: Inclusion Press.

Bunch, G., Lupart, J. & Brown, M. (1997). *Resistance and acceptance: Teacher attitudes to inclusion of students with disability*. Toronto: Faculty of Education, York University.

Bunch, G. & Valeo, A. (1997). *Inclusion: Recent research*. Toronto: Inclusion Press.

Carr, W. & Hartnett, A. (1996). *Education and the struggle for democracy: The politics of educational ideas*. Buckingham: Open University Press.

Carr, P. R. & Klassen, T. R. (1997). Different perceptions of race in education: Racial minority and white teachers. *Canadian Journal of Education, 22*(1), 67-81.

Chasnoff, D. & Cohen, H. (Producers). (1997). *It's elementary: Talking about gay issues in school* (video). Available from Women's Educational Media, 2180 Bryant St., San Francisco, CA 94110.

Cochran-Smith, M. & Lytle, S. L. (Eds.) (1993). *Inside/outside: Teacher research and knowledge*. New York: Teachers College Press.

Cross, B. (1999). Mediating curriculum: Problems of nonengagement and practices of engagement. In R. C. Chavez & J. O'Donnell (Eds.), *Speaking the unpleasant: The politics of (non) engagement in the multicultural education terrain* (pp. 32-55). Albany: State University of New York Press.

Darling-Hammond, L. (Ed.) (1993). *Professional development schools*. New York: Teachers College Press.

Davis, B. (2000). *Skills mania: Snake oil in our schools?* Toronto: Between the Lines.

Delpit, L. (1995). *Other peoples' children: Cultural conflict in the classroom*. New York: The New Press.

Duquette, C. (1996). Partnerships in preservice education: Perspectives of associate teachers and student teachers. *McGill Journal of Education, 31*(1), 59-81.

Entwistle, H. (1996). The relationship between educational theory and practice. In W. Hare & J. P. Portelli (Eds.), *Philosophy of education: Introductory readings* (2nd Edition) (pp. 19-28). Calgary: Detselig Enterprises.

Epstein, R. (1998). Parent night will never be the same: Lesbian families challenge the public school system. *Our Schools, Our Selves, 9*(1), 92-117.

Giroux, H. & McLaren, P. (1986). Teacher education and the politics of engagement: The case for democratic schooling. *Harvard Educational Review, 56*(3), 213-238.

Grant, C. A. & Zozakiewicz, C. A., (1995). Student teachers, cooperating teachers, and supervisors: Interrupting the multicultural silences of student teaching. In J. M. Larkin & C. E. Sleeter (Eds.) *Developing multicultural teacher education curricula* (pp. 259-278). Albany: State University of New York Press.

Hartnett, A. & Carr, W. (1995). Education, teacher development and the struggle for democracy. In J. Smyth (Ed.), *Critical discourses on teacher development* (pp. 39-53). Toronto: OISE Press.

Henry, F., Tator, C., Mattis, W. & Rees, T. (1995). *The colour of democracy: Racism in Canadian society.* Toronto: Harcourt Brace.

Howard, G., (1999). *We can't teach what we don't know: White teachers, multicultural schools.* New York: Teachers College Press.

Lieberman, A. & Miller, L. (1990). Teacher development in professional practice schools. *Teachers College Record, 92*(1), 105-122.

Liston, D. P. & Zeichner, K. M. (1990). Teacher education and the social context of schooling: Issues for curriculum development. *American Educational Research Journal, 27*(4), 610-636.

Lortie, D. (1975). *Schoolteacher.* Chicago: University of Chicago Press.

McIntosh, P. (1990). *Interactive phases of curricular and personal re-vision with regard to race.* Working paper #219. Wellesley, MA: Wellesley College, Center for Research on Women.

McIntosh, P. (1989). White privilege: Unpacking the invisible knapsack. *Independent School, 49*(2), 31-36.

McLaren, P. (1998). *Life in schools: An introduction to critical pedagogy in the foundations of education* (3rd Edition). New York: Longman.

McNeil, L. M. (2000). *Contradictions of school reform: Educational costs of standardized testing.* New York: Routledge.

Menter, I. (1989). Teaching practice stasis: Racism, sexism and school experience in initial teacher education. *British Journal of Sociology of Education, 10*(4), 459-473.

Narode, R., Rennie-Hill, L. & Peterson, K. D. (1994). Urban community study by preservice teachers. *Urban Education, 29*(1), 5-21.

Nehaul, K. (1996). *The schooling of children of Caribbean heritage.* London: Trentham Books.

Norquay, N. (1996). *Teaching social equity in pre-service education through partnerships with schools: A report on the placement of education 1 students at Maple Leaf Public School.* Unpublished report. York University, North York, Canada.

Ontario Ministry of Education and Training (1993). *Antiracism and ethnocultural equity in school boards: Guidelines for policy development and implementation.* Toronto: Queen's Printer for Ontario.

Ontario Ministry of Education and Training (1993). *The common curriculum: Policies and outcomes grades 1-9.* Toronto: Queen's Printer for Ontario.

Quinn, L. F. & McKay, J. W. (1998). *Professional development outcomes of multiple student teacher placements within a university/school partnership.* A paper presented at the Preservice Education Research Association meeting, San Diego.

Sears, J. T. (1994). Challenges for educators: Lesbian, gay, and bisexual families. *High School Journal, 77* (2), 138-156.

Sleeter, C. E. (1992a). Resisting racial awareness: How teachers understand the social order from their racial, gender, and social class locations. *Educational Foundations, 6,* 7-32.

Sleeter, C. E. (1992b). *Keepers of the American dream: A study of staff development and multicultural education.* London: Falmer Press.

Solomon, R. P. (2000). Exploring cross-race dyad partnerships in learning to teach. *Teachers College Record, 102*(6), 953-979.

Solomon, R. P. & Levine-Rasky, C. (1996). When principle meets practice: Teachers' contradictory responses to antiracist education. *Alberta Journal of Educational Research, 42*(1), 19-33.

Solomon, R. P. & Rezai-Rashti, G. (1997). *School-university partnership in teacher education for educational equity and diversity.* A paper presented at the Canadian Society for the Study of Education Conference. St. John's, NF.

Stoddart, T. (1993). The professional development school: Building bridges between cultures. *Educational Policy, 7,* 5-23.

Tatum, B. (1992). Talking about race, learning about racism: The application of racial identity development theory in the classroom. *Harvard Educational Review, 62*(1), 1-24.

Troyna, B. (1994). The 'everyday world' of teachers? Deracialised discourses in the sociology of teachers and the teaching profession. *British Journal of Sociology of Education, 15*(3), 325-339.

Troyna, B. & Williams, J. (1986). *Racism, education and the State: The racialization of education policy.* London: Croom Helm.

Zeichner, K. M. (1993). Connecting genuine teacher development to the struggle for social justice. *Journal of Education for Teaching, 19*(1), 5-20.

Zeichner, K. (1996). Teachers as reflective practitioners and democratization of school reform. In K. Zeichner, S. Melnick & M. L. Gomez (Eds.), *Currents of reform in preservice teacher education* (pp. 199-214). New York: Teachers College Press.

Chapter 10
Pendulum Swings and Archaeological Layers: Educational Policy and the Case of ESL

Nina Bascia

Besides First Nations peoples, Canada is a country comprised of immigrants and their descendents. Recurring patterns of migration have continually exerted pressure on educational systems and resulted in a wide range of educational reforms. The establishment of large bureaucratic school systems, first occurring in the 19th century in urban centres such as Toronto, was driven at least in part by concerns about the social control and occupational training of massive numbers of immigrants (Darling-Hammond, 1997; Harper, 1997). In the 20th century, the refinement of the educational program into different streams and even different types of schools – "academic," "collegiate," "vocational," "technical," and "commercial" – corresponded to assumptions about appropriate career futures for various immigrant groups (Curtis, Livingstone & Smaller, 1992). The second half of the 20th century saw a range of educational policy efforts to provide equal access to education and thus to higher education and careers; in the 1980s and 1990s, federal and provincial governments and some school boards emphasized the "celebration" or tolerance of difference through multiculturalism policies (Kehoe & Mansfield, cited in Harper, 1997). In Ontario in the 1990s, a host of policy strategies charged schools to become more responsive to culturally diverse students: encouraging school-based development of special programs for immigrant and racial minority students, making curriculum content and teaching strategies more culturally inclusive (e.g., Dei, 1994), connecting schools with other public agencies (Rusk, Shaw & Joong, 1994) and increasing the racial and cultural diversity of the teaching force to more closely reflect the diversity of the general population (Ontario, 1993a). Most recently, following trends in a number of other countries, Canadian provincial educational policies have mandated standardized curricula and large-scale assessments of student learning (Earl, Bascia, Hargreaves & Jacka, 1998). Even these sorts of reforms, so fundamentally different from the multicultural and antiracist policies they replaced, are couched, in part, on claims that "the same" education will ensure equality of opportunity for all students (Metz, 1989).

This chapter focuses on the current status of ESL (English as a Second Language) programs, one attempt by school systems to respond to these patterns of immigration. ESL programs are intended primarily for newcomers to Canada whose native language is not English – though they also sometimes include second generation students who live in linguistically homogeneous communities and have little opportunity to speak English outside school, and native English speakers who do not speak "standard" English. ESL courses are intended to develop students' reading and writing skills over a short period of time (usually a few months or years), with the expectation that they can then be readily assimilated into "regular" school programs. ESL often thus comprises the first encounter immigrant students have with Canadian schools. This chapter's close-up examination of the conditions of ESL teaching and learning emphasizes the impact of several generations of policy efforts intended directly or indirectly to improve the education of minority and immigrant children.

Educators' understandings about educational improvement tend to follow two distinct and opposing schools of thought. One is that there is "good policy" (for equity-minded educators; for example, policy that attempts to democratize educational processes and decision-making) and "bad policy" (for example, policy that reinforces social inequalities) and the goal is to discern and advocate for good policy while minimizing or countering bad policy. Another is that educational policy has little direct effect on what goes on in schools and classrooms (e.g., Cohen, 1991; McLaughlin, 1987; Smith & O'Day, 1991). According to this view, prevailing social dynamics such as those which maintain social status inequalities (between, for example, native-born, white, heterosexual males and all others) are persistent and powerful enough that policy makes little or no difference, and that the most productive route is through "grass roots," local, small efforts that help individuals cope with the worst excesses of these prevailing trends. The chapter's primary purpose is to problematize these common understandings about policy effects on educational equity by demonstrating policy's power, promise, and unpredictability, and the insufficiency of policy as it is currently conceptualized to bring about significant changes in educational quality.

The chapter first provides a conceptual framework that challenges conventional notions about how educational policy affects practice, then outlines the major policies that have shaped and reshaped ESL programs over the past decade. Next the chapter reports on the status of ESL programs in four public schools in southern Ontario, identifying the impact of historical layers of policy on ESL delivery. A final section discusses the implications for understanding policy and for seeking more promising solutions to the enduring challenges of educational practice for immigrant students.

The chapter draws on the conceptual research of Canadian and U.S. educational policy analysts whose work in the late 1980s and early 1990s has unfortunately been layered over and all but forgotten by more simplistic, harsher conceptualizations of policy. The chapter draws empirically on two studies conducted in the early and late 1990s on the work lives of Canadian teachers who have a particular responsibility for the education of immigrant students (Bascia, 1996a, 1996b; Bascia & Jacka, 2000a, 2000b; Thiessen, Bascia & Goodson, 1996).[1] The first study developed and contrasted the life and professional histories of nearly a dozen racial minority immigrant teachers who worked in public schools in Ontario and British Columbia during the early 1990s and who taught new immigrant students (Bascia, 1996b). The second study documented the nature of ESL teachers' work inside and outside of their classrooms in four public schools (three elementary and one secondary) in a large urban-suburban district in southern Ontario in the 1997-98 school year (Bascia & Jacka, 2000a, 2000b). The schools in both studies were typical in terms of their programs and also in terms of immigrant settlement patterns in larger Canadian urban centers: 75-100% of the students at each school were immigrants or second generation children. Students in these schools had come to Canada from over 60 countries and, together, spoke two to three dozen different languages at home. While our samples were limited in each case, our findings are consistent with other research on the work of racial minority teachers (e.g., Foster, 1992, 1994; Henry, 1992; Ortiz, 1982) and programs for racial and linguistic minority and immigrant students (e.g., Chambliss, 1997; Dorph, 1997; Eaton, 1997; Gebhard, 1997; Olsen, 1997; Wong, 2000). The two studies reveal some of the powerful, complex, and unpredictable effects of educational policy on teaching and learning. Devising policies that support practice in particular ways requires a finely nuanced understanding of the conditions in which teaching and learning take place.

Policy Dynamics: Change, Durability, Complications and Choices

Several overarching concepts are helpful in understanding the extent to which, and how, policy shapes pedagogical practices. One is the system's permeability to a wide variety of ideas about the purposes of schooling and the nature and context of educational programs. Another, seemingly paradoxical, is the enduring nature of certain structural features of the educational system. These two forces, working against each other in dynamic and shifting ways, shape and reshape how students and their teachers experience life in schools. At the same time, a variety of forces at all levels of the educational system challenge any attempts to reform practice by remote control policy. Finally, it is helpful to consider how a range of policy options have differential impacts not only on individual practice but on the educational system as a whole.

Change. North Americans routinely turn to the educational system to solve social problems both large and small. Changes in broader social and economic conditions often engender new expectations for schools. North American schools have been peculiarly permeable to a variety of ideas; schools can be seen as political arenas to which divergent ideas about preferred social futures are brought, and where they are integrated or contested. Waves of new courses, programs, and whole new forms of schooling have had their impact on North American schools for over a century (Coulter, 1996; Harper, 1997; Tyack, 1991; Werner, 1991). Recent decades have seen profound changes in who may legitimately participate in framing educational policy and practice, in who might become a teacher or administrator, and what the nature of those roles might be. Programs have proliferated. As a result, some view the educational system as fragmented and chaotic (Bascia, 1996d). Comprehensive secondary schools, in particular – what critical researchers have called the "shopping mall high school" (Powell, Farrar & Cohen, 1985) or the "multi-everything secondary school" (Campbell, 1996) – have attempted simultaneously to be many things to many people. Some policy analysts have suggested that this incremental adding on without fundamentally rethinking the purposes of schooling dilutes the potential impact of reform (Bascia, 1996c; McDonnell & Elmore, 1987; Timar, 1989).

The pendulum is an oft-employed metaphor used to describe the progression of social values that drive educational reform. A prevailing notion among practitioners and analysts is that sets of social values or concerns are replaced by their opposites, each a reaction to what preceded it, driving educational policies first in one and then in a diametrically different direction. Policy initiatives, for example, that seek to democratize the educational enterprise and expand the possibilities of educators' work may be challenged by different notions that restrict the range of people who may claim legitimate authority over educational practice. But despite these very real policy swings, close scrutiny of educational practice suggests that policy eras are not as discrete as they may appear: teaching and learning in any given time period has much in common with that which occurred before. This continuity between one policy era and the next is partly a function of the time lag between the initial publication of a reform idea, its manifestation in formal policy, program implementation, and enduring effects on educational practice. Ideas, rules, and changes in activity do not occur quickly; implementation is rarely complete or comprehensive; schools typically do not abandon one set of activities before assuming another (Bascia, 1996c; Clune, 1990; McLaughlin, 1987; Tyack, 1991; Werner, 1991). Even when official governmental policy changes radically, some values and practices endure. In this sense, teaching and learning take place in institutions permeated by history, a sort of archaeological dig, where layers of past policy may continue to exert some influence, part of the taken-for-granted scenery for those who live there but visible to those who have the skill to see them.

Durability. Attempts to democratize school programs have left their mark, but strong convictions and investments in traditional school processes have served to marginalize such efforts. While change is an important feature of the educational system, many structural and normative features have persisted over time. The large urban educational systems that first emerged about a century ago were shaped by a set of powerfully compelling ideas about organization and governance borrowed from business. Administrators who designed and governed new bureaucracies asserted the scientific "expertise" and therefore the authority to determine a standardized school curriculum and to designate job classifications at various organizational levels (Darling-Hammond, 1997; Gitlin, 1996; Larson, 1977; Smaller, 1991; Tyack, 1991; Urban, 1982). These initial efforts have been hard-wired, so to speak, into the educational system: the authority to shape and reshape the administrative order – who may teach, what may be taught and the relative breadth and diversity of various educational programs – ultimately is concentrated at the top of the hierarchy. This new bureaucratic structure has endured despite recurring challenges

(Curtis, et al., 1992). Policies, norms, and practices have maintained the dominant status of white male administrators, while the involvement of teachers in educational policy making has been inhibited (Carlson, 1992). Women have been restricted from managerial positions and positions of authority, and educators have remained overwhelmingly white and of northern European origin, even as Canada's population has continued to diversify (Ortiz, 1982; Reynolds, 1990). Such systemic inequities perpetuate the primacy of particular points of view within the educational system, serving to reinforce dominant interests in the larger society and to ensure that educational processes reproduce rather than challenge the social status quo.

Another powerful legacy of this bureaucratic order is the diversification of the curriculum into discrete categories. The sorting of students by age and ability, and the division of the curriculum into subjects, as well as its scope and sequence, the assignment of teachers by grade, subject, and student type, and the expectations for teachers' responsibilities for and relationships with students and colleagues have remained remarkably consistent across time and across schools (Miles & Darling-Hammond, 1998; Tyack & Tobin, 1994). These regularities are ensured and maintained by a range of policies, including requirements for university entrance, teacher certification, teacher education practices, job classifications, and collective agreements (Werner, 1991). There are important normative dimensions to these regularities as well, common understandings about what Metz (1989) and Hemmings & Metz (1992) call "real school," "real teaching," and "real learning." Most people, including teachers, agree about the set of school experiences every student should expect to have, and in many ways schools are organized and structured to meet these expectations (see also Louis, 1990; Meyer & Rowan, 1978).

Metz, an American sociologist interested in variations in teaching and learning, especially with respect to students' race and social class, contends that expectations for "real school" can be met when students have strong academic skills and believe in the value of schooling. But when students lack skills, experience, and/or economic resources, these expectations are more difficult to meet. Educational systems have attempted to compensate for the mismatch between expectations for "real school" and a diverse student population with curricular tracks or streams based upon differentiated expectations for students' life directions; and by establishing distinct programs such as special education, ESL, co-op, or vocational education. Such special programs are add-ons, pull-outs, and augmentations to the "regular" academic program, but they do not seriously challenge its primacy (Miles & Darling-Hammond, 1998). Tyack (1991) suggests that the programs that endure are those that do not seriously challenge the status quo (in terms of authority or competition for scarce resources), and that are championed by people with sufficient political power in the educational system. Like the inequitable patterns of access to positions of administrative authority described earlier in this section, the systematic marginalization of programs aimed at redressing inequality reproduces relations of power not only in the educational system but also in society at large.

Complications. The public and decision-makers alike place a lot of faith in policy edicts to effect educational changes but, as a generation of policy analysts have suggested, it's difficult to mandate what matters (McLaughlin, 1987). Walter Werner (1991) writes, "An assumed linear sequence of events – curriculum revision causes teachers to modify what and how they teach, thus resulting in changes in students learning – is fraught with many uncertainties" (p. 105). Beyond the characteristics of the policy development process delineated above, policy implementation is complicated by a range of forces. Talbert and McLaughlin (1994) see teaching and learning as occurring within a set of "nested" or "embedded" layers of influence, where national and state/provincial policies, professional norms, local communities, school district administration and school organization exert particular contextual influences. Nespor (1997) suggests that rather than emphasizing organizational boundaries, change processes occur across networks and human systems (see also Bascia & Hargreaves, 2000). As more than a decade of teacher development research has suggested, the act of teaching is shaped by teachers' social identities and life histories, as well as the contexts of their workplaces (see, for example, Bascia, 1996e). Rather than merely accepting policy edicts unchanged (or rejecting policies wholesale), perhaps what teachers and school organizations do is negotiate or co-construct them in relation to local priorities and perceived needs (Clune, 1990). Within schools, many individuals – especially administrators, support personnel, teachers, and students – contribute to the actual shape of practice through the range of values, skills, priorities, and experiences they bring to the interpretation of policy (see especially McLaughlin, 1987; Weatherley & Lipsky, 1977; Werner, 1991).

Policy choices. People often think of policies as regulations that require compliance. Mandates, however, are only one of several types of available policies. Lorraine McDonnell and Richard Elmore (1987) suggest several more. Inducements – that is, incentives that encourage the adoption of new or changed behaviors – are another. Recognition, rewards, resources and money are typical inducements. Policy can also be used deliberately to build capacity – providing the material of human capital with the promise of future added value – or "change systems" by granting or shifting official authority among individuals and agencies. These policy instruments have very different impacts on practice, both in the short and long term.

All of these policy choices have been employed in recent decades in Canadian educational systems. The policy instruments most frequently employed in recent years have been mandates, requirements for compliance which have been presented to educators without accompanying inducements or the sorts of infrastructural supports that would increase educators' capacities to change their practices. Amendments to provincial education acts which have shifted authority from the local to provincial level represent a sort of system changing. These choices differ from earlier attempts to devolve programmatic decisions to schools, to encourage teachers to assume curricular leadership roles, and to increase teachers' capacities to work effectively with diverse students.

The next section charts two recent policy eras in Ontario educational history that have left residual impacts on ESL programs. The following descriptions emphasize the interactions of endurance and change, the actual impact of policy on practice in specific schools and classrooms, and the consequences of the employment of a limited variety of policy instruments.

The Pendulum

Few policies are intended to solve single problems; those that have successfully passed the legislative process are those that appeal to a variety of stakeholders who believe they will resolve a range of concerns. The educational policy initiatives put forward by the province of Ontario in the early 1990s were directed at least in part, though not exclusively, toward improving the educational opportunities of immigrant students. Many of the educational policies initiated at the time were democratizing in their focus. Many were intended to enfranchise broader representation, including racial and cultural minority "community" groups, in developing school programs; many, rather than imposing a single universal program model, required school staffs to develop programs that were responsive to the needs of their particular student populations.

The policy most explicitly directed toward improving the education of immigrant students provided guidelines for promoting antiracism and ethno-cultural equity in schools boards (Ontario Ministry of Education and Training, 1993a). This set of recommendations was intended to "permeate all aspects of [a school board's] organizational structure" (p. 12) and targeted a wide range of educational practices. Administrative decision-makers were charged with "equip[ping] all students with the knowledge, skills, attitudes, and behaviors needed to live and work effectively in an increasingly diverse world, and encourag[ing] them to appreciate diversity and reject discriminatory attitudes and behavior" (p. 5). School boards were charged with developing effective working relationships with increasingly "diverse communities" (p. 13). The curriculum, conceptualized broadly as "all learning experiences the student will have in school" (p. 13), was to be modified to "ensure that the cultural and racial identities of all students are affirmed...to reflect the diversity of staff, students, parents, and the community" (p. 14). School boards were required to provide staff development "to ensure that...staff are aware that they are expected to broaden their expertise...through courses, workshops and community consultation" (p. 17). In a somewhat oblique nod to the racial and ethnic homogeneity of the teaching pool, hiring and promotion practices were to be modified to encourage greater racial and cultural diversity of school board staff (pp. 16-17). Language proficiency was another concern. The Antiracism and Ethno-cultural Equity document supported the expansion of ESL programming, noting that "research shows that most newly arrived immigrant students...require a minimum of five to seven years to become proficient...and to function academically like native speakers" (p. 14) and recommended providing "appropriate support programs for language learning" (p. 15).

Ontario's "Common Curriculum" for grades 1-9, also released in the early 1990s, supported and exemplified many of these intentions. Besides stating explicitly that implementation of the curriculum "must be linked to the development and implementation of policies on antiracism and ethno-cultural equity" (Ontario Ministry of Education and Training, 1995, p. 4), it noted that "the curriculum must reflect the diversity of Canadian society," and that "exclusions of the experiences of some social groups...constitutes a systemic barrier to success for students from those groups and often produces inequitable results" (p. 11). Language was one of four new integrated program areas; the Common Curriculum policy document noted that "a program that recognizes, respects, and values students' racial, cultural and linguistic backgrounds, as well as varieties of language, helps them develop a positive sense of self and motivates them to learn" (p. 47). It defined stages of linguistic proficiency, including learning outcomes in listening, speaking, and reading for grades 3, 6, and 9, and noting that only at the fourth and final stage would students be "able to participate fully in the academic program of the school" (p. 98).

These mandates, and many others released during the same time period, embodied a set of new intellectual and socio-emotional expectations for teachers' work (Bascia & Hargreaves, 2000). In order to develop and implement these new programs, teachers had to leave the relative autonomy of their classrooms in order to learn, plan, and sometimes even teach with their colleagues; they had to transcend the boundaries and comfort of their own subject matter expertise and competence with particular developmental stages in order to "teach the whole child" and take collective responsibility for the nature of school programs (Bascia, 1994; Cochran-Smith & Lytle, 1992; Hargreaves, 1994; Little, 1993). Administrators had to learn to "share power" with teachers (Lieberman, 1988). For many Ontario educators, these new activities, roles, and relationships were quite different from what they were accustomed to and quite challenging to put in practice.

These ambitious policies were conceptually coherent but practically inadequate. Some educators complained that they lacked both the specificity and explicitness that would allow them to understand the new concepts and design new practices. The new policies assumed practitioners possessed or could readily develop a deep understanding of intellectually challenging new ideas (Earl & Katz, 2000). There was little money for training and little time for planning and learning. They required new working relationships among teachers, and between teachers and administrators and teachers and parents, that challenged social and professional norms, revealed power differentials, and engendered sometimes painful and intractable conflicts (Bascia, 1994; Datnow, 2000; Little, 1995; Muncey & McQuillan, 1993; Oakes, et al., 2000; Zeichner, 1988). They were further challenged by political compromises in their inception (for example, the original plan to postpone streaming for students from grade nine to grade 11 was reduced to a single year within an other-

wise streamed secondary program), challenged in their implementation by their placement atop archaeological layers of practice that
had been laid down before. Interviews in the mid-1990s with teachers who worked with immigrant students noted that few of the new
school-based programs that sprang up in response to these mandates addressed issues of race, gender, or social class either directly
or indirectly (Bascia, 1994; Bascia, 1996b; see also Chambliss, 1997;
Dorph, 1997; Gebhard, 1997). Simply mandating antiracism and
ethno-cultural equity was clearly insufficient because of the durability of the traditional "grammar of schooling."

Many of the racial minority immigrant teachers we interviewed
had gone back to school and obtained ESL training; others had been
specifically assigned to teach courses in literacy and "life skills" for
immigrant students; and all were contending with expectations that,
because of their own immigrant, minority status, they serve as inter-
mediaries between the school and minority students. Each was
essentially working to compensate for the enduring mismatch
between traditional school programs and minority students, and for
their colleagues' lack of experience and conceptual capacity. In many
instances, not only were these teachers racial and linguistic "tokens"
in their schools, but they were the only individuals in these roles, or
one of two. Most felt they worked in hostile environments: "I try not
to go into [certain topics] too deep...[and] I'm not completely off
[my] guard," said one. When asked about workshops for teachers on
equity strategies, one of these teachers said, "You should hear the
guffawing that goes on whenever race-related issues are brought up.
This is a big joke" (Bascia, 1996b; Thiessen, Bascia & Goodson, 1996).
This relegation of racial minority and immigrant teachers to special
responsibility for the academic and social care of immigrant students seemed to partially compensate for, but also paradoxically to
contribute to, the marginalization of programs and services for
immigrant students.

Finally, the legislative passage of antiracist and enthno-cultural
and other democratizing policies collided with an increasingly
restrictive educational funding base that not only reduced the range
of necessary supports for such reforms – time for professional
learning and program development, training, materials, and supporting roles such as curriculum consultants and specialized staff at
the school level. They also exacerbated relations between teachers
and the educational system to the extent that teachers' federation
officials and administrators alike refused to endorse them, saying

they must "protect" teachers from any but the most traditional, classroom-based work (Bailey, 2000; Bascia, 1996d; Bascia & Hargreaves, 2000).

Educational reforms initiated in the second half of the 1990s by two governments, the New Democratic Party (NDP) and then the Progressive Conservatives (PC), seem antithetical to the democratizing reforms put forward by the NDP in the early 1990s. In general terms, they replaced school-based decision making and program design with centralized controls and standardized solutions. In this broad sense as well as in many of their specific features, they paralleled prevailing policy trends during the same time period across Canadian provinces as well as in the U.K., Australia, New Zealand, the U.S., and other parts of the world (Earl, Bascia, Hargreaves & Jacka, 1998; Whitty, Powers & Halpin, 1998). While not unique and not unprecedented in Ontario's educational history (Gidney, 1999), they nonetheless had a strong and decisive impact on the nature of teaching and learning, further reinforcing the primacy of "real school."

One of the cornerstones of the new educational reforms has been curriculum standardization. The Common Curriculum of the mid-1990s, which established learning outcomes but left curricular and pedagogical strategies to teachers' discretion, was replaced with "a challenging, high-quality curriculum...[with an emphasis on] measurable results" (Ontario Ministry of Education, 1999, p. 6). Instead of emphasizing social diversity and acknowledging community variation, the new policy documents emphasized courses that "provide all students with essential knowledge and skills" (p. 6). New province-wide assessments served both to drive and reinforce this standard curriculum. Ontario's exams differ from those used in many other jurisdictions in that they are designed to assess students' ability to reason deeply rather than merely to demonstrate competence in reading and mathematics; but, as in other jurisdictions, the high stakes impact of publicly published school-by-school comparisons result in troubling consequences (Earl, 1999).

At the same time, antiracism and ethno-cultural equity guidelines were dropped from use and employment equity policies, first passed in the 1980s, were repealed. Most Ontario school boards, strapped for funds, dropped equity officer positions along with other consultancies from their staffing charts. Racial, ethno-cultural, and linguistic diversity were rarely mentioned in the new policies. Another salient change during this time period was a return to traditionally circumscribed roles for teachers and school administrators and an intensification of hierarchical authority relations among educators. Administrators, who had been members of the teacher federations, lost that affiliation and their roles were redefined to emphasize managerial rather than instructional leadership. The Progressive Conservatives' policy documents, in particular, stressed compliance rather than program development. School boards and school leaders had less ability than before to craft practice according to local student needs because of centralized control over program funding and teachers' working conditions. As in many parts of Canada and the world, these trends occurred simultaneously with significantly reduced funding for education. All of these restrictions resulted in the reduction of "special" programs, including ESL (Galt & Sarick, 1999).

The Layers

When we visited Ontario elementary and secondary schools in the late 1990s, teachers told us that sudden and multiple shifts in provincial education policy had caused many significant changes to their work. In the fall of 1997, nearly every public school in the province had been closed for two weeks as educators protested the passage of the omnibus education bill that shifted much of control over educational decision making from schools and school boards to the provincial level. For teachers, the emotional toll of this publicly political protest was high. A new and more demanding curriculum for the elementary grades was scheduled for implementation for the next school year (though teachers had only a cursory sense of it by June), and a highly politicized curriculum development project was underway for secondary schools. This was the second year of a provincial assessment of grade 3 student learning, a massive effort that took two weeks out of regular programming during the spring term and culminated in school-by-school comparisons that were published in the newspapers. New reporting requirements had teachers "constantly testing." The decrease of educational funding resulted in an increase in class size. ESL teachers noted that their colleagues were "burning out" because of the simultaneous impact of all of these factors, exacerbated for some by teaching assignments they didn't want or feel qualified for, because new funding formulas left principals with less staffing flexibility.

In the schools we visited, the low status of ESL programs relative to the "regular" school curriculum was obvious. Even while administrators we spoke with expressed a personal commitment to ESL programming in their schools, its subordinate position was played out and reinforced by a variety of structural and normative factors. In the elementary schools this manifested in terms of the dominance of the prescribed curriculum and a lack of attention to linguistic and cultural diversity in "regular" classrooms. In the secondary school, teachers of sheltered subject classes identified their courses primarily in terms of subject content. In many ways, it seemed, "regular" teachers continued to own and determine the curriculum, and ESL teachers were expected to augment at best and at least to support their efforts. In cases where ESL was "integrated," teachers worked in "regular" classrooms, ESL teachers were expected to follow the regular teachers' lead and assist with designated curriculum, much like classroom aides. Some ESL teachers seemed comfortable assisting regular programming, "trying to support [regular] classroom work," but those who insisted on emphasizing foundational language skills development found themselves in conflict with administrators and experienced some dissonance in relation to "regular" teachers' intensified attention to standardized curricular goals.

The programmatic inequities were similar across the schools we visited, and were particularly poignant given the nearly universal immigrant experience of the student bodies. The space allocated to ESL programs was inadequate and of poor quality. In the secondary school, ESL classes were assigned to particularly shabby rooms and portables some distance away from the main building. In two of the elementary schools, two teachers shared a single room, either dividing the room in two or team teaching in order to manage the crowded space. In one school, since the program was intended to be fully integrated, ESL had no allocated space at all; the ESL teacher took small groups of students to the library or the staff room to find space to work. The space situation would only worsen; early in the next school year, the province announced a new formula that calculated school space-per-pupil in a way that did not account for special programs such as ESL.

Due to funding reductions, only students seriously lacking English language proficiency could officially be served by ESL teachers, and no student was entitled to more than two years of ESL programming. This marked a change from the recent past, where students assessed as moderately proficient had also received ESL teachers' attention. Because the non-English speaking immigrant population continued to increase, not only were ESL classes larger, but there was also a growing number of students whose ESL teachers were convinced had not received adequate language training and could only be accommodated informally, outside of regularly scheduled ESL time. ESL teachers found themselves spreading their work time more thinly among more students, working with different students at different times of the week and school year, and having to decide which students needed them most. They also struggled to reconcile the contradictions between their own sense of students' need to acquire a solid foundation in language skills and the new culture of standards and assessment, where all students were expected to learn the same skills and concepts at roughly the same rate.

The time ESL teachers spent with immigrant students was further restricted by egalitarian beliefs that all students should receive the "same" resources and expectations, and that ESL teachers not "play favorites." In the elementary schools, they were expected to help any students who sought them out or whom other teachers believed needed special help. When they worked in other teachers' classrooms, computer labs, or libraries, ESL teachers at School B were reluctant to "draw special attention" to or appear to advocate specially for ESL students or to "deny" their attention to any student. An ESL teacher who spent part of her time in "regular" classrooms said, "I probably help all kids. Let's face it, I'm a warm body and they need help. I feel bad about the loss of attention to ESL students but that's the reality." At the school where ESL was presumably fully integrated, "regular" teachers could assign any small number of students – ESL, special education, "needy," or just needing special attention that day – to the ESL teachers

Many of the teachers we encountered were new to teaching ESL. None had taught ESL for more than a few years. Several teachers, in fact, lacked permanent teaching contracts and would not necessarily return to the school the following year. In the high school, sheltered subject teachers (teachers in "regular" subject departments like mathematics and science who were assigned to provide "bridging" classes in these subjects to ESL students) received little ESL training; workshops that ESL-certified teachers had provided in past years were no longer possible because of budget cuts. There were often no departmentally-designed teaching materials or lesson plans to fall back upon, and there was little continuity of staff from year to year because many teachers had little desire to teach sheltered classes. Sheltered teachers spoke of discovering that the department head had "just put [the sheltered class] on my timetable." Sheltered subject teachers expected ESL teachers to assume primary responsibility for ESL students' problems. One sheltered subject teacher said, "Even though I have ESL on my ticket, and I'm teaching ESL, I'm not an ESL teacher, I'm a geography teacher teaching ESL students. So I think they have their own teacher, and I think they really look after that." Another said, "There's an ESL department, and they should be the ones that are helping those kids."

In addition to the development and delivery of curriculum and the assessment of student learning, ESL teachers often served as school liaisons and provided special assistance to parents of their students. They also acted as advocates for ESL students beyond their classrooms and, in some cases, supported additional students believed to need extra help. ESL teachers expected themselves, and were expected by others, to serve as special advocates for their current and former students to compensate for dimensions of teachers' practice and school procedures that did not take ESL students into account. In the elementary schools, ESL teachers characterized themselves as "a lifeline for new kids, the one person who specifically cares about them, a friendly face, reminding teachers of the reality of the energy required to learn a new language in a foreign place, that it takes five to seven years to learn a new language." Advocacy often involved interactions with other teachers: "I'm another set of eyes if they say 'What's going on with this kid?'" Despite assertions by regular classroom teachers that "everyone here is an ESL teacher," ESL teachers felt it necessary to provide cultural translations on behalf of ESL students: for example, "try to make teachers realize that when they do a food unit, not every kid has Rice Krispies for breakfast, and if a kid says he had rice for breakfast then he probably did, and he might not recognize a picture of a waffle."

ESL teachers were expected to help other teachers by providing ESL training. But many teachers were reluctant to admit when they need help, and teachers who believed they could be of some assistance "tread carefully" in order to avoid challenging their colleagues' competence (Bascia, 1996a; Little, 1990a, 1990b). This was the case in each of the four schools, though it played out somewhat differently in each one. At the secondary school, sheltered subject teachers believed that such assistance was available to them but seemed ambivalent about making use of it. The ESL teacher in one elementary school was able to "model" teaching in his work in other teachers' classrooms and develop and deliver team-taught curriculum units with them. He described his efforts as "making their work lighter, I know how strapped teachers are," characterizing himself to us and to other teachers as their "assistant." An ESL teacher at another school said, "It's not our role to tell teachers what to do."

ESL teachers were also expected to take responsibility for the infusion of multiculturalism in their schools more generally, especially in the elementary schools. This took the form of team-taught units, reading of multicultural literature, working in "regular" classrooms to deliver curriculum units around various holidays, maintaining "multicultural" display cases, coordinating a guest speaker series, lunches and assemblies around various holidays, a multicultural book fair, a "culture club" for students, and ordering dual language books for the school library. Such efforts seemed restricted to episodic events rather than having any serious influence on the broader curriculum. One teacher told us that its consistency with the curriculum she herself had experienced as a child was what "[made] teaching all worthwhile." On the other hand, the intensification and high expectations for ESL teachers made us wonder whether such programs are sustainable in the long run.

It was relatively easy for us to identify the impact of recent policy changes on educational practice. Teachers themselves were quite conscious of how curriculum standardization, assessment and reporting requirements, changes in authority relations, and reductions in educational funding had brought about changes in their working conditions. But attention to policy directives of the past decade suggests that policies that have been revoked or reversed may leave their mark on marginal programs such as ESL, even when teachers do not identify them as such. For example, school-based rather than centralized programming was still in effect to some extent when it came to ESL: in the district where our study took place, the nature of ESL programming (e.g., whether it was integrated into "regular" classroom activities or operated as a separate "withdrawal" program) was to be determined at the school level. In the return to traditional authority relations, this meant that principals could decide how ESL programs would operate without having to consult with teachers. Because administrators had the right to hire and fire ESL teachers without the due process available to other teachers, ESL teachers were particularly anxious about their principals' impressions of their work. While most teachers worked under a more restrictive, technically-based set of policies, ESL teachers' work seemed to be predicated on the previous, expanded model: while most "regular" teachers worked relatively autonomously and primarily on curriculum delivery in their classrooms, ESL teachers were expected to "pay attention to the whole child," to provide professional development for and to team teach with other teachers, and to work the margins between "the community" (social services, immigrant families) and the school. In this sense, while most teachers worked under a more restrictive, technically-based conception of teaching, ESL teachers' work seemed predicated on the model that had been in effect before the Progressive Conservatives came to power.

Teachers, in short, lived and struggled with several contradictory sets of beliefs and values with respect to the education of immigrant children. It was apparent to us that the democratizing policies of the first half of the 1990s had been successful in establishing a set of work expectations for a cadre of ESL teachers but had not been sufficient in shifting understandings and distributing responsibility for teaching new immigrants more widely across school staffs. The standardizing policies of the late 1990s appeared to decrease the likelihood that such recognition, skills development, and redistribution would occur. Thus were the layers of practice laid down by recent policy swings made evident to us.

Discussion and Implications for Policy and Practice

What does this description of teaching immigrant students suggest about the impact of educational policy, and what are the implications for efforts to improve the education of new immigrants? First, these descriptions remind us that policy-makers, who have several possible policy choices at their disposal, have recently restricted their efforts to two instruments – mandates and system changes – which essentially have reduced schools' and teachers' ability to respond effectively to immigrant students' academic needs. Policy attempts during the early 1990s to encourage educators to expand their professional repertoires through a range of teacher leadership positions (inducements), to increase their capacities to address diverse students' academic needs by providing opportunities (time, money, and structures) for ongoing learning (capacity building), and to encourage broader participation in school programs (system changing) were reversed in the second half of the 1990s. This loss of capacity, incentives, and authority has had real effects on individuals and school programs. Such an awareness of policy options and systemic influences is necessary for both decision makers and educators to understand the real constraints and potential directions for improvement.

Second, these descriptions over time suggest that, as powerful as policy can be, it is also confounded by individual and collective experience and values. Consider the work of teachers who had special responsibility for immigrant students during the early 1990s. Despite a range of policy efforts to encourage such work – the antiracist and ethno-cultural policy and *Common Curriculum*, as well as a range of attempts to rethink teachers' professional development through mentoring programs, team teaching, shared planning time, and action research – teachers we spoke with described themselves as lone rangers, fighting the enduring power of "real school" embedded in their colleagues' habits and attitudes. During the late 1990s, conversely, despite the lack of official support for ESL programming and the host of policy efforts that effectively crowded it out of the curriculum, ESL teachers persisted, working daily to support immigrant students. Policy is powerful, but it interacts with organizational and individual realities. Rather than concluding that the situation is completely bleak or relatively satisfactory, it is important to recognize how these contradictions and tensions play out in real school settings. The power of policy is real, but policy instruments are always blunt. Broader capacity building is important, but the actual programmatic solutions must be worked out school by school and teacher by teacher. As Blackmore and Kenway (1995) suggest in relation to gender reform efforts in Australia, top-down, rationalist policy perspectives are in "direct antithesis to the process by which much gender reform had occurred in most schools in our study...There has always been teacher[s]...who through their own initiatives, experience or individual and collective struggle have worked for gender reform in schools in a variety of schools. [Change] is inconsistent, time-consuming, contradictory, open-ended, and uneven" (p. 239).

Third, the snapshot portraits of teaching in two recent time periods illustrates the "drag" of notions about "real school" which reinforces distinctions between teaching, teachers, subjects, and students, and marginalizes educational programming for new immigrants. At the same time, we can still discern the presence of several sets of structures, routines, values, and understandings marked and embodied by teachers' professional and life experiences. Eras of policy change also leave their mark on schools.

Policy, in short, is powerful, but practitioners weave a complicated web of possibilities. Working to democratize schools requires steady work (Elmore & McLaughlin, 1988) and persistence across multiple policy eras. Supporting the improvement of education for immigrant students is not about advocating for a single solution but rather recognizing and creating of a range of opportunities at both policy and practical levels.

References

Bailey, B. (2000). The impact of mandated change on teachers. In N. Bascia & A. Hargreaves (Eds.), *The sharp edge of educational change: Teaching, leading and the realities of reform.* (pp. 112-128). London: The Falmer Press.

Bascia, N. (1994). *Evaluation Report: "Creating a Culture of Change" Initiative.* Report prepared for Ontario Ministry of Education and Training and the Ontario Teachers' Federation, June.

Bascia, N. (1996a). Teacher leadership: Contending with adversity. *Canadian Journal of Education, 21*(2), 155-169.

Bascia, N. (1996b). Inside and outside: The experiences of racial minority immigrant teachers in Canadian schools. *International Journal of Qualitative Studies in Education, 9*(2), 151-165.

Bascia, N. (1996c). Caught in the crossfire: Restructuring, collaboration, and the problem school. *Urban Education, 31*(2), 177-198.

Bascia, N. (1996d). *Evaluation Report: "Creating a Culture of Change and Educational Network of Ontario" Initiatives.* Report prepared for Ontario Ministry of Education and Training and the Ontario Teachers' Federation, April.

Bascia, N. (1996e). Teacher unions and teacher professionalism in the U.S.: Reconsidering a familiar dichotomy. In B. Biddle, T. Good & I. Goodson (Eds.), *International handbook of teachers and teaching* (pp. 437-458). Dordrecht, the Netherlands: Kluwer Academic Publishers.

Bascia, N. & Hargreaves, A. (2000). Teaching and leading on the sharp edge of change. In N. Bascia & A. Hargreaves (Eds.), *The sharp edge of educational change: Teaching, leading and the realities of reform* (pp. 3-26). London: The Falmer Press.

Bascia, N. & Jacka, N. (2000a). *When "every teacher is an ESL teacher" (not): The organizational context of ESL teaching.* Paper presented at the annual meeting of the American Educational Research Association, New Orleans, LA, April.

Bascia, N. & Jacka, N. (2000b). *Falling out and filling in: ESL teaching careers in changing times.* Paper presented at the annual meeting of the Canadian Society for Studies in Education, Edmonton, AB, May.

Blackmore, J. & Kenway, J. (1995). Changing schools, teachers and curriculum: But what about the girls? In D. Corson (Ed.), *Discourse and power in educational organizations* (pp. 233-256). Cresskill, NJ: Hampton Press, Inc.

Campbell, E. (1996). "The tensions within: Diversity in a multi-everything secondary school." *Alberta Journal of Educational Research, 42*(3), 280-292.

Carlson, D. (1992). *Teachers and crisis: Urban school reform and teachers' work culture.* New York: Routledge Chapman & Hall.

Chambliss, D. (1997). *Restructuring high schools and the response to student diversity.* Paper presented at the annual meeting of the American Educational Research Association, Chicago, IL, March.

Clune, W. (1990). Three views of curriculum policy in the school context: The school as policy mediator, policy critic, and policy constructor. In M. McLaughlin, J. Talbert & N. Bascia (Eds.), *The contexts of teaching in secondary schools: Teachers' realities* (pp. 256-270). New York: Teachers College Press.

Cochran-Smith, M. & Lytle, S. (1992). Communities for teacher research: Fringe or forefront? *American Journal of Education,* May 100 (3), 298-324.

Cohen, D. (1991). Revolution in one classroom. In S. H. Fuhrman & B. Malen (Eds.), *The politics of curriculum and testing: The 1990 yearbook of the Politics in Education Association* (pp. 103-123). Philadelphia, PA: Falmer Press.

Coulter, R. (1996). Gender equity and schooling: Linking research and policy. *Canadian Journal of Education, 21*(4), 433-452.

Curtis, B., Livingstone, D. & Smaller, H. (1992). *Stacking the deck: The streaming of working-class kids in Ontario schools.* Toronto: Our Schools/Our Selves.

Darling-Hammond, L. (1997). The limits of the education bureaucracy (chapter 2). In *The right to learn: A blueprint for creating schools that work* (pp. 37-68). San Francisco, CA: Jossey-Bass.

Datnow, A. (2000). Gender politics in school reform. In N. Bascia & A. Hargreaves (Eds.), *The sharp edge of educational change: Teaching, leading and the realities of reform* (pp. 131-155). London: The Falmer Press.

Dei, G. (1994). Anti-racist education: Working across differences. *Orbit, 25*(2), 1-3.

Dorph, R. (1997). *The construction and categorization of knowledge and assumptions about students.* Paper presented at the annual meeting of the American Educational Research Association, Chicago, IL, March.

Downs, A. (1972). Up and down with ecology - The issue-attention cycle. *Public Interest, 28,* Summer 38-50.

Earl, L. (1999). Assessment and accountability in education: Improvement or surveillance? *Education Canada, 39* (3), 4-6, & 47.

Earl, L., Bascia, N., Hargreaves, A. & Jacka, N. (1998). *Teachers and teaching in changing times: A glimpse of Canadian teachers in 1998.* Prepared for the Canadian Teachers' Federation. Toronto: International Centre for Educational Change, Ontario Institute for Studies in Education of the University of Toronto (OISE/UT).

Earl, L. & Katz, S. (2000). Changing classroom assessment: Teachers' struggles. In N. Bascia & A. Hargreaves (Eds.), *The sharp edge of educational change: Teaching, leading and the realities of reform* (pp. 97-111). London: The Falmer Press.

Eaton, M. S. (1998). *Teaching high school mathematics to English learners: Practice as policy.* Unpublished dissertation. Stanford, CA: Stanford University School of Education.

Elmore, R. & McLaughlin, M. (1988). *Steady work: Policy, practice, and the reform of American education*. Santa Monica, CA: RAND Corporation.

Foster, M. (1992). The politics of race: Through the eyes of African-American teachers. In K. Weiler & C. Mitchell (Eds.), *What schools can do: Critical pedagogy and practice* (pp. 177-202). Albany: SUNY Press.

Foster, M. (1994). The role of community and culture in school reform efforts: Examining the views of African-American teachers. *Educational Foundations, 8* (2), 5-26.

Galt, V. & Sarick, L. (1999). Schools shortchange non-English speakers. *The Globe and Mail*, Nov. 10, A9.

Gebhard, M. (1997). *Second language acquisition in restructured elementary schools*. Paper presented at the annual meeting of the American Educational Research Association, Chicago, IL, March.

Gidney, R. (1999). *From Hope to Harris: The reshaping of Ontario's schools*. Toronto: University of Toronto Press.

Gitlin, A. (1996) Gender and professionalization: An institutional analysis of teacher education and unionism at the turn of the twentieth century. *Teachers College Record, 97*(4), 588-624.

Hargreaves, A. (1994). *Changing teachers, changing times: Teachers' work and culture in the postmodern age*. London: Cassell.

Harper, H. (1997). Difference and diversity in Ontario schooling. *Canadian Journal of Education, 22* (2), 192-206.

Hemmings, A. & Metz, M. (1992). Real teaching: How high school teachers negotiate societal, local community, and student pressures when they define their work. In L. Valli & R. Page (Eds.), *Curriculum differentiation: Interpretive studies in U.S. secondary schools* (pp. 91-111). Albany: SUNY Press.

Henry, A. (1992). African Canadian women teachers' activism: Recreating communities of caring and resistance. *Journal of Negro Education, 61* (3), 392-404.

Larson, M. S. (1977). *The rise of professionalism: A sociological analysis*. Berkeley: University of California Press.

Lieberman, A. (1988). Teachers and principals: Turf, tensions and new tasks. *Phi Delta Kappan, 69*, 948-953.

Little, J. (1990a). The persistence of privacy: Autonomy and initiative in teachers' professional relations. *Teachers College Record, 91*(4), 509-536.

Little, J. (1990b). The mentor phenomenon and the social organization of teaching. *Review of Research in Education, 16*, 297-352.

Little, J. (1993). Teachers' professional development in a climate of educational reform. *Educational Evaluation and Policy Analysis, 15* (2), 129-151.

Little, J. W. (1995). Contested ground: The basis of teacher leadership in two restructuring high schools. *Elementary School Journal, 96* (1), 47-63.

Louis, K. S. (1990). Social and community values and the quality of teachers' work life. In M. McLaughlin, T. Talbert & N. Bascia (Eds.), *The contexts of teaching in secondary schools: Teachers' realities*, (pp. 17-39). New York: Teachers College Press.

McDonnell, L., & Elmore, R. (1987). Getting the job done: Alternative policy instruments. *Educational Evaluation and Policy Analysis, 9* (2), 133-152.

McLaughlin, M. (1987). Learning from experience: Lessons from policy implementation. *Educational Evaluation and Policy Analysis, 9* (2), 171-178.

Metz, M. (1989). Real school: A universal drama amid disparate experience. In D. Mitchell & M. Goertz (Eds.), *Education politics for the new century: The twentieth anniversary yearbook of the Politics of Education Association* (pp. 75-91). London: The Falmer Press.

Meyer, J. & Rowan, B. (1978). The structure of educational organizations. In M. W. Meyer & Associates (Eds.). *Environments and organizations*, 78-109. San Francisco: Jossey-Bass.

Miles, K. & Darling-Hammond, L. (1998). Rethinking the allocation of teaching resources: Some lessons from high-performing schools. *Educational Evaluation and Policy Analysis 20*(1), 9-29.

Muncey, D. E. & McQuillan, P. J. (1993). Preliminary findings from a five-year study of the Coalition of Essential Schools. *Phi Delta Kappan, 74* (6), 486-489.

Nespor, J. (1997). *Tangled up in school: Politics, space, bodies and signs in the educational process.* Hillsdale, NJ: Lawrence Erlbaum Associates.

Oakes, J., Wells, A., Yonezawa, S. & Ray, K. (2000). Change agentry and the quest for equity: Lessons from detracking schools. In N. Bascia & A. Hargreaves (Eds.), *The sharp edge of educational change: Teaching, leading and the realities of reform* (pp. 72-96). London: The Falmer Press.

Olsen, L. (1997). *Made in America.* New York: The New Press.

Ontario. (1993a). *Antiracism and ethno-cultural equity in school boards – Guidelines for policy development and implementation.* Toronto, ON: Ministry of Education and Training.

Ontario. (1993b). *The Common Curriculum Grades 1-9 working document. Version of parents and the general public.* Toronto, ON: Ministry of Education and Training.

Ontario. (1995). *The Common Curriculum Policies and Outcomes Grades 1-9.* Toronto, Ontario: Ministry to Education and Training.

Ontario. (1999). *Ontario Secondary Schools Grades 9 to 12.* Toronto, ON: Ministry of Education and Training.

Ortiz, F. I. (1982). *Career patterns in education: Men, women and minorities in public school administration.* New York: J. F. Praeger.

Powell, A., Farrar, E. & Cohen, D. (1985). *The shopping mall high school: Winners and losers in the educational marketplace.* Boston: Houghton Mifflin.

Reynolds, C. (1990). Hegemony and hierarchy: Becoming a teacher in Toronto, 1930-1980. *Historical Studies in Education, 2*(1), 95-118.

Rusk, B., Shaw, J. & Joong, P. (1994). *The full service school.* Toronto: Ontario Secondary School Teachers' Federation.

Smaller, H. (1991). "A room of one's own": The early years of the Toronto Women Teachers' Association. In R. Heap & A. Prentice (Eds.), *Gender and education in Ontario: An historical reader* (pp. 103-124). Toronto: Canadian Scholars' Press.

Smith, M. & O'Day, J. (1991). Systemic school reform. In S. H. Fuhrman & B. Malen (Eds.), *The politics of curriculum and testing: The 1990 yearbook of the Politics in Education Association* (pp. 233-267). Philadelphia, PA: Falmer Press.

Talbert, J. & McLaughlin, M. (1994). Teacher professionalism in local school contexts. *American Journal of Education, 102* (2), 123-153.

Thiessen, D., Bascia, N. & Goodson, I. (Eds.) (1996). *Making a difference about difference. The lives and careers of racial minority immigrant teachers.* Toronto: Remtel/Garamond Press,

Timar, T. (1989). The politics of school restructuring. *Phi Delta Kappan, 71*(4), 264-275.

Tyack, D. (1991). Public school reform: Policy talk and institutional practice. *American Journal of Education, 98*, 1-19.

Tyack, D. & Tobin, W. (1994). The 'grammar' of schooling: Why has it been so hard to change? *American Educational Research Journal, 31*(3), 453-479.

Urban, W. J. (1982). *Why teachers organized.* Detroit: Wayne State University Press.

Weatherley, R. & Lipsky, M. (1977). Street-level bureaucrats and institutional innovation: Implementing special-education reform. *Harvard Educational Review, 47*(2), 171-197.

Werner, W. (1991). Curriculum and uncertainty. In R. Ghosh & D. Ray (Eds.), *Social change and education in Canada*, 2nd edition (pp. 105-115). Toronto: Harcourt Brace Jovanovich.

Whitty, G., Powers, S. & Halpin, D. (1998). *Devolution and choice in education: the state, the school and the market.* Buckingham: Open University Press.

Wong, P. (2000). *New math, same old story: Standards-based mathematics curriculum and English language learners.* Paper presented at the annual meeting of the American Educational Research association, New Orleans, LA.

Zeichner, K. (1991). Contradictions and tensions in the professionalization of teaching and the democratization of schools. *Teachers College Record, 92* (3), 364-379.

Funding was provided by the Social Sciences and Humanities Research Council (SSHRC) of Canada, through the auspices of the "Racial/Ethnocultural Minority Teachers: Identities and Careers" and "Cultural Negotiation of Minority Students and Teachers" research projects.

Chapter 11
Educational Programming for Children Living in Poverty: Possibilities and Challenges

Bill Maynes

All Western democracies have imbedded within them perspectives on social justice that reflect what the particular society has accepted as an appropriate balance between social and individual responsibility. Of course, that balance is never static; always being "renegotiated." In Canada, the current re-negotiation is being heavily influenced by forces of globalization and the accompanying neoliberal orientation of "the new right."

Within that context, as has always been the case, schools are expected to be instruments of social justice in the sense that schools are expected to serve purposes related to social mobility. Canadians cling to the view that individuals, regardless of their circumstances of birth, can be successful in our society. Schools are expected to play a major role in ensuring that this is possible. This is a comfortable and encouraging view of schooling. With respect to education of children living in poverty, Canada's social responsibility is discharged through the provision of a uniform quality of schooling for all; to access the good life, individuals need only take advantage of this opportunity.

There are, however, less comfortable, less encouraging perspectives on the role of schooling in our society. Critical pedagogues have raised powerful and well-articulated critiques which position schools very differently with respect to matters of social justice. Critical theorists have exposed the role that schooling plays as one of society's key "sorting mechanisms" in which "select groups of students are favored on the basis of race, class and gender" (McLaren, 1989, p. 160). McClaren and others, such as Henri Giroux and Michael Apple, have put forward compelling arguments that "schools serve the interests of the wealthy and the powerful, while simultaneously disconfirming the values and the abilities of those students who are most disempowered in our society already: minorities, the poor and female" (McLaren, 1989, p. 163). Far from being instruments of social justice, schools are seen as serving the purposes of the dominant culture by helping transfer privilege from generation to generation.

These two radically different images of schooling – one embodying the popular view of schools as instruments of social justice; the other, the critical view of schools as instruments of hegemony – frame the contents of this chapter. The first image calls upon us to look for ways in which schooling can contribute to improving the life-chances of children living in poverty. The second image calls upon us to be alert to the substantial challenges inherent in pursuing those possibilities. The first image would have us examine matters of instruction. What do we know about educational programming for children living in poverty? What can be done? The second image reminds us that we need to view these possibilities in relation to structural matters. That is, we need to attend to political, economic, and curricular forces that limit the extent to which what is possible will be achieved.

In this chapter, I endeavor to keep both images on the surface, although in various sections one image is clearly more visible than the other. Early on, the focus on possibilities – on successful educational programming for children living in poverty – brings the first image forward; later the exploration of challenges which constrain such programming brings the second image forward. For the most part, however, I hope that by keeping practice at the center of the argument, I have been able to keep both images in view.

On Possibilities

Perhaps the first point to be made is that there is good reason to examine what can be done. To date, most Canadian children living in poverty have not been particularly well served by schooling. By any measure, collectively these children do less well in school than their non-poor counterparts. In grade school, they score substantially lower on standardized testing and are far more likely to be identified as "special needs" students (Levin, 1995; Ross, Scott & Smith, 2000). They are also more than twice as likely to drop out of school (Ross, Shillington & Lochhead, 1994) and up to four times less likely to access post-secondary education (Connell, 1993). A dismal record. But perhaps it need not remain so. There are bright spots; there are schools, such as Park and Lord Dufferin in Toronto, that have done much better. We now have a substantial body of well-researched knowledge about what can be done to make a difference for children living in poverty.

Schorr (1988), writing about social programming generally, provided a perspective on what can be done: "in the last two decades we have accumulated a critical mass of information that totally transforms the nation's capacity to improve outcomes for vulnerable children. The knowledge necessary to reduce the growing toll of damaged lives is now available" (p. xix). With respect to schooling, we now have strong research-based evidence that particular kinds of programming can make a substantial difference. Those with the strongest research support include: high quality pre-kindergarten programming (Barnett, 1998; Schweinhart, Barnes & Weikart, 1993), comprehensive school-wide programs such as Success for All (Slavin & Fashola, 1998), pedagogical approaches which focus on higher levels of thinking (what Knapp and Associates [1995] refer to as "teaching for meaning") and tutoring programs such as Reading Recovery (Slavin & Fashola, 1998, pp. 59-62). There are also encouraging results from a number of curriculum-specific programs in mathematics and in reading, writing, and language arts (Slavin & Fashola, 1998, pp. 43-55). We know what can be done to improve outcomes for children living in poverty.

Acting on this knowledge requires that school jurisdictions engage in more than the "regular" programming provided at all schools. In part, to get a sense of the extent of additional programming for children living in poverty Rosemary Foster and I (Maynes & Foster, 1998) surveyed all Canadian school jurisdictions each serving more than 18 000 students (15 000 for provinces east of Ontario). In doing so we identified 145 "Canadian Educational Poverty Programs." While such programs were in place in most urban centers, we found heavier concentrations in school jurisdictions that employed specialists to coordinate "inner city" programming (The School Council of the Island of Montreal, the Toronto Board of Education and Winnipeg School Division). *The Directory of Canadian Educational Poverty Programs* (Maynes & Foster, 1998) which resulted from that survey provides a broad and somewhat encouraging perspective on possibilities. There were quite a number of programs in place in Canadian jurisdictions. But the work also provides a perspective on challenges. In Maynes and Foster (forthcoming), for example, we noted that 91 of the 145 programs depended for their existence on temporary funding. We also noted that, with a few exceptions, much of this programming had either not been evaluated or the evaluations were done poorly. Together, these factors highlight the vulnerability of much current educational programming for Canadian children living in poverty. Programs that are not evaluated properly and that are not funded through base budgets are obvious targets for policymakers who find themselves having to balance budgets in times of fiscal restraint.

This draws our attention to the interplay between possibilities and challenges when programming is viewed from afar, at a distance from the school environments in which the programming is lived. We get a sense of the kinds of programs that can make a difference and a broad sense of jurisdiction- or policy-level challenges to initiating or maintaining such programs. I see this broad perspective, which elsewhere (Maynes, 1993a; 1993b; 1996) I have explored in some detail, as essential to understanding the discrepancy between what we could be doing and what we actually do in Canada to educate children living in poverty. But I also see it as limited by being distanced from the dynamics of the day-to-day interactions of those who bring the programming to life in schools. My purpose in this chapter is to construct what I see as a complementary view, a view of possibilities and challenges from the perspective of school-level practice. Accordingly, the remainder of this chapter is devoted to exploring lessons about possibilities and challenges that can be extracted from the experiences of two schools for which there is considerable evidence to support the claim that they provide exemplary education for children living in poverty. Park Public School and Lord Dufferin Public School are both part of the Project School Initiative in Toronto that is, perhaps, the most comprehensive Canadian educational poverty program, that has been thoroughly evaluated.

Toronto's Project School Initiative

The Toronto Board of Education introduced the Project School Initiative in response to a 1973 study which demonstrated that "a disproportionate percentage of children from Inner City schools were found in Vocational courses – now known as Basic courses" (TDSB, 1998, p. 1). The intent was to find the most effective way for the school district to use the additional resources which they had allocated to support inner city schools, and in so doing, to "help deal with the poor performance in schools associated with poverty" (ibid.). From the outset, enhancing equity for children living in poverty has been the central goal of the project school initiative. To facilitate their work toward this goal, project schools are assigned additional staff in the form of a "Project Resource Team" which coordinates project work and provides "on-going site based staff development" (Goldman, 1999).

Careful evaluations conducted by the Toronto School Board's Academic Accountability Unit have demonstrated that project schools have been successful in improving academic outcomes. Yau (1998), for example, said of the gains in literacy for the children at Lord Dufferin School: "For three consecutive years, the post-assessment results show a notable increase in the proportion of students performing at (Benchmark) Level 3 or above by the end of the school year" (p. 1). In making this point more generally, Goldman (1999) quoted Mary Low, then Executive Officer of the Academic Accountability Unit: "All of you [staff at Lord Dufferin] have demonstrated your accountability to the students and the parental community and you have done this in an outstanding way. Thank you for your care and commitment to children and their success. You are making a wonderful difference in their lives" (p. 4).

Such assessments led to the selection of the project school initiative for inclusion in a study of exemplary Canadian urban educational poverty programs. This in turn led to case study research in two project schools: Lord Dufferin and Park (Maynes, 2000). The case study reports, I contend, provide a sense of why children in these schools have been successful; a sense of what children experience in project schools that they may not experience in other schools. I hope that is not entirely lost in the manner in which I draw upon those reports in this chapter. Space limitations simply prohibit the presentation of the full reports. At any rate, I commend readers to those reports (Maynes, 2000) for a more "nuanced" view of the ways in which project schools fulfill their mandates, and for a description of the case study research methodology that led to the development of the reports.

With respect to methodology, I will note here only that I obtained and analyzed a substantial collection of district- and school-level documents related to the project school initiative and that, during two-day site visits at each school, I interviewed parents, classroom teachers, project teachers (including the project facilitators), non-certified staff, and administrative staff. In the following exploration of how schooling unfolds in Lord Dufferin and Park schools I have called upon the documents to clarify a number of technical or organizational matters. The words of those I interviewed are meant to serve grander purposes. Functionally, these words serve to convey meaning that is likely inaccessible without them. Context and practice are integrated seamlessly in the words of those who have lived the experiences of Lord Dufferin and Park schools. Without their words, what follows would be a sterile listing of activities. Schooling at Lord Dufferin and Park is so much more than that. A second purpose relates more to ownership. The stories of these schools belong to the people who lived the stories. I hope this is clear in the words I have chosen and that I have chosen in ways that honor the voices of the remarkable people who bring these schools to life.

The Schools

Lord Dufferin and Park are inner city schools, both serving families in Toronto's Regent Park Community. In each, the student complement of over 600 is richly multicultural, including more than 30 language groups. Seventy percent of these students have English as their second language.

Both schools are rated as "1A" inner city schools, signifying that they are among the schools that rate highest (or most in need) with respect to the criteria used to assess "inner-cityness" in Toronto. Given that they serve one of the lowest income communities, which also has one of the highest concentrations of subsidized public housing in Toronto, this is not at all surprising. Indeed, Yau (1998) referred to Lord Dufferin as "one of the most inner-city schools in Toronto," noting that "[m]ost of the students come from low-income families, with 1 in 3 living with a lone parent." The principal at Park simply observed that "The common factor that all the kids in this school have is that everybody is pretty poor."

Staff at both schools are keenly aware of the challenges they and their students face due to the nature of the school community. The results of an assessment of children beginning the Kindergarten program at Park during 1997 provide one perspective on those challenges. The assessment found that 37% of the Park children were "at-risk," compared to 3% in the general population (Yau, 1997). The level of student transiency at these schools provides another. In making this point, a teacher at Lord Dufferin spoke of a "Decade Club," membership in which requires that a student be enrolled in the school from junior kindergarten through grade 8. She observed that "two years ago, of the 55 who graduated, only 10 had been with us for the decade. Last year, out of 52 or so who graduated, only 9 belonged to the Decade Club." Teachers also spoke of the linkage between the extent of poverty in the community and student behavior, particularly their orientation toward violence. One observed: "The kids come with stories;...the sad thing is that they don't think it is unusual to have vagrants outside their window. They are totally desensitized. They will watch someone get knifed or kicked,…watch it like it is an everyday occurrence. And I think to myself, 'how many kids grow up with this kind of thing on a daily basis?'" Staff at Park also worry about the amount of violence in the community. This, however, they attribute to the drug dealing and prostitution which is practiced in the community by people who do not live in the community. As the principal observed, "they use the community as a place to deal drugs." But, irrespective of who the dealers are, the presence of drug dealers in the community does affect schooling and child rearing generally. In the words of a staff member who chooses to live in the community: "Success! What is success? Success to a lot of people in the community is keeping the children off drugs because the influence is so strong."

In the context of the many issues related to poverty and the nature of the community, staff at both schools see considerable strength related to diversity. The principal at Park, for example, noted that "there has been a concerted effort…in this community to build links between groups.…When you go to community meetings, just about all the ethnic groups are present and talking with and supporting each other." He also recognized the strengths brought to Canada through immigration: "People come with incredible credentials and experiences.…They provide leadership in the community." He illustrated this point by referring to one parent who was "educated as a doctor in Romania and then practiced medicine for four years in Cuba." He observed that many of Park's immigrant families place a very high priority on education, seeing education as a "stepping stone."

Certainly, programming at Lord Dufferin and Park is shaped considerably by the poverty-related issues confronting the children and families in the community. But so too is it shaped by the diversity in the community and by the strengths of those who live in the community.

Project School Programming at Lord Dufferin

Since its designation in 1993 as a project school, the goal of providing an environment within which students can achieve equity of outcomes has guided programming at Lord Dufferin. The teachers felt strongly that this could not be achieved simply by importing mainstream approaches to teaching and learning. As one said, "The traditional or old style, the factory model, whichever label you want to put on it, does not work [at Lord Dufferin]. You really have to look at alternative ways." Doing so is facilitated by Lord Dufferin's project school designation.

In addition to the resources assigned to all "1A" inner city schools, as a project school, Lord Dufferin is assigned extra staff resources to facilitate innovative programming and on-site professional development. One position is devoted to the role of "project facilitator," the others to the roles of "project teacher." Although overall leadership for the project is most directly the responsibility of the project facilitator, in practice, that responsibility is shared with the project teachers and the other administrative staff at the school.

Over the five years during which Lord Dufferin has been a project school, the school has sought to enhance equity through work in four overlapping areas: Social Skills-Problem Solving, Literacy, Math/Science/Technology, and The Arts. Figure 1 is a diagram similar to one the staff have used to illustrate the ways in which these areas relate to each other and to the central goal of equity of outcomes for students.

Figure 1: Project School Areas of Emphasis at Lord Dufferin

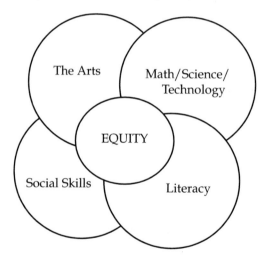

While these areas of emphasis have been addressed each year, the amount of attention devoted to each – the relative priority for action – has differed from year to year. There has been a kind of evolution, as each year's plan has been refined based on the previous year's experience. This process was described in the Lord Dufferin 1998-99 program plan:

> *There has been a shift in emphasis on past goals due to positive change and significant accomplishments as well as simply changing circumstances that influence our work. For instance, although discipline and safety issues are still being addressed, there have been significant pos-*

itive results in this area. The parents and staff four and a half years ago identified this area as critical. There was a sense that the school was acting in a crisis, reactive mode. These issues that were foremost in people's minds in 1993-94 during the consultation period, were barely touched on this year....I believe this is a major accomplishment ...[which] allows us to better facilitate and expend our energy and commitment on our ultimate goal and the main goal of the Project – improving the academic success of our students. (Lord Dufferin Public School, 1998, p. 2)

Successes experienced in the Social Skills-Conflict Resolution areas have allowed the school to focus on the other areas, with a very strong emphasis on literacy. This is not to suggest that the Social Skills-Conflict resolution area does not receive significant attention. It certainly does. But the school reviews (e.g., Biggs, 1999) and the recent program plans make it clear that, for the past several years, issues in this area have not been at anything near the "crisis level" at which they were at the beginning of the project.

Literacy initiatives have included such activities as "Reading Club extended to grade 6 classrooms," "Homework Club opportunities after school with volunteer tutors from Frontier College," "action plan to improve language acquisition as measured on EQAO [Ontario Education Quality and Accountability Office standardized tests]," and "First Steps Training for staff moving from Reading to Writing" (Biggs, 1999). There was also a major "Storytelling Project involving parents, students, staff and professional storytellers telling stories and writing stories for publication."

The storytelling project illustrates the "overlappingness" of the areas of emphasis illustrated in Figure 1 and highlights the multicultural orientation which is imbedded in all programs at Lord Dufferin. Prior to beginning the project, staff engaged in professional development activities focussing on narrative storytelling as a vehicle for enhancing literacy. One of the project teachers described how the storytelling project was then "kicked off by bringing in several professional storytellers." She observed that "the children listened to the professionals and the teachers listened to the professionals. Everyone was extremely excited. The kids were coming up to me and saying 'I remember that story in my country!'" Building on the enthusiasm generated from this beginning, the project teachers organized a "professional development session with teachers and provided them with a package that would guide their use of storytelling as a language arts strategy." The classroom work that followed led to a school-wide "storytelling festival" during which students had opportunities, in front of audiences of parents and community members, to tell the stories they had learned. This "retelling" phase of the storytelling process led naturally to the "reflect" stage in which students were asked to write their own stories. This stage connected very strongly with the "equity" emphasis. "We invited the community to share their family stories, the cultural stories for their heritage, their stories from growing up in Regent Park." Children and parents worked together in developing these stories. "We organized a way so that we could send the children home to collect the stories....Some of them are written in their first language. We got them translated, sent them home for revisions, back to school....It was a long process which took an entire term." A project teacher noted that the results were worth the effort: "Ultimately we had some of the most poignant and powerful stories" describing experiences which range from "star gazing in Regent Park to escaping from Vietnam in a boat with arms tied together because if we capsized and all washed ashore at least they would know to bury us together." The stories were published in *Family Stories from Lord Dufferin P.S.* (Lord Dufferin Public School, 1999).

Biggs (1999) reports that, in the Math/Science/Technology area, a new initiative was undertaken in the form of a "School-Wide Science Theme organized on the strand of 'Structures and Mechanisms' including; professional development, development of resources, cross-age teaching, teacher partnering, fieldtrips, speakers and a display of learning" (p. 3).

The program activity in the Arts area also illustrates that Lord Dufferin staff have been able to shift their energies from safety and security concerns to student programming. In addition to activities such as "student participation in Board events such as Dramafest and Music Camps," "support and modeling for integration of Arts across the curriculum" and "coordination of performances and special celebration assemblies," two major initiative were undertaken. One of these, "The Tamil Music Project," resulted in the publication of "Tamil children's songs sung by parents and transcribed by staff." The publication was illustrated by the children and the music was taught to all students in the school. This publication has now achieved a wider audience, including all Toronto schools with Tamil children, and a variety of schools across Canada.

While the aspects of the program that define Lord Dufferin as a project school can be separated from the rest of the program for reporting purposes, the staff and students do not experience such a separation. Consider what the principal said about special needs programs:

We have six programs in the school that serve kids with behavior issues, learning disabilities....We have a lot of interaction with various agencies. When you were going around, you met kids from George Brown College who are studying to become child and youth workers; there were Drama Co-op students from high school; we have volunteer tutors; the Sick Kids Hospital runs a program for kids who are at-risk....We designate one of our own staff members as a crisis intervention worker who works directly with families and students who are at-risk.

She then pointed out that they could do this "because we are a project school." A teacher made a similar point in relation to "the facilitation of special needs kids in our classrooms." She noted that "the project has helped us be more aware" and that "we have gotten a lot better in terms of early identification and actually doing something about it."

Each year, parents and community members have played a significant role in developing and monitoring the project school program plans. This is just one indication of the strong orientation towards, and support of, parent and community involvement as expressed in the school goal "to expand direct opportunities for parents' involvement in school initiatives and decision making and to increase their satisfaction" (Biggs, 1999, p. 6). Their considerable progress with the goal is evident in the high level of parent involvement in classroom activities, in school-wide projects, Adult ESL day classes, the Parenting Centre, and in School Council Meetings.

Staff spoke of parent involvement in classroom activities. The storytelling project outlined above provides one example of such involvement. Parent involvement in the school-wide science theme, "Structures and Mechanisms," provides another. In relation to this work in science, one teacher commented: "We have been successful in getting more and more parents involved." If this parent's comment is any indication, the involvement was very positive:

It was fun to have a chance to work with my son in class. We could both learn. It helped my concentration because we both had to pay attention to what we were building. It was a short day, but nice. Shaun really liked having me there and I hope to have another chance.

A teacher commented on the linkage between success in this area and their being a project school: "The parents are getting involved because of some of the programs that the project staff started....It is a big improvement for the school because the parents feel that they belong somewhere in the school with their children. It really does help."

Project School Programming at Park

In their 1993 proposal to achieve project school status, staff at Park wrote:

> *Park needs to recommit to the fundamental notion that our students, regardless of race, class or gender, have the ability and the right to achieve equity of outcome.*

Since that time, this has remained as the "goal and cornerstone of the Park Project" (Park Public School, 1998, p. 3). From the outset, "anti-racist curriculum" has served as a primary means of addressing this goal. This is clear in the following excerpt from the 1998 "Inner City Project Review."

> *[Anti-racist curriculum] is curriculum defined in the broadest sense to include what is taught, how it is taught, who the children see in the school, in books and on the walls and how we evaluate and are held accountable in our work. It is, as well, an integrated inclusive approach, global in scope with an emphasis on community links, integration of new technologies, continual professional development, self-esteem, creativity and academic excellence.*

> *Anti-racist curriculum is based on the belief that there is a very direct link between a child's sense of the importance of their own identity, its affirmation in school and the development of respect for all people, regardless of race, class, gender, ethno-cultural background and sexual orientation, and a child's self-esteem, academic success and development of life-long learning skills. (Park Public School, 1998, p. 3)*

Each year, several additional goals have served as complements to the focus on antiracist curriculum. Figure 2 illustrates the goals for 1999-2000, and the ways in which they relate to each other.

Figure 2: Park Project Priorities 1999 - 2000

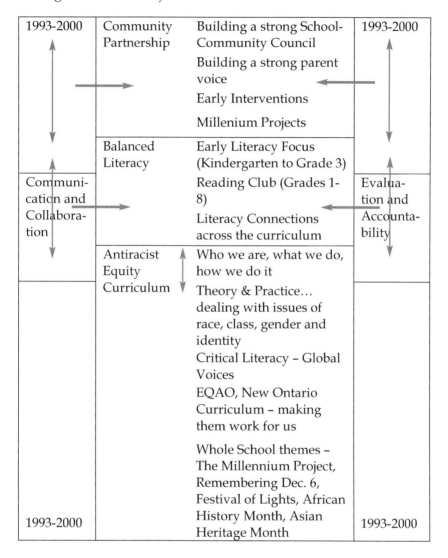

1993-2000	Community Partnership	Building a strong School-Community Council	1993-2000
		Building a strong parent voice	
		Early Interventions	
		Millenium Projects	
	Balanced Literacy	Early Literacy Focus (Kindergarten to Grade 3)	
Communication and Collaboration		Reading Club (Grades 1-8)	Evaluation and Accountability
		Literacy Connections across the curriculum	
	Antiracist Equity Curriculum	Who we are, what we do, how we do it	
		Theory & Practice… dealing with issues of race, class, gender and identity	
		Critical Literacy – Global Voices	
		EQAO, New Ontario Curriculum – making them work for us	
1993-2000		Whole School themes – The Millennium Project, Remembering Dec. 6, Festival of Lights, African History Month, Asian Heritage Month	1993-2000

The model displayed in Figure 2 conveys a picture of a very complex program with its components linked to three priorities. This is how the program for 1999-2000 was described in Park's 1999 School Profile:

> *Park Public School is an Inner City Project School with a commitment to equity and excellence for all students. As a Project School, the school has a Project Team of three and a half extra staff members, who*

act as curriculum resource teachers to teachers and students. This year Park School has committed itself to the Early Literacy Longitudinal Project and as such has an Early Literacy Co-ordinator and two teachers involved in working with Grade 1 students in Reading Recovery.

As a school our three major goals for this year are:

• *To build a balanced literacy program in all our classrooms.*

• *To build a strong school-community partnership.*

• *Develop antiracist curriculum and continue to build an inclusive school with a focus on equity and equity of outcomes.*

This year we are planning a special school-wide millennium activity called "The Stories We Have To Tell." This activity will allow us to concretely put into practice our learning around the three goals mentioned above. All students in the school will be involved in integrated studies where students will develop literacy, artistic, social studies and science skills around the theme of developing and telling our stories, that is, the stories that make each of us who we are. (TDSB, 1999a, p. 1)

Both the model and this summary statement from the 1999 School Profile convey the sense of "wholeness" and "connectedness" that is so important to understanding how children, parents, and staff experience the school program at Park. In the words of the project facilitator: "Everything that goes on in the school, we consider curriculum. Everything! No matter what; it is curriculum."

Inclusion. A commitment to inclusion serves as an underlying principle for all programming at Park. The teachers celebrate this as one of the qualities that makes Park, as one of them said, "truly unique." But they also know that inclusion requires support. The same teacher commented "kids with learning disabilities and behavior – it is amazing to me, having them fully integrated. We take it for granted. This is the way it is. To talk to somebody [from a different school] who teaches a behavior class with six kids and two assistants, I can't believe it. I don't think we could do it if it weren't for the project staff."

Both the sense of "connectedness" and the orientation toward inclusion can be seen in specific initiatives that characterize much of the work at Park School. In a report prepared for their annual inner city project review, Park Public School (1998) highlighted five of these initiatives; (1) role models and mentors, (2) whole school themes, (3) parent and community involvement, (4) reading club, and (5) behavioral advocacy.

Role Models and Mentors. Staff at Park have thought carefully about the ways in which role modeling provided by adults in the school – staff, volunteers, guests – can contribute to the goals of the school. In their words:

> *The importance for our students of seeing themselves in the diversity of people who are in our school – to visit, to work, to volunteer, to perform, to speak – is multi-purposed and cannot be over-emphasized. It enables us, as a school, to dismantle stereotypes, to break down gender barriers, to help foster respect and tolerance, and to provide life-long role models. (Park Public School, 1998, p. 4)*

Park also has a formal one-on-one mentoring program that serves purposes related to role modeling and to literacy.

Whole School Themes. Each year, the project team coordinates a number of school-wide events related to the project priorities. The major purpose of these events is "to ensure that everyone's identity (socio-cultural, race, gender, class) is valued and validated, their history recognized and affirmed, their academic, artistic, collaborative skills demonstrated, and a sense of belonging developed" (Park Public School, 1998, p. 5). They have held school-wide events to commemorate the victims of the December 6, 1989 Montreal Massacre, to commemorate Martin Luther King's birthday, and to celebrate African History Month, to name only a few. These are major events which call heavily on the time and energy of the project team.

Parent and Community Involvement. For each of its years as a project school, parent involvement and community outreach/involvement have been priorities. The results can be seen both in the presence that parents have in the school and in the partnerships Park has developed with other agencies. The level of parent involvement is already quite impressive, with parents participating in such activities as volunteering in classrooms and the library, helping with school teams, supporting school-wide events, and contributing to the Kindergarten intervention. Park also maintains a Parenting Centre which is well attended. With parent involvement as high as it is, the emphasis at Park has shifted to developing a "parent-driven Park School Community Council" with "parents sitting as key members not just on the Staffing Committee, but on the Curriculum, Anti-Racist and Community Outreach Committees as well" (Park Public School, 1998, p. 6). Staff at Park report moderate success with this goal, noting that progress is slowed, "not from a lack of willingness or ability on the part of the parents (that we have in abundance), but due to busy lives that have to balance family commitments, work, and, in many cases, job retraining and being back in school themselves" (ibid.). Continuing progress with this goal is evident in the principal's observation that, for 1999-2000, parent involvement in and ownership for school council activities was at its highest level ever.

Community partnerships have been established with Dixon Hall, the Regent Park Recreation Centre, the Health Centre, the African Women's Centre, parents for Better Beginnings, Focus Coalition, South East Asian Centre, the Metro Toronto Police 51 Division, and Upper Canada College. The staff at Park note the essential role these partnerships play in relation to their equity goals.

Reading Club. Reading Club is a literacy intervention now in place from grades 1 through 8. This initiative began in the primary grades in response to concerns about "literacy acquisition and, in particular, the number of children in the primary division who, for many reasons, were struggling readers" (Park Public School, 1998, p. 8). The design of Reading Club is intended to accommodate the commitment at Park to an "inclusive curriculum" while at the same time providing intensive instruction in reading to "at risk" readers. In one teacher's words: "That is why it is called Reading Club. Everybody is reading. They are just reading different things or they might be approaching it differently." With the entire class organized in groups and engaged in reading club, a group of at risk readers works with the Reading Club instructor who, based on individual students' performance provides "appropriate literacy activities and strategies" from the "First Steps Literacy" program (Park Public School, 1998, p. 8). The project facilitator summarized the purpose of Reading Club nicely: "Reading Club is where you are fostering a love of reading and helping your kids become confident."

Reading Club activities are done in support of the themes being addressed by all of the children in the classroom. One of the project teachers described how her work with Reading Club served to complement a teacher's classroom program built around a novel study and to allow the weaker readers to participate more fully in classroom activities. While the strong readers in the classroom had read the novel more or less independently, she read the novel aloud with her reading club group. "Because I read it to them, they were able to participate in the activities in the classroom. Once a week the teacher did a discussion or debate [about aspects of the novel]. So, because they had heard the story – they are all able to understand the book, they just can't read it – they were able to participate to a high level." She went on to point out that, "at the same time, on the other days when I wasn't in the classroom with that group, I did the remedial support with them – decoding, comprehension." Thus she was able to support the weak readers' inclusion in the classroom while also helping them develop the reading skills they will need to become independent readers.

In addition to providing a structure for implementing "balanced literacy" practices, Reading Club serves to support project school goals related to equity and antiracist curriculum, often by facilitating work related to school-wide activities. One group of teachers, for example, engaged in a "World History of Racism in Minutes" project through reading club.

Behavioral Advocacy. At Park, one staff member is assigned as "behavioral advocate" to support the school goal of integrating high-risk students. This person works directly with individual students experiencing behavioral difficulties, with small groups and in classrooms. The behavioral advocate also works with teachers, school administrators, and outside agencies to coordinate efforts on behalf of children experiencing behavioral difficulties and their families.

In addition to providing support for high risk students, the behavioral advocate facilitates a preventative peer conflict mediation program (Peacemakers). Staff at Park measure the success of their Peacemakers program in terms of their "relatively conflict-free recesses" (Park Public School, 1998, p. 11).

The five initiatives described above serve to convey a sense of the work that is central to the Project School Initiative. They do not, however, convey adequately a sense of the breadth and complexity of the overall programming at Park. Consider, for example, that the "Park Public School Proposed Program 1999-2000" report lists 51 initiatives in 11 program areas.

School-Level Perspectives on Possibilities and Challenges

Since its inception, the Project School Initiative has pursued related goals of improving the academic performance of children living in poverty and providing for equity of outcomes for these children. There can be no question that the academic performance of the children has improved. This is reflected in the results of provincial standardized tests used to assess performance, and in the anecdotal evidence provided by staff at the schools. While it is unlikely that anyone would claim that children in the project schools have achieved completely all that is implied in the phrase "equity of outcomes," it is clear that the children served by Lord Dufferin and Park schools have come much closer to that goal. Because these schools demonstrate that we can successfully educate children who live in poverty, we can extract from them lessons about possibilities for educating children who live in poverty. From the day-to-day experiences of those in these schools who have passionately pursued what is possible we can extract lessons about challenges.

A Sense of Wholeness

It would be convenient if the lessons about what is possible could be reduced to a straightforward listing of what schools should do. They are, however, more complex than that. Perhaps the central lesson is related to the sense of "wholeness" present in each of the schools. In both, everything that happens seems to be connected and to depend for effectiveness on everything else. Nothing in either school is "disposable." I suspect that this sense of wholeness is present because the project schools, in part through their annual program review and planning activities, have evolved very thoughtfully over the years. Nothing has been added on, eliminated, or changed without carefully considering how doing so would fit with what was already in place and with the school and community contexts. This has resulted in the two schools being similar in many ways, but also unique in ways that reflect their differing histories and contexts. The Project School Initiative is not a "one size fits all" approach to school improvement. It shares with other successful approaches to school improvement in high poverty schools the quality of being adaptive (see, for example, Slavin & Fashola, 1998).

Maintaining a sense of wholeness while also being constantly in the process of adapting is no mean feat, particularly in view of the complexity of the programming at both schools. I see three key structural features of the Project School Initiative at Lord Dufferin and Park as central to their ability to "hold it all together": the ways in which leadership is effected, their capacity to support in-school professional development, and additional resources.

Leadership

Leadership – more accurately, the ways in which leadership has been understood and practiced at these schools – has been central to the success of Lord Dufferin and Park. Teachers spoke of leadership in these schools as being democratic, based in notions of collaboration, and distributed among many in the school. They also felt that the principals played key roles in enabling these orientations toward leadership. Both principals were acknowledged to be excellent leaders with strong commitments to clear visions of what is important to schooling children living in poverty. At Park, for example, staff spoke of the principal's educational beliefs and values, including a strong belief in inclusive education and a "commitment to inner-city students." One teacher, who came to Park "because [the current principal] was here," described how the principal creates an environment in which teachers feel safe in taking risks, suggesting that this "makes the school much more collaborative." Another noted how "[the current principal] is very good about telling us that we make a difference." Yet another observed that: "One of the biggest boosts for this school is the principal and the administrative team that is in place. The staff feels fully supported and that is a key to making everyone in the school feel comfortable. The teachers want to be here." Similar sentiments were expressed by staff at Lord Dufferin. One teacher, for example, commented that the "administration and leadership is the kind that supports and encourages collaborative work....I think that the school is only as good as the principal." Teachers expressed admiration for her "democratic approach." They also felt affirmed professionally. As one said, "she trusts us." Or another: "she recognizes quality." This teacher also noted that staff appreciate [the principal] "giving people the opportunity to take on leadership roles."

Staff saw these principals as enabling and supporting collaborative work while sharing leadership with others. Both were admired for their democratic approaches and both were successful in creating an environment in which staff felt supported and affirmed. These principals' orientation toward democratic and shared leadership enabled the leadership of others in the school. Leadership was shared broadly, with project facilitators and project teachers playing key roles, but almost everyone was involved in one way or another.

Collaborative Cultures and In-School Professional Development

At Lord Dufferin and Park, collaborating with colleagues and working in teams are simply understood ways of doing things. Consider this observation from a teacher at Park:

There is a certain feeling in this school – whether it is because of the team approach that is fostered by the administration and the whole idea of the project school,...this is the first place I have worked where being part of the team was on the table up front and the understanding was that you will work as a team member.

And this comment from a first year teacher:

It is very rare that I would walk down the hall and feel uncomfortable about walking into anybody's classroom and saying, "What is going on?" Or even just walking in and sitting and watching for a few seconds to get ideas from somebody else and see how somebody else does it. Everybody is so helpful. It might be just the fact that I am a first year teacher...but I sense that people are really committed to working together.

Both staffs attribute much of their success to the collaborative ways in which they work. Collaboration seems now to be understood by all as simply "the way we do things around here"; as part of the school culture. I have noted above how the ways in which leadership is practiced in these schools contributed to the growth of such a culture. Their professional development practices have been just as important.

Due to their involvement in the project school initiative, both schools have the capacity to provide ongoing in-school professional development. The project facilitators and project teachers work directly with teachers in classrooms, and meet with them regularly to talk about improving teaching and learning. The adaptations chosen are worked out collaboratively and in the context of current school and classroom practice. These adaptations work because everyone understands them and can see the ways in which they will contribute to improved practice. This form of professional development is in sharp contrast to traditional approaches, which tend to have external "experts" telling teachers what they ought to be doing. Given the support in the literature for collaborative approaches to professional development (e.g., Darling-Hammond, 1996), we should not be surprised that this makes such a difference at Lord Dufferin and Park.

Resources

As the staffs were quick to point out, Lord Dufferin and Park would be very different without the additional resources allocated to them as project schools. Certainly, the capacity to provide for in-school professional development depends upon additional resources. Even the ways in which leadership is practiced at these schools depends upon there being additional resources to support the structuring into the work of those at the school opportunities for collegial activity. The point that additional resources have been essential to the success of these schools can be made generally by contrasting the experiences at Lord Dufferin and Park with those at many other inner city schools. The wide range of intense educational, social, and emotional issues that face educators in every inner city school often prevents them from moving beyond the "dailiness" of their work. Educators in these schools risk becoming "trapped" in this dailiness, spending most of their energy responding to crises. The additional staff resources at Lord Dufferin and Park have enabled them to escape this trap. Consider, for example, the ways in which those at Lord Dufferin, during its first year as a project school, were able to address directly the crisis-level issues they were facing with respect to safety and security. They have since been able to divert their energy to matters related more closely to teaching and learning.

Curricular Orientations

While the structural features noted above (leadership, capacity for in-school professional development and additional resources) have been critical to the successes at Lord Dufferin and Park, the program features themselves, and the curricular orientations embedded within them, have been just as important. For example, the additional resources have allowed for appropriate adaptations of curricula in the "traditional" areas, with a very strong emphasis on literacy education. Both schools do an excellent job of helping children living in poverty perform better on the standardized tests which measure achievement in relation to traditional curricula. But, at both schools, staff also recognize that curriculum is broader than what is expressed in the syllabuses which establish the parameters of traditional curricula. As one teacher said, "everything we do is curriculum." They recognize that, in the context of traditional "middle class" schooling, the children they serve are marginalized because such schooling reflects neither these children's life experiences nor their diversity. At Lord Dufferin and Park such matters are consciously addressed in the overt and in the "hidden" curriculum. Both schools embrace diversity as a strength and openly address issues related to difference. They treat problems related to equity and to social justice as natural topics for the overt curriculum. The "antiracist" curriculum at Park is one illustration of this. They also attend thoughtfully to the ways in which matters related to equity and social justice are reflected in the hidden curriculum. We see this in their attention to staffing practices. In describing the outcome of "affirmative hiring practices" at Lord Dufferin, the principal observed that the staff now has representation from "visible minorities, people of various faiths and socio-economic backgrounds" and many of the language groups found among the student population. She feels very strongly about the contribution of this affirmative hiring strategy to the success of Lord Dufferin:

> *I cannot emphasize how significantly this changed the culture and tone in the school! The staff openly express pride in their diversity and cohesiveness. The parents and children are excited and encouraged to see staff members they can relate to....I believe this was one of the most significant contributions to the project's success.*

She then noted that "50% of Toronto's children will soon be visible minorities," and that schools need to reflect that makeup. "That is the essence of an inclusive school."

Attention to the hidden curriculum is also apparent in the ways in which parents and community members are engaged within the schools. Parents have played key roles in major curricular projects such as the Storytelling Project at Lord Dufferin. Each school has physical space set aside for parents. Parents play key roles in the governance of the schools. No words need be spoken for the children in these schools to know that their parents are valued and respected members of the school community, and that the life experiences of their families are honored. Unlike many children in inner city schools who are in many ways "outsiders" looking in at a middle class curriculum to which they cannot relate, students at Lord Dufferin and Park see themselves and their experiences reflected in the curriculum.

Orientation Toward Student Achievement

In sustaining their approach to curriculum, staff at Lord Dufferin and Park have had to come to terms with pressures associated with the province-wide program of standardized achievement testing. They have done so in similar ways. At both schools, staff think carefully about the results of these tests. At Park, for example, I observed a meeting in which the "school team" reflected upon the results and developed action plans to address the areas they selected for improvement. They take the results very seriously. But they do so knowing that standardized tests disadvantage the children they serve. One teacher, for example, observed that the tests being in English creates disadvantages for ESL students, then made this point about the "middle class bias" of standardized tests:

> *Our kids find that [standardized tests] harder because of poverty. There are few resources and fewer experiences that our kids tend to have as part of their family background. Our kids are not the ones who can afford a computer in their home, or a science subscription to Owl Magazine, or a family trip to the museum or the science centre. They are just not getting the background that is taken for granted in the curriculum.*

They also worry about district test results being published in newspapers with very little explanation of the contexts of the schools. They know that most who see their results in the newspaper are not able to make informed decisions about whether the results are poor, good, or excellent. Readers see only that achievement test results from Lord Dufferin and Park are lower than those from schools located in more affluent communities. This, of course, is a common theme these days. Many inner city schools have diverted their curricula almost entirely to the task of improving achievement test results. McNeil (2000), for example, notes that in the context of the Texas Assessment of Academic Skills program, classrooms in many inner city schools devote enormous amounts of energy and time to preparing students to write the exams. McNeil points out that "scores go up in these classrooms, but academic quality goes down. The result is a growing inequality between the content and quality of education provided to white, middle-class children and that provided to those in poor minority schools" (2000, p. 730). While perhaps the emphasis in Ontario on improving test scores is not as extreme as it is in Texas, the pressure associated with the testing program is very real and felt by the staff at Lord Dufferin and Park. It is to their credit, and to the credit of the district-level administrators who have supported them, that they have not allowed the achievement testing program to divert their attention from other matters that are just as important to schooling children living in poverty.

On School-Level Lessons

These six "lessons" correspond to "themes" I drew from the case study research conducted at Lord Dufferin and Park schools. I see them as complementing the broad perspective on possibilities and challenges to which I referred early in the chapter. From that broad perspective, exploring possibilities is about identifying what to do.

It is about identifying programs for which there is strong research support. I should note here that this broad perspective has had considerable influence on schooling at Lord Dufferin and Park. Both schools have attended to the research. They have pre-kindergarten programs, emphasize teaching for meaning, have tutorial programs such as *Reading Recovery*, and are engaged in comprehensive school-wide programming very similar to *Success for All*. Knowing what to do is crucial. The contribution of the school-level lessons is that they call upon us to consider that HOW programming is enacted may also be crucial. They call upon us to consider that the cultures of collaboration, nurtured in environments emphasizing democratic leadership, have as much to do with the successes at Lord Dufferin and Park as does what they do; to consider that orientations toward curriculum and testing may be just as important; and to consider that resources play a key role in enabling schools to provide more equitable programming for children living in poverty.

The school-level lessons also offer perspectives on challenges. We see dedicated teachers struggling to deal with the complexity of poverty-related issues. They are challenged by a middle-class curriculum that diminishes the experiences of the children and families they serve. They are challenged by the standardized testing programs that measure their students in relation to that middle class curriculum. They are challenged by their uncertain future.

Concern for the Future

The structural supports for schooling at Lord Dufferin and Park have enabled the development of very complex and integrated programs. Students in these schools, engaged in curricula that reflect their needs and their life experiences, have thrived. This same environment has generated intense pride among the staff and, with that, extremely high levels of dedication and commitment. In recent years, however, this has been mitigated by a sense of extreme vulnerability. Staff at both schools are deeply concerned that all they have worked for during their years as project schools is soon to be lost. In particular, they are very concerned about the consequences of reduced educational funding and the recent amalgamation of Toronto school boards. In the words of the principal at Park:

> It is quite possible at the end of this year, if things go the way they are going and if the province doesn't give in at all in terms of giving more money, it looks like we could lose a vice-principal, lose a secretary, lose a caretaker, lose the 3 1/2 project teachers, lose the 3 inner-city teachers, lose all of the para-professionals, lose 2/3 of our educational assis-

tants. It would become a place where you would not want to be.

The principal was not alone in stating this concern. As one of the teachers commented: "I can't imagine working here without the extra support. I don't think it would be the same school. I don't think we could do a fully integrated program, which makes this school really unique."

A teacher at Lord Dufferin observed that the political will to sustain the project school initiative may no longer exist in the recently amalgamated school district:

> *It doesn't look like inner city is receiving any kind of strong attention. It is competing against French Immersion and quite a few other programs: the Art School, that kind of thing. These are all being looked at together. Right now I don't think there is a political will to keep the project schools going.*

Another teacher commented that "the [old] Toronto Board actually was involved with significant differential funding to inner city schools." The teachers noted that much of this is at risk due to amalgamation and the resultant mechanisms for funding schools. They read much into the recent loss of the district-level inner city coordinator's position. In addition to their concerns about loss of the resources associated with their project school designation, they worry about the funding for the paraprofessionals in the school, for their special education programming and for their senior kindergarten program.

Those at Lord Dufferin and Park are hardly alone in feeling vulnerable. As Bennis (1997) and others have pointed out, every public service is currently under siege. Having been defined as **"government"** and, therefore, as wasteful and a drain on the economy, public services are struggling for their existence. Bennis refers to this as "the inverted trust factor," observing that the public have somehow become convinced that the trust they once had in government now is better placed with private enterprise, particularly with major multinational corporations (pp. 19-30). Objectively, it may seem strange that the public has shifted their trust to a sector that has as its sole purpose the making of profit for shareholders and away from a sector that pursues purposes more associated with the public good. Even the names – private enterprise; public service – convey that clear distinction. But the logic aside, subjectively, that is what has happened. It is difficult to have a week pass without hearing the neo-liberal mantra of "small government" which can only be translated into a call for reductions to public service. These are unfriend-ly times for any kind of social programming.

Elsewhere, I have argued that educational poverty program-ming is particularly vulnerable in these times (Maynes, 1993). The communities served by such programming tend to have weak polit-ical voices, policymakers tend to have very little direct knowledge of issues related to inner city education, and few are aware of the research evidence to support the high quality programs which are in place. The neo-liberal orientations which now pervade most policy making circles in Canada only serve to highlight this vulnerability. That we know what to do to successfully educate children living in poverty does not guarantee that it will be done.

With the recent amalgamation of the Toronto area school boards, those at Lord Dufferin and Park have had direct experience with the move toward small government. They see challenges related to this amalgamation. They had achieved project school status under the old Toronto School Board which had a history of placing a very high priority on inner city programming. They worry that poverty-relat-ed issues are becoming lost in the multitude of other issues con-fronting policy makers who are now responsible to much more geo-graphically and economically diverse communities. They know that, without strong advocates among educational leaders in the district, inner city issues may not receive the consideration that might be given issues more central to the education of the non-poor. The recent elimination of the district-level position of Inner City Coordinator is an indication that their worries are well founded. Despite their well-documented successes, those at Lord Dufferin and Park are deeply concerned that they will lose the additional resources that have allowed them to create and maintain the school environments in which those successes have been achieved. I hope they are wrong. Toronto's project schools are a bright light among Canadian programs for children living in poverty.

As I reflect on the title of this book, it strikes me that critique and possibilities are not necessarily separable. Indeed, that we know the possibilities serve to sharpen the critique. I think that this is the point that Ron Edmonds was making when he wrote:

> We can, whenever and wherever we choose, successfully teach all chil-dren whose schooling is of interest to us; we already know more than we need to do that; and whether or not we do it must finally depend on how we feel about the fact that we haven't so far. (Cited in Lord Dufferin Public School, 1993, p. 11)

It seems to me that we are in the process now of finding out what Canadians feel about the fact that we haven't so far.

References

Barnett, W. S. (1998). Long-term effects on cognitive development and school success. In W. S. Barnett & S. S. Boocock (Eds.), *Early care and education for children in poverty: Promises, programs and long-term results* (pp. 11-44). Albany, NY: State University of New York Press.

Bennis, W. (1997). *Managing people is like herding cats.* Provo, UT: Executive Excellence Publishing.

Biggs, D. (April, 1999). *Project school review: Lord Dufferin Public School 1995-2000.* Technical report. Toronto, ON: Toronto District School Board.

Connell, R. W. (1993). *Schools and social justice.* Philadelphia, PA: Temple University Press.

Darling-Hammond, L. (1996). The right to learn and the advancement of teaching: Research, policy, and practice for democratic education. *Educational Researcher, 25*(6), 5-17.

Goldman, N. (1999). *Lord Dufferin program review, year 4, external review feedback report. Technical report.* Toronto, ON: Toronto District School Board.

Knapp, M. S. & Associates. (Knapp, M. S., with Adelman, N. E., Marder, C., McCollum, H., Needels, M. C., Padilla, C., Shields, P. M., Turnbull, B. J. & Zucker, A. A.). (1995). *Teaching for meaning in high poverty classrooms.* New York, NY: Teachers' College Press.

Lord Dufferin Public School. (1993). *Lord Dufferin Public School proposed program 1993-1994.* Technical report. Toronto, ON.

Lord Dufferin Public School. (1998). *Lord Dufferin Public School proposed program 1998-1999.* Technical report. Toronto, ON.

Lord Dufferin Public School. (1999). *Family stories from Lord Dufferin P.S. Technical report.* Toronto, ON.

Levin, B. (1995). Educational responses to poverty. *Canadian Journal of Education, 20*(2), 211-224.

Maynes, W. G. (1993a). Child poverty in Canada: Challenges for educational policymakers. *Canadian Review of Social Policy, 33*(1), 13-28.

Maynes, W. G. (1993b). Educating urban poor children: Challenges for educational policymakers. *Canadian Administrator, 33*(1), 1-12.

Maynes, B. (1996). Inner city education in the world of the new right. *Canadian School Executive, 16*(5), 12-18.

Maynes, B. & Foster, R. (1998). *Directory of Canadian educational poverty programs.* Edmonton, AB: Department of Educational Policy Studies, University of Alberta.

Maynes, B. (2000). *Toronto's Project School Initiative: Case studies of Lord Dufferin and Park schools. Technical report.* Edmonton, AB: Department of Educational Policy Studies, University of Alberta.

Maynes, B. & Foster, R. (forthcoming). Educating Canadian children living in poverty. *Canadian Journal of Education.*

McLaren, P. (1989). *Life in schools: An introduction to critical pedagogy in the foundations of education.* White Plains, NY: Longman.

McNeil., L. M. (2000). Creating new inequalities: Contradictions of reform. *Phi Delta Kappan, 81*(10), 729-734.

Park Public School. (1998). *Continuing our commitment to equity, excellence and literacy: Highlights of Park's project school initiatives: Inner city project review. Technical report.* Toronto, ON.

Ross, D. P., Scott, J. S. & Smith, P. J. (2000). *The Canadian fact book on poverty – 2000.* Ottawa, ON: Canadian Council on Social Development.

Ross, D. P., Shillington, E. R. & Lochhead, C. (1994). *The Canadian fact book on poverty – 1994.* Ottawa, ON: Canadian Council on Social Development.

Schorr, L. B. (1988). *Within our reach: Breaking the cycle of disadvantage.* New York: Doubleday.

Schweinhart, L. J., Barnes, H. V. & Weikart, D. P. (1993). *Significant benefits: The High/Scope Perry Preschool study through age 27.* Yipsilanti, MI: High/Scope Press.

Slavin, R. E. & Fashola, O. S. (1998). *Show me the evidence! : Proven and promising programs for America's schools.* Thousand Oaks, CA: Corwin Press.

Toronto District School Board. (1998). *Moving toward the year 2000: Rethinking the inner city project school model and mandate. Technical report.* Toronto, ON.

Toronto District School Board. (1999). *Lord Dufferin Junior and Senior Public School, 1999 school profile. Technical report.* Toronto, ON.

Toronto District School Board. (1999a). *Park Junior and Senior Public School, 1999 school profile. Technical report.* Toronto, ON.

Yau, M. (1997). *Individual kindergarten student profile results: Park Public School, Fall 1997. Technical Report.* Toronto, ON: Toronto District School Board.

Yau, M. (1998). *Lord Dufferin Public School: A three-year snapshot, 1995-1998. Technical report.* Toronto, ON: Toronto District School Board.

Chapter 12
An Argument for the Progressive Possibilities for Public Education: School Reforms in Manitoba

Dick Henley and Jon Young

Introduction

One of the great regrets of many progressive educators in Canada today, as they engage in what often appears to be a rear-guard struggle to combat policies promoted by a new generation of neo-liberal school reformers, might be that the social welfare state that was constructed during the 1960s and early 1970s was not more successful in ensuring that Canadians fully appreciated their responsibility as citizens to attend to its maintenance. Social programs in the areas of health care, public insurance, pharmaceutical drugs, hospitalization, and the like, which took years of struggle to bring under public control, are now openly assailed. School systems throughout the country, no less than any other public institution, have become prey to the imperatives of economic globalization: unlimited growth, a seamless global consumer market, corporate rule, deregulation, privatization, and free trade. Clearly, contemporary Canadians are confronted with two conflicting models of democracy as they enter the third millennium. These models we refer to here as "a market democracy model" and "a pluralist moral democracy model" (Carr, 1991; Bruno-Jofré and Henley, 2000). While both are rooted in the historical development of liberalism, they hold up radically different roles for the public school.

The purpose of this chapter is to look critically at school reform initiatives in the province of Manitoba, as they were proposed and implemented during the 1990s. We will do this against a backdrop of these competing versions of democracy and public schooling, and the historical development of liberalism in Canada. The analysis that we will develop is that the reform initiatives of the 1990s – albeit considerably less radical than in some other Canadian provinces such as Ontario and Alberta – were intended to provide the foundation upon which a neo-liberal market democracy would eventually be constructed. Here primacy would be afforded to the largely unfettered rights of the individual, superseding earlier efforts in the 1960s and 1970s to forge a pluralist moral democracy where primacy was given to issues of equity over those of individual liberty. Our argument will be that, despite claims that the educational reforms introduced in Manitoba in the 1990s are "common-sense," or "a necessary response to the irresistible pressures of globalization," they are far from inevitable – evidenced by the choices made in other jurisdictions (Deen, 1994) and their contested nature within the province (Wiens, 1995; Hesch, 2000). Nor, we argue, are they a desirable direction for public education in a compassionate liberal democracy. The chapter argues that "progressive possibilities" are to be found in: (i) the egalitarian reforms of the 1970s and 1980s, (ii) the more moderate approaches to reform taken by the ruling Progressive Conservative Party during the 1990s, and (iii) some early initiatives taken by a newly elected New Democratic Party.

A Conceptual Framework: "The Liberal Project"

McKay (2000a; 2000b) has argued that Canadian history ought to be approached from a new intellectual perspective, one which replaces the traditional "nation-building" and the more recent "state formation" constructs with a broader and more inclusive paradigm which he calls "the liberal project." This interpretive model asserts that the real priority of political decision-makers was to fashion a liberal social order, a grand project that aimed to unify the inhabitants of Canada through a shared ideology. McKay sees it as first taking hold in urban pockets of eastern British North America during the middle years of the 19th century and from there being projected over time and space to contemporary Canada, notably through institutions constructed by the state authority. In its classical form, liberalism accorded the right of citizenship only to those deemed in full possession of themselves and capable of exercising independent action. Liberty, initially enunciated in terms of the natural right of an individual and subsequently extended to concepts such as free labor, free speech, and free trade, represented the first of three core ingredients of liberalism. The second element, equality, was granted on the contingency that the rational individual had achieved independence. The third was the right to own property, a fundamental ingredient of liberalism because it was only through private property that one established ownership of the self.

It is McKay's contention that it is the struggle over the hierarchical ordering and re-ordering of liberty, equality, and private property that distinguishes the historical forms which liberalism has taken in Canada and which has found different expressions in different regions of the country at different historical moments. The struggle to afford priority to principles of equality over liberty, or vice versa, lies at the heart of our analysis of school reform and of our argument for "progressive possibilities." It is a market model of democracy that asserts the primacy of individual liberty and private property and a pluralist moral democracy that argues otherwise for the primacy of equity, inclusion, and social justice. This distinction is derived from the work of British philosopher Carr (1991) whose work lays out the essential character of "moral democracy" as distinguished from "market democracy." It is extended by Canadian academics Kymlicka (1998) and Bruno-Jofré and Henley (2000) who integrate the Canadian experience of multiculturalism and inclusion into the model to develop the notion of a "pluralist moral democracy."

Carr (1991) refers to "market democracy" as a form of neo-liberalism that either openly or implicitly contends that all life, not least public institutions, must be open to market forces. Market democracy envisages the citizen as essentially a self-regarding consumer who spends waking time in pursuit of his or her self-interest. The concept of a collective public good in the market model is limited because nothing should transgress upon private individual liberty. Carr describes the ideal social conditions of market democracy as follows:

> *Democracy flourishes in an individualist society with a competitive market economy, minimal state intervention, a politically passive citizenry, and a strong political leadership guided by liberal principles and circumscribed by the rule of law. (Carr, 1991, p. 11)*

Market democracy does not pursue the goal of social equality beyond universal franchise rights. In every other respect, access to power and position are perceived to be quite properly determined on the basis of individual initiative. The foundation of social justice in a market democracy is the sanctity of private freedom from state/public interference.

Moral democracy, by way of contrast, treasures public space because it is only through public agency that the goal of social justice, its core principle, can be realized. In a moral democracy government pursues the public good, often in the face of entrenched private interests, in full knowledge that the collective need takes precedence over private wants. The ideal society is home to an active self-conscious citizenry and can only flourish among people who are well educated and well-versed in the tenets and practices of moral democracy (Carr, 1991, p. 9). The idea of a pluralist moral democracy extends Carr's model to encompass Kymlicka's (1998) and Bruno-Jofré and Henley's (2000) concept of Canada as a multi-national and poly-ethnic society in which a fluid pluralistic citizenship is encouraged and difference is not merely tolerated but celebrated.

Much has been written about the educational responsibilities of schools within a liberal democracy. Tom Symons (1975) offered what we consider to be a clear and compelling definition of education when he suggested that "self-knowledge" lies close to the heart of what it means to be educated. The development of self-knowledge, he suggested, involves a process of actively and critically constructing an understanding of ourselves as individuals and as members of a wide social community – who we are, where we are in time and space, where we have been, where we are going, and what our responsibilities are to ourselves and to others. Extending this, Young and Jones (1995) have argued concretely that the ideals of accessibility and inclusion, participation and accountability, make a particular demand on that educational agenda. They do not allow for a system in which only certain students are educated and come to know themselves in the fullest and most advantageous ways. Nor can such a system justifiably restrict some children's education by presenting them with (a) deformed histories, (b) biased and stereotypical representations of who they are and what they can become, or presenting some students with negative expectations and self-images. Neither can this system legitimately allow only certain students the opportunity to actively and critically engage in the construction of their own identities and knowledge of themselves, while others have that knowledge imposed upon them in a narrow and limited way. Rather, public education requires that our curriculum materials and school practices be informed by the diversity of human knowledge and experiences in Canadian society and in the world, and a commitment to challenging practices inside and outside of school that unfairly place limits on some children's chances of being truly educated.

Such notions of a pluralistic moral democracy, we believe, hold three broad implications for public school systems that provide the basis for this chapter's discussion of recent changes in Manitoba public education. First, as *public* institutions, schools must be held up to the light of public scrutiny and provide a structure of governance that encourages meaningful participation from all sections of the population and recognizes the pluralistic nature of Canadian society. Second, as *educational* institutions, schools have a particular curricula and pedagogic responsibility in the development of the human potential of all of its students and the development of the knowledge, skills, and critical dispositions consistent with the requirements of democratic citizenship in a global society. Connected to both of the preceding, we would argue, is a third requirement that public schools are afforded broad-based support and *legitimation* measured in part at least in terms of the resources devoted to them and the regard which their teachers are afforded by their publics.

It is these three touchstones against which we structure our analysis of school reforms in Manitoba during the 1990s, after first examining something of the development of public schooling in Manitoba during two key stages of its history: its early beginnings between 1870 and 1920, and, the construction of a modern pluralist school system between 1960 and the early 1990s.

The Historical Context

1. Constructing the Manitoba Public School System (1870-1920)

Manitoba came into existence through the Manitoba Act of 1870, which created a bilingual (French and English) province; recognized Aboriginal rights through the provision of a land scrip for Metis children; and established a dual (Protestant and Roman Catholic) system of schools. This constitutional arrangement was arrived at through negotiations which had been forced on the Dominion government by the seizure of power in Red River by Louis Riel and his followers. This development forced John A. Macdonald to compromise his liberal agenda for colonizing at least the eastern portion of the Canadian prairies. Uncompromising opinion in Ontario had the effect of denigrating the 1870 constitutional arrangement, however. This was subsequently compounded by questions about the loyalty of communitarian Roman Catholicism to the British Canadian liberal project, arising out of the Jesuit Estates controversy of 1888, which led to the complete undermining of the Manitoba Act in 1890. Protestant immigrants from Ontario had by 1890 become the dominant force in Manitoba politics and in that year the provincial government dissolved the dual school system and established a single non-denominational public school administration. The founding of the 'national' school system, and the accompanying legislation which declared the province officially unilingual, was intended by its sponsors to signal the closing of the era of 'institutional distortion' that had been foisted on the province by Riel and the opening of a 'more advanced regime' built upon the liberal traditions of the now numerically dominant British population.

We have to be careful of applying the language of democracy to the politics of 19th century Manitoba because the right of franchise was limited to property-holding, adult males, who were British subjects (by birth or naturalization). Excluded from the rights of citizenship were women and all First Nations people. The latter had been officially declared 'other' through the British North America Act of 1867. During the 1870s, through the numbered treaty process, their Aboriginal title to the prairies had been stripped away, their occupancy reduced to pockets of collectively-owned reserve lands, overseen by federal agents. After 1879, a system of residential schools, jointly operated by the Dominion government and the mainstream churches in Canada, were constructed with the intent of 'civilizing' First Nations children to make them into fit subjects of liberal rule (Titley, 1986; Miller, 1996; Canada, 1996; Milloy, 1999). Women were excluded from citizenship by virtue of their gender that, according to Victorian separate spheres ideology, deemed them subordinate to their husbands. Property-holding males alone expressed the political opinions of their families.

For those fortunate enough to hold the right to participate in the political process, where the Public Schools Act of 1890 and its amended form in 1896 were concerned, citizens who felt strongly about one side of the issue or the other were active participants in the making of school law. The majority of them cast ballots in support of the Thomas Greenway Liberal government twice in the 1890s. In doing so they registered their support for a single public school system dedicated to the promotion of what educational historians have labelled Anglo-conformity, an ethnocentrism constructed on the foundation of liberalism.

Resistance to the 1890 legislation gave rise to a struggle which took on national significance, the Manitoba Schools Question – pitting an aggrieved religious minority led by its Francophone bishops against an arrogant majority, which coalesced behind its protestant clergy and elected politicians. The Laurier-Greenway Compromise of 1896, which Canadian historians continue to claim resolved the issue, did nothing to address the original Catholic grievance, however; nor did it serve as an acceptable basis upon which to build the new liberal order. Its major flaw was that it contained a bilingual education clause which threatened to stymie the Anglo-Saxon majority's ambition to use the public schools to impose its Anglo-conformist social and political agenda in the province until it was revoked in 1916 during the heated ethnic tensions of the Great War years.

The defeat of the Greenway Liberals in 1899 considerably altered the political dynamics of public schooling in Manitoba. The new Conservative government, having promised to uphold the terms of the 1896 compromise prior to their election, attempted to do just that shortly after coming to office. Catholic parents in Winnipeg began operating their own tuition-financed schools in 1890 and throughout its decade and a half long tenure in office, the Conservative regime attempted to re-establish Catholic schooling without altering the existing school legislation. This was thwarted by the Winnipeg School Board, that claimed that the segregation of Catholics into its own school system was not legally possible. By taking this stand, school trustees in the city became staunch defenders of the liberal project, underlined by the promotion of policies (notably, compulsory school attendance) which posed a direct challenge to those formulated by provincial politicians. By 1916 it had become clear that provincial authority was far from absolute in the area of public education (Henley, 1993).

Meanwhile, the development of centralized educational bureaucracies at the provincial and Winnipeg School Board level after the turn of the century conferred a new social status on its chief administrators. These were men who may have staked out positions on the Manitoba Schools Question in the 1890s but who were nonetheless comparatively minor players in that unfolding constitutional struggle. However, by the 1910s men like Daniel McIntyre, who had served as superintendent of Winnipeg schools since 1885, and William A. McIntyre, the Principal of the Winnipeg Normal School since 1893, had clearly established themselves as Manitoba's leading educational experts (Osborne, 1998-99, p. 5; Wilson, 1981). Their views on such issues as compulsory schooling and bilingualism, while decidedly supportive of Anglo-Saxon and Protestant ascendancy, were projected on loftier and more acceptable grounds; they appealed for educational progress and greater administrative efficiency, which made their discourse seem less partisan in the charged atmosphere of Manitoba electoral politics. Their neutrality may have been more apparent than real; nonetheless, it introduced an important new dimension to the politics of education in the province. Although their positions favored one ethnic group over the rest, their essential ethnocentrism (and gender bias) was justified on the grounds of bureaucratic necessity and the need to reform the curricular program of public schooling in order to attend to the social and economic needs associated with modernization.

By 1920 women had won the vote and in Manitoba, the culmination of the Winnipeg General Strike of 1919 had turned back the communitarian ambitions of organized labor in the city, and the foundation had been laid for a liberal democracy based on Anglo-Conformity (Bruno-Jofré, 1996; 1998-99). Central to this model of society was a compulsory public school system, similarly committed to Anglo-Conformity, with a strong system of local school boards, and a professional bureaucracy interested in notions of modernization and efficiency. This tradition of liberal democracy in education was to remain in large part unaltered for the next 40 years.

2. The Forging of a **Pluralistic** Vision for Public Education, (1958-1994)

In his synthesis of the 20th century, Hobsbawm (1995) describes the period of 1945 to 1990 as a time of social revolution in world history. He highlights the mass migration of people away from rural farm life into burgeoning urban centres; the demand for universal high schooling and a greatly expanded post-secondary education sector; a waning of class consciousness among industrial workers; and a tremendous expansion of the number of women in the workforce as defining characteristics of world-wide social change (pp. 287-391). Manitoba and the rest of Canada experienced this sweeping transformation where politicians responded by adopting a significantly revised version of liberalism that led to the construction of the welfare state featuring universal social services paid for by new, progressively graduated, taxation schedules. Grounded in an invigorating ethic of equality, the social welfare state became the means, however partial, for redistributing material wealth. This new moral democracy (its pluralist character came later) was embraced by all of the mainstream political parties in the province, each of them vying to win the support of a population that had high expectations for the future well-being of themselves and their children. In Manitoba, Black and Silver (1999) have identified what they call a somewhat collectivist strand in Manitoba's political culture (p. 31) which found government expression during much of the 30-year period between the election of Roblin's Progressive Conservatives in 1958 and the defeat of Howard Pawley's NDP in 1988. They describe the orientation in the following terms: "strong support for public education and public health care, public ownership of certain industries, robust labour legislation, and a strong and effective social safety net" (p. 31).

The Manitoba public school system that was in place by 1920 proved to be remarkably durable, but it was not so impregnable that it could withstand the effects of modernization when it finally arrived in the province in the 1960s. Educational change was a nation-wide phenomenon during this decade and Manitobans, like most other Canadians, were swept into the rising tide of public opinion which ultimately determined that a completed secondary education was essential to success in life. This new universal expectation brought with it a demand that public education be provided fairly to all children. Initially, the Manitoba government concentrated its efforts on improving the educational opportunities for rural children through the construction of regional schools that were proclaimed as highly enriched learning centres compared to the old one-room-school buildings. Improved road networks and the modern school bus made the projects viable and, ultimately bought an end to traditional models of rural schooling. The second important feature of transformation of Manitoba schooling during the period was a decentralization of administrative authority in the province. Among other things, the reign of the school inspector was concluded, as was the system of annual, standardized, provincial high school examinations. Both of these developments contributed to the elevation of the status of the teaching profession in the province. Higher teacher certification standards were introduced in conjunction with the closing of teachers' colleges and the expansion of university faculties of education – a move which anticipated a new emphasis on the education, and less on training, of new teachers. Greater responsibilities brought improved material benefits, developments which should not be disassociated from the vitalization of the Manitoba Teachers Society.

A second major current of social change during this period culminated in the re-definition of English-Canadian identity. In the post-war years, the demise of the British Empire/Commonwealth; the rise of aggressive nationalism in Quebec; and, the arrival of hundreds of thousands of new immigrants, many from non-European countries, all contributed to an identity crisis by the 1960s. The old Anglo-Conformist ideology of the past became seen by many as an increasingly inappropriate social ideology for the country. A host of federal royal commissions undertaken during the 1960s confirmed this. The Official Languages Act of 1969, the Trudeau Statement on

Multiculturalism within a Bilingual Framework in 1971, and the federal government's acceptance in principle of the National Indian Brotherhood's 1972 declaration, "Indian Control of Indian Education," all contributed to a contesting of Anglo-Conformity and the re-definition of Canada as a pluralist society.

This new reality slowly percolated into the provincial school system through policy and curricular changes, some attention to employment equity and inclusion, and a new emphasis on inter-cultural education in teacher education (Manitoba Education, 1990; Winnipeg School Division, 1989). But this demand for recognition and legitimacy did not end with ethnicity. From the 1970s through to the early 1990s, issues of race, gender, sexual orientation, and disabilities all sought recognition and acceptance in society, particularly through the public school (Levin, 1996; Tavares, 2000). Public schooling enjoyed a high level of public confidence (Livingstone & Hart, 1995), and consistent increases in funding, as the teaching force, effected by public pressure and characterized by increased professional status, began the process of dismantling the system's Anglo-Conformist hegemony, and building in its place a tradition of a more broadly-based and inclusive educational system (Winnipeg School Division, 1989; Smith & Young, 1996). Although one can hardly claim that the politics of difference achieved the kind of acceptance its sponsors hoped for, nonetheless, the tendency in that direction was strong enough to make the claim that Manitoba had established itself as a pluralist moral democracy by the early 1990s. The middle years of the decade brought what many perceived as a powerful challenge to that perception (Bruno-Jofré & Henley, 2000; Young & Levin, 2000).

Educational Reform in Manitoba in the 1990s: "New Directions"

Gary Filmon and his Progressive Conservative Party squeaked into power in Manitoba in 1988, forming a minority government in the midst of the campaign by the Mulroney government in Ottawa to convince Canadians of the benefits of free trade with the Americans. During the subsequent three terms in office that ended in 1999, the Conservatives embarked on a new economic strategy which aimed to balance the budget and reverse the collectivist orientation of the previous 30 years. Black and Silver (1999) write that there were two essential elements in the plan: "cut public spending to enable tax reductions to create a more competitive environment for private investment in Manitoba; and increase exports to the large American markets to the province's south" (p. 4).

Against this backdrop, public education in the province witnessed a great deal of government intervention. This intervention was characterized by a very rapid stream of policy initiatives, heated and at times vitriolic debate, and some significant changes to the face of public schooling. Central to the changes in education in the province was the release by the government of three key policy documents: *Renewing Education: New Directions – A Blueprint*; *Renewing Education: New Directions – The Action Plan*; and *Renewing Education: New Directions – A Foundation for Excellence* (Manitoba Education and Training, 1994a, 1995a, 1995b).

Introduced as representing "the Government's commitment to revitalize the public education system for current and future generations of students" (Manitoba Education, 1995a, p. 4), the documents detailed six priority areas for action: Essential Learnings (the development of an outcomes-based curriculum for all schools in the province); Educational Standards and Evaluation (the development of standards tests mandated for grades 3, 6, 9 [Senior 1], and 12 [Senior 4]; School Effectiveness (the defining of teacher and parental roles and rights and the introduction of the requirement for all schools to produce an annual school plan); Parental and Community Involvement (the establishment of Advisory Councils for School Leadership and the widening of parental choice); Distance Education and Technology; and Teacher Education. These three documents laid out a strategy of school reform that in large part guided government involvement in education for the next five years until the Progressive Conservative government was defeated at the polls in September 1999. In addition, three Reports commissioned by the government during the 1990s contributed significantly to the educational debate in the province even when their main recommendations were, ultimately, not adopted by the government. These reports covered a review of school division boundaries (Manitoba Education and Training, 1994b), teacher preparation (Manitoba Education and Training, 1996b), and the teacher compensation process (Manitoba Education and Training, 1998).

These policy proposals, which marked the government's effort to establish an educational order more reflective of a market democracy, without doubt signalled a shattering of the "educational settlement" (Taylor, 1996) of the previous 30 years in the province. No longer was policy to be directed by the educational establishment.

Table 1: Manitoba Reforms – A Chronology

1989 July	Report of the Winnipeg School Division Task Force on Race Relations published.
1990	Manitoba Education releases "Multicultural Education: A Policy for the 1990s."
1990 September	Progressive Conservative Government led by Gary Filmon re-elected with a narrow majority.
1991 September	Children of the Earth High School opens.
1993 December	Manitoba, Saskatchewan, Alberta, British Columbia, Yukon and Northwest Territories sign the *Western Canadian Protocol for Collaboration in Basic Education.*
1993-1997	Provincial funding for education is reduced or frozen for five years. Teachers are required to take days off without pay (Filmon Fridays).
1994 July	*Renewing Education: New Directions – A Blueprint for Action* released.
1994 November	Final report of the School Districts and Divisions Boundaries Review (The Norrie Report) released.
1995 January	*Renewing Education: New Directions – The Action Plan* released.
1995 April	Progressive Conservative government led by Gary Filmon re-elected for a third term with a majority.
1996	Shapiro Report on Teacher Education released.
1996 Fall	Several pieces of legislation passed that increase substantially the powers of the Minister, limit teachers' rights in collective bargaining, provide for parental choice of schools, and require schools to have public annual plans.
1998 February	Scurfield Report on Teacher Compensation released.
1999 September	Progressive Conservative government defeated. New Democratic Party under Gary Doer form majority government.
2000 May	Government issues consultation document on Grade 3 Assessment.
2000 June	Bill 42 introduced on collective bargaining.
2000 July	Ministerial letter to educational partners identifying government priority areas.

Rather, the educational agenda was now to be set by a provincial government that would not wait upon approval from the leadership of education's "internal stakeholders" (i.e., teachers, administrators, trustees, and the universities), but which sought instead greater input from "external stakeholders" or "the clients" of public education (i.e., parents and business).

Many of these proposals were contested, often vigorously, by the Manitoba Teachers' Society, and by the New Democratic Party opposition, and on occasions even internally within the ruling Progressive Conservative Party and its constituents. As a consequence, while some policies such as standards testing were pushed forward in spite of considerable opposition, others were slowed down or modified, while some were abandoned entirely.

In looking critically at these developments, we now return to the notions of: (i) an active and inclusive public participation in the governance of public schools; (ii) the educative notions of democratic citizenship; and (iii) the importance of public support and legitimation for public schools, outlined at the beginning of this chapter as being central aspects of a pluralist moral democracy.

1. School Governance – School Boards, Advisory Councils for School Leadership, and School Choice

If 'participation,' 'education,' and some notion of 'the public good' lie close to the heart of public school governance in a pluralist moral democracy, 'efficiency,' 'accountability,' and 'choice' are the watchwords of a market democracy. Our argument thus far has been that in the Canadian and Manitoban design of education, locally elected school boards have historically provided a cornerstone for public participation, representation, and accountability – albeit one significantly bounded by the influences of race, class, and gender and one not always characterized by vigorous public participation. Furthermore, some notion of "the common school," where students from all walks of life met together in the public space of the school – again bounded by the geography of class, the biases of curriculum, and the provisions for private schooling – has historically been an important element of the democratic ideals and traditions of Canadian education. School reform in the 1990s in many Canadian provinces has seen a substantial weakening of the role of school boards as well as some erosion of the notion of the common school with the increased support given to provisions for parental choice in the schools that their children will attend (Pierce, 1998).

School Boards

Manitoba has, to date, provided an important exception to this pattern of reduced authority for school boards. The government commissioned a review of school boundaries in 1993 (Manitoba Education and Training, 1994b) but then chose not to act on the Commission's relatively modest recommendations on amalgamation. Chaired by a respected former mayor of the city of Winnipeg, Bill Norrie, the Commission's recommendations gave a strong endorsement of locally elected school boards. It concluded:

The Commission believes the best form of governance accountability can be achieved through democratic election of local representatives. To be effective in providing its choice of education programs within provincially approved curricula, the board should have special levy taxing powers to finance those things it feels are appropriate to its area. (p. 127)

This endorsement was accompanied by the recommendation that the existing 57 school divisions (ranging in size from over 30 000 students to less than 500 students) be consolidated into 21 divisions, where the smallest rural divisions would have some 2000 students and the largest urban divisions up to 35 000 students.

These proposals for government-mandated amalgamation met with considerable opposition, particularly from rural divisions, which were the traditional sources of support for the government. In June of 1996 the Minister of Education announced that the government would work to promote voluntary amalgamation and collaboration across divisional boundaries rather than unilaterally redrawing division boundaries, and to date two urban divisions and two rural divisions have completed mergers, while discussions are ongoing among several others.

The newly elected New Democratic Party government in 2000 has increased the pressure on school boards to consider seriously voluntary amalgamation or face government intervention (Caldwell, 2000b). In addition, the merits of school boards' powers to raise education taxes locally has become a controversial issue, with some trustees warning that unless the province re-instates traditional funding levels for education, boards should refuse to levy property taxes at all (*Winnipeg Free Press*, Friday, October 20th, 2000, A10). It is doubtful that any school board would actually go as far as to carry out this threat, and as things stand, boards remain a strong and vital part of the public structure of educational governance in the province.

Advisory Councils for School Leadership

Public voice and professional expertise have found formal expression at the provincial level through both the elected Minister of Education and the professional bureaucracy of the Department of Education and Training. At the local level, these structures are paralleled by School Division Trustees and the personnel of the Superintendent's Office. At the level of the individual school, formal structures that provide for public voice have been largely absent with formal authority residing with the principal and the teaching staff.

Along with all other provinces in Canada, the 1990s saw in Manitoba an increase in parental and community involvement in education promoted by the mandating of Advisory Councils for School Leadership. These were conceived as advisory bodies that would present parental and community concerns and perspectives on matters related to programs, school planning, budgeting, and school management to the principal and staff of the school. Membership was originally tightly defined to ensure that parental representation constituted a clear majority on all councils. Moreover, it was also specifically aimed at limiting teacher participation – even as parents of children attending the school. Stated clearly in *Renewing Education: New Directions – The Action Plan*, this was to be a parent and community voice:

> To ensure that parents' views are clearly represented, a minimum of two-thirds of the advisory council's positions must be filled by parents who are not employed by the division and whose children attend the school. To provide the view of the community at large, up to one-third of representatives on the advisory council may be residents who live within the school catchment area, but do not have children in the school. The principal and one teacher representative are to serve on an advisory council as ex-officio members without voting privileges. Only one teacher can be elected to sit on a council as a community representative with voting privileges. Where a student council exists in the school, the president will automatically become part of the community representation. (Manitoba Education and Training, 1995a, p. 25)

When regulations regarding Advisory Councils for School Leadership were finally released in March 1996, more open provision was made for teachers and school staff who were also parents or community members to comprise up to one-third of the council, or, by the wishes of those voting for the council, up to 50% of the council.[1] The regulations required that a council consist of a minimum of 7 elected members, at least two-thirds of whom must be parents of children attending the school and not more than one-third community members who do not have children attending the school. In High Schools with Student Councils one member of the Student Council was automatically a member of the Advisory Council, and the principal and a teacher representative were ex-officio members (Manitoba Education and Training, 1996a).

Within the context of this chapter several points are worthy of note: (i) that Councils, while given quite wide ranging roles and responsibilities, had a strictly advisory function; (ii) that in its proposals for the establishment of these councils the government also announced the intent to provide the Minister of Education with the authority to dissolve any parent council "that does not serve the best interests of the students and the community" (Manitoba Education and Training 1995a, p. 25); and (iii) that the representativeness of these councils of the views and interests of all segments of the local community was seen by the government as unproblematic.[2]

Advisory Councils for School Leadership in Manitoba serve neither as draconian forms of teacher accountability nor as romantic models of community schooling. While in many schools the introduction of legislation related to these councils merely served to formalize existing structures, in others they have provided a forum for the development of a more open and ongoing dialogue between teachers and parents.[3]

From the standpoint of a pluralist moral democracy, elected advisory councils represent, at best, a weak form of community participation. More exciting and vigorous examples of broadly based community involvement, developed without the support of government regulation and support (and at times in spite of them) exist within the province, usually dependent upon the leadership provided by individual school boards, such as Winnipeg School Division #1, and of particular groups of teachers and parents. In the early 1990s, for example, following up on the report of its Task Force on Race Relations published in 1989, the Winnipeg School Division established an Urban Aboriginal Education Advisory Committee that in the first half of the decade became a powerful voice for Aboriginal education and was instrumental in the establishment of two Aboriginal-focussed schools in the division – Children of the Earth High School and Niji Mahkwa Elementary School. Also within Winnipeg School Division during the 1990s, William Whyte Community School served as a powerful model of wide-ranging and effective inner city parent and community involvement. Here, community involvement was developed on the basis of two central priorities. The first involved using the school as a focus for community economic development strategies intended to strengthen the neighborhood economic base (i.e., hiring teacher aides and teachers whenever possible from the community, purchasing supplies locally, and developing a Family Centre for the community). The second focus on community education created for members of the community more opportunities for voice and a sense of agency and responsibility for action in the education of their children (i.e., active participation in school planning and decision-making) (Hunter, 2000, p. 116). At the same time on a larger scale, the Manitoba School Improvement Program (MSIP) – a school improvement network of some 30 high schools in the province – provided support for high schools to engage their communities in the development of their schools and, in particular, to increase the place of student voice in educational decision-making (Earle & Lee, 1998; Hickcox, 2000; Levin, 2000a).

Strengthening the participation of parents and communities in education has been identified as a priority of the new government, particularly with reference to improving educational outcomes for Aboriginal students (Caldwell, 2000a, 2000c). *Healthy Child Manitoba* (Manitoba, 2000) represents a focal point for this priority to date. Structured to promote inter-sectoral collaboration between six provincial departments – Education and Training; Family Services and Housing; Aboriginal and Northern Affairs; Culture, Heritage and Tourism; Health; and Justice – the initiative focuses on the development of parent-child centres, pre-natal and early childhood nutrition, nurses in schools, FAS/FAE prevention, and adolescent pregnancy prevention. Government attention here has shifted away from changing governance structures to efforts to improve early childhood supports for parents, an approach that research is suggesting has significant potential both for improving the quality of life for all children (McCain & Mustard, 1999) and for lowering the differential impact of socio-economic class and poverty on school success (Hertzman, 2000).

School Choice

Maximizing parental choice in terms of the schools that their children can attend fits well within a market democracy perspective, while its compatibility with the ideals of a pluralist moral democracy becomes far more controversial and problematic. In Manitoba, particularly in the urban centre of Winnipeg, accommodation of cultural and linguistic diversity saw the establishment during the 1970s and 1980s of a variety of different programs (French Immersion, Ukrainian-English Bilingual Programs, German-English Bilingual Programs, Aboriginal Focused Schools, etc.) that provide choice in the interests of inclusion and the structural recognition of multiculturalism. Yet the concerns that individual choice comes at the expense of a broader public good and serves best those parents with the resources to effectively exercise a choice contradicts the equality tenet in a pluralist moral democracy.

New Directions reforms in Manitoba moved modestly to increase parental choice by removing barriers within and across school divisions in terms of selection of schools to attend. *Bill 47, The Public Schools Amendment Act*, passed in 1997, allowed for parents to enrol their children in schools other than their designated school, either within or outside of their school division, without incurring any fees provided that there was space available and that requests were filed by May 15th prior to the beginning of the school year. The initial impact of this legislation was to encourage the recruitment efforts of a small number of urban schools and school divisions and those bordering on urban centres, particularly with regard to adult learners, but overall the changes appear to have done little to significantly change the face of public education in the province.

Private/Independent schools occupy a special place in the Manitoba education system, owing to the treatment of Catholic education in the 1890 school legislation. Ever since, church leaders have tenaciously maintained that they had a constitutional right to public funding. In 1980, through a series of legal threats, the development of strategic alliances and the promotion of an ideology of parental choice, legislation was introduced by the short-lived Sterling Lyon government which provided direct grants to all educational institutions operating under an umbrella organization called the Manitoba Federation of Independent Schools, which had been established in 1974. During the Filmon years, while the budgets of public schools were being reduced, independent schools, which included among them high-tuition, elite institutions, were receiving grants on the basis of a per pupil funding formula negotiated between the Federation and the government (Stapleton & Long, 1999). Private schools increased their enrolments during the 1990s, rising from

10 280 (5.4% of the total student population) in 1989 to 14 240 (7.3% of the total student population) by 1999 (Manitoba Education and Training, 1989, 1999).

2. *Curriculum Renewal and Student Assessment*[4]

Curriculum renewal and student assessment constituted a central element of Manitoba's *New Directions* reform initiatives (Manitoba Education and Training, 1994a, 1995a, 1995b). A striking feature of these documents is the lack of *any* explicit ideological justification for the substantial changes, curricular or otherwise, that they called for. Nevertheless, a central theme of each of these documents was the claim that the school system generally is not graduating students ready to take on the requirements of citizenship in the 21st century, in particular the academic competencies deemed necessary for the province's and for Canada's economic well-being. Without a discussion of *which* students are under-achieving and with no clear statement on the significance of issues of race, culture, class, and gender to school achievement, or to competing visions of what qualities might in fact be deemed desirable in graduates, these shortcomings of the public school system were seen as stemming primarily from: a lack of uniformly applied definition of basic education/essential learning; a lack of rigor and relevance within the existing curriculum; and, a lack of accountability within the system for student achievement.

The response of *New Directions* was built around the definition of essential learning from Kindergarten to Grade 12 (Senior 4), with a priority placed upon implementing a revised curriculum based upon grade- and subject-specific outcomes for compulsory core subject areas – language arts, mathematics, science, and social science. Crucial to this definition of essential learning was the development of complementary educational standards that describe the expected level of student performance in relation to grade- and subject-specific outcomes, with standards tests administered at the end of Grades 3, 6, 9 (Senior 1), and 12 (Senior 4). According to *The Action Plan*, these test scores were meant to form a part of all students' final mark at each stage, with the exception of Grade 3, reported to parents as a gauge of their children's progress and made public on a school-by-school basis.

The language of *New Directions – The Action Plan* is the language of "success for all," pitched as a means of raising academic performance through a more tightly structured and more demanding curriculum. It is, we would argue, in the words of Hatcher (1998), a language of "abstract universalism and deracialized individualism" that discounts the significance of how students' (and parents' and teachers') gendered, racialized, and class-based experiences have shaped their views of the world, including their understandings of the relationships between school and learning, and their conceptions of curriculum relevance.

The third of the *New Directions* policy documents, *A Foundation for Excellence*, released shortly after *The Action Plan*, lays out in detail the curriculum development and assessment processes. Still embedded in the broader rhetoric of "success for all," this document does give significant mention of diversity and the importance of "respect for human diversity." This document cites equity, defined as "ensuring fairness and the best possible learning opportunities for Manitobans, regardless of background or geographic location" (p. 3) as one of eight guiding principles for curriculum development. Equity and inclusion get taken up in the document in two important places: through *representation* in the curriculum development process and through a model of curriculum *infusion* in curriculum design.

As part of the *Western Canadian Protocol: Collaboration in Basic Education*,[5] curriculum development in the areas of mathematics, language arts (English and French), science, and social studies is designed to follow a process of curriculum development teams, review panels, field validation, authorized provincial use, and continuing updating. Central to this process are curriculum writing teams made up of a departmental project manager, a professional writer and a team of exemplary classroom teachers "who work extensively in the subject/course under development, who are knowledgeable about curriculum planning and design, pedagogy, and assessment and evaluation, and who can work well in a group, discuss and synthesize within strict time limits" (Manitoba Education and Training, 1995b, pp. 10-11). Further, with regard to membership, the *Foundations for Excellence* document requires that "each curriculum development team has appropriate representation (e.g., geographic, gender, Aboriginal)" (p. 11). However, the extent to which such a loosely defined gesture towards inclusion and "balanced representation" can, in fact, lead to the production of a curriculum that truly understands the significance of diversity, and is grounded in principles of inclusion, would seem from the outset fraught with conceptual and practical problems.

In a clear statement of an infusion model of curriculum development, *A Foundation for Excellence* outlines ten elements to be incorporated into all curriculum documents: foundation skill areas (literacy and communication; problem solving; differentiated instruction; curriculum integration; Aboriginal perspectives; gender fairness; appropriate age portrayals; human diversity; antiracist/antibias education; and sustainable development). That these priorities find their way into this generative document on school reform for the province must be acknowledged and may be seen as signalling the intent to embed across the curriculum a particular perspective on the issue of diversity in schooling.

These equity themes find expression in the Language Arts Framework documents and a degree of prominence in the Social Studies documents that have been produced to date. Nevertheless, our argument is that the overall effect of curriculum reform has been, perhaps paradoxically, to significantly reduce, not increase, the significance of diversity within the enacted curriculum of schools across the province (Young and Graham, 2000). Several factors have contributed to this. First, none of the reform documents contain any analysis – or what Dei and Karumanchery (1999) refer to as a "grounded discussion" (p. 116) – of equity questions. This absence both masks the contradictions that may be inherent in the competing priorities claimed in the documents and fails to provide teachers with any elaboration of the complexities of inclusive and antiracist education. Second, it would be our contention that the rapid-fire dissemination of curriculum documents closely tied to 'high stakes' testing has demanded teacher attention in a way that has eroded the previously developing levels of involvement in professional development work related to equity issues. Third, funding cuts that have accompanied school reform in Manitoba have seen a significant reduction in positions such as Multicultural Education, Race Relations, and Employment Equity consultants at the provincial and school board levels. Such reductions take out of the school system a critical source of advocacy and professional development and render impotent the policy rhetoric of inclusion (Young & MacKay, 1999; Rethinking Schools, 2000).

The Standards Debate in Manitoba

The re-introduction of province-wide, mandated assessment as a part of *New Directions* has been highly controversial. Opposition has been provoked from a wide range of different directions: (i) the process of publishing assessment results on a school-by-school basis ("league tables"); (ii) whether the tests would be marked locally at the school level or centrally, and whether teachers would be paid for their work as markers; (iii) whether standards tests, written by Manitoba teachers and based upon outcomes defined in Manitoba's curriculum documents, would inhibit the creative classroom work and lead to an increasingly narrow "teaching to the tests"; (iv) whether tests that were more summative than diagnostic were of value in supporting student learning; (v) whether the very large costs associated with the assessment process could be justified in a climate of funding cutbacks across the system; and (vi) whether the tests would become an inappropriate form of teacher evaluation (Manitoba Teachers' Society, 2000).

Within a context of quite vigorous public debate and professional resistance, the Progressive Conservative government remained committed to these tests until its defeat at the polls in 1999. However, the weights to be assigned to these tests in reporting a student's final grade for the year and the sequence of tests to be administered at each designated grade level was subject to constant adjustments.

In its 1999 election platform, the New Democratic Party committed to review the processes of provincial standards testing. Its initial stance since coming into office has been: (i) to seek the replacement of the existing Grade 3 assessment process with a classroom-based, teacher-administered assessment plan carried out at the beginning of the year rather than the end, having as a central objective the communication to parents of clear and meaningful information about their children's reading and literacy skills; (ii) to make assessments at grades six and senior one optional at the school divisional level; and (iii) to retain standards tests in English language arts, Français, and Mathematics at the senior four level that will be administered province-wide and marked locally (Levin, May, 2000b; Manitoba Education and Training, 2000a, 2000b).

3. The Professional Status and Autonomy of Teachers

The third dimension of public education in a pluralist moral democracy, we maintain, is the matter of broad-based societal support and legitimation for public schools and public school teachers. This is not to say that schools should not be subject to critique or that they do not require adequate vehicles for professional and public accountability. The critical consideration is that these dimensions of critique and accountability be contained within a broader climate of support.

In Manitoba in the 1990s the professional status and autonomy of teachers and the level of public support for public education was put under strain by a number of government policies, but equally distressing was the rhetoric of the public debate over education (Livingstone and Hart, 1995; Guppy and Davies, 1999). Ultimately, we believe, this attack on the professional status and commitment of teachers may have been the most damaging element of school reform.[6]

At its most basic level, public support for education is reflected in the annual budget allocated to public schools. For most of the 1990s, provincial government grants for education failed to keep up with inflation and in some years actually declined from the previous year. Black and Silver (1999) report that during this period the provincial government took $100 million out of education. The primary justification for these budgets was articulated as the need to balance the provincial budget while holding steady or reducing levels of taxation. Closely linked to this was a rhetoric of efficiency/inefficiency that suggested that the level of funding being provided was adequate if school boards spent their budgets more wisely. A critical consequence of this was that during the course of the 1990s, local property taxes came to shoulder a significantly larger proportion of the costs of public education (see Table 2). Relatively large annual increases in local school taxes characterized the 1990s. School boards were caught between a provincial government tightening its funding allocations and local communities where strong and often conflicting pressures existed both to maintain existing school programs and to contain local taxes. Collective bargaining, carried out at the local level in Manitoba, became a focus of this pressure.

Collective bargaining in Manitoba is subject to the provisions of the *Public Schools Act*, legislation that prevents teachers from taking strike action or school boards from locking teachers out and instead provides for a system of binding arbitration. While this system had been generally non-controversial for many years, in the financial context of the 1990s, outlined above, Manitoba school trustees became increasingly critical of this system which they saw as taking out of their hands the ability to properly manage the financial affairs of their boards. To respond to this pressure, the government in 1996 revised the *Public Schools Act* requiring that an arbitrator take into account a community's "ability to pay" in coming to an arbitration

Table 2				
Manitoba Educational Funding 1990-91 to 1998-99 (Operating Budget)				
Year	Total Expenditures	Revenue Source		Enrolment*
		Province	Municipal	
1998/99	$1 162 219 630	61.3	33.9	192 204
1997/98	$1 126 197 460	62.0	32.5	191 764
1996/97	$1 099 345 968	62.9	31.8	192 133
1995/96	$1 092 091 491	63.9	30.8	192 037
1994/95	$1 090 944 481	65.2	29.4	191 627
1993/94	$1 079 367 565			
1992/93	$1 063 962 693	67.3	27.4	186 233
1991/92	$1 024 982 228	67.8	26.7	185 865
1990/91	$1 010 550 851	69.2	25.5	186 492

*Enrolments – Actual, September 30th, K-S4
Source: Manitoba Education and Training FRAME Reports.

award as well as limiting the number of matters that could be referred to arbitration.

This legislation was bitterly opposed by the Manitoba Teachers' Society and the then opposition New Democratic (NDP) party as a uniquely unfair attack on teachers' salaries. One of the early acts of the NDP on forming the government in 1999 was to repeal this legislation – to the delight of the Teachers' Society and the "profound opposition" of the Manitoba Association of School Trustees (Manitoba Association of School Trustees, 2000). Also in its first budget, the NDP increased provincial funding to public schools by some 2.8%, the largest increase since the funding cuts of the mid-1990s.

Several authors (for example, Barlow and Robertson, 1994) have drawn attention to the ways in which manufacturing a sense of crisis in public schooling in the 1990s was seen as strategically necessary in order to justify the changes being sought by the advocates of a school system driven by the priorities of a market democracy. While less extreme than in other provinces, the 1990s were without doubt a period of sustained scrutiny of teachers and schools in Manitoba. While this scrutiny produced strong supporters of public schooling, it also promoted attacks on the profession that did considerable damage to the public standing of teaching and to the morale of teachers. The NDP government has moved to return to a more positive and collaborative relationship between government and educators, although it has already had its disagreements with the trustees – over collective bargaining – and with the Teachers' Society – over its implementation of new assessment procedures for Grade 3 students. What the new government is unlikely to seek to curtail is the increase in parental participation and public consultation around education policy that developed during the 1990s.

Conclusion

Kenway (1995), cited in Dei and Karumanchery (1999, pp. 119-20), suggests that when state policy begins to be driven by the commercial interests of a market democracy, four main movements will develop as fundamental aspects of school restructuring: *devolution, deregulation, dezoning,* and *disaggregation. Devolution,* Kenway suggests, refers to the reduction in state funding as well as efforts to decentralize government responsibilities for schools while simultaneously centralizing curriculum and assessment processes. *Deregulation* suggests moves that weaken existing constraints on the market such as moving control out of the hands of elected officials in favor of government appointees, thereby weakening the power of teachers', and other, unions. *Dezoning* seeks to remove major structural barriers that constrain the market, opening up parental choice in schooling, so that "quality education becomes a matter of affordability." *Disaggregation* incorporates market ideals of competition into schooling in lieu of collectivity and co-operation. It would be quite wrong to suggest that the education reforms that were implemented by the Progressive Conservatives during the 1990s presented the province with the kind of radical agenda described by Kenway. What the Filmon government did do, however, was to introduce a number of measures which we contend were designed and implemented in an effort to shift the prevailing pluralist moral democratic tendency of the previous 40 years to a market democracy model of education. Concern over health care may have been the most important single issue in the recent provincial election, but it is not too much of a stretch to suggest that the Tory defeat was brought about, in part at least, by popular concern that the new direction in education might only be a precursor to the full blown abandonment of what had become by the early 1990s, the traditional pluralist moral democratic thrust of public education.

Where does the new NDP government stand on the question of building a pluralist moral democracy in Manitoba? Traditionally, the party has shown a marked inclination for the promotion of social equality, and this tradition is certainly recognizable – if at times tentatively – in its early statements of educational priority (Caldwell, 2000a, 2000c). Meanwhile, in much of the rest of Canada, particularly in Ontario and Alberta, a school reform agenda driven by the dictates of a market democracy is being aggressively put in place. Is it realistic to think that a small province like Manitoba cannot only resist this national and global tendency but further provide a model of how things can be otherwise? We believe that it is for a number of reasons.

In the first place, although the concerns of urban Winnipeg have often overshadowed those of the rural areas of the province, the city has never achieved hegemonic domination over them. Many elements of the market agenda of school reform (issues such as school choice and the elimination of meaningful roles for elected local school boards) have little resonance in the relative isolation of northern communities, for example. While the new Minister of Education has made it clear that he would like to see some alterations to existing school division boundaries and the government is reviewing existing arrangements for local education revenue generation and distribution, school boards appear to be an enduring feature of the Manitoba education scene, and a robust vehicle for democratic involvement.

Manitoba is a pluralist society and its demographic character continues to find political expression through public institutions like its school boards, where its citizens can participate meaningfully in the decisions and processes of educational policy making. This has encouraged an approach to school administration in which there is a rough (and at times uncomfortable) balance between public and professional authority.

One area which has proven difficult for the NDP in the past is the question of the funding of private schools in the province. It grates on many party supporters that public funds are allocated to private educational institutions, as is currently the case. Does the Manitoba Schools Question legacy provide a sufficiently compelling, or inescapable, justification for the existing situation? The matter may be complicated in a more critical manner by the current round of World Trade Organization (WTO) negotiations on services – the General Agreement on Trade in Services (GATS) – which may have serious implications for Manitoba whereby the provincial government finds itself compelled by the current funding arrangements to support any private consortium which requests it.

Finally, if a pluralist moral democratic agenda is, as we would contend, the appropriate direction for public schooling, the curriculum needs to reflect and support that orientation. Tightly prescribed curricula that prioritize training for an existing, or predicted global, labor market over broader ideals of education and emancipation cannot be consistent with public schooling in a moral democracy. Manitoba's curriculum reforms and the assessment requirements that accompanied them may not invite teachers to engage this active, political, and emancipatory ideal of education, but neither do they exclude this possibility. In a more supportive public context, teachers may once again be empowered to take up this challenge: a truly public education.[7]

Notes

[1] The public debate surrounding this proposal serves as one of several instances the government's proposals were quickly taken as evidence of what was seen as their broader concern with challenging at every opportunity the authority of the profession in educational decision-making and "breaking" the Teachers' Society. Whether or not this was ever a part of the government's plans on this issue, they only contributed to the galvanization of this perception which was to remain throughout the government's tenure.

[2] A final section of *Renewing Education: New Directions – The Action Plan* contains government responses to a series of hypothetical questions related to the policy proposals. Included among these was the question: "How can we be sure that all parents' voices are heard?" The documents answer was: "It is up to parents and community members to ensure that candidates who are nominated and elected represent their points of view" (p. 54).

[3] Fine (1993), writing of developments in the USA, distinguished between at least two stances that parents on such councils may take: an oppositional, parents' rights perspective rooted in a history of non-trusting and adversarial relationships, and a more collaborative orientation that seeks to work with teachers towards a collective vision of a school community. Both of these stances may be seen as important to the notions of educational democracy.

[4] Parts of this section of the chapter are drawn from a broader analysis of the 'deracialization' of education associated with school reform initiatives in Manitoba in Young and Graham, "School and Curriculum Reform: Manitoba Frameworks and Multicultural Teacher Education," *Canadian Ethnic Studies* XXXII, I (2000). Here these issues are taken up with specific reference to the Language Arts curriculum and pre-service teacher education.

[5] In December 1993, ministers of education from the Northwest Territories, the Yukon, British Columbia, Alberta, Saskatchewan, and Manitoba signed The Western Canadian Protocol for Collaboration in Basic Education (Kindergarten to Grade 12). Recognizing that the provinces shared many common educational goals, and seeking to achieve "greater harmonization

of ways to achieve them" across provincial boundaries as well as "making optimum use of limited educational resources," the Agreement has seen the development of a number of initiatives including the development of curriculum frameworks for mathematics, English language arts, and social studies. Manitoba also participates in the Pan-Canadian Science Project coordinated by the Council of Ministers of Education, Canada (CMEC). These developments are significant in the ways in which, within a constitutional framework of provincial autonomy, they allow for a more regional and national "harmonization" of curriculum.

[6]The origins of this "attack" on public education and the professionalism of teachers are not unambiguous and it is, we believe, simplistic to attribute this simple agenda to the various Ministers of Education. As we have noted earlier in this paper, Manitoba reform documents are largely devoid of any ideological justifications. Clayton Manness was the Minister of Education most identified with implementing the reform agenda and seen as leading the attack on teachers. Yet his statements in Hansard and in the press are more often complimentary towards teachers and couched instead in the rhetoric of reform to meet the demands of a changing world (see Levin & Young, 2000). The "social construction" of this climate of critique and public dissatisfaction has to be understood more broadly in terms that include, at least, government initiatives in other arenas and in educational reforms underway in other jurisdictions that informed the Manitoba debate.

[7]In this regard, the NDP government was reminded of its democratic principles by one of its candidates, Lawrie Cherniack, after narrowly failing to win his constituency:

Whether we win or lose a particular election there is only one speech. It is a speech about personal, social and economic liberation. It is a speech about dedication through adversity. It is about principles not practicality. We live in a world of tremendous inequalities and inequities. If we had won, I would therefore have said that the struggle is not won. Now we have lost this election in this constituency, I tell you that the struggle is not lost. For we are part of a world-wide movement that seeks to change our society from one based on greed and competition to one based on giving and co-operation. And that movement began centuries before our time, and will, for better or for worse, be continuing past our time. In some countries members of our movement are engaged in real life and death struggle, where the forces that oppress them have the power to kill them. As always, it is less dramatic in Canada. We can work within the electoral system. We can spread our message to people who can read and write, who are generally more secure than the majority of people in other countries. We don't have to take to the hills to fight our battles. But our struggle is no less serious and no less important.

References

Barlow, M. & Robertson, H. (1994). *Class warfare*. Toronto: Key Porter.

Black, E. & Silver, J. (1999). *A flawed economic experiment: The new political economy of Manitoba.* Winnipeg, MB: Canadian Centre for Policy Alternatives.

Bruno-Jofré, R. (1996). Schooling and the struggles to develop a common polity, 1919-1971. In R. Bruno-Jofré and L. Grieger (Eds.), *Contemporary issues in education policy and administration in Canada: A foundations perspective* (pp. 71-108). Winnipeg: University of Manitoba.

Bruno-Jofré, B. (1998-99). Citizenship and schooling in Manitoba, 1918-1945. *Manitoba History, 36,* 26-36.

Bruno-Jofré, R. and Henley, D. (2000). Public schooling in English Canada: Addressing difference in the context of globalization, *Canadian Ethnic Studies, XXXII* (1), 38-53.

Carr, W. (1991). *Becoming a citizen: Civic education in a democratic society.* Paper Presented at the International Symposium on Human Development and Education, Universidad Complutense de Madrid, Madrid, October, 1991.

Caldwell, D. (2000a). Minister's Letter to Educational Partners. July 10th, 2000.

Caldwell, D. (2000b). Minister's Letter: School Board Amalgamation. September 25th, 2000.

Caldwell, D. (2000c), Minister's Letter: An Education Agenda for Manitoba. October 20th, 2000.

Canada (1996). *The report of the Royal Commission on Aboriginal Peoples. Vol. I.* Ottawa: Ministry of Supply and Services.

Deen, R. (1994). Free marketeers or good citizens? Educational policy and lay participation in the administration of schools. *British Journal of Educational Studies, XXXXII* (1), 23-37.

Dehli, K. (1998). What lies beyond Ontario's Bill 160? *Our Schools, Ourselves, 9* (4), 59-78.

Dei, G. & Karumanchery, L. (1999). School reform in Ontario: The "marketization of education" and the resulting silence on equity. *Alberta Journal of Educational Research, XLV* (2), 111-131.

Earle, L. & Lee, L. (1998). *An evaluation of the Manitoba School Improvement Program.* A Report prepared for the Walter and Duncan Gordon Foundation, Toronto.

Fine, M. (1993). [Ap]parent involvement: Reflections on parents, power and urban public schools. *Teachers College Record, 94* (4), 682-710.

Guppy, N. & Davies, S. (1999). Understanding Canadians' declining confidence in public education. *Canadian Journal of Education, 24* (3), 265-280.

Hatcher, R. (1998). Social justice and school improvement. *Race, Ethnicity and Education, 1* (2), 267-289.

Henley, R. (1993). The school question continued: The issue of compulsory schooling in Manitoba. In R. Bruno-Jofré (Ed.), *Issues in the history of education in Manitoba* (pp. 47-72). Lewiston: Edwin Mellen Press.

Hertzman, C. (2000). The case for an early childhood development strategy. *isuma: Canadian Journal of Policy Research, 1* (2), 11-18.

Hesch, R. (2000). Mass testing and the underdevelopment of inner city communities. *Alberta Journal of Educational Research, XLVI* (1), 49-64.

Hickcox, E. (2000). *Searching for community.* A Report prepared for the Manitoba School Improvement Program and the Manitoba Association of School Trustees, June, 2000.

Hobsbawm, E. (1995). *Age of extremes: The short twentieth century 1914 –1991.* London: Abacus Press.

Hunter, H. (2000). In the face of poverty: What a community school can do. In J. Silver (Ed.), *Solutions that work: Fighting poverty in Winnipeg.* Winnipeg: Fernwood Publishing and The Canadian Centre for Policy Alternatives – Manitoba.

Kenway, J. (1995). *The marketisation of education: Mapping the contours of a feminist perspective.* Paper presented to the British Education Research Association Conference, Bath, September, 1995.

Kymlicka, W. (1998). *Finding our way: Rethinking ethnocultural relations in Canada.* Toronto: Oxford University Press.

Levin, B. (Forthcoming). *Reforming education: From origins to outcomes.* London: Routledge Falmer.

Levin, B. (2000a). Putting students at the centre of education reform. *Journal of Educational Change, 1,* 155-172.

Levin, B. (May, 2000b). Provincial standards testing schedule. Correspondence to Superintendents of School Divisions and Districts and Principals.

Levin, B. (1996). Moving away from the common school? In R. Bruno-Jofré and L. Grieger (Eds.), *Contemporary issues in education policy and administration in Canada: A foundations perspective* (pp. 33-53). Winnipeg: University of Manitoba.

Levin, B. & Young, J. (2000). The rhetoric of educational reform. *Journal of Comparative Policy Analysis, 2* (2), 189-209.

Livingstone, D. & Hart, D. (1995). Popular beliefs about Canada's schools. In R. Ghosh & D. Ray (Eds.), *Social change and education in Canada* (3rd edition), (pp. 16-44). Toronto: Harcourt Brace.

McCain, M. & Mustard, J. F. (1999). *Reversing the real brain drain: Early years study final report.* Toronto: Ontario Children's Secretariat.

McKay, I. (2000a). A note on "region". Writing the history of Atlantic Canada. *Acadiensis, XXIX* (2), 88-101.

McKay, I. (2000b). The liberal order framework: A prospectus for a reconnaissance of Canadian history. *Canadian History Review, 81* (4), 617-45.

Manitoba (2000). Speech from the Throne. Second Session of the 37th Legislature of the Province of Manitoba. December 5th, 2000.

Manitoba Association of School Trustees. (2000). A Brief by the Manitoba Association of School Trustees (MAST) to the Law Amendments Review Committee on *Bill 42, The Public Schools Amendment and Consequential Amendments Act.* Winnipeg: MAST.

Manitoba Education. (1989). *Enrolments and transportation report.* Winnipeg: The Department of Education.

Manitoba Education. (1990). *Multicultural education: A policy for the 1990s.* Winnipeg: The Department of Education.

Manitoba Education and Training. (1994a) *Renewing education: New directions: A blue-print for action.* Winnipeg: Manitoba Education and Training.

Manitoba Education and Training. (1994b). *The report of the Manitoba school divisions/districts boundaries review commission (the Norrie report).* Winnipeg: Manitoba Education and Training.

Manitoba Education and Training. (1995a). *Renewing education: New directions: The action plan.* Winnipeg: Manitoba Education and Training.

Manitoba Education and Training. (1995b). *Renewing education: New directions: A foundation for excellence.* Winnipeg: Manitoba Education and Training.

Manitoba Education and Training. (1996a). Regulation 54/96. Advisory Councils for School Leadership.

Manitoba Education and Training. (1996b). *Manitoba teacher education programs: An option for the future (the Shapiro report).* Winnipeg: Manitoba Education and Training.

Manitoba Education and Training. (1998). *The teacher compensation process (the Scurfield report).* Winnipeg: Manitoba Education and Training.

Manitoba Education and Training. (1999). *Enrolments and transportation report.* Winnipeg: Manitoba Education and Training.

Manitoba Education and Training. (2000a). *Grade 3 assessment in reading and numeracy: Educator consultation document.* Winnipeg: Manitoba Education and Training

Manitoba Education and Training. (2000b). *Grade 3 assessment in reading and numeracy: Parent consultation document.* Winnipeg: Manitoba Educ. & Train. (http://www.edu.gov.mb.ca/metks4/curricul/assess/index.html)

Manitoba Teachers' Society. (2000). *Position paper on student assessment.* Winnipeg: The Society. (http://www.mbteach.org)

Miller, J. (1996). *Shingwauk's vision: A history of Native residential schools.* Toronto: University of Toronto Press.

Milloy, J. (1999). *A national crime: The Canadian government and the residential school system 1879-1986.* Winnipeg: University of Manitoba Press.

Osborne, K. (1998-99). One hundred years of history teaching in Manitoba schools. Part 1: 1897-1927. *Manitoba History, 36,* 3-25.

Pierce, M. (1998). *The future of school boards: The Canadian experience.* A presentation to the NSBA Executive Directors' Summer Institute, Quebec City. <http://www.cdnsba.org/govern/NSBA_Quebec_Workshop1998.asp>

Rethinking Schools. (2000). Multicultural education: What now? A special rethinking schools report. *Rethinking Schools, 15* (1), 3-12.

Smith, J. & Young, J. (1996). Building an anti-racist school: The story of Victor Mager School. In K. McLeod (Ed.), *Multicultural education: The state of the art national study, report #3.* Toronto: Faculty of Education, University of Toronto.

Stapleton, J. & Long, J. (1999). The Manitoba independent schools question, 1957-1996. In G. Friesen and R. Lebrun (Eds.), *Saint Paul's College, University of Manitoba: Memories and histories* (pp. 304-324). Winnipeg: St. Paul's College.

Symons, T. (1975). *To know ourselves. Report of the commission on Canadian studies, Vols. 1 and 2.* Ottawa: Association of Universities and Colleges of Canada.

Tavares, A., (2000). From heritage to international languages: Globalism and western Canadian trends in heritage language education. *Canadian Ethnic Studies, XXXII* (1), 156-171.

Taylor, A. (1996). *Education for 'post-industrial purposes: Understanding the context of change in Alberta schools.* Unpublished Ed.D. thesis. Graduate Department of Education, University of Toronto.

Titley, B. (1986). *A narrow vision: Duncan Campbell Scott and the administration of Indian affairs in Canada.* Vancouver: University of British Columbia Press.

Wiens, J (1995). *Education reform and the globalization of the economy.* A paper presented at the American Education Finance Association annual meeting, Savannah, Georgia, March 9th – 12th, 1995.

Wilson, W. (1981). *Daniel McIntyre and the Winnipeg schools.* Winnipeg: University of Manitoba.

Winnipeg Free Press. (October 20th, 2000). Pool taxes for schools. *Winnipeg Free Press,* p. A10.

Winnipeg School Division. (1989). *Report of the task force on race relations.* Winnipeg.

Young, J. & Graham, R. (2000). School and curriculum reform: Manitoba frameworks and multicultural education. *Canadian Ethnic Studies, XXXII* (1), 142-155.

Young, J. & Jones, B. (1995). *Focus on bias: A resource for teachers.* Unpublished Resource Document. Winnipeg: Manitoba Education and Training.

Young, J. & Levin, B. (2000). Education in transition: Canada. In D. Coulby, R. Cowen & C. Jones (Eds.), *World yearbook of education 2000: Education in times of transition* (pp. 50-62). Kogan Page: London.

Young, J. & MacKay, T. (1999). Multicultural in-service teacher education in a period of school reform: A survey of western Canadian teachers. *Multiculturalism/Interculturalisme, 18* (1), 5-16.